An Introduction

AN INTRODUCTION TO
PLATO'S *REPUBLIC*

BY
JULIA ANNAS

CLARENDON PRESS · OXFORD

Oxford University Press, Walton Street, Oxford OX2 6DP
Oxford New York Toronto
Delhi Bombay Calcutta Madras Karachi
Petaling Jaya Singapore Hong Kong Tokyo
Nairobi Dar es Salaam Cape Town
Melbourne Auckland
and associated companies in
Berlin Ibadan

Oxford is a trade mark of Oxford University Press

Published in the United States by
Oxford University Press, New York

First published 1981
Seventh impression 1991

British Library Cataloguing in Publication Data
Annas, Julia
An introduction to Plato's Republic.
1. Plato. Republic.
I. Title
321'.07   JC71.P6   80–41901
ISBN 0–19–827429–7 (Pbk)

Printed in Hong Kong

Preface

Like most books on the *Republic*, this one emerges from years of teaching it that have revealed how much there is to learn about it. Since my first encounter with the work I have followed the progress most of us make from initial shock and disgust, to fascination with the parts, to some kind of understanding of the whole. I am not sure that this is not exactly what Plato intended. This book attempts to share one understanding of the *Republic* in a way helpful to those reading it in English as part of their introduction to philosophy. I have avoided technicalities, and, while I have tried to do justice to the seminal importance of many of the parts, I have concentrated on bringing out the lines of the main moral argument.

I have more intellectual debts than I can easily name. One very long-standing one is to G. E. L. Owen, from whom I first learned to question received and easy opinions about knowledge in the *Republic*. Over the years I have learned a great deal from Myles Burnyeat, both from his writings and from his example of sustained and incisive dialectic. My debt to him in the discussions of knowledge and understanding, and of the virtuous agent and virtuous actions, is part of a larger intellectual debt in the understanding of ancient philosophy. He has read a typescript of the book and made many helpful comments. Gregory Vlastos has, in discussion and correspondence, forced me to clarify and greatly to improve my views on the form of Plato's argument and its relation to modern theories; and I have benefited greatly, and most enjoyably, from his deep understanding of the *Republic*. Christopher Gill has not only read a version but has helped me greatly over the years in the understanding of ancient views of character, and in appreciating the form of a Platonic dialogue and the implications for the way it should be read. I have been helped a great deal, in matters both of content and of style, by comments on an earlier draft by Jonathan Barnes and John Ackrill, and by discussion of various issues with Charles Kahn. I should mention also Terry Irwin's book *Plato's Moral Theory*, with much of whose work on the *Republic* I found myself in enthusiastic agreement and which made my own ideas much clearer as a result of working through his argument. I am pleased also to find much agreement with Nicholas White's book *A Companion to Plato's Republic*, a book which, with a rather different format and emphasis, puts similar stress on the coherence of the main moral argument. I am indebted also for helpful discussions of various points to John Cooper, Alexander Nehamas, Anthony Long, and Martha Nussbaum. And there is, finally, an enormous debt to all the pupils I have taught over the years, who have, in their essays and tutorials, raised the questions that needed answers.

The book originates in lectures given in Oxford, and took its present form in the summer of 1979, when the first version was written in a pine cabin overlooking Lake Rosseau in Ontario, where my father-in-law's books were written some years ago. I am grateful to my husband's family for being so patient with an impatient writer. And I am most grateful to my husband, David Owen, for his loving support with the book as with all else. The book is dedicated to him with gratitude, and with love.

St. Hugh's College, Oxford   J.A.

Contents

Chapter 1

Introduction

The *Republic* is Plato's best-known work, and there are ways in which it is too famous for its own good. It gives us systematic answers to a whole range of questions about morality, politics, knowledge, and metaphysics, and the book is written in a way designed to sweep the reader along and give a general grasp of the way Plato sees all these questions as hanging together. So our reaction to it, at least on first reading, is likely to be over-simplified; we may feel inclined to accept or reject it as a whole, rather than coming to grips with particular arguments.

But the *Republic*, though written with single-minded intensity, is a work of great complexity. And this is the best reason for studying it in detail. For when we do, we find, with pleasure and profit, that it is a work of great subtlety. Plato *is* writing a manifesto, but he is too good a philosopher not to raise important and difficult philosophical issues in the process, and sometimes to develop a point at the expense of his declared aims. The *Republic* is in fact a work in which a grandiose plan covers a number of struggles and tensions.

The richness of the book can be seen from the very different interpretations that it has produced. Plato has been seen as a revolutionary, a conservative; a fascist, a communist; a fiercely practical reformer and an ineffective dreamer. Some of these interpretations are more fanciful than others, but they all have *some* footing in the text. A book which gives rise to such extreme disagreements over what it is saying is not a simple and easily comprehended book, however much Plato's own style of writing may try to persuade us that it is.

Our first response is likely to be simple; it is also likely to be hostile. We are almost all going to find many of Plato's views unacceptable, even repellent. His ideal society is highly authoritarian. His ideal person is dedicated to a social ideal, and identified with a social role, in a way that we feel denies the importance and interest of the individual. His theories of knowledge and of value conflict with many of our fundamental assumptions.

But we should not underestimate Plato here. He is a sophisticated literary artist who is aware of the effect he is producing. The *Republic* is *meant* to startle and shock. Plato was not out to conciliate his contemporaries; they would have been just as offended by the book as we are – indeed more so if anything, since we live in a world more inured to various political and social forms of collectivism than they did. Plato is passionately concerned about a number of issues, and prefers to jolt us into awareness of them and their shocking consequences, rather than keeping the discussion at a harmless level. One result of this is that it is impossible to be neutral about the *Republic*. If we really grasp what Plato is saying, then we are bound to respond to it. If we disagree with some shocking conclusion, we are bound to ask why, and to be thrown back on arguing in defence of our view. And this is what Plato is basically after; he wants us to think, to do philosophy, rather than to fall in dully with what he says. In spite of his dogmatic tone, he does not want ready, unreflective agreement; indeed, the possibility of unreflective agreement is one of his reasons for distrusting books, as we find from a famous passage in another dialogue, the *Phaedrus* (274b–277a). Books cannot answer back and respond to the objections they provoke; there is no real dialogue of minds between writer and reader, only between two people actually engaged in philosophical discussion. Plato is deeply influenced by the idea that true knowledge is something that can only be gained by each individual in his or her own case, by thinking things through and questioning everything accepted. There is no short-cut to understanding by passively reading a book. None of this implies that the *Republic* is not seriously meant; Plato makes the most of the means at his disposal to further his own ideas. But it encourages us to think of the book as consciously and deliberately provocative, and to think that Plato would be less disturbed by an articulately hostile objection than by a passively uncritical acceptance. He is giving us the truth as he sees it; but it is a truth that each of us must rediscover for ourselves before we can properly be said to possess it.

To understand the *Republic* it is helpful to know something about Plato's background. I shall not say much about it here, because it is covered in useful detail in many easily available books; I shall merely pick out a few points relevant to interpreting the *Republic*.

Plato was born in or about 427 BC and died in 347. He belonged to an old and powerful Athenian family and was closely related to some influential political figures of the day. In the natural course of events he would have taken an active role in Athenian politics. As it was, he became a full-time philosopher, founding a philosophical school, called the Academy after the gymnasium near whose grounds it met. (Opinions differ greatly over how formally organized an institution it was.) Of course there were many influences on Plato leading him to choose the life he did, but we can usefully pick out two: the influence of Socrates and Plato's disillusionment with contemporary Athenian politics.

Socrates was an older contemporary of Plato's, an extraordinary person who made a strong impression on everyone coming into contact with him, and yet who had such an elusive personality that the accounts we have of him diverge to an amazing degree. The comic playwright Aristophanes ridiculed him in his play *The Clouds*; the historian Xenophon wrote long and uninspired reminiscences of him; and Plato was so influenced by him that he made him the main speaker in nearly all his philosophical dialogues. There is an obvious problem, how far do the views of 'Socrates' in Plato's dialogues represent the views of the real Socrates, who made it his life's business to engage in philosophical discussions, but never wrote a book? In the main, scholars agree that Plato's practice altered. In the early dialogues, which are short and genuinely dramatic, Socrates appears in a role suited to the historical Socrates; he questions people and deflates their pretensions to knowledge, but puts forward no explicit systematic doctrine of his own, and represents his own task as being merely that of goading people into realizing the confused and baseless nature of many of their beliefs. He himself claims to be ignorant of

everything except awareness of his own ignorance. The other
characters in these dialogues sometimes complain that this
enterprise is a merely destructive one, and that they are left
stranded, free from vain pretensions certainly, but with no
idea what to do next. In Plato's 'middle-period' dialogues this
figure is replaced by a Socrates who has plenty of positive, even
dogmatic things to say. The dialogue form loses the character
of a real philosophical interchange and becomes little but a
device to break up the flow of monologue into palatable chunks.
(The late dialogues raise problems of their own, which there is
no scope to go into here.) The general consensus is that Plato
moved from presenting something like Socrates' actual
procedure to putting forward his own views, which went
beyond anything he derived from Socrates; but that he
continued to use Socrates as his mouthpiece, because he
regarded his own ideas as the result of Socrates' influence, and
as carrying on his intellectual and spiritual task.

The *Republic* is especially interesting in this connection
because it is overtly transitional. Book 1 has the form of a
Socratic dialogue like the early ones; but the rest of the book is
a continuous exposition of what we can only take to be Plato's
own views on people and society. In the discussion of Book 1
I shall revert to the significance of this, and to what some have
seen as the irony that it is Socrates who puts forward theories
which seem to be the negation of everything that the historical
Socrates stood for.

It may have been Socrates' example that persuaded Plato
that philosophy was worth doing as a full-time occupation.
In another dialogue, the *Gorgias*, we see Plato defending
philosophy as a way of life, against a worldly-wise politician
who holds that it is silly and immature for a grown man to
spend his time discussing abstract questions of right and wrong,
rather than participating in the social and political life of his
city, and organizing his practical life to the best advantage.
Plato never wavers from his belief that Socrates was right, and
that the real foolishness is to spend one's time on practical
matters when one is in confusion about the state of one's soul –
or, as we would put it, the meaning of one's life.

And yet there is a certain ambivalence about Plato's attitude
to the life devoted to study. For by his activity, Socrates had

laid himself open to dislike and enmity, and in 399 was executed on a trumped-up charge. Plato never forgot this; it crops up again and again in the dialogues; and though he writes with admiration of Socrates' unworldliness he never managed to emulate it himself. Throughout his life he hoped, with varying degrees of optimism, that philosophy might change the world for the better. His writings reflect the ups and downs of this belief. The *Republic* is often thought to represent a high point of optimism, indeed to be a blueprint for a coming society; but in fact Plato's attitude is not so simple. As we read the book, we can hardly avoid asking various pertinent questions. Does Plato seriously believe that philosophers can be rulers? How realistic are his proposals for their education meant to be? What is the point of their highly theoretical knowledge, and how is it to be applied in practice? We shall see that the answers to these questions do not always cohere. Plato is ambivalent; he never agrees that theory may be sacrificed to pragmatic needs, but neither is he interested in working out a political ideal with no practical relevance.

Plato's disillusionment with the politics of his own day is a matter of controversy, and I shall only touch on it here. There is extant a long autobiographical letter (the 'Seventh Letter'), purportedly by Plato, which gives an account of his original hopes for a political career and subsequent abandonment of them. Unfortunately, there are the strongest grounds for thinking that this letter is not genuine. But even if it is forged, it is close in date to the events it describes and presumably does not falsify the major happenings of Plato's life too grossly, or it would lose all hope of acceptance as Plato's work. Without relying on the authenticity of the Seventh Letter, we can still give a very general background to Plato's writings.

The Athens that Plato grew up in was a democracy of a universal and direct kind. All adult male citizens could and were expected to play a part in decision-making and the business of governing. (Slaves and women were totally excluded from any such activity.) The city was proud of its democratic mode of government, and Athens's military and commercial expansion in the fifth century, to the point where she effectively ruled a large number of other Greek cities, was seen as confirmation of its excellence, and its superiority to more authoritarian and oligarchic forms of government (typified in the current ideology by Athens's rival Sparta). But the democracy was disliked by many members of aristocratic families, including some of Plato's close relatives, and when in 404 Athens surrendered to Sparta at the end of a long and demoralizing war, they collaborated in imposing a dictatorship of thirty oligarchs (including Plato's cousin and uncle). They started a reign of terror and ruled so badly that we can believe the Seventh Letter's claim that Plato was glad when they were overthrown and the democracy eventually restored. He had had a demonstration, uncomfortably near home, of the extent to which political power corrupts individuals, and may well have thought that the best prospect lay in trusting established institutions, even ones he disliked and which had proved fallible. But he was in for further disillusionment when in 399 Socrates was tried and put to death, ostensibly for corrupting the young by his teaching, but really because he had been associated with some of the most notorious enemies of the democracy. It is very plausible that Plato decided at this point that political institutions could be as badly corrupted as powerful individuals, and despaired of any prospect of improving his society by his own practical efforts.

This may not have been the end of Plato's political involvements, however. He made three journeys to Sicily, in 387, 367, and 362. According to the account in the Seventh Letter, which formed the basis of the ancient tradition, the last two visits were attempts to do something like realize the plan of the *Republic*. Dionysius II, the new ruler of Syracuse, showed some interest in philosophy, and according to tradition Plato tried to bring about the rule of philosopher-kings by turning a king into a philosopher. But the tradition has been questioned; and anyway if Plato did attempt any such thing, it failed completely. It would not have been unexpected for Plato to take on some such gallant but hopeless task. For, as we shall see, he wants to combine the values of intellectual perfection, which demand that one's life be devoted to study, and the values of practical activity, which demand that one improve the political world which is in such a mess. Plato sees the force of both claims and does not want to admit that they are irreconcilable. We are told that various members of the

Academy were not satisfied by improving the world indirectly through philosophy, but became political revolutionaries in some cities; we do not know whether Plato encouraged them.

Plato's dialogues are nearly all set in the late fifth century (much earlier than the time of their composition), at a time when Athens was feeling strongly the tension between a way of life built on the acceptance of traditional values and styles of life, and the intellectual questioning of these values resulting from a situation where Athens had taken on a more cosmopolitan role. Exposure to other ways of life led many Athenians to become detached if not alienated from the values of their own culture, and made popular a kind of cultural and moral relativism. Great attention was devoted to the question of the roles in human life of *nomos* and *phusis* – usually translated 'convention' and 'nature'. Many traditional values and patterns of behaviour, hitherto treated as 'natural', part of the inevitable order of things, were now suddenly thought of as conventional, part of fallible human endeavour which might well have been ordered otherwise (and was, in other parts of the world). We can see from the works that survive that there was not much agreement over what 'convention' and 'nature' exactly meant, and that the contrast between them had different implications in different contexts. None the less, we can see how strong an impact was produced by the idea that important features of life like governments and other social institutions were, however hallowed by long custom, all the same products of 'convention', and might have been different. Many people, in particular those we might be inclined to think of as intellectuals, began to question the way their social and political lives were ordered, and to refuse to trust the values of their predecessors. There was a very noticeable weakening of social and moral continuity and consensus.

These tendencies could lead rapidly to cynicism and scepticism about there being right and wrong answers in matters of value; and they were confirmed by a group of intellectually prominent people usually called 'the sophists'. These were not a school of thought, but a collection of professional teachers who lectured and gave instruction in various cities, and who claimed expertise in the lessons needed for people to get on in life. What they taught varied, but they nearly all taught the skills of speech-making and debating necessary for someone aiming at a public career. They offered the nearest thing to further education available in the ancient world until Plato's own school. Plato presents some of them in his dialogues, usually in a hostile or ludicrous light. They angered him because they had pretensions to knowledge about how to live one's life, which on examination usually turned out to be useless or vacuous; but much more because they regarded matters of moral importance as being a matter of amoral expertise, teachable by them for a fee. They tended to dismiss worries about right and wrong as being without substance, merely the product of one's upbringing; the most famous of them, Protagoras, held a kind of relativism about values and much else. In Plato's view the sophists' influence tended to produce relativism and scepticism about questions of value, and to replace the question of how to live a good life with the question of how best to get on in the world.

One very widespread way of interpreting the *Republic* is to see Plato as concerned mainly or exclusively with the task of refuting the moral sceptic. On this view, what dominated Plato was the fragmentation of accepted moral consensus, and the erosion of confidence in familiar moral values, that he could see around him. The job he saw as primary was that of showing, against the sceptic, that there *are* objective moral truths, and that it is worth while accepting constraints on one's self-aggrandizement because the moral order can in fact be relied upon. Traditional confidence in traditional values is to be re-established.

Now there is something to this interpretation. The bulk of the book is put forward as an attempt to answer Thrasymachus, who claims that the life of injustice is more worthwhile than the life of justice; and he is one of the sophists whom Plato regards as producing scepticism about the value of justice. Thrasymachus derides conventional moral standards; nobody with any intelligence, he maintains, would pay any attention to them if he could get away with violating them. Justice, the behaviour commonly regarded as right, is a mug's game, because it can only benefit others; it is not rational to act against your own interests, and so no-one with any sense would take morality seriously. This is the point of view reformulated by Glaucon and Adeimantus as the challenge Socrates has to meet, and most of the rest of the book is taken up by Plato's attempt to show that it is wrong. And he takes care to claim that anyone just by his account would also be just according to the common moral understanding of the term. So there is indeed some temptation to see Plato, as he is on this interpretation, as a *conservative*, who thought that what was wrong in existing society was the corrosive scepticism produced by Thrasymachus and his like, and who offered the remedy of a social ordering that would reweld the shattered moral structure of society and make people unable and unwilling to question the truth of objective and accepted moral judgements.

Now undoubtedly Thrasymachus is an important opponent. And yet he, and the sophists in general, do have the virtue of questioning what people have been brought up to accept. To that extent, they are intellectually liberating. If the result is scepticism, maybe the moral is not that we should refuse to think, but that we should think a little deeper. After all, Plato does put forward his views in the mouth of Socrates, whose main contribution was that of upsetting people and getting them to question accepted moral views. Some people have found it highly ironic that Socrates, who was famous for his fearless and free questioning, should be made to put forward the authoritarian proposals of the *Republic*. But the fact that Plato does this shows that he does not think of his project as being opposed in principle to the free search for truth, or as an anti-intellectual flight to security. And his proposals are not in fact conservative; he is the sort of ally that conservatives least want. If he reinstates ordinary moral views, it is on a new basis which is remote from anything that the ordinary person would dream of. When we look at the proposals for society that made the *Republic* notorious, it is hard not to think of him as *revolutionary*.

In fact what makes the *Republic* most interesting is the revolution it effects in moral theory, a shift of perspective on the whole question of the right way to live, one which was to be extremely influential. It turns out that the sceptic has a point in rejecting ordinary morality the way this is understood by most people; what Plato gives us is an entirely new kind of theory. And it is important that Thrasymachus is not the only opponent. The dialogue opens in the house of a wealthy and respectable family, and it is their moral views which provoke the whole discussion in the first place and which produce Socrates' first, and devastating, criticisms. Cephalus and Polemarchus are untouched by scepticism about the value of justice; yet their views on it are demolished before the sophists are so much as mentioned. Traditional views, held in their traditional form, are unsatisfactory: they lead to a kind of complacency which is as important a target as scepticism.

And the nature of Plato's systematic proposals makes it entirely clear that he would be a strange kind of conservative. He does appeal to society's moral intuitions for support; but he also proposes arrangements that would outrage most of his contemporaries: common possession of property, sharing of sexual partners, rule by experts. These radical ideas are not eccentric whims, excrescences on a basically conservative scheme. Plato is radically challenging the way we conceive the good life.

So the *Republic* is not what it is often presented as being: a boringly obsessive attempt to put the clock back. Its target is not simple and its response is not simple either. It may well, of course, turn out to be hopelessly over-ambitious, for Plato is combining two projects which are easily regarded as anti-thetical. Attacks on moral scepticism tend to rely on moral consensus and intuition and to give weight to established attitudes; what the sceptic attacks is the truth of accepted moral views, and attacks on him tend to be inherently conservative in so far as it is to be shown that this attack is needless, or wrong. Attacks on moral complacency, on the other hand, tend to emphasize the limitations of moral views which are accepted because of the way they fit in with people's established attitudes; they tend to be inherently revolutionary in so far as they insist on the need to revise and reform our ways of thinking about right and wrong. Plato is making the brave attempt both to establish that there are objective moral truths and to under-take a considerable overhaul of what those objective moral truths are.

One matter must be discussed before we turn to Book 1, because it affects our interpretation of the whole dialogue. What is the *Republic* about? The answer might seem to be easy: it is about justice. *Justice* is the usual, because the only reasonable, translation of the Greek work *dikaiosunē*, which is the word Plato uses for his subject-matter. But does the concept of *justice* really correspond to that of *dikaiosunē*? Does the *Republic* give us a 'theory of justice' in the way that, for example, Rawls's *A Theory of Justice* does?

Dikaiosunē, it is sometimes claimed, can cover a wider area than *justice*, and be used for right conduct in general. Plato appears to support this idea when he makes Socrates at 352d describe the search for justice as a search 'for the right way to live'. Hence it is often suggested that *dikaiosunē* should be translated as 'righteousness' or the like, and that it corresponds more closely to 'morality' than to 'justice'.

Two points of terminology are important here. Firstly, we would naturally distinguish justice from other virtues by reference to *rights*: rights are often the basic or key concept in a modern theory of justice. Plato has no word for 'rights'. He and his contemporaries distinguish justice as a particular virtue rather by means of the notions of equality and of keeping to what is one's own. The vice it is opposed to is called *pleonexia* – having and wanting more than one is entitled to. The ordinary view, in the person of Polemarchus, is that justice is giving everyone what is owing, that is, what is due or appropriate. We shall see whether what Plato says about justice can be reformulated in terms of rights; the fact that he lacks the word does not mean that he is not talking about what we do when we talk of rights.

Secondly, I have opposed justice to the wider notion of 'morality'; but nothing crucial is meant to hang on this word. There is no Greek word which answers comfortably to 'moral' (one reason why translators suggest archaisms like 'righteousness' and the like), and this is no accident; our use of the word and many of the distinctive assumptions often brought with it derive from a tradition foreign to the Greek one. I shall try not to use it in a loaded sense; 'moral' is not meant to suggest a strong and exclusive contrast with, for example, 'prudential'. I shall use 'morality' for the area of practical reasoning carried on by an agent which is concerned with the best way for a person to live.

It is commonly suggested that *dikaiosunē* should not be

rendered by 'justice'; but it is worth noticing that people who make this suggestion seldom stick by it. It is very common for a translation or commentary on the *Republic* to say on the first page that 'justice' is, for example, a 'thoroughly unsuitable word' to translate *dikaiosunē*; and then to go on to talk of 'justice' throughout. But to do this is to risk getting Plato's subject-matter wrong, for if *dikaiosunē* means something like 'morality' then the *Republic* is not in fact a book about *justice*.

This problem arises independently of translation. Aristotle, Plato's greatest pupil, points to *dikaiosunē* as a star example of a word which is ambiguous (*Topics* 106b29), and discusses the point at length at the start of Book 5 of his *Nicomachean Ethics*. The word, he says, has two different but related senses: it can be used for law-abidingness and virtuous behaviour to others in general, or for the more specialized virtue which we would call justice, and which is opposed to *pleonexia*. He probably has Plato in mind here, and is voicing a criticism which has been repeated; that the *Republic* is a muddle, because Plato slides between a broad and a narrow sense of *dikaiosunē* and it is never clear whether he is talking about justice or about morality in general.

So a lot hangs on the question, whether the *Republic* really is about *justice*. In fact, I think that it is, and that Plato is not guilty of shifting between a broad and a narrow sense of *dikaiosunē*. He is talking about justice throughout. He makes justice more important than we might expect, and his theory of justice has a much wider scope than some; but that is another matter. Even if *dikaiosunē* has two senses, as Aristotle supposes, this does not affect Plato's argument; and the instincts of translators who use 'justice' as a translation for it are sounder than their qualms in their prefaces.

It would be surprising if Plato were to confuse justice and morality; for one thing, in earlier dialogues justice is always treated as one virtue among many, and as 'part' of virtue as a whole. In the *Republic* itself, the challenge that Socrates is set at the beginning of Book 2 concerns the narrow notion: Thrasymachus had claimed that it is better to be unjust, meaning by this, having more than one's rightful share, and Glaucon renews the point in the context of equality and fairness, justice and injustice being characterized as abstaining, or not abstaining, from what is another's (360b,d). And Plato's own analysis of justice does not let it usurp the role of virtue as a whole; it is carefully distinguished from another social virtue, moderation, which appears to cover the same ground.

But of course by the time we get to the end of the *Republic* we have had more than a theory of justice in the narrow sense. We have been told a good deal about the good life in general. This is because Plato has what can be called an expansive theory of justice. He does not think that matters of what is just and unjust can be settled in a way which will leave untouched other central moral questions that arise in a society. One might hold that injustice occurs in a society only if people's specific rights are violated, or antecedently recognized laws are being broken. But an expansive theory, like Plato's, holds that a society is unjustly run if it fails wider moral requirements, for example if wealth is honoured more than desert. Hence it will hold that the needs of justice require wholesale moral reform. Plato believes that once we get clear about the nature of justice, we will see that for a society to be just it must be drastically reorganized in every department, not only in its enforcement of the laws. Injustice cannot be corrected by merely righting a few past wrongs; the whole distribution of wealth, honours, and goods within society must be made to conform to fundamental moral requirements. And hence the just life turns out to be the moral life after all – but not through any confusion of terms; rather through an insistence on the centrality of justice and the wide extent of its requirements.

Justice is a virtue which regulates our relations with others. An expansive theory of justice will therefore make our relations with others central to the moral life, and tend to stress the individual's relations in society as partly constitutive of moral attitudes. Conversely, a theory which pays great attention to the uniqueness of each individual and the autonomy of his moral decisions will tend to give justice a restricted scope, and deny that the removal of injustice requires a moral reordering of the whole of society. Because Plato's is an expansive theory, we can suspect from the start that he is going to pay less attention to individuality than western liberals have come to expect.

FURTHER READING

The *Republic* is available in several translations, most of them
in paperback. The most easily available are those of Grube,
Lee, Lindsay, Cornford, and Bloom. Jowett's classic Victorian
translation is also available in paperback. The Loeb edition, in
two volumes, has the Greek text facing a translation by Shorey.
I have mainly used the translation of Grube (Hackett), but
sometimes make my own translations; I comment whenever
the translation makes a difference to the way a passage is taken.

A good introduction to Plato's historical background can be
found in J. K. Davies's *Democracy and Classical Greece*. C. Rowe's
An Introduction to Greek Ethics gives a short introduction to
Plato's intellectual background, and a descriptive account of
Plato's and Aristotle's main works. K. J. Dover's *Greek Popular
Morality in the Time of Plato and Aristotle* is a substantial and
fascinating book which brings together evidence from contemporary sources for popular attitudes with which Plato
would have been familiar. Background on Socrates and the
fifth-century intellectual movements can be found in W.
Guthrie's *History of Greek Philosophy*, vol. iii. (This is available
as two paperbacks, entitled *Socrates* and *The Sophists*.)

Accessible introductions to the *Republic* for those without
Greek are Cross and Woozley's *Plato's Republic, a Philosophical
Introduction* and N. White's *A Companion to Plato's Republic*. A
good survey of the dialogue and relevant literature is in
Guthrie's *History of Greek Philosophy*, iv. 434–561. I. Crombie,
An Examination of Plato's Doctrines, in two volumes, is invaluable
on every point in the *Republic* and has a chapter devoted to it
in the first volume. A densely written but rewarding book is
T. Irwin's *Plato's Moral Theory*, in which the theory of the
Republic is contrasted sharply with the work of Plato's earlier
period.

Good collections of articles, for those wishing to follow up
various points, are: Vlastos (ed.), *Plato*, vols. i and ii, and
Platonic Studies, and Allen (ed.), *Studies in Plato's Metaphysics*.

The problem about 'justice' and '*dikaiosunē*' is lucidly
discussed in Vlastos, 'The Theory of Social Justice in Plato's
Rep.', forthcoming as part of a larger work and now available
in H. North (ed.), *Interpretations of Plato*.

Readers are referred to the chapter on the *Republic* in Irwin, *Plato's Moral Theory*, for a particularly thorough coverage of the main philosophical and scholarly literature and their bearing on the issues raised in this book.

There is a Bibliography at the end of the book.

Chapter 2

Book One

It is clear to any reader of the *Republic* that Book 1 is different from the rest of the work. It opens with an elaborate scene-setting, and is rich with dramatic indications. Socrates maintains that he himself has no knowledge, but does his best to undermine, by his questioning, the confidence of the people he is talking to. The conclusion is negative; Socrates has argued his interlocutors into silence, but nothing replaces their previous beliefs. In all this Book 1 contrasts sharply with the rest of the *Republic*, where in spite of the dialogue form there are no strongly characterized interlocutors, and Socrates delivers what is essentially a monologue. Book 1 does, however, resemble the early, Socratic dialogues, and falls into the pattern that many of them exemplify: Socrates talks to a character about some moral quality – courage in the *Laches*, piety in the *Euthyphro*, friendship in the *Lysis* – and uncovers the fact that the beliefs he holds about it are inadequate, or even incoherent. Usually the discussion arises out of some practical problem or moral dilemma, and frequently this arises because the character in question either has, or appears to have, the moral quality under discussion. The discussion in the *Euthyphro*, for example, arises from the fact that Euthyphro is a seer and therefore something of a professional expert on piety and right behaviour to the gods, and yet is proposing to do something which strikes Socrates, and most of his friends, as shockingly impious. The general lesson of these dialogues is that people who possess or claim to know about a moral quality are quite likely to have wrong or unsatisfactory beliefs about it, and to be unable to withstand intellectual probing on the matter. The characters concerned often suffer an experience which the reader sometimes shares: irritation that their confident beliefs have been removed when nothing is offered to replace them. This is what happens in *Republic* Book 1. A discussion with a rich man who believes that riches help one to be just sparks off a discussion of justice, which exposes common beliefs about it as radically wrong, but concludes that we are still in the dark as to what it is.

It is not surprising that many scholars have concluded from the contrast of style between Book 1 and the rest of the work that this Book was written earlier than the rest of the *Republic*, and had led a life of its own as a separate dialogue. There is one interesting bit of external evidence for this. In Book 1 a character called Cleitophon intervenes to make an unsuccessful attempt to help Thrasymachus. There exists among Plato's works a short dialogue called *Cleitophon* (usually labelled spurious, but for no very good reasons), in which Cleitophon is given more of a say. There, he complains to Socrates that, although he would prefer to go to him for instruction, he is thrown back upon Thrasymachus, because at least the latter has definite and helpful views about what justice actually is, whereas Socrates is merely negative: he knocks down other people's accounts of justice, and implores them with great passion to live the life of real justice, but offers them no help at all about what this real justice actually comes down to; they are left baffled as to what the first steps in living the good life could be. Now this makes no sense at all as a reaction to the complete *Republic*; but it does make sense as a reaction to Book 1 on its own.

Why, however, should Plato re-use an earlier dialogue? We know that he took great pains over the literary shape of his work, and could easily have written a new introduction if he had wanted to. Surely he is aware of the contrast, and it is meant to serve some purpose. We shall see that, even if Book 1 was written separately, this does not matter; it forms an entirely suitable introduction to the main discussion. I shall return to this when we have looked at the arguments.

Book 1 gives us the only dramatic indications that we get, and it is worth examining them, because Plato does not begin his philosophical arguments about justice in a vacuum: he presents them as arising naturally out of a concrete situation. Right at the beginning we are shown that philosophical investigation does not take place in abstraction from the real world, but arises to expose inadequacies in the way we actually think. Plato does sometimes incline towards the view that the philosopher does not really live in the same world as other people (and there are dialogues, like the *Theaetetus* (172c–177b) where he says this), but the *Republic* at any rate begins from the premise that philosophers should not ignore the problems of the imperfect world around them; they should become aware of them and do something to solve them.

CEPHALUS AND POLEMARCHUS: MORAL COMPLACENCY

Socrates and Glaucon are visiting the Piraeus, the port of Athens, for a festival, and are jokingly forced to visit the house of Cephalus and his sons Polemarchus and Lysias. Cephalus is not an Athenian citizen; he is a 'resident alien' from Syracuse who has grown rich from trade and manufacture. In Athens the citizens in the main made their living from land; trade and most of what we would call commercial forms of moneymaking were in the hands of Greeks from other cities, who lived in Athens without citizen rights. Cephalus is a man who has chosen to spend his life making money by living in a foreign city and renouncing all the rights, duties, and activities of a citizen, things vitally important to the self-respect of most Greeks. By the end of the *Republic* we know in the harshest terms just how low Plato puts the life dedicated to moneymaking, but even in Book I we see his contempt for it and for the complacency it engenders.

It is often said that Plato's picture of Cephalus is sympathetic, that we are supposed to respect the dignified old man sitting in his household enjoying a tranquil old age free from lusts and cares. But things are not so simple. We should remember here that the *Republic* was written much later than the time it depicts. Plato was writing for an audience that knew that the security based on wealth which Cephalus had spent his life building up, and which is so much stressed here, was wholly illusory: only a few years later, when Athens fell, the family was totally ruined, Polemarchus executed, and Lysias driven into exile. (Lysias later became a professional speech-writer, and in his speech *Against Eratosthenes* we can read a vivid account of his family's ruin.) Money cannot provide even the kind of security it promises, and a life devoted to the pursuit of money is a life whose highest priority is something which can be lost through the actions of other people. We shall see later why it is wrong to care about external things more than the state of one's soul, which is something one cannot lose. Meanwhile we see the shortcomings of those who do care principally for money. There are enough malicious touches in Plato's picture of Cephalus to show us that we are being presented with a limited and complacent man.

He begins by saying that Socrates really ought to visit more often, because he himself finds that he enjoys discussion ever more as he loses the capacity for bodily pleasures. This is, to say the least, a back-handed compliment. For Socrates, discussion and philosophy are the most important and urgent things in life – 'the unexamined life is not worth living'. Cephalus is saying, in a tactless and insensitive way, that this sort of thing is fine once you have nothing better to do. 'Philosophy' is thought of as something old men do when they look back and make vague and complacent comments about Life. Cephalus is better than most in that he at least does not resent old age and the waning of desire; this is the nearest someone like this can get to philosophical detachment. But Socrates probes a bit further: is Cephalus able to achieve tranquillity because of his temperament, or because he is well-off? Cephalus' answer shows the limitations of his mind. Riches, he says, are not actually sufficient for a man to be just; but they do help. It is very hard for a poor man to be just throughout life, though rich men also can fail to be just (330a). (We are presumably meant to notice the insensitivity of this; Socrates' concern with philosophy kept him poor, something brought out later when Glaucon offers to pay Thrasymachus on Socrates' behalf.) Money is very important to Cephalus; though he avoids the more vulgar obsessions of most *nouveaux riches* he has spent his life building up the remains of a fortune spent by his father.

The chief consolation of riches, Cephalus says, is that a man can die in tranquillity. Even someone who sneered at tales of rewards and punishments in the next world when he was young, starts to worry about them when he gets older, and it is a great help to have had the aid of wealth in avoiding wrongdoing; the rich man need never lie or keep what was not his, so he can have a clear conscience. Cephalus is not an unscrupulous businessman who has got rich by not being squeamish about his methods; he is concerned about living rightly. But his ideal of the right way to live is a very limited one. His notion of doing right consists in observing a few simple rules or maxims like 'don't lie' and 'give back what isn't yours'. He thinks of them in a very external fashion: what matters is whether or not you perform certain actions, like sacrificing to the gods, and not the spirit in which this is done: the rich man, he says, can die knowing that he has not deceived anyone 'even unwillingly'. This is why he thinks frankly that it is harder for a poor man to be just; he may owe someone money, or owe the gods a sacrifice, and not be able to afford it, and so may die having done wrong, though unwillingly. Right and wrong consist for him in the performance of certain actions (which riches help you to do): the *kind* of person you are does not matter. For someone like this, morality is something entirely external, a matter of rules to follow and duties to perform; and these are taken over without questioning whether these are the right things to do – whether, for example there *should* be duties which the rich can perform better than the poor – or questioning the spirit in which they should be done – whether, for example, they *should* be such that you could fail to do them even unwillingly. It is not surprising that someone who thinks of morality as externally as this has no particular motive to be moral except fear. Cephalus is quite frank that most people only perform their duties because they fear punishment – if not here, then after death. He is superior to most people not in that he genuinely desires to do what is right without any fear, but in that he is better prepared and more rational about it than most; he has not been caught short at death's door with debts unpaid, but has taken care to pay them all beforehand. But basically he does not care very much about morality. He has no intellectual interest in the matter at all. He enjoys a chat about it with Socrates, but as soon as the latter asks questions which force him to think, he loses interest and goes away with the polite fiction that he has to attend to the sacrifice (which is in fact over).

I have spent some time on Cephalus because Plato does, and

because the picture of him is important: it depicts the view which Polemarchus will articulate, the ordinary person's view of justice. Cephalus is someone who has never had to become self-conscious about the matter, whereas Polemarchus has given it some thought, but they agree in thinking of justice very externally, as a matter of sticking to a few rules and maxims; motives are unimportant, for what matters is that the debts be paid, in whatever spirit. The only reason for being just is that, perhaps in the very long run, it is better for you. If you neglect justice, you may be tormented in your old age by fear of hell-fire; and who knows, maybe there *is* a hell-fire.

What is wrong with this view? In Book 1 we see three rather striking things wrong with it. Firstly, it leads to complacency. Cephalus and Polemarchus both have no doubt that they are just men; justice is not perceived as something *difficult*, which might involve effort, and which you might not be sure you had achieved. Secondly, precisely because justice is not thought of as needing much effort, no need is felt to think about it much, and so people like this are very quickly reduced to silence by Socrates; their beliefs have no intellectual backing. Once complacency is shaken, it leaves a void. And thirdly, that void is all too plausibly filled by scepticism – it is not for nothing that Polemarchus is followed by Thrasymachus. Once your confidence is shaken that justice is sticking to a few simple rules, there is nothing to put in its place except the sceptical view that justice is nothing but a racket; in Book 1 nobody envisages any other coherent alternative.

What Socrates picks Cephalus up on is the claim that justice is telling the truth and giving back what is not yours (331c). 'Yes, but this thing justice, are we to say without qualification that it is truth-telling and giving back what one has received?' Socrates at once objects that there may be occasions when telling the truth and giving back what one has received may not be just. If you borrow a weapon from someone and then he goes mad it would not be right to give it back when he asks for it; nor is it always right to tell the truth to someone not in their senses. This is a move of a kind often made in the Socratic dialogues. Somebody who appears to have a particular virtue is asked what it is, and replies by specifying actions of a certain type. Euthyphro, who is a supposed expert on piety, is asked what that is, and replies, 'the pious is just what I'm doing now, prosecuting for murder and temple theft and everything of that sort' (*Euthyphro* 5d–e). Similarly, Cephalus, whom most people think a just man, characterizes justice as performing a few basic duties like telling the truth, not deceiving people, and not keeping what is not yours. The trouble in these cases is always the same: Socrates comes up with circumstances in which the supposed case of *X* is a case of the opposite, or else a case in which *X* is displayed in a radically opposed kind of situation. Euthyphro's action is pious for the reasons he gives; but it is also impious because prosecuting your father is, in a strongly patriarchal society like fifth-century Athens, impious. The actions which are commonly just can be unjust, in odd enough circumstances. The moral is the same: you cannot say what a virtue is by giving a list of kinds of action, for the same kind of action might not display that virtue, and the virtue might be displayed in other kinds of action.

It is sometimes objected that Cephalus did not intend to define justice or say what it is; Socrates has picked on his stray remarks and unfairly elevated them into a definition. No doubt Cephalus did not intend to 'define' justice, but it is clear that on his conception, justice can be no more than the performance of a list of duties, and Socrates is forcing him to recognize this, and to see that this cannot be right. In fact I do not think that it is useful to discuss the argument in terms of 'definitions'. There is no harm in using the word as long as it is taken to mean something like an account of what justice is, not to be a precise piece of philosophical terminology. Plato does sometimes take an interest in definitions (in the *Meno*, for example) but it is wrong to think of him as being obsessed with what we would call a search for definitions. Questions about definitions are for us questions about the meaning of words. But Plato's general enterprise of asking what justice, or courage, or whatever, is, does not fit well into the mould of asking about words. He is not interested in examining how most people use the word – no doubt most people would agree with Cephalus, and the question is whether they are right. Nor is he interested in stipulating his own meaning for 'justice' – that would lack point in a discussion which is to keep contact with the original moral dilemma. But if he is not concerned with words in these ways, then it seems as though he must, somehow, be concerned with 'things'; and it is often said that he is trying to produce a 'real definition', which is a definition but somehow defines a thing. Not surprisingly, this has been found mysterious. The truth is that Plato does not think that there is a sharp difference of kind between what we can find out through investigating the meanings of words, and what we can find out by investigating what is true of the things our words refer to. This is not, of course, to deny that Plato could make the distinction on an everyday level, merely to deny that he lays philosophical weight on it. What he is doing is investigating *what justice is*; and this is a comprehensible task, one undertaken in books like Rawls's *A Theory of Justice*, but one not usefully described as giving a definition of justice. As we shall see later on, the meaning most people give to 'justice' does not determine the content of Plato's account. So Cephalus has not mistaken the nature of the enquiry, only given an inadequate answer.

We cannot, then, say what justice is by listing a few duties like truth-telling. At this point Polemarchus takes up the argument. He does not question the idea that justice must be characterized by the doing of certain actions; he merely thinks that they must be specified on a higher level of generality so as to avoid counter-examples like the ones Socrates has just given. Quoting the poet Simonides he suggests that justice is giving everyone 'what is owed'. Socrates makes him be more precise, and he says that this is a poetic way of saying what justice is: giving everyone what is due or appropriate. This suggestion is taken seriously. It is not obviously weak and inadequate as was Cephalus' attempt. It is taken as the best the ordinary person can come up with when challenged to reflect on what justice is. Socrates brings four objections to it. They are commonly taken to be feeble if not sophistical; but in fact they are quite effective. For they show up the inadequacy of the notion that one can say what justice is by specifying kinds of action at all. Later in the *Republic*, when we find what Plato's own account is, we shall see that he moves away entirely from the doing of certain actions, and instead characterizes justice as a state of the agent. The primary questions will turn out to be those about the just person, and questions about which actions are just actions will be in an important way secondary. The arguments with

Polemarchus clear the way for these views, for they show the hopelessness of trying to characterize justice by appealing first to just actions.

Firstly (332a–333e) Socrates forces Polemarchus to admit that, if what he says is true, justice is trivial, because there is no special field for it to be concerned with. Medicine is the skill concerned with remedies and cures for the body; cookery is the skill concerned with producing palatable food. What field is the skill of justice concerned with? Once the question has been put this way, Polemarchus is gradually cornered. The characteristic scope of justice, he says, is to do good to your friends and harm to your enemies. But to help your friends you have to help them in some specific way. But the best person to help you when you are ill is a doctor, and the best person when you are at sea is a navigator. The just man has no expertise of his own. Polemarchus retreats to the claim that the just man is specially useful in business, where his honesty can be relied on. Yet even this is limited; for any specific purpose, someone else will always be better at using the money or goods or whatever it is that is required. The just man is only really useful when they are being deposited with him, not when they are being used. 'So in all spheres justice is useless when you are using things, and useful when you are not?' Polemarchus is forced to the conclusion that 'justice is not a very serious thing'.

The fault in this argument seems to be the way Polemarchus accepts the idea that justice is a skill, on the basis of the analogies with other skills. It is Socrates who introduces this idea; Polemarchus himself never said that justice was a skill; one's reaction is that he should have rejected the analogy and said that justice is a matter of following certain rules, perhaps, but not a matter of expertise. And worse: later on in the book Socrates gets Thrasymachus into trouble by using the very same analogy which he had got Polemarchus to accept in order to make trouble for him. So it looks as though the very first argument in the book combines the faults of being unfair and ineffective. Neither objection is justified: but to see why not, we need to look more closely at the notion of a skill.

The word translated 'skill' is *technē* (whence 'technical'), which is sometimes also translated 'art' or 'craft'. The notion of a skill is prominent in Plato, and his use of it rewards examination; his most sustained discussion is at *Gorgias* 462–3, where he contrasts a skill with an empirical 'knack' or 'know-how'. Put very generally, *technē* or skill is an organized body of knowledge of the ways to achieve a certain end. Some skills are practical, like cooking, while others are not, like doing mental arithmetic. Most skills have products – shoemaking, weaving, cookery again – while others are not naturally so described, for example playing a musical instrument. Some are more specific than others – ploughing is more specific than farming; and some fall under others because they are more specialized ways of achieving the end of the more general one, as with ploughing and farming again.

What strikes Plato is interesting about a skill is the intellectual element, the fact that the craftsman *knows* what he is doing. If he is a good potter, then he uncontroversially knows how to make pots, and understands what is a good and what a bad pot, and why. In the *Apology*, we find that Socrates was extremely impressed by this. Craftsmen undoubtedly know what they are doing; something that struck him as contrasting with the shakiness of people's assumption of knowledge in other spheres. In the early dialogues, Socrates often develops the idea that virtue, or a particular virtue, is or is like a skill, and what attracts him seems to be the point about knowledge. His confidence in the analogy is not constant. Sometimes (as in the *Protagoras*) he shows considerable optimism about the notion that virtue is, properly, a skill, in which the experts are distinguished by their superior knowledge and expertise. In other places (the *Charmides*, *Hippias Minor*, *Euthydemus* 288–292) he shows more reservations over the comparison of virtue to a skill. But the crucial point of the analogy seems always to have been the intellectual grasp a skill involves, and the consequences of this, such as that skills are impartible, and involve an element of generality. A master can pass on his trade to a pupil because he can teach him general rules about what to do in types of situation; the pupil does not have to work things out afresh every time. Aristotle developed this point in his own terms by saying that skills are the first step up to knowledge because instead of just coping with the particulars as they come along, as the man does who has merely experience and a knack, the man with skill is dealing with the universal which is present in all the instances he deals with. Later on in Book 1, when Socrates is arguing with Thrasymachus, the point about knowledge and intellectual grasp seems to be the aspect of skill which he has in mind in comparing justice to skill.

But there is another important aspect of the skill analogy too, less attractive for the idea of treating justice like a skill. A skill has a determinate end and finds means and methods of attaining it; the reasoning involved is means-end reasoning. It is no part of a skill to question what its own end is, though of course this can be questioned from other points of view, including the viewpoints of other skills. The ploughman has to work out how to plough, not whether he should plough, though if he is a farmer he may well question whether ploughing is the best thing to do. A good doctor can heal the sick, but it is not his business as a doctor to question whether the sick ought to be healed. Of course, in his private capacity he may be faced with the question whether to let a patient die; but that is a matter of medical ethics, not of medicine; and skill in medicine is no guarantee that he will answer it in the appropriate way.

It is a matter of some controversy how aware Plato was, in the earlier dialogues, of the importance of this feature of the skill analogy, and how far he welcomed it. However, all that matters in the present context is that it is this aspect of the analogy which Polemarchus allows to be foisted on him, and which gets him into trouble. It is true that it is Socrates' idea and not his own; but he never protests, and we should take it that this feature is implicit in Polemarchus' notion of justice, but that he has not thought it out; he is unhappy with its consequences when Socrates draws them out. Polemarchus has never questioned the idea that justice consists in doing certain simply specifiable actions, following some simple rules or maxims which say what these are; Socrates brings out that he is implicitly thinking of these like the rules of a skill, a means of achieving an antecedently determined end. But given this, justice is on his conception of it trivial, for it does not seem to be an expertise that achieves anything important. What is it that justice helps us to produce or achieve? Nothing very much, Polemarchus admits unhappily.

We may think that Polemarchus has collapsed too quickly; there are two very different moves he could have made, which would have saved him from being forced to Socrates' conclusion. Firstly, he could have said that justice is a skill aiming at an end, but that this end is not trivial – it is happiness or a satisfactory life: a very general aim which we try to achieve in exercising more specific skills, and which therefore includes the exercise of the specific skills rather than being pushed out by them. But it is not surprising that this does not occur to Polemarchus; for it is not a very natural reaction from the viewpoint of the ordinary moral agent. We have already seen that for Cephalus and Polemarchus justice *is* fairly trivial, certainly not something that structures their lives as a whole.

Another move would seem the obvious one to someone impressed by the Kantian claim that *moral* rules and maxims have an unmistakeably different status from the rules of skill and of prudence. A Kantian would say that Polemarchus goes wrong right from the start in letting the maxims of justice be compared to those of skills. A skill is dependent on its end; if you don't want to achieve the end then you lose any reason for exercising the skill. But moral rules have an unconditional force; they apply whether you want to achieve any given end of yours or not. So Polemarchus goes wrong in thinking of justice as a skill with a trivial end; in fact it is not a skill with an end at all but a system of rules which do not depend for their force on the achieving of any end. But again it is not surprising that this does not occur to Polemarchus. The fact that Greek lacks any word for 'moral' only underlines the fact that he is unacquainted with the idea that *moral* rules and maxims have an absolutely unconditional force that other rules lack, and that it is somehow obvious that this is the case. Polemarchus thinks of what we would label 'morality', and its rules and maxims, as part of the practical reasoning an agent carries on; he sees it as quite legitimate to treat rules of skill and rules of justice alike and demand a differentiating feature. We are, I suspect, closer to Plato than to Kant on this point, and are no longer comfortable appealing to the ineffable force supposedly possessed by *moral* rules.

And so Socrates' argument is fair enough: he brings out the fact that someone like Polemarchus is implicitly thinking of justice as being like a skill with a given end – but with the defect that in this case there is no *important* given end that justice helps us to attain. And, as we have seen, this is the conception of justice shared by Cephalus and Polemarchus: they respect justice, but it is not an important part of their lives.

Socrates' second argument goes from 333e to 334b. The man who can cure can also bring about disease; the man with an ability to keep a thing safe can also steal it. A skill is always a skill for 'doing opposites': if you are skilled in doing X you are also skilled in doing the opposite of X. So on Polemarchus' conception the just man, who is good at keeping things safe, will also be good at appropriating them, and so will turn out to be 'a sort of thief'. Polemarchus does not like this conclusion, but he admits that this is where the argument leads (334a9). He is of course wide open to this objection: there is nothing to prevent a competence being used to attain a goal which is quite opposed to the goal it is meant for. What comes out sharply here is that Polemarchus sees nothing in his concept of justice to distinguish it from mere means–end reasoning; it does not have built into it the notion that a just action must be aimed at some good. Of course he does in fact believe this: he is very upset when he is forced into saying the opposite. But he fails to fasten on to the fact that it is not essential to his notion of justice that as a virtue it must have a good aim.

We can see from this that Plato does think that it is essential to justice that you are aiming at some good in performing a just action; it is not a neutral means to a variety of ends. Put thus baldly, this may sound platitudinous. But it is significant that Polemarchus' notion does not include it. And it is worth remembering when we get on to the central books and find the stress laid by Plato on reason and reasoning in the good life. Plato's good person is a person in whom reason is supreme; but we can see from this argument that he does not mean by reasoning, mere means–end reasoning, the efficient calculation of the technocrat.

Polemarchus is confused, but prepared to stick to his basic idea, and restates his position (334b): justice is to help your friends and harm your enemies. Socrates picks him up: what exactly does he mean by 'friends' and 'enemies'? Polemarchus says that a man's friends are those he thinks good, his enemies those he thinks bad. But, Socrates points out, this can run him into trouble, for what happens when he is wrong? He may think

a man bad when he really is good, in which case he would seem
to be committed to saying that it would be right to harm the
good.

Polemarchus is very shocked by this conclusion; there must
be something wrong with the argument, he says, if it shows
that. What Socrates has done is to show him that his own
intuitions about what is just run ahead of the primitive morality
he claims to believe in. Polemarchus would not be unusual
among people of his time in saying that justice is helping your
friends and harming your enemies; this is a view natural in a
world where desirable goods are in limited supply and people
are predominantly perceived by others as being in competition
for them. In such a world, the qualities and virtues most
admired will be the 'competitive' ones, as they have been
labelled, rather than the 'co-operative' ones, and the moral
world will be perceived as being divided between relations with
one's friends (not necessarily people you like, but people who
are on your side, co-operating in your enterprise) and one's
enemies (again, not necessarily people you hate, but people
who are in your way, preventing you from getting what you
want). A great deal of stress has been laid on the extent to which
the ancient Greeks emphasized the importance of competitively
valuable qualities, and seem to have been less inhibited than
we are in extolling strength and power regardless of the agent's
worth in other respects. (Some have gone so far as to claim that
this happens to such an extent that the Greeks lacked our
notion of morality; but this is a vexed question which raises
the problem of what, if anything, is the core meaning of 'moral'
and related concepts.) What matters in the present context is
that Polemarchus, when asked for the usual or sanctioned
view of justice, replies in terms of the crude view of the poets: it
is helping the people on your side, and doing down the other
side; but this does not in fact answer to his own best intuitions.
He is shocked by the idea of harming someone who is in fact
good, even if on the other side; so he does instinctively think of
justice as something possibly involved in his dealings with
anyone. There is not one set of standards for one group of
people and another for another; justice is not dependent on or
created by social position or relationship to one's group.

But this conflicts with what he puts forward as his considered view, and so Socrates has shown up an incoherence in his moral viewpoint. And the real point of the exchange is probably to show us this, not the laudability of Polemarchus' intuitions. We have been shown another inadequacy in the unreflective moral viewpoint: if you think of morality as a set of rules that you must obey, but which you think of as external demands, then these may be implicitly contradicted by the felt results of your experience. Polemarchus is thus vulnerable: Socrates produces an argument which shows that his avowed views lead to something he rejects violently, and he can only respond that the argument is wicked if it leads there, but can neither fault the argument nor adjust his avowed view to the way he actually sees things. It does not take much imagination to see that Plato's target is again moral complacency; Polemarchus has accepted justice as a set of rules governing a not very basic part of his life, and the result is that he has an unreflective and external attitude to them, and they are not integrated with the way he actually lives. No wonder his beliefs about justice collapse at the first query.

Two points are worth noticing here. Firstly, Thrasymachus is going to go on to champion the idea that life is, in fact, a competition where everyone is, whether they like it or not, trying to do everyone else down, and he emphatically rejects the idea that justice is really an impartial notion that might require one to recognize virtue in an enemy and wickedness in a friend. Polemarchus is inconsistent; but if you hold inconsistent views it is open to you to reject either of them. Plato clearly thinks that what Polemarchus should retain are the intuitions that justice concerns a person's goodness or badness, not their contribution towards one's own projects; but before having this expounded we hear Thrasymachus, who clearly thinks that what Polemarchus should jettison are the intuitions, which he would characterize as merely sentimental, and stick to the view that justice in one's dealings is entirely derivative from the perception of one's self-interest. The result of realizing, after reflection, that one's moral beliefs are incoherent is likely to be scepticism.

Secondly, the ease with which Polemarchus is flattened prepares us for the immense stress which Plato lays later on the notion of *knowledge* in connection with goodness. The good

person must be someone with knowledge, and we shall find
that this puts severe constraints on what is to count as being
just; at the very least good people must be articulate about
what they are doing and why. For Plato, there is no such thing
as 'natural virtue', an untrained disposition to do the right
thing unaccompanied by any ability to explain and defend
what is done.

The last argument (335b–e) is the most dubious, though in
some ways the most interesting. Polemarchus has been cornered
into admitting that justice cannot merely be helping your
friends and harming your enemies – your friends must be good
for it to be just to help, and your enemies must be bad for it to
be just to harm them. This presents itself to him as a view that
he is happy to hold (335b). Socrates, however, now gets him
to admit that justice cannot involve harming anyone at all,
even one's enemies. The conclusion (336a) is that the view that
justice is helping friends and harming enemies cannot be the
thought of a wise man, but rather of some jumped-up and
morally coarse dictator, of which type some examples are
given.

The argument goes as follows. Polemarchus maintains that
the good man will harm some people at any rate, namely the
wicked (335b). Socrates replies by producing counter-
examples: a horse when harmed is a worse horse, a dog when
harmed is a worse dog. They are worse precisely in those
respects in which a horse or dog is a good horse or dog, worse
specimens of their kind. So men when harmed become worse
specimens of their kind, worse in respect of human excellence
(335c). Here we should notice something which makes it easier
for Plato to argue as he does: in Greek the word I have
translated 'excellence', *aretē*, is also the word that we translate
as 'virtue'. There is no sharp distinction between moral and
other kinds of excellence. A good specimen of a horse shows
aretē, and there is no unbridgeable difference of kind between
dispositions that make people morally good and those that make
them good in other spheres. So Socrates' next move comes more
naturally to him than it would to us. Having got Polemarchus
to agree that people who are harmed are made worse in respect
of human excellence, he gets him to admit that justice is the
human excellence (335c) – a move he is happy to make, seeing

no sharp break between this case and the other kinds of excellence just mentioned. Socrates goes on to say that if this is so, then those who are harmed must become more unjust; for to be harmed is to become worse in respect of one's characteristic excellence, and ˉin the case of people this is justice. But it would be very odd if justice operated in such a way as to produce its opposite. Those who possess musical skill do not, by the operation of that very skill, make others deficient in it. Nor do those who possess skill in horsemanship make others deficient in it precisely by the exercise of that skill. So those possessing justice cannot, by the operation of that very skill, make others deficient in it, i.e. more unjust. More analogies are produced to back this up. Heat makes things hot, not cold. Dryness makes things dry, not wet. Excellence makes things excellent, not the opposite (335d). So the just person cannot operate so as to make others more unjust; and, given the steps of the argument already accepted, this means that he cannot harm anybody. Injustice must be produced by the unjust person, so it is he who will do any harming that is done.

This is an irritating argument, because even if one agrees with the conclusion, it is hard to go along with the steps of the argument. Commonly it is said that the argument fails because it trades on an ambiguity. What Polemarchus meant when he talked about harming enemies was damaging their interests, not making them worse men; the word Plato uses, *blaptein*, is thus ambiguous between 'hurt' and 'harm', and Socrates draws a conclusion about harming when Polemarchus was talking about hurting. This seems to be the wrong approach, however. It is true that one can hurt someone without harming them, but this is clearly not a difference that interests Polemarchus; he is concerned with hurting one's enemies and possibly harming them in the process. In ordinary cases one does harm people by hurting them, and it is presumably ordinary cases that concern us here.

The real fault in the argument, as often in Book 1, is not an easily locatable ambiguity. There is nothing formally wrong with the argument. The problems lie rather in interpreting the premises.

Firstly, Polemarchus agrees without argument that justice is the human excellence or *aretē*, that is, that justice is to people what being a good specimen of its type is to a horse or a dog. This is rather a breath-taking assumption. Surely a good specimen of humanity is distinguished by good health and functioning and a great many more features than the performance of just actions. Of course, justice might be seen as the characteristic excellence in that the capacity to be just *distinguishes* humans from other animals. But even so, it is unrealistic to expect justice to be as agreed-upon as the less controversial excellence of horses and dogs. In Socrates' defence it may be said that by the time we have read the *Republic* we shall see that for him justice *is* the human excellence; someone defective in that virtue will be defective in the business of living. But that comes later; Socrates is not entitled to put forward the claim here as though it were obvious, before we have seen what any of the grounds for it might be.

Secondly, the analogies offered are rather odd. Justice cannot make people unjust, we are told, in the same way that heat cannot make things cold and musical skill make people unmusical. The general idea is that a power cannot produce its opposite. But the analogies of heat and dryness are not examples of rational powers or capacities: they apply to things as much as to people and leave out the element of agency altogether. Perhaps, however, they are not seriously meant as analogies, but merely as examples to make vivid the idea that no power can produce its opposite. Even so, the more realistic examples of musical skill and skill in horsemanship are problematic, for they do not apply to people the way justice does. These are examples of skills which are impartible and can be passed over from one person to another without regard for any motivation other than the sharing of the requisite common aim. Justice is not a skill that can simply be passed over in this fashion, irrespective of motivation; making people just is not like making them musical, for reasons that have become clear already in Socrates' interchange with Polemarchus. The obvious response to this is to point out that Polemarchus accepted that justice was like a skill in the crucial respects, and so this argument is merely pressing further an analogy that he accepts. This point is fine as far as it goes: Socrates has shown that even on Polemarchus' conception of justice, it cannot be right to harm the bad. However, the argument was presented as though Socrates were not merely pointing up another inadequacy in Polemarchus' conception but were making a point that he holds himself. And so there is some awkwardness, for Socrates accepts the conclusion of the argument, but he does not accept Polemarchus' conception of justice which is used to reach it. It is not clear what the point is of proving a conclusion he accepts on the basis of something he does not accept. The main point of these arguments is to show how unsatisfactory is Polemarchus' notion of justice; and right at the end Plato slightly blurs this point by showing that even on this view something is true of justice which he accepts anyway.

Socrates' arguments against Polemarchus are not, then, as feeble as they have sometimes been thought; nor are they merely *ad hominem*. Polemarchus represents the best that common sense has to offer about justice, and in Plato's view (unlike that of some moral philosophers) this is not very much. We have been shown the limits of moral complacency, and in the process we have had a glimpse, by contrast, of the form that Plato's own views will take. We know already that he will not think of justice as a matter of following a few rules that specify types of action to be done and avoided; justice will not be something that the agent can think of as external, a set of demands to be fulfilled without regard for the motive. Nor will it be something that one could possess in an unreflective way. We have been to some extent prepared for Plato's own definition of justice as a matter, not of the performance of certain defined actions, but of the state of a person's soul. Whatever it is, it will be internal, not external, and a matter of knowledge, not of blindly following convention.

Polemarchus is silenced and at this point (336b) Thrasymachus breaks in. He is an entirely different matter; unlike Polemarchus he does have a thought-out theory about justice and is a real intellectual challenge. His position is very different from Polemarchus', but can be seen as a natural reaction to it.

THRASYMACHUS

The arguments with Thrasymachus are in some ways odd; everyone agrees that what he says is extremely important, for the rest of the *Republic* sets out to answer the challenge set by what he claims. This is made explicit at 358b–c. Unfortunately, there is much less agreement over what it is that Thrasymachus does say.

The problem is that in the course of Book 1 Thrasymachus says several things which together form an inconsistent set. Is the inconsistency deep or merely superficial? That is, are we meant to see him as holding a basically coherent position which he begins by formulating badly until he is prodded by Socrates into coming up with a consistent formulation of it? Or are we meant to see him as fundamentally confused, and driven from pillar to post by Socrates' criticisms? And if he does have a coherent view, which is it – the one he starts out with or the one he ends up with?

He claims, with a great deal of noisy rudeness, that justice is merely the advantage or interest of the stronger. After some deliberate misunderstanding by Socrates, designed to make him clarify his claim, he says that justice is obeying the laws. Socrates produces objections to this, there is some argument and then in a long speech Thrasymachus maintains that justice is 'another's good', i.e. behaviour which benefits another, whereas injustice benefits the agent. There has been a good deal of disagreement over which position best represents the essence of his view. Some scholars hold that he is not clear what he believes, and shifts from one position to another in such a way that no single defensible position can be recovered. Plato's reason for doing this would be to show up the moral sceptic as a shallow and stupid person. Thrasymachus was, after all, a real person about whom we have some evidence, and there are enough touches in the picture of him to make it clear that Plato intends us to dislike and despise him. He is shown as rude and overbearing, insulting Socrates in the grossest manner and accusing him of hypocrisy, losing with a bad grace and vulgarly demanding money. Obviously the real Plato detested the real Thrasymachus. But there are two reasons for being dissatisfied with this interpretation. One is that we do not have enough evidence about the historical Thrasymachus to say whether his ideas were anything like those in the *Republic*, or whether Plato is creating a deliberately confused position for him to hold. The second is that there is an unavoidable pointlessness about this procedure. It is clear from the beginning of Book 2 that Plato took Thrasymachus to be defending a theory which was a real and dangerous alternative to what we took to be the truth about justice. If he were deliberately presenting the opposition as being weaker than in fact he took it to be, he would be guilty of intellectual dishonesty.

But what then is Thrasymachus saying? There are two views each of which he puts forward at some point and both of which Plato would have seen as opposed to his own. One is conventionalism (which in the context of laws is called legalism or legal positivism). This is the idea that justice is nothing but obeying the laws. We do in fact conform to the laws and institutions that we live under, and we do so because we have to – if we do not we will be punished or subject to various forms of social pressure. But if we think that justice is anything over and above this *de facto* conformity, we are being subject to a kind of illusion. 'Justice' is a misleading name we use for certain behaviour, which varies from country to country, depending on the institutions: misleading because it leads us into thinking that there is something over and above conformity to the laws which exists in all cases of such behaviour and which has an independent value. But in fact talk about justice is really, if we look at the facts, talk about power and who holds power. On this interpretation, Thrasymachus is giving a reductive account of justice. He is directing our attention to the realities of power that lie behind the fine show of talk about justice, and saying that strictly speaking that is all that is going on. This is the view of the cynical realist who claims that in spite of all the high-minded talk one hears about justice, really there is nothing to it other than the fact that most people, in fact, obey the laws and conform to the social pressures of their society.

But on the other hand, Thrasymachus has been seen as holding that justice and injustice *do* have a real existence independent of any human institutions, and as making a decided commitment to injustice. I shall label this view 'immoralism' (at the risk of confusing 'moral' and 'just', because there is no convenient word 'injusticism'). Whereas the conventionalist thinks that there is nothing behind our talk of justice and injustice, the immoralist holds that there is an important question about justice, to be answered by showing that injustice is better. Justice has a real existence all right, and is embodied in some laws and institutions, but anyone with any sense will see that conforming to it is a bad thing from the agent's point of view. The conventionalist tells us that justice is not what we think it is. The immoralist tells us that it is exactly what we think it is, but that we are wrong to think it is a virtue; there is nothing admirable about it. It benefits the weak, and what is so good about benefiting the weak? On this interpretation, Thrasymachus' view has affinities with that put forward by a character called Callicles in the dialogue *Gorgias*. Callicles claims that by nature it is just for the strong to rule and exploit the weak; it is only by convention that it is just for the weak to restrain the strong. His position has been called 'Nietzschean', and the comparison is just, though it cannot be pushed very far in detail; both overturn standard moral evaluations by rejecting outright what most people would regard as the very basis of morality. For it is a fundamental moral assumption that superior strength and intelligence do not in themselves *entitle* their possessor to whatever he or she can get by exploiting them. Thrasymachus differs from Callicles in that he does not talk in terms of natural and conventional justice (a point to which we shall return), but on the immoralist interpretation his message is basically the same: justice has a real existence independent of convention, but there is nothing admirable in it.

Any position which lends itself to two such different interpretations is, to put it mildly, complex. I shall discuss the arguments in a way which I hope will produce at least clarity. Firstly, I shall look at the question of what Thrasymachus' position actually is. As they stand, his statements certainly do not add up to a consistent position. But, as I see it, he is not presented as basically changing his mind, but as being driven from a muddled and misleading formulation of what he holds to a clearer and more defensible statement which reveals the core of his position more obviously. His real position is the immoralist one, but he begins by stating it in a confused way which appears to lead to conventionalism, and Sócrates' initial arguments are directed at making him clarify what he really holds and reveal it as immoralism. Once this is clearly laid out,

Socrates presents three arguments against it. I shall look at these and ask whether they are really as feeble as they seem. Then I shall return to the question of why Socrates is made to argue here in so weak a way and in a fashion so different from that of the rest of the work.

First, an important preliminary point. The discussion with Polemarchus arose from the difficulty of saying adequately *what justice is*. And Thrasymachus also begins by attacking the question, What is justice? – Justice, he says, is nothing but the interest of the stronger. But all through the discussion, the question of what justice is becomes intermingled with the question of whether justice benefits its possessor, for Thrasymachus spends much energy insisting that it does not: what benefits the agent is injustice. This fact means that we can expect some complexity and difficulty working out exactly what Thrasymachus is saying, for it is neither a straight answer to the question of what justice is, nor a straight answer to the question of whether justice benefits its possessor. It also means that we can rule out right from the start as unhelpful attempts that have been made to determine what Thrasymachus is saying by examining each of his statements about justice to see whether it has the status of an 'analytic' claim about the meaning of justice, or of a 'synthetic', informative statement about justice. As already pointed out, Plato does not lay philosophical weight on the distinction between what we know by virtue of knowing what '*X*' means, and what we know by virtue of knowing facts about *X*s.

But Thrasymachus is presented as a hasty and confused thinker. Does this mean that his running together the two questions, of what justice is and of whether it is worth having, is intended as a sign of his muddle? We might think so when we get to the end of the Book, for at 354b–c Socrates claims that the reason the discussion has got nowhere is precisely that they have mixed up the two questions and got on to discussing whether justice is worth having, before finding out adequately what it is. This may make us think that *Plato* is quite clear that the two questions are distinct, and that the mixing of the two in Book 1 is a sign of Thrasymachus' confusion, and is avoided by Socrates.

There is, however, something odd about this passage at the

end of Book 1. The demand to get clear about what X is before discussing various facts about X is one that is common in some other dialogues. In the *Meno* Socrates lays particular weight on this, and says that he cannot really tell whether virtue can be taught until he knows what virtue is. But although Socrates is made to repeat the point dutifully about justice in the *Republic*, it doesn't seem to correspond to anything that he actually does. We could say that Books 2–4 are one long attempt to define justice or say what it is; but they are introduced by Glaucon's demand that Socrates show that justice is something that we should want to have; and at the end of Book 4 we are told that once you know what justice is, you can see that it is something that you would want to have. So Socrates does not keep the two questions separate any more than Thrasymachus does. The whole of the *Republic* is in fact based on the idea that the two questions belong together: a thorough investigation into what justice is, cannot avoid raising the question of whether it pays, and no answer as to whether it pays can be adequate unless we are assured that we really know what it is. So Thrasymachus' mistake is not really that of treating the two questions together; and Socrates' statement at the end of Book 1, which claims that the definitional question has to be settled first, is misleading; it seems to belong to a 'Socratic' investigation like those of the early dialogues, and to be out of place in the *Republic*.

Thrasymachus' opening claim, crudely emphasised, is that justice is the interest of the stronger (338c1–2). How are we to take this? There are a number of indications that initially this is to be taken as a reductive analysis, an account of what justice is which reduces it to facts about power. So he starts off in a way which would naturally be taken as committing him to a form of conventionalism. He says at 338c1–2 that justice is 'nothing but' the interest of the stronger. And one would expect him to be putting forward his own candidate for what the essence of justice is, since it was Socrates' failure to do this that angered him before. Further, when he expands on his brief formula, he does so in a way suggesting that his analysis is a reductive one. At 338e–339a he says: Every government sets up laws in its own interest. A democracy sets up laws of a democratic spirit, and analogously for oligarchies, tyrannies, and so on. In making these laws they declare that this is just for their subjects, namely what is in their own interests, and they punish the man who transgresses them *as a lawbreaker and unjust man.*

Thrasymachus is expanding his formula in political terms, in a way that Polemarchus did not: justice is analysed in terms of the relationship of government to governed, not in terms of 'how one ought to live' in general. But nobody questions this; both here and later Plato is building on the fact that for him and for his contemporaries there was not such a sharp break as there is for us between the 'moral' and the 'political'. Justice is a virtue that covers both personal and civic dealings, and should not be considered as if it were confined to one or the other. By focusing right away on social and civic relationships, Thrasymachus makes it easier to take what he has to say in a conventionalist way; he strongly suggests that there is nothing to justice over and above obeying the laws which in any state are set up in the interest of the rulers. The sole content to injustice which he is prepared to consider is the breaking of these laws.

So, no sooner has Thrasymachus introduced the formula 'Justice is the interest of the stronger', than he appears to present it as equivalent to the formulation 'Justice is obeying the rulers'. This is what Socrates assumes at 339b7–8, and it is not questioned. – 'You say it's just to obey the rulers?' – 'Yes.' So he seems to understand his own formula as follows: the stronger is the ruler, and the interest of the stronger comes down to the fact that rulers rule in their own interest. So there is nothing more to justice than obeying the laws of one's own state, whatever that is. Justice turns out to be what the rulers say it is; and this certainly looks like conventionalism.

Socrates deals with this by forcing Thrasymachus to see that his two formulations can conflict, and to choose between them. This bit of argument goes from 339b7–340c9.

Thrasymachus admits, when asked, that rulers may make mistakes. So they may make the laws, which are in their interest, badly. We may get a situation, then, where the rulers make laws which are *not* in their interest. But if justice is obedience to the laws, it is just for the subjects to obey the rulers' laws whether they are in their actual interest or not. So justice may lead to one's doing not only what is in the interest of the stronger, but its opposite – namely, what is in fact against the interest of the stronger, but has been ineptly made law by the rulers.

What Socrates has done is in fact extremely obvious: by treating his two formulations as equivalent Thrasymachus was assuming that the ruler will always be the stronger: that is, that the existing legal and social structure always accurately reflects the distribution of power. Socrates pulls the two apart and makes Thrasymachus choose. Is he going to tie justice to what is, at any given time, actually in force and legal? Or is he really interested not in the ruler as such but in the *stronger*? The latter turns out to be the case. Thrasymachus was interested in the ruler only as long as he unreflectingly assumed that the ruler would be, in fact, the man who was the stronger, the one with the greatest command of resources and power. It is, in fact, fairly natural for Thrasymachus to make this assumption. Governments do not usually last long if they cease to control the sources of power; a weak government is, on the whole, a government on its way out. By the time we get to the end of the Book we can see why it was especially natural for Thrasymachus to make this assumption, for he tends to think of people as constantly in competition, and of governments as ruling by force because if they gave the opportunity for competition they would be unseated. None the less, Socrates is quite entitled to press Thrasymachus on the matter of whether it is the notion of the ruler or of the stronger that is essential to his analysis of justice.

Thrasymachus' choice is made more dramatic by the intervention of Cleitophon, who speaks up for the first and last time. He suggests (340b6–8) a way that Thrasymachus can avoid the problem of reconciling his two formulations, (1) justice is the interest of the stronger, and (2) justice is obeying the laws. According to Cleitophon, Thrasymachus meant by 'the interest of the stronger' simply 'what the stronger *thinks* is in his interest', and adds, 'this the weaker must do, and that is what he defined the just to be' (Grube).

Cleitophon's suggestion sounds a bit naïve, but we can take it as an attempt to close the gap threatening to open between Thrasymachus' two formulations in terms of the stronger and of the ruler. According to Cleitophon, justice is merely whatever the laws do enjoin you to do – justice really is nothing but the rules and regulations laid down by whatever institutions are the ones enforced at any given time. Whether or not this happens to be in the interest of the stronger is not to the point. Cleitophon is in fact suggesting that Thrasymachus explicitly adopt conventionalism. So even though his intervention is comically brief, Cleitophon is important: if Thrasymachus had taken up what he suggested, he would have been committing himself to a conventionalist position. But in fact he violently rejects this and will have nothing to do with it. This means that he does not want to hold a conventionalist position. And since we have seen that there were reasons for taking what he said in that way, we are presumably meant to think that he has begun by mis-stating his position and has been forced to recognize this. He rebuffs Cleitophon's helpful offer by saying, 'do you think I call someone who is making a mistake "stronger" just when he is making a mistake?'; and once he has done this he is committed to rejecting any form of conventionalism, for he has chosen to stick to the notion of the stronger rather than that of the ruler, i.e. the actual authorities at any given time in any given state.

Some people have thought that Thrasymachus would have done better to adopt Cleitophon's suggestion. If he had, he would have at least maintained a consistent position, instead of being driven to change what he had said. And further, since this was the only way in which we were invited to understand Thrasymachus' position, once he rejects it we are left without any clues as to what on earth he could mean by 'justice is the interest of the stronger'. All we have found out is that he holds this even when the interest of the stronger does not coincide with what is actually being enforced by law, and we gather that he believes this because he glorifies success and admires powerful people; but this is not very informative.

Worse, the way in which Thrasymachus reacts to Cleitophon's suggestion forces him to go back on his claims. He now has to reply to Socrates' objection about rulers making mistakes by saying that strictly speaking rulers do not make mistakes at all. Strictly speaking, no-one who practises a skill does so while and in so far as he is making mistakes in it. The doctor or ruler who goes wrong *eo ipso* ceases to be a doctor or ruler in that respect. This is a very counter-intuitive position, and Thrasymachus is probably only forced into saying this about skills in general because he finds it plausible as a position to hold about the stronger in any situation. He is thinking of the obviously true point that the man who has the upper hand cannot afford to make mistakes, or he will soon cease to have the upper hand. He saves the consistency of his position by a verbal move that makes this true of all rulers and all practitioners of any skill. But this flouts our beliefs about doctors, rulers, etc., and it is clear that he has essentially given up the idea that the stronger can be equated with the ruler.

This still leaves us with very little idea of what he does mean by 'the stronger'; but we find out more in his reaction to Socrates' next move (341a–343a). Socrates takes advantage of Thrasymachus' distinction between rulers in a normal sense and rulers in his strict sense, and argues that each skill in the strict sense has its own object and sphere of activity, and works for the good of this and its interest; its own interest does not come into it. If ruling is a skill, and a skill in the strict sense as Thrasymachus has insisted, then the ruler exercises it not in his own interest but in that of his subjects. Plato sets some store by this argument, for it is summed up at 343a as having turned the account of justice round into its opposite: Thrasymachus had claimed that justice was obeying the laws of rulers who ruled in their own interests, whereas Socrates has shown that ruling, so far from being essentially self-interested, is essentially not self-interested: in so far as a ruler is self-interested he is not strictly speaking a ruler. The argument is somewhat artificial, and it is hard to know how we are to interpret the claim that a skill works in the interest of its subject-matter. We feel the same discomfort as in the last argument against Polemarchus: justice is not exercised on people in the same way as a skill is exercised on its subject-matter. But the argument at any rate serves its immediate purpose, because by claiming that ruling is essentially concerned with the welfare of the subjects and not the ruler, it provokes Thrasymachus into making a response which reveals at last with some clarity what his true view of justice is.

His speech is a long one (343b–344d) and it is signalled as important in various unsubtle ways. Thrasymachus is made to insult Socrates before launching into a long speech, after which he tries to leave without being questioned about it. The contrast here occurs elsewhere in the Socratic dialogues too: a character is made to show off with a long speech to impress the audience with various rhetorical devices, and this is contrasted with the method of Socrates, who insists on short questions and answers which are aimed at discovering the truth, however inelegantly, rather than at playing to the gallery. Thrasymachus' behaviour here is meant to suggest that he is not intellectually serious, and that he wants agreement to bolster his ego, but is not confident that his views can stand up to cross-questioning. The picture is very overdrawn and one gets the impression of cheap tricks on Plato's part; but all the same the long speech does give us a coherent view. And what it presents is not the conventionalist position we suspected but a revisionary and immoralist view, which praises injustice.

Thrasymachus compares the ruler to a shepherd or herdsman: he takes care of his flock, but his attitude is basically exploitative. Taking this as his model he concludes that in general justice is 'another's good' (*allotrion agathon*, 343c3) and injustice is 'one's own good' (*oikeion agathon*). The unjust man seeks his own good, whereas the just man does not – he acts in such a way that his actions are to the advantage of others. The just man pays taxes, the unjust avoids his. The just man acts honestly in public office and so damages his own affairs, while the unjust man uses public office as an opportunity for corruption and nepotism. So Thrasymachus identifies the unjust man with the man who successfully forwards his own interests. And because he assumes throughout that most of the time most people's interests will inevitably conflict, the unjust man who forwards his own interests before anything else will necessarily come into conflict with the interests of others. He is bound to outdo others, chiefly the just, who lay themselves open to such exploitation. Thrasymachus admires the unjust man as being strong, self-reliant, and intelligent. He is even prepared to admire criminals if they are successful: petty wrongdoers are not admirable, but crime on the scale of the Mafia is something that demands respect. But the man he chiefly admires is the tyrant or dictator, the man who pushes his own interests at others' expense in such a ruthless and successful fashion that he gets into a position where nobody can challenge him. Injustice, if it can attain such a position, is 'stronger and freer and more masterful' than justice (344c5–6). In other words, justice is acting in a way which defers to and promotes the interests of others, and injustice is acting to promote your own interests, at others' expense if need be, which it probably will be. This makes injustice seem overwhelmingly reasonable. Why let others take advantage of you, when you could be defending your own interests? Why not admire the man who uses his brains on his own behalf?

This speech is, I think, the one taken as expressing Thrasymachus' real view – certainly it is the view which Socrates argues against for the rest of Book 1, and it is the view that has the consequence which most troubles Glaucon and Adeimantus, namely that it pays to be unjust, and that justice is foolish. The rest of the *Republic* will be devoted to arguing that this view is wrong.

However, if Thrasymachus' real view is that justice is having less than you could, and is another's good, how is this related to his earlier statement, viz. that justice is the interest of the stronger?

Formally it conflicts with it. For if justice is another's good, this will hold whether the agent is the weaker or the stronger party in the situation. And this has implications for what Thrasymachus said, particularly about politics. If justice is acting in the interests of another, then for the ruler justice will be acting in the interests of the *weaker*, the subject who is ruled. For the subject, justice will be acting in the interests of the stronger, the rulers. Injustice will be, for the ruler, the interest of the stronger, but for the subjects it will be the interest of the weaker, themselves.

This conflict need not worry us too much, however. For we can see 'justice is another's good' as an expansion of the original claim that justice is the interest of the stronger, made by someone who has seen that the original claim was made in too limited a context. Because he began by thinking only of strong and successful rulers, Thrasymachus defined justice in a way that strictly only applied to their subjects, who by acting justly are serving the interests of their rulers, the stronger, and who are acting in a way that is to the interests not of themselves but of others. Under pressure Thrasymachus comes up with another formulation which applies to rulers as well as to their subjects. Strictly speaking it conflicts with the first formulation, but it takes it over in spirit. For underlying all his changes in wording runs the thought that acting justly is not in the agent's interests. Thrasymachus shifts in his attempts to say what justice is, but they are controlled by the thought that whatever it is, it is not worth much. From the point of view of the subject of a strong ruler, justice is acting in the stronger's interest. From anybody's point of view, it is acting in the other person's interest. The common idea is that whoever I am, justice is not in *my* interest.

So a plausible account of the development in Book 1 goes as follows: Thrasymachus' real position is that justice is another's good, whereas injustice is acting in the vigorous pursuit of your own interest. At first he gives a formulation of this which only applies to subjects of competent rulers: 'justice is the interest of the stronger'; and this way of putting it leads him into saying 'justice is obeying the laws'. This is misleading since it suggests that he holds a conventionalist position. Only when Cleitophon faces him with explicitly adopting this does he reject it and come up with a much broader formulation – 'justice is another's good' – which encapsulates what he really wants to say. The way he is driven from a partial and muddled to a clear formulation is no doubt meant to show, unsubtly, that he is an over-hasty and confused thinker who needs lessons in rigour from Socrates.

There are three points which support this picture of what is going on. Firstly, right at the end of his long speech (344c7–8) Thrasymachus sums up by saying, 'and as I said at the beginning, justice is the interest of the stronger – and injustice is what profits oneself and is in one's own interests.' The earlier and the later formulations are juxtaposed in a very abrupt way which shows that Thrasymachus is trying to claim that his position is consistent overall; at the same time we can see a verbal conflict. The same situation is described both as being just, from the point of view of the subjects who are serving the interests of another, and as unjust, from the point of view of the ruler who is exploiting them in his own interests. Thrasymachus is being undermined by being made to express himself in a clumsy way.

Secondly, after the long speech, Socrates says that he is delighted to know what Thrasymachus really thinks, but asks him to stick to what he says or change it openly (345b7–9) – 'stick to what you say, or, if you change, do so openly and don't deceive us.' This points up the idea that Thrasymachus is confused, but has finally been forced by Socrates' criticisms to say exactly what he does mean; he does not in fact change what he says any more.

Thirdly, after the long speech Socrates puts forward a rather artificial argument to the effect that no skill or art includes the idea of doing well for oneself out of it, so that it positively excludes self-aggrandizement. No skill, he says, includes as part of itself the skill of making money, for this is a quite separate skill; thus rulers do not rule in their own interests, for if they get anything out of ruling it is not *qua* ruler. This is rather an artificial way of making the undoubtedly sound point that rulers do not as such rule in their own interests, since making money is not part of any skill considered as such. Plato clearly regards this as a strong point. There is a little interchange about it with Glaucon (which looks very much, incidentally, as though it came in after Book 1 became part of the *Republic* as a whole, for not only does Glaucon not appear again as a speaker till Book 2, but some of Socrates' claims about rulers read very oddly unless we have the central books in mind, cf. 519d–521b, 540d–541b). Socrates turns to Glaucon (347e) and says that he disagrees with Thrasymachus over justice being the interest of the stronger, but much more important is the point Thrasymachus has raised, namely whether justice is to one's advantage or not. So according to Plato, once Thrasymachus has got straight what he is claiming, the main interest of it lies in the claim that justice is 'another's good', something no sensible person would want. In the light of this, the claim that justice is the interest of the stronger is seen to reduce to a more trivial claim, that rulers always rule in their own interest. *This*, Plato thinks, can be met by a fairly short argument, and Socrates therefore counters it with the claim that money-making is a separate skill and not part of any skill like ruling, so that rulers do *not* (*qua* rulers as Thrasymachus insisted) rule

in their own interests. This is all that is required to refute the
claim that justice is the interest of the stronger, and Socrates
can now get down to dealing with the revealing formulation of
Thrasymachus' view: justice is something in the interests of
others, and therefore a mug's game.

Thrasymachus thus comes out holding a view which is rather
similar to that put forward by Callicles in the *Gorgias*: the
admirable life is the life of the person who disregards justice and
goes ruthlessly and unjustly after his own interests. There are,
however, two revealing differences between them.

Callicles distinguishes sharply between 'natural' and 'conventional' justice. By convention it is just that the weaker
should restrain the stronger, but natural justice demands that
the strong should make use of their strength and exploit the
weak. Thrasymachus does not make this distinction, and this
makes his position more difficult to state. While both admire the
successful tyrant, Callicles can say that his activities are
naturally just though conventionally unjust, whereas
Thrasymachus has to say that they are unjust but still
admirable. Because he glorifies qualities which are generally
thought undesirable, and still calls them by the accepted
unfavourable words, he gets involved, as Callicles does not,
in an attempt to 'revalue' the moral terms in which justice is
appraised. Plato brings this out in a very interesting passage
at 348c–d. Would he go along with the common view, asks
Socrates, that when we are talking about justice and injustice
we are talking about a virtue and a vice? Yes, of course. Is
justice a virtue or excellence, and injustice a vice or defect?
Thrasymachus can hardly go along with this – how can
something be a virtue or excellence if it benefits you not to have
it? He cannot consistently call justice a virtue or excellence
when he recommends its opposite. Is it then, asks Socrates, a vice
or defect (*kakia*, the opposite of *aretē*)? Here Thrasymachus
baulks. He should say, but cannot bring himself to, that justice
is a vice or defect. After all, he thinks that it is something that it
is never a good thing to have. But all he can say is that it is
'noble good nature' – words which conventionally are favourable, but which he uses to suggest a simple-minded kind of
goodness. Well, persists Socrates, if justice is *good* nature,
injustice must be *bad* nature or malevolence. No, says

Thrasymachus, refusing to accept the unfavourable word, it is shrewdness and sagacity. In fact he is in a thorough mess over his use of ethical and value terms. He cannot bring himself to make a clean break with the normal use of terms like 'good' and 'bad' and say straight out that justice is a bad thing, a defect, and injustice a good thing, an excellence. This confuses what he says. Callicles, by sharply distinguishing his own sense of 'just' from the ordinary one, is able to make his own moral position more clear. He does this, though, at the price of cutting himself off from normal moral appraisals. Thrasymachus keeps closer to the reality of what most people say when he praises injustice rather than openly scorning 'conventional' justice but distinguishing this from 'natural' justice.

Secondly, Callicles thinks in terms of the strong individual imposing himself on others and giving free rein to his desires. He thus thinks of the agent as seeking to gratify all his desires regardless of others, and Socrates traps him by arguments designed to show that this is an unacceptable view of desire. Thrasymachus avoids this because his thinking is resolutely political: his ideal is always the successful *tyrant*. He avoids Callicles' difficulties because he thinks not of gratifying desires but of getting as much *power* as possible. In this respect too he is more realistic. But it is fair, I think, to say that his ideal is the same as Callicles', but expressed in terms of political power.

So much for Thrasymachus' position; what of Socrates' arguments against it? There is not much to say about the two pieces of argument that go from 341a–342e and from 345e–347e – in fact we have looked at them already. They are both attempts to force Thrasymachus to make clear exactly what his position is. He had insisted on regarding ruling as a skill in the strict sense, and Socrates takes this up and claims that if you think of ruling like this, then ruling cannot be essentially in the ruler's interests. He overstates his case: he claims that all skills are practised for the benefit of their objects and not of their practitioners, and this seems absurdly optimistic. And the claim that money-making is a separate skill is very artificial. But the basic point is sound: regarded as a skill, ruling is not essentially exploitative, as Thrasymachus had claimed. No skill is as such essentially exploitative; it can be practised from a variety of motives. Of course it does not follow from this that ruling is always carried on in an unselfish spirit either. In fact Socrates admits that good people will rule not because they want to, but as avoiding 'the greatest punishment', that of being ruled by men worse than themselves. (It turns out, though, that what they do, although described in terms of self-interest, is not self-interested in the ordinary way; this kind of self-interest is better described as a concern for what is good rather than as a concern to get something for themselves.) Meanwhile all that matters is that Socrates has shown that ruling as such, the actual business of signing forms and sitting on tedious committees, does not appeal to any ordinary notion of self-interest.

So these arguments bring out Thrasymachus' mistake in thinking of all ruling as essentially exploitative: but neither does, or is meant to, touch the heart of his claim that injustice pays. This thesis is only confronted in Socrates' three arguments at the end of the Book.

It is these arguments that are worrying, for although formally they succeed and Thrasymachus concedes defeat, no reader of the Book is convinced by them, and Socrates is left alone congratulating himself on his success at the end. This is disturbing because it suggests that Socrates, having taken such great pains to isolate and confront Thrasymachus' position, has no strong arguments against it. The thesis that injustice pays is not, after all, far-fetched or unconvincing; the problem is rather that it is all too convincing and that is why philosophers have always worried about the moral sceptic, the person who questions the value of being just and claims that the just person is a fool under a kind of illusion, and that one should recognize frankly that it is injustice that pays. Yet Socrates' arguments against this thesis are all weak and unconvincing to an amazing degree.

The first one goes from 349a–350e. Thrasymachus has characterized the unjust man as the man who will always want more than he ought to have. He is not satisfied with what he is entitled to and shows *pleonexia*, the state of always wanting to have more (*pleon echein*). Thrasymachus also wants to say that the unjust man is the intelligent man, the one who uses his brains, whereas the just man is the fool. Socrates' argument is designed to pull these two ideas apart and show that if your motive is always to 'have more' then you are precisely *not* being intelligent; the praiseworthy quality of cleverness belongs, contrary to Thrasymachus' claim, to the just man.

Socrates again uses skill as an analogy, but this time to justice, not to ruling. Naturally, the points of comparison he wants to press are not those that threw Polemarchus; he is not claiming that acting justly is like following rules that lay down the means for the successful accomplishment of some determinate end. Rather what he wants to stress here is that justice is like a skill in involving intellectual mastery of the material involved; the stress is all on the *knowledge* which marks off the expert from the non-expert. The expert musician or doctor, claims Socrates, will not want to overreach or outdo (*pleon echein*) the other experts. Two expert doctors will agree on the right dose, and two expert musicians will agree on the right tuning, and neither will try to outdo the other in respect of their skill. It is only the non-expert, the ignoramus, who will try to outdo both experts and non-experts. Therefore the analogue to the unjust man is the ignoramus, not the expert, for the ignoramus tries to outdo both the experts and other ignoramuses, and the unjust man was agreed to be the man who tries to outdo both the just and other unjust men.

One's first reaction is to conclude that the argument is simply fallacious, because it depends on an ambiguity in *pleon echein* (and *pleonexia*), one which shows up rather painfully when it has to be translated as 'outdo'. For the unjust wants to outdo the just in the sense of *having more* than he does, whereas the ignoramus tries to outdo the expert in the sense of *doing better* than he does. The unjust man is greedy; the ignoramus is simply over-ambitious. This is not, however, the root of the matter. Perhaps Plato is in fact using the words here in a rather strained way. But what is wrong with the argument is not a simple mistake located in one word, but something rather deeper that would persist even if the argument were reformulated. The trouble is that Socrates is representing the difference between the just and the unjust as one of expertise – this is the idea lying behind the use of *pleon echein* – whereas it does not seem to be such a difference. He wants the unjust man to be trying unsuccessfully to be what the just man is; but this can only be done by presenting them as competing in the same race, with the just man winning. Thrasymachus is not given the chance to protest, but surely should have said that the analogy does not hold. Injustice is not a ham-handed attempt to do what justice succeeds at doing; the unjust man is someone who has different priorities from the just man. By letting Socrates' analogy go through, Thrasymachus lets him win the argument by virtually begging the question: the conclusion is that it is the just man who shows more intelligence, but the obvious reply is that the unjust man would not recognize the terms of the competition.

But Socrates is allowed to win; and we are told that Thrasymachus blushed as he reluctantly conceded victory (350d). This sounds odd to us; in our culture we usually blush with embarrassment, and Thrasymachus has not done anything very embarrassing. But for the ancient Greeks blushing was a sign rather of humiliation, and the little dramatic touch is presumably meant to picture the moral of the argument. Thrasymachus, who thinks of argument in terms of aggressive competition and showing off, has been publicly shamed by losing to Socrates; he is meant to be the ignoramus who tries to do better than the expert, but fails because his over-reaching has made him 'too clever'. But of course the reader is not satisfied that Socrates has in fact won the argument; Thrasymachus has no come-back, but he is not convinced, and henceforth takes no serious part in the argument, but merely sulks.

The second piece of argument goes from 351a–352c. Thrasymachus wants injustice to be associated with strength; the unjust man achieves great things, and in particular, rule over a city. Socrates maintains that in fact it produces weakness rather than strength, because it precludes co-operation. If everyone is known to want to outdo the others, nothing will ever get done, because nobody can trust anyone else to refrain from pushing their own aims at the expense of whatever common good it is that they are co-operating to achieve.

Socrates' point is a good one as far as it goes: nobody can develop purely competitive virtues if he needs the help of others to achieve his ends. However, Thrasymachus could retort that he is not interested in the achievement of ends that require genuine co-operation; he is interested in the unjust individual, the would-be tyrant. And *he* doesn't need justice; all he needs is the common sense to persuade people to rely on him as long as they won't thwart his ends. At most he needs to pretend to be just. To become a successful tyrant you need to simulate justice to a judicious extent, but there could be a successful and ruthless individual tyrant who was uninterested in justice.

All Socrates can say to meet this point is what he does say at 352a5–8: injustice, he claims, pulls apart not just a group but an individual. The unjust man cannot achieve anything because he is always in potential internal conflict. He rebels against himself and becomes hateful to himself as well as to others. The individual is throughout described in terms that we would normally use only of a group. But why should we accept this strange idea? As thrown at us here it is just extraordinary. We will get, later on, a theory that the soul has parts and that the individual must be thought of as characterizable in the same ways as groups, but at this point nothing indicates this. What Socrates says here is merely unconvincing rhetoric, no better than the immediately following claim that the just man is better off because he is dear to the gods. But if we discount the rhetoric, the argument does not refute Thrasymachus' position.

The third argument goes from 352d–354b, and is the most notorious, because it employs the notion of a thing's *ergon*, a word usually translated 'function'. Socrates first establishes that various things have a function, and that whatever does, has a corresponding excellence or virtue (*aretē*). The soul has a function: directing and guiding the body and being its principle of life. The excellence of the soul is agreed to be justice. Therefore the good soul will live well, and to live well is to be happy. So justice will make us happier than injustice will. Justice is not only a better sign of intelligence than injustice, it is a better bet if you want to live well and be happy.

This argument has been found particularly scandalous, and there are many obvious points for dissatisfaction.

One common objection is that it is wrong to talk of people having functions, because only artefacts have functions. If a thing has a function, it has it because it was given one, made for a purpose; so if you think of people having functions, you must be thinking of them as having been made, presumably by God, for some purpose. This objection is feeble, because while it may be true of 'function', it is not true of *ergon*, and shows only that *ergon* has not been properly understood. *Ergon* is what a thing does *qua* a thing of that kind. As applied to people referred to by what they do, it means 'job' or 'work'. As applied to a natural kind like men, it means little more than 'characteristic behaviour'. But it is important to remember than *ergon* covers sculpting, the sculptor's job, and the characteristic behaviour-patterns of species; artefacts made for a purpose are only a subset of things that have *erga*. Socrates gives criteria for *erga*, but in doing so makes no mention of purposes – a thing's *ergon* is that which only it can do, or which it can do best. And his examples include eyes, ears, and horses as well as artefacts.

However, he may seem to lay himself open to this bad objection by the way he talks of the *ergon* of the soul (353d). He asks whether the soul has an *ergon* 'which you could not do with anything else' as though it were an instrument used by the person. But this is only careless expression: Plato's real view is just the opposite – he tends to think of the body as the instrument of the soul and not vice versa.

There *is* a problem about the soul in this argument, however. At 353e10–11 Plato says blithely, 'so the just soul and the just man will live well, and the unjust man badly.' However, what lives well is the just *man*, but what the argument was about was the just *soul*. Ultimately, Plato believes that a person *is* his soul, so he sees no gap because he sees no ultimate gap between talking of a person and talking of his soul. But here this is a very strong assumption to make, and we have seen not a glimmer of argument for it so far. Aristotle took over the argument from *ergon* in Book 1 of his *Nicomachean Ethics*, but he avoids at any rate some of Plato's problems here because he talks consistently about the function and excellence of *man*, not the function and excellence of *soul*.

It is often said that the argument is fallacious because it trades on an ambiguity in 'live well': between living in an efficient and well-ordered way, and living a virtuous life. But here again there is no ambiguity that can be located in a single word; rather, Plato is working with a systematic set of assumptions which we might want to query, but which make it more plausible for him to argue as he does. Just as there is no gap, for him, between excellence of the kind which leads to good living and excellence of other, more technical kinds, so there is no great difference of kind between living well in the way of having a good example of a life – one that displays human excellences to the full – and living well in the way of living the life of a good person. We may question this set of assumptions in general, but it is not very useful to claim that the argument rests on ambiguity; the problem would remain if the argument were reformulated.

In fact, the argument is formally all right, and succeeds in making its point, on a very high level of abstraction, if we allow Plato to move between talking about a person and talking about his soul. The major problem lies rather in the step taken at 353e7–8. Living has been agreed to be the function of the soul, what it characteristically does. What then is the soul's virtue or excellence? Socrates says, astoundingly, 'Now we have agreed that justice is excellence of the soul, and that injustice is vice of soul?' 'We have so agreed,' says Thrasymachus (Grube). But where? and how? Presumably Thrasymachus is referring to the outcome of the first argument, but that is not precisely what was proved there, and anyway it is made entirely clear that Thrasymachus is agreeing only out of sulkiness, and is not really convinced. But this matters. For the whole argument depends on this premise, and collapses if it is not accepted. Yet it has not been argued for; Thrasymachus accepts it only to get the argument over; and if one thinks independently that it is true, then one is in no need of conviction by the argument from function. So in the end the argument is futile, for it depends on a premise which there is not the faintest chance that anyone would accept unless they already accepted the conclusion.

None of these arguments, then, carries any conviction. They all seem to beg the crucial question. The first employs an analogy acceptance of which carries acceptance of the conclusion; the third depends on a premise which is entirely question-begging. The second makes only a limited and not very effective point, unless one is prepared to accept a very contentious set of ideas about the unity of the person. The arguments are not formally flawed, but they make no real impact on Thrasymachus' position.

Can Plato have been unaware of this? I think not, and there is one strong indication of this. After the first argument, Thrasymachus gives up arguing and merely chimes in 'yes' and 'no' in an insultingly obsequious manner. At 350d–e he says in an obnoxious way that this is all he will do with Socrates' questions; he is uninterested in their content. And right at the end he says (354a) when the final argument has concluded with an apparent victory for Socrates, 'Well, have a good time – it's a holiday.' The more Thrasymachus stresses that he couldn't care less what is said, the more earnest Socrates becomes and the more passionately he insists on the importance of what they are talking about. At 352d he says with deep seriousness that they are discussing the most important topic that there could possibly be – the right way to live.

The same thing happens in the *Gorgias*, where Socrates is talking to Callicles, whose view is similar to Thrasymachus'. Callicles loses the argument, but he is not convinced; he retreats to the lofty view that Socrates' fiddling little arguments are a waste of time to someone who is interested in the realities of life and of power. The more insultingly he goes along with Socrates, feeding him the answers he wants because he is not interested, the more personal and emotional become Socrates' appeals to him to take the matter seriously.

Now Plato is writing both parts; and presumably some point is being made. And most plausibly it is something like this: Plato sees the emotional force of the idea that it is injustice which is the rational choice and that the just person is losing out on life. He sees this so well that he sees also that someone deeply convinced of the truth of this would never give in to the purely intellectual appeal of arguments like those of Socrates. There is no reason to think that he considered these arguments fallacious, or realized how bad they are, but he did see that a Thrasymachus or a Callicles would think them only trivial and quibbling. Socrates' opponents lose the argument, but they are not convinced, and they say so; the only result of their being worsted in argument is that they become dismissive of argument, regarding it as a silly waste of time and a diversion from the real issues. Socrates may be right, but his methods of discussion and argument are not adequate to deal with someone who disagrees with him in a basic and systematic way. In Book I of the *Republic* we see the ineffectiveness of Socratic methods in dealing with the powerful claim of the moral sceptic, that there is really no reason to be just, and that one should, if one is rational and intelligent, look after one's own interest. Plato took the point, and realized that it was not only particular people like Thrasymachus who were not convinced. In the rest of the *Republic* we move to a different style of arguing. There are no more snappy little arguments with disputable premises. Instead of that, the discussion is expanded; Plato's defence of justice is built up against a large and rich background theory of the nature of the person and society. The claims which Socrates failed to make convincing are fleshed out and become part of a much larger discussion which makes appeal to the philosophical imagination as well as to the narrower kind of cleverness tested by Socrates' methods of arguing.

It is sometimes said that it is a pity that the lively dialogue of Book I gives way to the more solid exposition of the rest of the work. But even people who make this complaint do not in fact think that political philosophy is best done by means of Socratic dialogue. In going on from Book I to the rest of the work, Plato is passing from an unsuitable method of meeting Thrasymachus' challenge to a more suitable one. When we think of the immense influence that the *Republic* has had, and reflect that Book I on its own would never have had that effect, we can only conclude that he was right.

FURTHER READING

A sympathetic discussion of the arguments with Polemarchus is given in H. Joseph, chapter I of *Essays in Ancient and Modern Philosophy*. The analogy of virtue and skill is discussed in a stimulating way, often differing from the account given here, in Irwin's book and in T. Penner, 'Socrates on Virtue and Motivation' in *Exegesis and Argument, Phronesis* Supplement I.

The debate on how to interpret Thrasymachus' position is well summed up in Nicholson, 'Unravelling Thrasymachus' arguments in the *Republic*', *Phronesis* 1974, where the considerable secondary literature is well discussed. A useful extended discussion of Book 1 can be found in Sparshott, 'Socrates and Thrasymachus', *Monist* 1966. Macguire, in 'Thrasymachus . . . or Plato?', *Phronesis* 1971 defends the view that no coherent position can be attributed to Thrasymachus because Plato is mixing up the views of the historical Thrasymachus with his own. Henderson in *American Philosophical Quarterly* 1970 gives a vigorous 'Defense of Thrasymachus'.

Chapter 3

The Form of Plato's Argument

At the start of Book 2 Plato makes clear his dissatisfaction with the methods of Book 1. Glaucon says that he is unhappy with the way that Thrasymachus has been reduced to silence, claiming that he had been 'bewitched' into giving up (358b2–3). Glaucon himself and his brother Adeimantus restate forcefully the challenge that they realize has been posed; they do not themselves believe that injustice pays and that justice appeals only to the foolish, but they appreciate the intellectual power of the thesis, and demand at length that Socrates answer the problem more satisfactorily (357a–358d). Socrates' response constitutes the rest of the *Republic*.

This opening passage is important for several reasons. It is of interest dramatically, for it attaches the 'Socratic' Book 1 to the rest of the *Republic* and makes clear what the rest of the discussion will be like. Because the brothers are fundamentally on Socrates' side, the question for truth is now removed from the area of competitive argument, and becomes the object of a longer, cumulative, and co-operative enquiry. This may lessen the dramatic tension, but it increases our sense of the size and importance of the problem.

But the passage is most important because it shows us vividly right at the start how distinctive is the form of Plato's reasoning in what we would call a moral argument. Glaucon begins by distinguishing three kinds of good things, and raising the question of where, in this division, justice belongs. The distinction is important, and must be set out in full (357b–d):

Tell me, do you think there is a kind of good which we welcome not because we desire its consequences but for its own sake: joy, for example, and all the harmless pleasures which have no further consequences beyond the joy which one finds in them? . . . Further, there is the good which we welcome for its own sake and also for its consequences, knowledge for example and sight and health. Such things we somehow welcome on both counts . . . Are you also aware of a third kind, such as physical training, being treated when ill, the practice of medicine, and other ways of making money? We should say that these are wearisome but beneficial to us; we should not want them for their own sake, but because of the rewards and other benefits which result from them. (Grube)

The division then is:
(1) things we find desirable in themselves
(2) things we find desirable in themselves and for their consequences
(3) things we find desirable only for their consequences.

Glaucon and Socrates agree that most people would put justice into the third class, the goods pursued and found desirable only for their consequences; they do not think that justice itself has anything to recommend it. They themselves both agree that justice belongs in the 'fairest' class, the second, among things like health. (Much is later to be made of the comparison of justice with health.) But neither has seen any good argument to show that this is so. The brothers now expand, in two long speeches, on what such an argument must show. But before considering the speeches, it is worth pausing over the threefold division itself.

Nobody questions either the nature of the threefold division, or the ready agreement that justice belongs in the second class and that this is the 'fairest' of the three. Yet a little reflection shows that this is a very different kind of assumption from what would be granted at the start of most modern discussions about morality. Socrates rejects the idea that justice is to be welcomed only for its consequences; but he also does not seriously entertain the idea that it is to be chosen without regard for its consequences. And so without hesitation Socrates takes up ground which is widely regarded as untenable by both sides in a great many modern discussions of justice.

A modern moral philosopher, trying to show someone that they ought to choose to be just rather than unjust, is likely to assume that the argument must take one of two forms: *deontological* or *consequentialist*. (I am using these terms here as labels for kinds of moral argument, not for complete moral theories; and I consider only what is relevant to Plato's argument.) In a deontological argument, justice, if it is to be recommended from a *moral* (as opposed to a prudential or self-interested) point of view, is to be shown to be something one would choose regardless of consequences. For on this view the properly moral appeal of justice must come from its own nature, not from anything it can offer in the way of consequences. The contrast tends to be stressed in deontological terms by saying that, whatever the consequences, it is our *duty* or *obligation* to be just. Plato (revealingly) has no terms that answer happily to the notions of moral duty and obligation; but the point can be put in his own terms by saying that if Plato's argument is a deontological one, he would have put justice in the first class, goods desirable for themselves without regard to their consequences. In fact Plato seems, judging by the examples, to have thought this class comparatively trivial from the moral point of view. And by firmly putting justice in the second class, including its consequences as reasons for its desirability, Plato shows clearly that his argument is *not* a deontological one. For in a deontological argument no consequences of justice could give one a *moral* reason to pursue it. Indeed, many who perceive this, but think that a moral argument must be a deontological one, have thought that the entire *Republic* is a mistake, and that Plato, in showing us that justice is desirable for its consequences, particularly happiness, is giving us a reason to be just all right, but not a *moral* one. Plato of course does not recommend justice *only* for its consequences: it is put in the second class and not the third. But in a deontological argument consequences cannot play *any* role in a moral justification; to show that justice is desirable 'in itself and for its consequences' is to offer a confused mixture of moral and non-moral reasons for being just. I shall not here examine the deontological assumption, that a moral reason cannot be one with any reference to consequences, an assumption that is far from self-evident.

Someone who thinks that a moral argument must be a consequentialist one holds that a moral justification is provided only by pointing to desirable consequences. There are many positions available to someone with this assumption, depending on what the items are that are being considered (whether, for example, they are actions, institutions, states of persons), what counts as a desirable consequence (pleasure, happiness) and whether the consequences to be considered are those affecting the agent or society. The commonest position within which a moral argument must be a consequentialist one is utilitarianism, according to which an action is right if it maximizes happiness. (It is, however, seldom held as a moral theory in this straightforward and unmodified form.) Now since Plato's argument is so clearly not a deontological one, and since it is often assumed that a moral argument can only be deontological or consequentialist, there has been a general tendency to interpret the *Republic* as a consequentialist argument, and in particular as a utilitarian one, since the consequence of justice is argued to be the agent's happiness. But this is not the form of argument that Plato offers. If it were, justice would be put in the *third* class, things desirable only for their consequences. For in a consequentialist argument moral justification comes only from consequences; the claim that something has moral value 'in itself' is either wrong or has to be interpreted as a misleading way of saying that it has good consequences (in which case it is at best redundant). Plato's claim that justice belongs in the second class makes as little sense if his argument is taken to be a consequentialist one as it does if it is interpreted as a deontological one.

Plato carefully distinguishes three classes, not two, and deliberately (if briefly) places justice in the second. And so, if we take the form of his argument seriously, we cannot interpret it as being either a deontological or a consequentialist one. In both of them, for different reasons, the second class is not a real option. For in a consequentialist argument, consequences are not just put forward, in a more or less common-sense way, as one of the factors relevant to the moral appraisal of, for example, an action. They are taken to be the *only* factor that is morally relevant. And similarly, what is characteristic of a deontological argument is not just the claim (again, more acceptable to common sense) that consequences do not have more moral weight than the nature of what is done; the claim is that consequences have *no* distinctive moral weight. Both kinds of argument are, therefore, committed, simply by being the distinctive kinds of moral argument that they are, to ruling out serious consideration of Plato's second class as a class of morally good things. (It is interesting that in this respect both of the basic forms of argument in modern

moral philosophy are, in their unmodified forms, more revisionary than Plato's.) Rather than forcing the argument to fit,
and discussing it in terms whose application depends on modern
assumptions, we should try to stand back from modern debates
and try to learn from Plato. For Plato is certainly offering us a
moral argument in a recognizable sense of 'moral'. He also
claims that he will show justice to be desirable both for itself
and for its consequences. We should therefore try not to criti-
cize him in ways that rest on assumptions about moral argument which defeat his project before it starts. If we assume that
the form of a moral argument must be *either* deontological *or*
consequentialist, then Plato's task is doomed, for the two parts
of his argument will either exclude each other, or collapse into
one.

We have more than scholarly reasons for wanting to bring
out the distinctive nature of Plato's argument; it may help us,
in moral philosophy, to find new and more fruitful ways of
looking at the basic issues. For it is very commonly assumed
that a moral argument must proceed either by showing that
justice, say, is desirable or valuable purely in itself, or by
showing that it is valuable solely because of its consequences.
It is true that nowadays few moral theories proceed on the
assumption that consequences are either *never* relevant, or
exclusively relevant, to establishing the moral goodness of
something. That is, few moral theories rely entirely on either
deontological or consequentialist ways of arguing. But they
avoid this crudity only by combining the two kinds of argument,
usually by employing them at different levels. For example, a
rule utilitarian may hold that all that is relevant to the rightness
of actions is good consequences, but that these consequences
must include some facts which in a deontological argument
would have value in themselves. So moral theories tend to
proceed by compromising between the two ways of arguing
rather than by looking for a genuine alternative. What is
interesting about the *Republic's* argument is that it offers just
such an alternative. Socrates will show us, he claims, that
justice is worth having both for itself and for its consequences;
and the two parts of this task are to be genuinely distinct, and
not in conflict. If this can really be done, it is obviously something worth doing. So far, of course, the claim has just been

baldly stated. For all we know, there may not be a single argument that brings both the intrinsic nature of justice and its consequences into one demonstration that is worth having. But it is worth insisting that this, and no less, is what Plato intends to show.

Glaucon and Adeimantus now go on to put the case for the superiority of injustice with as much force as they can muster. Glaucon begins: most people, he claims, practise justice only for what they can get out of it, and because there is no better available alternative; but he wants to know what justice and injustice are, and what power each has in the soul, leaving aside rewards and consequences (358b4-7). What most people think is that justice is a second-best, and they think this because ideally people would prefer to be free to wrong one another. However, in a situation where one is free to wrong others one stands a high chance of being wronged oneself, and because of the contingencies of fortune one can never feel really secure. So people reach a compromise neither to wrong nor to be wronged. Justice is thus satisfactory as a second-best which stabilizes the conditions of life, but it is not what anyone would choose if he could get away with being unjust without the attendant risks. In essence this is Thrasymachus' view: it is injustice that pays if one is clever enough to avoid the consequences of getting caught, and these exist because of the collective fears of the weak and vulnerable, who stand to lose most in a situation where all are free to get away with what they can.

The fact that just and unjust alike regard justice as only a second-best is shown, claims Glaucon, by the fact that as soon as he can get away with avoiding the bad consequences of being unjust, the just man will exploit his situation every bit as much as the unjust. To illustrate this Glaucon tells the story of Gyges' ring. Gyges was an insignificant man who found a ring that made him invisible whenever he wished, and who used this device to usurp a kingdom. Now if a just man came into possession of such a ring, claims Glaucon, he would use it to do exactly what the unjust man does – kill his enemies, have sex with anyone he fancied, get his friends out of danger, and all with impunity. This shows that the just man is only just 'through compulsion'; as soon as he can get away with it he will act unjustly. And this shows that what is actually valued is not being just, but only seeming to be just; as long as one can seem just the life of injustice is clearly better, whereas it is futile to *be* just regardless of appearances. Glaucon puts the point graphically by sketching the lives of the just man who appears unjust, and ends up persecuted and tortured, and the unjust man who appears just, who ends his days in peace and prosperity. How then could anyone with any sense prefer justice for itself, regardless of appearances?

Adeimantus chimes in to complain that Glaucon hasn't stated the case completely. In fact what he adds is relatively minor (and certainly doesn't warrant the length of his speech). He points out that parents and teachers, people who nominally side with justice, still recommend it not for itself but for its rewards, and that this is true of religious teachers also; they say that while the gods do not positively approve of injustice, none the less they can be bought off. From all the sources that surround and form a young man's sensibility, he gets the same message: what matters is the appearance of justice and not the reality. The personal dilemma of people like Glaucon and Adeimantus is movingly brought out at 366c–d: even someone who does not believe all this feels, all the same, 'full of forgiveness' to those who do think this way. For he knows that 'only a man of godlike character whom injustice disgusts, or one who has superior knowledge, avoids injustice, and that no other man is willingly just, but through cowardice or old age or some other weakness objects to injustice, because he cannot practise it.' (Grube) There are a few isolated saints who reject injustice, but it is not clear even to those who approve of them that it is reasonable, or in accordance with human nature, for everyone to try to do the same.

The two speeches unfortunately raise quite serious problems as to what exactly their import is. What precisely is the challenge that Socrates has to meet in the rest of the book?

Firstly, Glaucon and Adeimantus clearly believe that they are making the same point, the second speech filling in details not made prominent in the first. But are the two speeches consistent?

One striking thing is that Glaucon stresses the need to praise justice for itself, whereas Adeimantus stresses the need to bring out the beneficial results of justice. In Glaucon's speech we find over and over again the request to praise justice 'itself by itself' (358b5–6, d1–2, and cf. 361b–c). Adeimantus, on the other hand, closes his speech with an impressive four-times repeated request to show that the effects of justice are beneficial to the person who has it (366e5–9, 367b2–5, d3–4, e3–5.) Now prima facie it may look as though Glaucon wants to exclude all consequences from the defence of justice, whereas Adeimantus wants to let in the beneficial consequences, and this makes it seem as though only Adeimantus wants to put justice in the second class (as he demands in so many words at 367c) whereas Glaucon's demand is really the deontological one, that justice be put in the first class. But there is not really a conflict, and there only appears to be one if we retain the assumption that showing justice desirable for itself must *exclude* showing it desirable for its consequences. Neither of the brothers assumes this; they are merely stressing different parts of the task of putting justice in the second class. When Glaucon insists that Socrates must defend justice itself, he is not opposing justice itself to its consequences. He wants to defend being just as opposed to merely *seeming* to be just; consequences are only excluded insofar as they could follow from the appearance of justice as well as from the reality. And Adeimantus refers back to this point (367b): Socrates must exclude the reputations that might equally well follow the appearance of justice as the reality. So, although the emphases of the brothers' speeches are different, they are making the same demand.

But this raises a second problem. How can the brothers' requirement be squared with the initial demand that justice be put in the second class? For we have seen, in showing that there is no conflict between them, that they agree in excluding *some* consequences. They both demand exclusion of the 'rewards and reputations' (*doxai*) of justice, and make it clear why – they can go to the person who seems to be just but is not. I shall call these (following the terminology of an article by M. B. Foster) the artificial consequences of justice. They are artificial because they depend on the existence of human practices and conventions, and would not accrue to the possession of justice in the absence of these. This is connected to the second important point about them: they can sometimes follow the mere appearance of justice without the reality, because humans are gullible and their institutions are defective; they do not flow inevitably from the mere possession of justice.

Now the brothers are firm that *these* consequences must be excluded from a successful defence of justice. But this produces a problem in fitting their demands in the speeches to the initial threefold division, as we can see if we turn back to it and consider the examples used there. Knowledge, sight, and health, which were put into the second class, don't *have* any rewards in the sense of artificial consequences. Health and sight have natural benefits, but there are no prizes conventionally instituted for seeing, ones that one might equally well get for putting up a convincing show of seeing when one lacked the ability. The third class is equally difficult. It is said that items in it have rewards, but again these cannot be rewards in the sense of *artificial* consequences. There are no conventionally instituted prizes for dieting or having operations, which one might get by successful pretence. The distinction between natural and artificial consequences, which emerges from the two speeches so insistently, simply does not fit the earlier threefold division.

Perhaps Plato has just been careless. But the problem is not merely one of artistic composition; it concerns the form of question which Socrates will answer in the rest of the *Republic*. We can respond in either of two ways. We can accept that the threefold division does not fit the demands made in the speeches, and conclude that one or the other is a mistake and that we find the real form of Glaucon's challenge by looking at only one or the other. Many interpreters of the *Republic* have done this; on the whole they have tended to downplay the threefold division and assume that it is superseded by the challenge made in the speeches. We can, on the other hand, try to find a consistent challenge in the two passages; and I think that this can be done.

Are the demands of Glaucon and Adeimantus actually in conflict with the original division of goods? As we have seen, their demand that the artificial consequences of justice be excluded does not fit that division happily. But why is this? The original division, as set up, was quite general. Glaucon gave a few examples to show us the kind of thing that was meant in each case; we therefore expect them to be uncontroversial

examples, as they are. When the question is raised, into which
class justice falls, there is an extra complication. For justice,
unlike knowledge and health, has two kinds of consequences,
the natural and the artificial. This is simply a fact about justice,
one which makes it a more difficult and controversial case than
health, say; but it need introduce no new principle of division
between goods. It simply is the case that justice has artificial
consequences and the other examples do not, because justice
depends for its existence on social conventions more than health
or knowledge does, and because people more often have good
reason to simulate justice than they do to simulate health or
knowledge. So in demanding that Socrates exclude the
artificial rewards of justice, the brothers are not setting him a
new task, but narrowing, and making harder, the task he has
already been set. It would have been easier to show that justice
falls into the second class if he had been allowed to count in the
rewards one gets by being just which are artificial in the sense
explained; but neither brother would be satisfied with this,
for the reasons they detail at length. Socrates has accepted a
more difficult job than before, but it is not a different kind of
task from the one he initially undertook: show that justice falls
in the second class. And Adeimantus says as much at the end of
his speech (367c–d).

The upshot of our long discussion of the speeches is that they
have not altered the nature of the demand made right at the
beginning in the threefold division; the brothers want, and
Socrates offers to deliver, a defence of justice that is neither
deontological nor consequentialist (indeed we have no one
jargon word for it). The two speeches have made it clearer why
they want an answer of this form; but for all we know so far it
might be an impossible demand. We learn more of Plato's
methods of arguing from Socrates' answer to Glaucon's
challenge than from the challenge itself, and we shall return at
the close of the main argument (the end of Book 9) to the form
of argument offered by Plato, and to its adequacy to answer
the pressing question: Why be just, if you can get away with
merely seeming to be just while in fact reaping the rewards of
injustice?

There is a further question to be faced. *Should* Socrates have
accepted the further demand that he exclude all the artificial

consequences of justice? He certainly goes out of his way to do so. He agrees not only to ignore the rewards that conventionally attach to justice and injustice, but positively to reverse them. He will show that it is desirable to be just even with all the penalties that attach to an appearance of injustice. And he will show that it is undesirable to be unjust even with all the rewards that conventionally attach to the appearance of justice. Following Glaucon we can sum the matter up by saying that Socrates undertakes to show that it is not worth being unjust even if you have Gyges' ring – that is, even if you can get away with your injustice as far as the rest of the world goes.

But isn't this an absurdly strong demand? Why does Socrates think that it is even relevant to the defence of justice?

It makes a great difference in moral reasoning whether one is or is not prepared to take on a task which is defined by examples that are avowedly unreal or fantastic. Socrates undertakes to show that even Gyges with his ring has reason to be just. But why not exclude Gyges? We can imagine what I shall call the 'realistic response' to Glaucon's challenge. '*If* Gyges had his ring, then perhaps he had no reason to refrain from the wicked acts that brought him success; *ex hypothesi* there was no way he was going to suffer for them. But it is no part of a defence of justice to show that *Gyges* has reason to be just. We live in a world where we have to take into account the natural and artificial consequences of injustice, and it is merely silly to ask what we would do if we escaped these by having magic rings. It isn't a fault in a defence of justice that it doesn't apply to someone who *ex hypothesi* escapes all those features of the human condition that make justice important to us. A realistic moral theory doesn't have to cope with fantastic examples. They fall outside the area that it purports to cover. Further, a theory that *is* designed to cope with them is likely for that very reason to be unrealistic, and not give the right answer in central everyday examples. Showing why Gyges with his ring ought to be just is likely to be irrelevant to showing why Joe Average ought to be just.'

Plato, we should note, is not unaware of this kind of response. In the bulk of the *Republic* he does try to answer the question in exactly this form: show that one has reason to be just *even if* one had Gyges' ring. But in Book 10 (612–613) he ends this defence and asks permission to restore to the just man the reputations and rewards that he could reasonably expect. In fact, he says, the just man does usually win through in the end. The unjust man is like an over-ambitious runner who cannot make it to the finishing-post. This is presented approvingly as the common-sense answer to the problem: honesty is the best long-run policy. Now it is questionable whether Plato is entitled simply to *add on* the 'realistic response' after arguing for eight books that even Gyges does have reason to be just; he seems not fully to realize that he is not throwing in an extra clinching argument but using a totally different kind of reasoning. But leaving this aside, Book 10 is important because it shows us that Plato was aware of this kind of response and did not think that it would do on its own. He accepts the challenge in the form offered by Glaucon: show that it is desirable to be just even if one has an absolute guarantee that one's injustice will not be found out.

So we can see right at the beginning that Plato's account of justice is not going to be 'realistic' in the sense of answering to common-sense intuitions about justice. It is designed to hold for extreme hypothetical cases as well as for what actually happens in the real world. We should not be too surprised, then, when his account of justice involves giving a picture of the 'ideal' state and 'ideal' human nature (though ideal in what sense we have yet to see). We have already seen that moral consensus is not enough for Plato, and he thinks that answers based on it will not satisfy the thoughtful. Later, when he has given his own account of justice in state and soul, we shall find Plato also worrying about the extent to which his account does in fact answer problems that arise for the concept of justice as we have it; he is not as ready to cut free from common sense as we might suppose here from his refusal to be satisfied with the 'realistic response'. But at the start the challenge to defend justice is posed in such a way that it cannot be met satisfactorily by any answer already available to common sense.

FURTHER READING

The article by J. Mabbott, 'Is Plato's *Republic* Utilitarian?' (originally written for *Mind* 1937, rewritten with additions for Vlastos (ed.) *Plato* ii), gives a clear picture of deontological and consequentialist interpretations of the *Republic's* argument. (This refers to the article by Foster that introduces the term 'natural' and 'artificial' consequences in this regard.) See also C. Kirwan, 'Glaucon's Challenge', *Phronesis* 1965; Irwin, *Plato's Moral Theory* ch. 7, sections 4–5; N. White, *A Companion to Plato's Republic* pp. 74–82, for different resolutions of the difficulties raised by the brothers' speeches.

Chapter 4

The Just Society

Socrates, having agreed to meet Glaucon's difficult challenge, starts his answer indirectly. He turns abruptly (363d) to justice in the city. While we are not clear about justice in the individual, he says, we would do well to turn to justice in the city, for there we will find the same thing only written in larger letters, and so easier to make out. Thus Plato begins his extended parallel between just person and just city. Two points are worth making about this at the start.

Firstly, Plato talks throughout about cities, but his claims are, in modern terms, about states or societies. The Greek word for 'city', *polis*, is often translated 'city-state' to emphasize the fact that for an ancient Greek the political unit was the city, not the nation. Different cities had very diverse systems of government and cultures, and though the Greeks did think of themselves as having a common nationality this meant little to them in comparison with citizenship in the *polis*. Where Plato talks about the city, I shall often talk about the state, or society, because he is talking about the unit, whatever it is, that determines an individual's political status and cultural background.

Secondly, the idea that justice in the city can illuminate justice in the individual only gets off the ground if 'justice' has the same sense as applied to both. Otherwise the argument would founder through the fallacy of equivocation: Plato would be making points about the justice of a city and then using them to talk about the justice of an individual, without noticing that 'justice' was not used in the same way in the two contexts. (This point can be made by saying, either that 'justice' has two senses, or that justice takes two different forms.) We may be surprised that Plato does not even consider the possibility at the outset that justice in the case of cities, and collections of individuals, might be a very different matter from justice in the case of an individual. His failure to do so has implications which become obvious later. When Socrates says at 368e7–8 that there will be *more* justice in the city because it is bigger, and so it will be easier to see, he is assuming that there will be more of the very same thing, whatever it is, that there is less of in individuals. Indeed, it is largely because of this assumption that he finds it more obvious a move than we do, to discuss the city as a way of establishing conclusions about individuals.

THE FIRST CITY

To examine justice in the city, we must ask about the nature of a city. What is essential for the existence of a *city* (as opposed, say, to a random group of mutually unconcerned people)? Socrates tries to find this by looking at the way a city would naturally be formed. He is not writing *a priori* history, or any kind of history. He is starting from given facts about individuals and asking what would have to be the case (in history, or now) for a state to exist among these people.

The basis for a state, he says, is the association of people based on *need* (369b–c). People aren't self-sufficient, and they have varied needs. We get a state when we have a group of people whose self-interest is far-sighted enough for them to specialize and divide their tasks. Thus the farmer will spend all his time farming, and exchange his produce with the shoemaker, who spends all *his* time making shoes; and this forms the basis of a simple market economy. A minimal state will consist of, say, four people (a farmer, a builder, a weaver, a shoemaker) whose competences are specialized in such a way that the needs of each are best fulfilled. Thus is introduced what I shall call the Principle of Specialization, the idea that one person should do one job.

Plato is not merely claiming that division of labour is needed for economic efficiency and development. He does think that if one person does one job greater efficiency results and things are better made (370b–c), but he is claiming more than that. In any association, even one as small as four people, the needs of all are best met if each can 'perform his own work as common for them all' (369e); and *this* is impossible, Plato claims, unless each person does only one job. He is not interested in efficiency as such, only efficiency in an association where people's lives are interdependent, and they do not merely 'feed side by side like animals' as Aristotle later put it. Once people stop seeing everyone else as in competition for what they need, and start to co-operate to fulfil their needs, specialization of labour is required for the needs of all to be fulfilled in the best available ways.

Socrates claims that the specialization of labour is *natural*; at any rate he supports it by claiming (370b) that 'each one of us is born somewhat different from the others, one more apt for one task, one for another' (Grube). The Principle of Specialization turns out to be basic for the structure of Plato's own ideally just state, and so it is important for him to show that it answers to what is found in nature and is not merely a conventional way of arranging matters; if it were, then the justice found in the ideal state would have no better claim to be what justice really is than what Thrasymachus suggests. But what is meant by this claim that each of us differs 'in nature' from other people?

One thing Plato does *not* mean is that *individual* differences between people are important and that society benefits when these are developed and encouraged. Later he often expresses the Principle of Specialization by saying that each person should *ta heautou prattein*, and a good literal translation of this is that everybody should 'do their own thing', but Plato does not mean what the modern phrase has come to mean, namely that each person should live the kind of life which he or she has freely chosen, rather than living according to other people's desires or expectations. For us, 'doing one's own thing' suggests spontaneity and individuality, the idea that the sheer fact of difference between people is enough reason for encouraging choice of life-styles that develop variety. But for Plato, 'doing one's own' implies a great deal of conformity and identification with a role shared by others. This is because the differences of aptitude that interest him are not the differences which distinguish one person from everyone else, but differences which suggest that people come in different types suited for different kinds of life.

Plato is often misunderstood here. The Principle of

Specialization has been one of the *Republic*'s features that has been found most repulsive, and hostile interpreters have sometimes claimed that Plato actually thought, through stupidity or snobbishness, that some people actually *like* doing boring routine jobs. But Plato was as aware as we are that most people prefer variety of occupation; he is not denying obvious facts, but claiming that there are important differences of kind between people, whatever preferences they actually express. It turns out later that he is not interested in what makes a person a shoemaker and not a farmer, but in much wider differences of type.

Plato's basic thought is that natural differences between people indicate differing complementary roles they play in and for the community as a whole. Diverse aptitudes are seen as differing means for co-operation. Plato sees people as essentially social; he is interested, not in what makes a person unique among everyone else, but the ways in which he or she is distinctively fitted to co-operate with others in joint efforts. He does not begin by stressing what makes each person concerned to live his or her own life as he or she sees best, and then ask how such people might co-operate. Rather he sees individuals as finding their natural place in some co-operative association; he sees it as simply obvious that each individual is not self-sufficient (369b) and therefore needs some place within a society to live a life that fulfils his or her potential. And so even in the first city, differences of talent are seen solely as means towards the greater good of the whole. That is why Plato does not bother to ask whether the farmer, although he is good at farming, would not prefer to do something else occasionally. For him this is irrelevant, because the farmer *needs* to specialize if he and the others are to have an adequate life based on their joint co-operation. Indeed, if the farmer were to insist on a variety of activities because he preferred this and found specialization boring, this would be irresponsible, because the needs of all would thereby be worse met. For him to neglect the task that he can best do, just because he yearns to do a bit of shoemaking occasionally, would for Plato be self-indulgence at the cost of the common good.

It is important that the Principle of Specialization is introduced in the context of the first city, which is based on *need*. For it does have plausibility in the context of pressing need. If the good of others does depend on my doing what I can best do, and I neglect this just because I don't fancy doing it, then this is immature and selfish behaviour. Furthermore, it not only penalizes others, it lessens my own welfare, since I would have done better also if I had co-operated fully with others by doing my own proper job as well as I could. Now Plato thinks that this is always the right way to think of the Principle of Specialization, even when (as in the ideally just state) pressing need is not in question. He thinks that someone who follows his or her own personal inclinations, rather than the inclinations that spring from the social role for which they are best fitted, is always irresponsible and immature, and that the person who is unwilling to co-operate as fully as possible in producing the common good is always selfish. This is not at all plausible where co-operating to stay alive is not at stake. Plato never argues for his assumption that even when need is not in question people may still reasonably be expected to live lives that are determined by their ability to contribute to the common good.

The first city is allowed to develop, and becomes corrupt, in a very odd way, which forces us to ask what is the point of the first city in the *Republic*'s argument. Socrates says that the principles established will lead to the city's expansion, for the more needs we have to take into account, the more competences we will have to have in order to fulfil them, and there will be more needs just because of the circumstances of any city, including the need to trade with other cities (370e–371b). There will thus be various kinds of farmers, sailors, and tradesmen. Socrates then draws a picture of how the people described so far will live (372a–d), one obviously meant to recall pictures of the Golden Age. His citizens will sit around in idyllic country surroundings living on plain fare.

At this point Glaucon interrupts to say that this is no more than a city of pigs (372d4–5): they ought to have more civilized comforts. Socrates takes his point and allows in many more sophisticated needs, though warning that the first city was the true and healthy one and that the city now considered is luxurious and 'inflamed'. He goes ahead, though, and we get hunters, service professions like those of barbers and confectioners, more doctors, and, interestingly, performers (*mimētai*, 373b5). Catering for all these needs means that more territory is required, so we get an army. A good army, however, must be specialized as much as any other trade, if not more. So Socrates expands on the qualities that these soldiers need; gradually we find that the soldier class are called the 'Guardians', and interest shifts to the training necessary for them to be, not just good soldiers, but good organizers and rulers of the city. In fact being a good Guardian involves such stringent conditions of life that later at 399e Socrates comments that they have in the process 'purged' the luxurious and inflamed city with which they began.

The ideally just state, then (for such the city of the Guardians turns out to be) develops not from the first city but from the purging process that gets rid of what is unhealthy in the luxurious city.

So what is the first city doing? It was presented as the true and healthy city, and nothing about it made it inevitable that it would decline to the luxurious one; this step is rather contrived, since Plato does not have to have Glaucon interrupt.

Many have been naturally led to think that we are meant to take seriously the claim that the first city is the true one and the allusions to the Golden Age in the description of it. On this view, the first city is a picture of human association given an ideal picture of human nature – for in it only necessary human needs are met; and as long as this is the case, there will be no corruption. Plato, however, was aware that it is no good basing a political theory on the optimistic assumption that people will limit their demands to what they have natural and necessary needs for; they just won't. So Socrates' acquiescence to Glaucon's demand is in effect a recognition that people will always go on to demand unnecessary gratifications; and the ideally just state is developed from a realistic theory of human nature rather than an impossible ideal. This comes out graphically in the way the Guardians develop from the army. They turn out, eventually, to illustrate the highest development of human reason; but they begin, prosaically enough, as the army needed for aggressive expansion if the city is to have enough resources to meet the citizens' needs. (Plato is probably

making a pun at 374a; the Guardians are needed to protect the
city's *ousia* or 'substance' in the sense of property; *ousia* is the
word he uses later for the essence of a thing, and possibly we are
meant to reinterpret this passage in the light of later developments.)

This is an attractive interpretation, and it does answer to
important indications in the text. But it runs up against at least
two difficulties.

Firstly, the original city is built up purely on the basis of
self-interest; at 369c Socrates says that each will give and
receive from the other, when he does so, thinking that this will
be best for him. Self-interest may well be an entirely respectable
motive; but these people are motivated in their association
entirely by self-interest, and this isn't the most glorious way of
presenting *ideal* human nature. It is true that the first city
fulfils only necessary needs, but even this leads to the existence
of trading and marketing, which Plato regards as a function of
the lowest side of human nature; the corruption of the luxurious
city differs only in the type of needs satisfied. There seems no
reason for making a sharp cut-off between the kind of people in
the first city and the kind of people in the luxurious city; they
share the same kind of motivation.

Secondly, there are two small indications in the text. At 369a
Socrates says that if they look at a city coming into being they
will see the growth of justice *and injustice*; then after introducing
the luxuries, he says (372e) that they now have a swollen city,
but can still perhaps see in it where justice *and injustice* come
from. This suggests that both the first, 'true' city and the
corrupted city are put forward for us as models of human
nature in association which display both justice and injustice,
to be contrasted with the ideally just city, which displays only
justice.

So the attractive interpretation does not quite work. None
the less it is very plausible, and if it does not work (as I think it
does not) we have to conclude, though reluctantly, that Plato
has not given the first city a clear place in the *Republic*'s moral
argument. The real argument starts from facts about human
nature and co-operation which we see at work in the luxurious
city – needs which lead to a specialized army which becomes
the Guardians. The first city adds nothing, except a context in

which the Principle of Specialization is introduced in a plausible way.

A final point about this passage. When Socrates is discussing the kind of army needed by the city, he says that soldiers have to be specialists at their tasks just as much as other craftsmen; and we expect an appeal to the idea that this is better for all, and demanded by the nature of the common task. But instead we find at 374b6 the sinister sentence: 'We prevented the cobbler trying to be at the same time a farmer or a weaver or a builder, and we said that he must remain a cobbler . . .' (Grube). This is the first mention of compulsion in the state, and Plato offers *no defence of it whatever.* He simply takes it for granted that the fact that the common good would be furthered if people did something legitimizes forcing them to do it. Admittedly he is referring not to authoritarian measures within the state, but to the way the state was first specified. Still, there is un-mistakeably a reference to compulsion.

We find this absence of argument surprising and shocking, for we are used to the idea that the state is not automatically entitled to enforce measures which make individuals do things which they would not otherwise do, even if it is agreed that these would be for the common good. We shall have to consider this issue in more depth later when we come to the question of whether Plato recognizes that individuals have rights. But it is worth noticing that one of the most controversial features of Plato's moral philosophy rests entirely on unargued assumption.

It is often said that Plato lived in a time when it was taken for granted that the city-state had a perfect right to enforce, by law or informal sanction, a large measure of conformity in opinion and behaviour. But this does not wholly explain away Plato's procedure here; for his ideally just state involves compulsion on a scale that was as shocking to Plato's contemporaries as it is to us. We just have to face the fact that Plato is too ready to move from the needs of the common good to the use of compulsion and manipulation.

EDUCATION AND PHILOSOPHY OF EDUCATION

Having established the need for a specialized army of 'Guardians', Socrates shows, at 374–376, that these people could in fact have natures that combine the seemingly opposed characteristics of fierceness and docility. Then at 376d he turns to their education, which occupies him till 412b, where he claims briefly that the Guardians should be the rulers in the state. He takes it as uncontroversial that the city should be ruled by the best people for the job (we shall come back to the question, why he thinks it so obvious that anybody should be ruler); the Guardians are, he claims, the best people; and this claim is filled out, and made non-trivial, by the long account given of their education, which shows us what it is for people to be brought up to have qualities that fit them to rule. Throughout the *Republic* he recurs to the theme that the state depends on the Guardians' education and stands or falls with it (e.g. 423–4). So the discussion of education is a structural part of Plato's argument; he is not offering a detachable 'philosophy of education' that can safely be extracted from the argument about the state. On the other hand, he apologizes for its leisurely nature (376d), he is clearly indulging some of his pet concerns, and his account of education is in fact of interest even to those who reject his fundamental political assumptions. Plato has been led by the needs of his argument to think hard about the nature of education; and while many of the details of his proposals (for example, his censorship of Homer and his concern with kinds of musical instruments) are of interest only to the student of Greek culture, his proposals about the form and content of education raise issues in philosophy and education that are clearly relevant today.

One preliminary point: it is disconcerting to find that the sole ground that Plato puts forward to support his claim that there are people who are educable to be Guardians is an analogy with animals (374–6). Having compared young warriors with pedigree dogs (375a) Socrates then says (375d) that this image or model provides the answer to our difficulty: the same person *can* be both fierce and gentle, and the answer lies in training the intelligence to control their responses, for trained dogs discriminate in their behaviour and are gentle or fierce depending on whether or not they know the person that they confront. The analogy is meant seriously, since the Guardians are compared to dogs in several passages (416a–b, 422d, 451d, 459a ff., 537a). But although Plato does think that animals' behaviour suggests possibilities for human behaviour, the passages should not be read (as they have sometimes been read) as showing that Plato thinks that people should behave as animals do, following a biological imperative; Plato is not foreshadowing anti-rational and fascist theories of political association, since no-one could stress more than he does the value of reason as what is specifically human. When he says that a trained dog is 'wisdom-loving' (*philosophos*, 376a11–12), using the word he will later use for his philosophers, Plato is making a pun, the point of which is presumably to claim that wisdom and desire for knowledge in people is not something recherché, but is continuous with the exemplification in the activities of all animals of intelligent, as opposed to undiscriminating, behaviour. This is appropriate in beginning a discussion of the education of children, in whom reason is undeveloped. But all the same it is odd that the analogy with animals should be our sole clue to the Guardians' educability, for their way of life turns out to be based precisely on what distinguishes people from animals – developed and articulate reason. Plato's argument here is provisional; he is trying to get us to accept the idea of training people in a certain way, without examining its basis too closely – that is something we do later, on the basis of a deeper understanding of the subject. He warns us here that the animals' behaviour is only an 'image' (*eikōn*, 375d5); and later we shall find that truly philosophical reasoning excludes all such appeals to experience and imagery, and provides a rigorous basis for what we were initially induced to accept by appeal to experience. After we have read the *Republic* as a whole, we see that a person with full understanding of what education is knows that the behaviour of animals is not the real justification for the Guardians' education; it is only an analogy that makes the idea easier for a person knowing nothing of the subject to assimilate. This is our first introduction to a theme that will be developed later in the discussions of knowledge: there is a great difference between learning about something for the first time and having a full understanding of it, and it is often a good idea for the learner to use aids, like visual aids, which can be discarded later when he or she has mastery of the subject-matter and its central concepts. The 'image' of animal behaviour is one such 'visual aid' to the person learning for the first time about the principles behind proper education – something comparatively new to Plato's first readers.

For Plato, education covers not just the content of what you learn, but the forms in which what is learnt is presented – the kind of music you listen to, the sort of exercise you take, the type of objects that surround you. He is far from identifying education with *what goes on in school*. For him it covers the whole of a child's development.

It follows that for education to be done properly, aspects of life regarded (in ancient Greece as now) as separate from 'schooling' must be brought under control of the educators. If education is, as Plato takes it to be, a total training of character, an education of all aspects in which children are educable, then education has a greater scope than we might have suspected. The rather disturbing implication is that there is no clear and defensible line between private life and public schooling. In the *Republic* the details of how the life of the young is to be organized are left vague; in a much later work, the *Laws*, Plato indulged his obsessions on this subject, and we find that he would begin before birth, by making pregnant women take certain exercises, and continue by regulating children's games and trying to produce ambidexterity in all children. In the *Republic* we have only an outline sketched, but even so we can see from a passage at 401b–402a how extensive Plato takes the scope of education to be, and how far he is from identifying it with acquiring information or skills:

Is it then the poets only whom we shall command and compel to represent the image of good character in their poems or else not practise among us, or are we to give orders also to the other craftsmen, and forbid them to represent, whether in pictures or in buildings or in any other works, character that is vicious, mean, unrestrained, or graceless? We must not allow one who cannot do this to work among us, that our guardians may not, bred among images of evil as in an evil meadow, culling and grazing much every day from many sources, little by little collect all unawares a great evil in their own soul . . . Are not these the reasons . . . why nurture in the arts is most important, because their rhythm and harmony permeate the inner part of the soul, bring graciousness to it, and make the strongest impression, making a man gracious if he has the right kind of upbringing; if he has not, the opposite is true. The man who has been properly nurtured in this area . . . will praise beautiful things, rejoice in them, receive them into his soul, be nurtured by them and become both good and beautiful in character. He will rightly object to what is ugly and hate it while still young before he can grasp the reason, and when reason comes he who has been reared thus will welcome it and easily recognize it because of its kinship with himself. (Grube.)

We shall pick up later two striking points in this passage: the authoritarian stress on commanding and forbidding, and the prominence of the arts. Several points stand out first as relevant to Plato's conception of education as a training of character.

What may surprise us most is the total absence of any reference to academic achievement. Neither here nor elsewhere is there any reference to exams or grading; the children are tested for strength of character (413c–d) but education is not thought of as a process of absorbing information or skills which can be periodically tested. The well-educated person is not a prodigy in any subject, or a range of subjects; the criterion of successful education is a morally mature and, as we say, 'healthy' outlook on the world. Nowadays this is often called 'moral education' and it is increasingly held that schools, rather than parents, should provide it; but it is rarely allowed to dominate the entire curriculum as it does for Plato.

Plato describes the training of his Guardians' characters in terms that are as much aesthetic as strictly 'moral'. Education is to produce people who are attracted to good and feel repulsion for evil, finding it ugly and vulgar. We must not think that this emphasis on the aesthetic point of view indicates a detached and 'arty' attitude; rather Plato thinks that there is no sharp distinction between aesthetic and moral attitudes. His point is made more forcibly in Greek because the word he uses for 'beautiful' or 'fine', *kalos*, is used of what is admirable and good of its kind. Goodness or fineness of speech, music, form, and rhythm follow on goodness of character, he claims, and lack of form, rhythm, and harmony are akin to poor language and poor character (400e, 401a). Plato stresses the aesthetic terms here because he is thinking of young children to whom 'reason has not yet come', that is, who do not fully understand the reasons they are given for commands and prohibitions, or the whole practice of giving and asking for reasons. And here he is strikingly realistic. Modern educators often recommend that children be simply trained to obey certain moral rules or precepts without understanding why, and later have reasons given. But Plato is aware that this process may only produce a Polemarchus, with rigid principles and no real understanding of them. Children may have no grasp of or interest in moral rules or concepts, and rather than force them to learn them Plato suggests that we develop in young children attitudes of attraction to what they will later see as morally good and repulsion to what they will later learn to be morally bad. Rather than be told flatly that certain behaviour is wrong, without knowing why, they will learn that it is ugly and that people who do it are horrible, and later appreciate that it is wrong. If this process is successful, then instead of having a baffled and resentful attitude to morality, they will 'greet reason as a friend': morality will be to them a comprehensible extension and reinforcement of the attitudes that are familiar to them already. Morality will thus be a natural and comfortable part of everyday life, not something that people forget about most of the time, or respect but have problems living up to. Plato is concerned that morality should have a hold on the feelings and attitudes in a way that is integrated with the whole of one's life, and should make sense in terms of the basic attachments that children make. We are familiar with the problems of a white who thinks it is wrong to discriminate against blacks, or a man who thinks it is wrong to discriminate against women, but who have trouble living by these beliefs because their education was so conditioned by racist and sexist stereotypes that they have tendencies which they disapprove of, tendencies for example to think that it is somehow objectionable or absurd for blacks or women to have positions of authority. Plato would see this as a fault in education: these people have been brought up to find the wrong things attractive and repulsive, and the result is a chronic conflict in the moral personality. Many of Plato's actual educational suggestions (including some which seem absurd to us) are designed precisely to avoid such a conflict.

Although so much is made of the character which is trained by education, the notion of *character* itself is not dealt with very specifically in this section of the book. Plato is content to put forward a general idea which could be refined in practice; the most he says is that there are two crucial aspects of character: what is developed by physical training and what is developed

by what he calls *mousikē*, which is best translated 'training in
the arts' and which covers the rest of the curriculum (again we
see how little emphasis is put at this point on academic
achievement). A long passage at 410–412 insists on a balance
between intellectual and physical training to produce the right
kind of character, and moderation is stressed in general as
necessary (401–3, 410e, 412a). Plato's basic point is just
common sense: those who devote all their time to sports become
philistine and boring, while those who neglect them entirely
become precious and ineffective. But what this implies is
important, namely that the character that is to be trained has
both a physical and a non-physical aspect. He does say at 410c
that even physical training is for the sake of the soul and not the
body, but this does not imply that the soul might become
detached from the body: the body is something that has to be
considered in the education of the whole character. Later in
the *Republic* Plato says things that are hard to reconcile with
these passages. In some passages he will urge us not to identify
ourselves with any of the desires or interests of the body. And
when he has produced his own account of human personality
and its divisions, he refers back to this passage (441e–442b)
saying that both physical and moral education affect only two
of the soul's parts, while the desires that arise from the possession
of a body are not educable but have merely to be restrained.
This is much more puritanical about the body than the actual
discussion of education, and we have to conclude, I think, that
in Books 2 and 3 Plato works with a rough but serviceable
notion of character to be trained which does not coincide with
what he says later about the relation of soul and body.

Another result of Plato's casualness about the character
that is to be trained is that he never distinguishes between
what is required for an undeveloped character and what is
appropriate for a more mature one. In spite of his emphasis on
development and progress he never considers the possibility of,
say, censoring children's reading but leaving educated adults
to choose for themselves. But it is one thing to protect young
children from the bad effects of racism and sexism in their
reading, and quite another to forbid an adult, after extensive
education, to read D. H. Lawrence. This is, precisely,
paternalism, treating adults as though they were children.

Plato is a paternalist, and this is one reason why it is important for us to separate his views on educating children from his political theory as a whole. We are readier than he is to think that a point comes when we must have faith in the reason that the child has developed, and let go.

Plato is the first thinker systematically to defend the notion that education is a training of character rather than an acquisition of information or skills, and while this idea has always been found interesting it has, in the twentieth century, been increasingly put into practice, so that discussion of it is far from an academic exercise. In America children's education is run on Platonic lines. As far back as 1918 the National Education Association listed seven main objectives for education in secondary schools: 'health, command of fundamental processes [i.e. the Three R's], worthy home membership, vocation, citizenship, worthy use of leisure, ethical character.' As in Plato, there is no great emphasis on the development of the intellect at this stage, or on the intrinsic interest and value of certain studies. During the twentieth century the pattern of American education has more and more come to be that of a secondary schooling which emphasizes the acquiring of moral and social values and relationships with one's peers, with intellectual and academic developments deferred until tertiary education. (This is not to say that children don't learn *anything* academic in school, only that academic values do not determine the curriculum and their importance is subordinated to that of learning to act in accordance with approved social and moral values.) The fact that Platonic ideas about education actually do work, can be put into practice, is highly significant for at least two reasons.

Firstly, the country whose educational system comes closest to the Platonic ideal (for a variety of reasons) is America, a country which has always stressed the value of liberty and individual initiative as ideals. In the Soviet Union, on the other hand, education has remained rigidly academic. This is one indication that there is no necessary connection between Platonic theories of education as a training of character, and totalitarianism, or a repressive view of the function of the state. The matter is much more complicated than that.

Secondly, the fact that it is possible to institutionalize a system whereby early schooling is dominated by training in group values whereas at a later stage what is required is dedication to academic ideals by an élite group, points up a problem that faces Plato. At a later stage, a minority of those receiving the initial education will go on to a rigorous and lengthy course of further education in predominantly mathematical studies. At this point what is stressed is intellectual capacity and creative imagination. Education is not, Plato says, a transfer of knowledge into the soul, like putting sight into blind eyes; it is more like turning the eye to the light (518b–c). All the educator can do is to provide the conditions in which the right kind of mind can develop its capacities. Throughout the long discussions of the mathematical studies which precede philosophy proper, there is constant stress on the need for all the intellectual virtues: breadth of vision, justness of judgement, sharpness in argument, and appreciation of what is relevant. The final products of the Guardians' further education are the philosophers in whom reason is most fully developed and whose rule is based on the claim that their understanding of matters important for the welfare of the state surpasses that of everyone else.

But why should people whose early years have been moulded by training in accepting the moral values of their society have preserved the capacity for intellectual rigour and creativity required by these further studies? This is a real problem, and it worries many educationalists, some of whom think that a child's intellectual autonomy is destroyed by too thorough a training in accepting group values at an early age. Plato, however, faces the problem in an especially acute form. For he does not think that children should be made aware of alternative values, or encouraged to question the ones they are presented with. In the ideally just state, moral education will involve a large amount of conformity, both in learning to conform to standards accepted already, and in learning to conform to what others of one's own age do. Why should people who are (crudely put) brought up to be moral conformists suddenly turn out to be intellectual pathbreakers in later life? And yet Plato goes out of his way to stress both the early conformity and the later intellectual honesty and rigour.

Some interpreters have solved this problem for Plato, rather backhandedly, by claiming that he does not really mean to encourage intellectual honesty and academic progress even at the later stage. They have been so unfavourably impressed by the moral uniformity to be produced by the early stages of education that they have flatly denied that any product of it could, or could be expected to, come out with new ideas, especially about morality. They think that Plato thought that the truth could be discovered once and for all, and that later generations would merely go through a charade of discovering new truths. But this is obviously wrong, not only because Plato does stress the importance of commitment to the truth and to following the argument where it leads, but because of his faith in the powers of reason in general.

But all the same, why would the education that Plato describes produce people capable of innovative and original thought? The more one stresses the unity of attitude and feeling with moral belief, the harder it is to see how the products of such a system could be genuinely open-minded about alternatives differing greatly from their own experience.

The problem is eased a bit if we point out that Plato thinks that further studies begin with mathematics, and that this is the road to philosophical thinking. For it might seem that capacity for creative work in mathematics is more likely than any other to survive an enforced conformity in values. Plato says some things at 536e–537a which support this. There he says that arithmetic and geometry and other mathematical studies must be introduced to the children, but not made compulsory: 'no free man should learn any lesson in a slavish way' (536e1–2). Enforced exercise doesn't harm the body, but enforced learning never stays in the soul. It looks as though Plato is especially concerned that the capacity for mathematical thinking should not become dulled, to the extent of insisting that early exercise of it should be encouraged by play and not forced – in a way not apparently true of any other study. So perhaps Plato thinks that the kind of thinking which is to develop later, provided it is not squashed by bad teaching, is of a pure and abstract kind which is relatively independent of the results of the early moral training. This would explain why he thinks that early docility and identification with the group's values do not preclude a later development of original thinking.

This thinking will be applied to moral matters, but it originates in more abstract mathematical studies. It cannot be said that Plato solves the problem here (and his glorification of thinking and the intellect turn out to be hard to fit with the emphasis in the account of early education on the development of the whole person, mental and physical). But at least it is clear, from the *Republic*, just where the problems lie.

We must now come back to the two points set aside earlier, the authoritarian nature of Plato's education and his emphasis on the arts.

Plato's programme of education is authoritarian in two ways. It is the only education offered; there will be no works of art other than the ones deemed beneficial, and *a fortiori* there will be no alternative schools. Plato is quite frank about the prevention of alternative systems, or the presentation of alternative values as desirable. And further, people are not to be brought up to question their beliefs. It is made clear that free intellectual inquiry is to be limited to the élite who have come through the long secondary education; nobody else is to be encouraged, or allowed, to put forward ideas that have political import. When the children mature, they are to greet reason as a familiar friend which is akin: reason is to reinforce the beliefs that have been brought about already, not to induce a questioning and critical attitude.

Now it would be wrong to think that Plato intends education to be a process of brainwashing which will instil the right beliefs and ensure that they are held, whatever the intellectual state of the person holding them. If all Plato cared about was bringing it about that the right beliefs be held, he would not have thought of education as a training of people's characters, for this would be unnecessary; all that would matter would be the effective implanting of the right moral beliefs in the young, and there are more direct and effective ways to do that than the character training Plato recommends. All the same, it is undeniable that his educational system aims to impose on children a single set of values in such a way that they will not be seriously sceptical about them either at the time or later in life. We feel unhappy about this; and most educational theorists would hold that this cannot be the proper function of education. Education, it is widely held, must aim to produce people who are autonomous in that they can think independently and can ask themselves whether they find it better to continue to hold the values in which they were brought up, or to choose to live by another set of values. We tend to think that education has failed just to the extent that children when grown up do not (at least) question the values that they were taught by some authority in childhood; we take this as a mark of dullness and conformity. We have already seen that Plato does not think this; he thinks that receptiveness to accepted moral values in youth can co-exist with an intellectually adventurous mind in maturity. But it is not at all obvious that this is so, and so Plato is not entitled to take for granted the acceptability of an authoritarian approach to education.

Because we disagree so strongly with Plato here, it is important to get straight just what his grounds are, because he has often been both attacked and defended on the wrong grounds.

Plato is not saying that the reason that people should be taught moral views in a way making them unlikely to question them is that there is such a thing as moral truth and we can be sure that we know it. Sometimes it is said that the only reason we are unwilling to bring about unquestioned acceptance of moral beliefs is that we are not sure of their truth, and it is implied that Plato's main reason for refusing to tolerate a plurality of moral teachings is that he thinks both that there is a moral truth to be known, and that we can be sure that we have it. But this cannot be the only reason, for one might hold both of these beliefs, and still think that it is bad for people to be brought to hold the truth in an unquestioning way. For one might hold (as Mill does) that it is only the consciousness of alternatives that makes one's possession of a moral belief something that has any hold on the imagination, rather than a dull and remote dogma.

Nor does Plato think that people should not be brought up to question their moral beliefs because doing this will make them less happy than they would otherwise be. This suggestion is often put forward by people who think that Plato was aiming at the return of a tribal or 'closed' society where people were brought up to be unquestioning and unselfconscious about their beliefs and roles. On this view, Plato thought that people should not be critical about their beliefs because this would make them alienated and anomic, whereas what he wanted was a society in which people felt secure and integrated into their roles. Encouraging people to be critical of received beliefs would seem to him to promote useless worry and unhappiness. As it stands this suggestion is clearly wrong, for the idea that people are necessarily shaken and made unhappy by acquiring a critical attitude to their beliefs shows a primitive fear of reason that may characterize a tribal society, but hardly the author of the *Republic*, who shows an amazing degree of confidence in the powers of rational inquiry to settle disputed moral matters and find out the truth. (On the other hand, we shall find some pessimism about the intellectual capacities of the mere producers in society, and correspondingly greater readiness to allow them to be manipulated into holding beliefs that will make them happy.)

It does seem true, however, that Plato does not attach importance to educating people to be autonomous, that is, to be critical of their beliefs and accept them because they are convinced of their rightness, rather than relying on authority. He does not see any great virtue in *my* insisting that *I* decide what I shall accept as convincing in moral matters. He thinks that it is a good thing that a small élite, who have been selected for their intellectual competence, should go through a process of asking for the grounds for all beliefs accepted on any authority. But this is because such people are well placed to get somewhere by their inquiries; there is some point in their doing this since they will advance to further comprehension and may produce valuable results. However, what about ordinary, intellectually mediocre people who will not make any important contribution to the subject? Plato sees no point in their having any tendency to question their beliefs: such criticism is for him justified only by its results in furthering understanding for everyone. We might object that it is valuable for any individual to go through a process of self-doubt and self-questioning; indeed we tend to assume that this is actually necessary for a secure sense of self. Plato takes no account of this. He attaches no value to an individual's coming to hold his or her beliefs for himself, as a result of his or her own thought; it matters more that one should have the right beliefs, live a life dominated by correct perceptions of oneself and one's capabilities. As we have seen, this is not the same as caring only that the right beliefs be held, for whatever reason. But Plato does not think that there is any intrinsic value to criticism and questioning of established ideas unless this is done as a means to further progress, by people who have had a long intellectual training and will not stop at the stage of being critical.

There is thus an important sense in which Plato's education does not develop what we think of as the individual personality: people are encouraged to develop in such a way as to hold firmly the beliefs appropriate to the kind of person they are, rather than to set up their own individual judgements as a test of what each will find acceptable. We shall come back to Plato's lack of interest in individuality and the importance of what is unique to a particular person. In the present context it emerges further in a passage at 405–409. This is a polemic against the need for the extensive services of doctors and lawyers, and it is so cranky and unsympathetic that it seems at first to be just an example of the non-professional's dislike of doctors and lawyers which crops up in literature from Molière to Raymond Chandler. But in fact it is more significant; it shows us Plato's proposed way of dealing with the failures of his system – those who despite the intensive training fail to have healthy bodies or a 'healthy' moral outlook. And in three rather chilling ways his proposals show the extreme unimportance to him of the individual's own viewpoint on his or her life. Firstly, the judge's role is made extensively parallel with the doctor's; people who oppose accepted legal and moral norms are not given the dignity of being rebels, but are thought of as 'defective and incurable in soul' (410a); they are thought of as having something wrong with them which should be dealt with regardless of their opinion on the matter, just as cancer should be dealt with even if the patient for some reason thinks that there is nothing wrong. Secondly, Plato is very rigid about applying his ideal of what is normal; somebody with a chronic and debilitating illness, he says, cannot have a life that is worth living (407a–408b). He never considers the possibility that an individual might find sources of value in his or her life other than the approved, standard ones. Because of this he can see no value at all in supporting the handicapped; he thinks that no individual can 'practise virtue' if he cannot lead a normally healthy life (407c). It is not that he believes in killing off the handicapped because they are no use to society; rather he thinks that they are prevented from leading a life that is virtuous and worth having for them. It is sometimes thought that Plato wrote this passage because of natural callousness towards the sick, but I doubt this; we should compare 496a–c, where mention is made of a friend of Socrates called Theages, who practised philosophy full-time because he had some chronic illness preventing him from going into public life. He is mentioned as one of those who 'deservedly consort with philosophy', with no apparent irony. It is not from personal hardness, but from reasoned conviction, that Plato denies that an individual life can be valuable to the person if he or she is 'deviant' (physically or morally) from the approved norm. Thirdly, Plato thinks that even an individual who has led a healthy normal life will lose any reason for living if he or she ceases to be 'normal' even physically. In a notorious passage (406d–407a) he gives as an example a carpenter who develops a chronic disease. There is no point, says Plato, in his supporting what is left of his life with the help of medicine; it is better for him to die and 'be rid of his troubles', because 'his life is of no benefit to him if he does not perform the job he has'. (Strictly, I suppose, it would be all right if he could stop being a carpenter and become something less physically demanding; the point is not that he is so devoted to carpentry that he cannot live without it, but that he is fitted to do manual work and cannot live without following some trade of that sort.) Plato does not say this because he happens to be hard-hearted; that would be of no philosophical interest. Nor is he advocating a programme of euthanasia (though the passage is often so interpreted). He is not saying that the state might as well get rid of this man because he is no use any more. But what he is saying is, if anything, even more chilling: he thinks that the carpenter's life is not worth living if he cannot fulfil the social role that structures his life, and this implies that the carpenter's own personal point of view on the matter is not relevant. Presumably he wants to go on living, and his family agree, but this is not even considered; whatever *he* thinks, Plato implies, his life just *has* lost its meaning and it is better for *him* not to go on living. This passage is a remarkable one; it shows that Plato's great emphasis on character and its proper development co-exists with the belief that many of our actual concerns and relationships with other people, based on caring for individuals, are likely to be misguided or lack proper justification, and that this may be so even with our concern for our own lives.

Plato is very sketchy about the curriculum of his education in all aspects except what we would call 'the arts'; he talks about these at great length, particularly poetry. Poetry is the most important art form for two reasons which do not apply to poetry in our society. It formed an extensive part of children's education, especially Homer, which was learned and recited in children's formative years. Poetry involved performing, because it was always recited or sung, not read silently, and it formed a major part of children's education. Plato, in fact, thinks of prose as marginal – the only prose works he mentions are children's stories and fables told by mothers and nurses (cf. 377a–c). His concern is with popular culture, the culture that surrounds children as they grow up; in a present-day setting his concern would be with novels, movies, and TV. Another point is that because epic and dramatic poetry had such high status and influence in Greek life, Plato thinks of poetry as especially influential on people's *beliefs*. He is more concerned about people having faulty and limited beliefs picked up from the poetry and literature they know, than with their being insensitive to natural or artistic beauty.

It is in terms of poetry that Plato makes a famous distinction which he uses to delimit the field of good art. This is the distinction between poetry which is, and that which is not, an example of *mimēsis*. *Mimēsis* is usually translated 'imitation' and I shall follow this, but it is an elusive term, and when Plato reverts to discussing it in Book 10 we shall find that it seems to be used in a different way. In Books 2–3 it is introduced in the context of the performing arts, and we might find it more natural to translate it as 'represent' or 'express', whereas in Book 10 it is introduced in the context of painting, and 'imitate' is a better rendering. So as not to beg any questions I shall use the traditional 'imitation' throughout for *mimēsis*, and discuss the difficulties in connection with the Book 10 argument.

Imitation is introduced ostensively at 392d, where Plato distinguishes carefully between imitation and narration in a passage from the *Iliad*. Narration is the poet telling what happened in his own person; imitation is taking on the character of another. In an epic poem like the *Iliad* this happens in the passages which are, as we put it, 'in direct speech'; a play is entirely made up of imitation. Here it helps to remember that for the Greeks all poetry was performed aloud (usually to musical accompaniment) so that reading poetry would involve taking on the role of the person represented. Plato is very concerned about the effects of imitation on the person imitating, and this may seem odd to us if we think in terms of modern culture, which is dominated by movies and TV and printed books, and in which the consumer is more passive; it is helpful to think of Plato's worry about confusion of roles as applying to acting rather than to silent reading or watching.

One problem is that, as he introduces it, imitation has clear application only to recited poetry. We can understand the difference between narration and acting a role only for this case, which involves performance. But he makes the distinction between imitative and non-imitative poetry the basis for his distinction between good and bad poetry, since he thinks that imitation is dangerous and bad. We are then told, however (401 ff.), that all the arts, not just poetry, show this distinction between good and bad kinds, between the kinds that sustain and the kinds that undermine and fragment good character. Now presumably we are to understand the distinction in these cases also as being based on the difference between being or not being imitative. But how can we carry over the distinction between narration and role-acting to the other arts that Plato mentions – painting, weaving, the applied arts, and architecture? We have no idea how we are to think of a good rug or house as akin to narration and a bad one as akin to role-acting. Plato has not thought the problem out for their case; he is not very interested in these arts and simply carries over to them terms that have application only to recited poetry, so that we really have a theory of the place of poetry in education rather than a theory about the place of the arts. This is something that often happens in discussion of the arts (or of Art) where one art is, more or less consciously, made the model in terms of which all the arts are discussed.

Why does Plato think that imitation is dangerous? He thinks that it has potentially bad effects on the person who imitates or acts a role, who may become like the person he or she imitates, and thus risks becoming morally worse, or split and disunified, 'many people' instead of one. The Guardians must strive to be singlemindedly excellent, and imitation, if freely allowed, might upset this.

But is this not rather simple-minded? In what sense do actors 'become like' kings, or cowboys? A standard objection is that Plato is ignoring the difference between life and art. We are aware of the difference between ourselves and the characters imitated, whether we or others are doing the imitating: fiction and the theatre depend on recognizable conventions. Now there may be something to the charge that Plato does not think that we really do distance ourselves and our lives from the performance involved in acting or reciting. But I do not think that this is his real objection. What he dislikes is that in imitating I am putting myself in the place of another. Plato thinks that this is dangerous and morally dubious, and I think that he would hold this even if the character imitated were real and not fictional. He is not concerned with the dangers of life imitating art, but with what happens when I identify with another person. Imitating fictional characters is dangerous only because fiction is the context where this usually happens. We can appreciate Plato's concern because, although we do not often 'imitate' aloud the way the Greeks did, we are encouraged in our reading of novels, biographies, and some poetry to 'identify with' characters, and this is his real target.

Still, what is wrong with it? In putting oneself in the place of another character, one comes to see things from their point of view. To act the part of Achilles convincingly, I have to come to understand what it would be like to be Achilles – that is, what it would be like to be a Homeric warrior in a certain situation, who is led to say and do certain things. My experience, whoever I am, is likely to have been very different from Achilles'. I have to imagine what it would be like to lack certain experiences and to have had others, to have very different attitudes and responses, to be someone to whom certain ways of acting, foreign to me, are natural. In the process

I will come to understand why Achilles thought it all right, indeed required by honour, to do things which I would find cruel and senseless. To imitate Achilles successfully (whether acting or silently empathizing) is to understand why he did what he did, the situation being now seen from his point of view.

We tend to think that this phenomenon is valuable because it extends our moral horizons and makes us more open-minded and flexible than we would be purely on the basis of our own experience. Reading novels is taken to be a source of moral growth. Plato, however, is against it. He expresses two objections and we can find, implicitly, a third. Imitation, he claims, both lowers the character (395c–396b) and fragments it (394e–395b). It improves the character to imitate good people, to put oneself in the place of someone doing a glorious deed; but equally it may expand the horizons for the worse to identify with someone doing a callous or revolting or treacherous deed. Plato thinks that not all experience is worth having, even vicariously. This is at least not obviously false, and it has the merits of taking seriously the effects of imitation on the character. Literature *does* change people, and enlarge their experience, and it is not clear that this is always good. (But to admit this is not necessarily to agree with Plato that there ought to be censorship.) And because people are affected by what they read, or see at the movies, as well as by what they themselves do, Plato has a point also in claiming that imitation tends to undermine unity of character. Here we may agree that he is right while disagreeing that it is necessarily a bad thing. Entering into the experience of another person makes me able to see both sides of the question where he is concerned, to see something as problematic from his or her point of view which would not be so from mine. We tend to think that awareness of a plurality of moral outlooks is healthy and that it is a good thing to understand the point of view of both St. Francis and Napoleon. (But Plato has a point in that there are dangers in having conflicting role models; one cannot try to *be* like both St. Francis and Napoleon.) Plato quite rigidly sets his face against his Guardians even enlarging their imaginative experience; they are to be single-minded rulers, and so he sees no point in their imitating even craftsmen (396a–b); he thinks that it is not good for them to understand what a craftsman's life is like, because that will not help them in their own kind of life.

We can see here a reason why Plato is so consistently hostile to tragedy and epic, although he never makes it explicit. The force of much of tragedy (and of parts of the *Iliad*, though not the *Odyssey*) lies in the moral conflict embodied in what happens. When we read Hector's farewell to his wife, or the ransoming of Hector's body by his old father, or watch the story of Oedipus, part of the way we are affected lies in the fact that we cannot sum up what happens as being, all told, good or bad, right or wrong. We can see why the protagonists come into irreconcilable conflict, or destroy themselves, without being able to reduce the outcome to a moral plus or minus. We are left feeling the force of both, or all, points of view. We cannot make a single moral judgement which will dispose of everything that we have been made to feel the force of. We are left feeling that there is no single statement of moral truth which does not leave out something vital. Later we shall see that it is fundamental to Plato's moral theory that there is a single finally correct moral point of view, from which justice is done to the situation and character of everyone. For him, conflict at the moral level is never final; it is always, at least to some extent, a matter of appearance, of faulty or partial viewpoint. In the end, moral truth transcends tragedy, because what appeared to be moral conflict is resolved. For such a point of view, epic and tragedy must be dangerous, because they encourage us to empathize with different characters and therefore feel very forcibly the validity of irreconcilable points of view. All the dramatic resources of poetry make us feel the impossibility of giving a single finally right moral appraisal of certain situations; and for Plato this is wrong, and dangerously wrong, because it encourages us to stay at the level of drama and theatre rather than to persevere in the search for moral truth. And so Plato is bound to be against imitation in poetry as he understands it, not only because it may lead people to have conflicting personal ideals and so a confused life instead of a well-organized one, but because even without leading to action it may encourage our imaginative capacities to frustrate the intellectual search for a single rational answer to moral problems.

Because Plato's objections to the effects of imitation do not apply with any precision to all poetry (never mind the other arts), his strictures leave room for the existence of *good* poetry to be helpful in the ideally just state, creating an emotionally sustaining background to the training that will make the Guardians good people. However, he is surprisingly vague and wavering over the role of good poetry. He is much cooler about the prospect than one would expect given the enthusiastic passage at 400–401 about the effects produced by good art. At 395–7 Socrates discusses with Adeimantus the extent, if any, to which the Guardians shall imitate. He has previously (394c) distinguished three styles, (a) that of pure imitation, (b) that of pure narration, and (c) a mixed style employing both. He now makes a new distinction, between (1) the good man's style, which will use little imitation, and that only of good people, and (2) that of the bad man, who will set no bounds at all to his imitating. All seems clear if the two distinctions are kept separate; both good and bad men use the mixed style which employs some imitation and some narration. But then at 397d, Socrates asks which style we shall have in the city – one of the pure ones or the mixed one? Adeimantus replies that he would prefer the unmixed style imitating the good man; and this is what they accept, though Socrates says that the mixed style, its opposite, gives more pleasure to the mob. There seems to be muddle; (b) has got confused with (1), and (c) with (2). As a result, there is uncertainty over whether Plato does in the end allow there to be any good, imitative poetry in the ideally just state. His muddle here is irritating, but understandable. Like other people with strong reforming views about art (Tolstoy, for example) he is very sure what is bad, but less sure about what is good. He is caught between the idea that imitation is all right as long as only morally certified models are imitated, and the idea that there is something morally fishy about imitation as such.

Some interpreters have thought that Plato is not confused here, but making a deep point. The good man's poetry, they claim, *is* both imitative and non-imitative. It is imitative in a good sense, and not imitative in a bad sense. Bad poetry and art imitate in the sense of merely copying the appearances of things (a theme that returns in Book 10). Good poetry and art, on the other hand, imitate in the sense of giving a perceptible representation of ideals and concepts in a form that can be appreciated by those who would not be capable of purely intellectual understanding. This interpretation rests mainly on a passage at 402b–d, where Socrates says that just as in learning to read we need to recognize the letters both in their normal manifestations and in their reflections, so to be properly educated it is necessary to 'recognize the different forms of moderation and courage, of generosity and munificence, their kindred qualities and their opposites too, as they occur everywhere, and perceive wherein they occur, both themselves and their images, and do not despise them in small things or in great, but recognize that this is part of the same craft and training' (Grube). The word for 'form' here will occur later in the book in contexts that are taken to be part of the 'theory of Forms' and concern the objects of the philosophers' studies, and this has encouraged some to think that Plato took the good artist to make the subject-matter of philosophical study manifest to learners not yet capable of the purely intellectual ascent to it. However, Plato is quite capable of using the non-technical word 'form' in contexts where he does not make his own rather special use of it, and it would be strange if there were a reference here to ideas that have not been broached yet. Furthermore, the distinction between a good and a bad sense of imitation does not answer to anything in the text and is a most implausible interpretation of it. And we shall see that Plato's account of philosophical knowledge and understanding does not allow the artist to function in any way parallel to the philosopher; despite what he says here, he thinks of the arts as being essentially marginal, and of use only in educating the young and immature.

However, this interpretation, though wrong, points to something interesting: in Books 2–3 the arts are presented as being very *important*, indeed a crucial part of education. We have seen that this comes from Plato's stress on the formation of character rather than academic development; and it is also not surprising in a revolutionary manifesto about the contemporary state of the arts. Plato thinks that the arts are very important because of their effects; he is very hostile to the central cases of what people around him thought great art; and he is uncertain as to what could replace it (he tries to censor Homer, but clearly not very much will survive the blue pencil).

We find the same combination of attitudes in Tolstoy's *What is Art?* (indeed reading this gives us some idea of the effect on Plato's contemporaries of his attacks on Homer; Tolstoy is not afraid to say that Shakespeare and Beethoven are bad, corrupt art). Plato and Tolstoy are enthusiastic, in the abstract, about the role and importance of the arts. But they find it hard to say, concretely, what good art will be, and the importance of art does not lead to their envisaging an important role for the artist.

A SKETCH OF THE IDEAL STATE

The passage from 412b to 427d (which cuts across the division of Books 3 and 4) is at first sight a strange and untidy mixture. A number of diverse and contentious issues are briefly raised and then dropped; some of them are picked up again later. What holds this section together is that it gives a sketch of the ideal state, the way it is ruled, and the basis for that rule. Plato, in giving us an outline of 'the ideal state', is not developing a complete picture of utopia; if he were, it would be hard to see why he passes over the issues in this section so lightly. He is concerned with the ideal state only in the sense of the *ideally just state*, and does not dwell on any of its features except in so far as these are relevant for establishing its justice. (For example, he thinks of war and conflict with neighbours as being a permanent feature of life, hardly an ideal one but compatible with the state's being ideally just. Cf. 422a–423b, 452a, 470a–c.) The sketch of the state is needed so that we can distinguish its three most important functional components, and see that its goodness and virtues come from the relation of these. This in turn is necessary for developing the account of the individual, and Plato's idea that the individual is like the state in having three parts, and in having virtues which are to be found in various relations between them. It is only when the virtues of both state and soul have been discussed, and Plato has drawn from this his own remarkable conclusions about justice, that he turns back to say more (in Book 5) about the more controversial provisions for the state.

At 412b Plato finishes off the Guardians' education and takes it as uncontroversial that the products of this education will be best fitted to rule the state. It has actually been assumed already

that there will be rulers (cf. 389b–c, 390a), and the only real
question is seen as being which of the people so trained will rule.
Plato does not seriously argue that the rulers should be a
minority, or that they should be older (his provisions are
always 'ageist', favouring the old as a group over the young).
He takes these points to be obviously acceptable (why, is a
puzzle; they were not uncontroversial in contemporary
Athens). The class educated in the way described, hitherto all
called 'Guardians', are now divided; some will advance no
further, and will function predominantly as warriors. They are
usually called the 'Auxiliaries' (*epikouroi*). Those selected as
Guardians proper (*phylakes*) have the city's interest most at
heart because they see it as identical with their own. (Much
more will be made of this later in the central books.) After
separating Guardians and Auxiliaries, Plato suggests (414b–
415a) that the rest of the citizens be told by the Guardians what
he calls a 'noble falsehood' to the effect that while all the citizens
are siblings, being born of the same mother, the earth, they are
different in kind, some having gold in their souls, some silver,
and some iron and bronze. It is of the greatest importance that
the metals, that is the classes, not be mixed or confounded. This
myth is meant to sum up what has been claimed about the
differences between the classes, and at the same time to
legitimize them by providing an emotionally satisfying vehicle
for the belief. (Of course it is very crude, but then so are most
myths when baldly stated.) The city is then notionally
established, and Plato adds, in a surprisingly perfunctory way,
that the Guardians must own no private property and have no
dealings with wealth. They will live in common, with no
private houses, rather as if in a camp (416d–417b). Adeimantus
complains that then they will not be very happy, and Socrates
replies that, although they may turn out to be the happiest of
all, still the relevant point is the state and its happiness, not
the happiness of one class in it (420b–d). The whole state can
be happy only when all do what is appropriate. If the potters
and farmers, he says patronizingly, were left to find their own
notion of happiness, they would laze around in a way that
would make them all happy as they see it, but which would not
be appropriate to their social role and real interests and so
would not produce the most happy state. (We shall return to

the question of whether Plato thinks that the state and its happiness is something over and above all the citizens and their happiness.) In fact, he allows, it does not matter so much if members of the productive classes neglect or combine their jobs; but if the Guardians neglect the Principle of Specialization and seek inappropriate tasks and ways of being happy, then the state as a whole is doomed (421a–c). They must preserve the state by preventing extremes of wealth and poverty. Only if this is done is there a state at all; states so-called are often really two or more states, if they contain mutually hostile groups like rich and poor. The Guardians will also protect the state against other states, by ensuring that the citizens are tough fighters uninterested in gaining wealth from war, and thus more attractive as allies than as opponents. They will also keep the city at a suitable size, not growing beyond the point which would destroy its unity (421c–423c). They must ensure the purity of the three classes by ruthlessly redirecting unsuitable children into other classes, and above all guard the education, preventing novelties in games or art forms which would undermine the stability of the children's cultural background. Emphasis on initiative and innovation in games will undermine the obedience to the laws which is the basis of the adults' law-abiding behaviour (423c–425a). Finally, Plato remarks that if the education is properly maintained, there will be no need of care over minor regulations about behaviour in public or styles of hair or clothes, or rules for markets. On the other hand, if the citizens' education is neglected, no amount of regulations will produce a well-ordered state. Politicians who spend all their time trying to remedy abuses do not realize that they are wasting their time, because abuses will always recur as long as the citizens are badly brought up and put their own interest before that of the whole society (425a–427d).

So we have a sketch of the ideally just state, in which three main points are stressed: its unity; the fact that this is maintained not by laws and rules but by the Guardians' characters and the education that produces this; and the fact that this will involve some manipulation of the ruled by the rulers. These are worth pausing over before we go on to the city's virtues.

Plato lays great stress on the city's unity, but in two rather different ways. He appeals to common sense: the city must not be *too* big or *too* small, it must not contain *extremes* of wealth or poverty. Aristotle repeats these points, and they are compatible with the city's containing a certain amount of conflict between different groups, as long as this is not chronically disruptive.

But Plato goes further; he also thinks of unity as what *defines* a city. A *real* city is a unity and not divided (422e). A city containing important groups which are at odds with one another because their interests conflict is not really a city. A city is a group where there is unity of interest; so only Plato's state is really a city, because only there are all the citizens at one in finding harmony between the interests of the city as a whole and their own interests as members of their own group. Actual cities are by this test not really cities, because they contain groups that see themselves as having conflicting interests (like rich and poor).

Plato's insistence that unity is *constitutive* of a state leads him to recommend measures (to which he will return in Book 5) that are avowedly designed to destroy a great part of that privacy and separateness that we take to define our individual lives. The common possession of property and the removal of nuclear families are designed to make the city more of a unity on the grounds that that is what is required of an ideal city. These measures have been criticized for their lack of realism about human nature, and indeed some have held that Plato's political measures are so unrealistic that he is not interested at all in politics in our sense of the term. For politics is often defined as the area in which major conflicts of interests are resolved, and political measures and theories are those that try to do this in various ways. But Plato does not want to regulate or cope with conflicts of interest. He wants to remove them altogether. This takes what he says out of the area of practical politics, and renders it either unpolitical, or, if one is not strict about the term, political but highly ideal. Plato's claim that a true city is a unity with no radically conflicting groups has, for example, the consequence that a pluralistic society must be considered as a failure – taking a pluralistic society to be one which recognizes, and tries to cope with in its institutions, the fact that its citizens will primarily see themselves as belonging to some smaller ethnic or religious group within the state, one with clearly defined interests opposed to those of other such groups. We are familiar with the idea that compromises between such groups are something the state should take into account and try to organize peacefully. If Plato is right, then any such compromises are an indication that the state is not a real state at all and radical measures would be appropriate to change it. This means that right from the start his political suggestions are of little interest to those who are pragmatically inclined and think of politics as the art of the possible.

Plato solves the question of who is to run the state in his account of the Guardians' education; he takes it for granted that once we are convinced that people could be brought up to be healthy and balanced, with sound knowledge, we would accept these as the people to run the state. He has, understandably, been accused of side-stepping the prior question, whether *anybody* should rule in the state. He proceeds as though our reluctance to set people in charge of our collective affairs stemmed only from our distrust of their abilities and motives, and that as soon as we were presented with disinterested and capable people we would put the state happily into their management. There is much that is just in this criticism: Plato does not, in the *Republic*, give enough attention to the importance of law in setting up and regulating the institutions of a state, regardless of the roles of capable people. There is nothing corresponding to a constitution, or a code of laws or an established legislature. Plato assumes that none of these are necessary once the Guardians are in charge. He uses the word for 'law' quite often, and talks of the citizens as obeying the laws, but the only laws that he thinks it important to protect are those that establish and organize the education of the Guardians (cf. 425a, 502b–c; the interlocutors of the dialogue are thus called the city's 'lawgivers', 458c, 497d). But these laws establish conditions for the production of rulers; they do not define citizens' rights and duties. Plato thinks of written laws as settling not matters of principle, only trivial matters of administration and organization which clearly derive from principles already established (425e). This means that Plato (quite in defiance of the political realities familiar to him) has in effect taken the education of the Guardians to *replace* the part played in public life by a constitution, or a code of statutes. He thinks that once we have the right people to do the job, laws will turn out to be fairly trivial (as at 425e). This leaves us feeling uncomfortable. The citizens in the third class will have no bill of rights, or written laws, as safeguards against exploitation and abuse. Plato thinks that this is not necessary because their rulers will be good people who will not exploit or abuse them. (In fact he seems to think that it would be a positive hindrance to the Guardians since legalistically minded citizens would have something to appeal to against them, although this would be against their own real interests which only the Guardians perceive.) But this only sounds like a good solution to political problems if there is a real chance that there could be such rulers; for to the extent that the rulers are corruptible, the other citizens will be worse off than people in even a badly run city who have laws to protect them. Plato sees clearly that putting so much emphasis on having the right people to rule, and so little emphasis on a constitution or code of laws to constrain what they shall do, is laying a great weight on the possibility of there being people who want to, and do, identify their interests with those of the city as a whole. That is why he worries, throughout the *Republic*, as to whether his ideal state is feasible, and why he sees the problem of the state's feasibility as being simply the question of whether there could be people who could rule without being corrupted. In later dialogues, when he loses faith in the possibility that there might be uncorrupted rulers, he comes to see laws as not merely a convenience for administration, but as defining the status of the citizens.

Plato's repeated insistence that the city stands or falls with the Guardians' education, and that the role of laws is fairly minor, plays an important part in his belief that the state and the individual person are analogous in their nature and virtues. We shall see that there is an important analogue in the case of the person: to be virtuous a person must be a person of a certain kind, and detailed duties are not laid down in advance to be followed come what may, but are thought of as minor, on the grounds that they will be obvious to the fundamentally virtuous person.

The Guardians rule by doing what is best for the city as a

whole, and thus for each of the classes in it. They are not constrained by a constitution or laws, and the other classes have no part in decision-making or even administration; they are simply not consulted. Now even if what is done is really in their interests, and even if they really do not mind this state of affairs (and Plato will argue that both of these are true) this must strike us as manipulative. The Guardians think of the others as inferiors who have less knowledge of their own real interests than they themselves have. Although the rulers are not condescending, they treat the others in ways they do not treat each other. The most notorious example of this is that while they are fanatically truth-loving among themselves they will lie to the others if their interests demand this. Plato not only does not try to cover this up, he draws attention to it several times. He does not yet raise the question of how their knowingly telling lies is compatible with their having truth-loving natures; we shall return to this when we have discussed justice in the individual (pp. 166–7). For the moment he only makes clear that they will not hesitate to deceive others if they know, because of their superior expertise, that this is a good thing, as an expert doctor or navigator may lie to patient or passengers to prevent useless panic. This comes out clearly at 389b–d: the rulers are justified in using lies 'medicinally' whereas the other citizens are in the wrong if they lie to them. This flouts our ordinary moral assumptions; we do not think that possession of superior knowledge gives one the right to lie. At 382c there is an odd attempt to distinguish two kinds of lie, the 'real lie' or lie in the soul, which no-one will willingly tolerate, whereas the 'lie in words' can be quite useful sometimes. Here Plato talks as though as long as one takes care not to be deceived oneself, telling falsehoods to others is not really lying, but a mere 'image' of lying. This would be a useful defence of what the Guardians do, but unfortunately it does not work, for one could avoid the lie in the soul by lying with *bad* intent as much as by lying with *good* intent.

It is in the light of these passages that we should read the famous 'noble lie' or 'noble falsehood' passage at 414–415. In the interests of unity, the citizens are to be brought to accept a story which is avowedly not true. Some interpreters stress that the word used, *pseudos*, does not imply 'lie', but simply means what is not true; but this does not explain away anything in Plato's position, since the earlier passages are so uncompromising in their acceptance of lying. Also, Plato seems to envisage the Guardians as eventually believing it themselves, so we do not have a straight case of manipulation by them of the others; but the rulers are surely thought of as believing the myth on a rather different level from the others. So there is, at the least, a double standard. And while the myth may strike us as fairly harmless (all states acquire their myths of identity) we should notice Plato's readiness to legitimize the telling of lies in the interests of some higher end. It is an early sign of what will become more prominent: his readiness to revise the content of morality in the interests of establishing morality.

Chapter 5
Parts and Virtues of State and Soul

At 427d Socrates remarks that the city has been sketched in sufficiently for them to start looking for its virtues, particularly justice. This is done in the passage up to 434d; then, after discussing the way that justice in the state can cast light on justice in the individual person, Socrates turns to the person and finds three parts and four virtues corresponding to those of the state. He ends Book 4 by applying the findings about justice in the person to the defence of justice as something worthwhile for a person to have. I shall follow Plato in dealing with the parts and virtues of the state before those of the person. But I shall alter his order in one way. He discusses the relation of justice in state and person before discussing the individual. I shall keep the difficult matter of the relation between state and individual until after the discussion of the individual, in order to get a clearer perspective on a baffling part of the argument.

Plato has shown, briefly, that there are three classes in the state, Guardians, Auxiliaries, and the Productive Class. He now sets about finding four virtues. At the end of the discussion, however, he remarks (435c–d) that they will never attain precision by use of methods such as the ones they have employed; there is a longer and fuller way, though perhaps the present attempt will suffice for its purposes. Here again we meet the point that the best way into a new topic may not be the way that most accurately reflects the nature of the subject; that may be clear only to someone who has spent much time and effort on the matter. At 504b, just before he begins his account of what is required for full understanding of anything, Plato reverts to this passage, emphasizing that someone with true knowledge would have a much fuller comprehension of the virtues than is sketched here. However, we are never shown what such a fuller comprehension would be like; Book 4 is in effect Plato's last word on the subject to us. The *Republic* never gives us an understanding of virtue that does not appeal to our experience and what we find clear in it.

Plato's methodology here does leave something to be desired, and is questionable at three points at least. Firstly, he says at 427e7 that the state will have all the requisite virtues because it is 'completely good'. But what are his grounds for saying this? Presumably they lie in the long description of the Guardians' upbringing. Why, however, should we agree that *this* sort of organization makes a city completely good? Plato is not appealing to intuitions about the goodness of cities, as might appear from the way he puts this point; he is *insisting* that his city is a paradigm of goodness.

Secondly, he says that if the city is completely good, then 'clearly' it will have the four virtues of wisdom, courage, moderation, and justice (427e10–11). What is so 'clear' about the claim that goodness or virtue is found in precisely these four forms? Some commentators refer to a standard or well-known doctrine of the 'four cardinal virtues'; but far from appealing to common sense Plato seems to be innovating. In an earlier dialogue, *Protagoras*, where the unity of virtue and its relation to its 'parts' is discussed at length, it is assumed, as a matter of course, that there are *five* virtues making up the whole of virtue, the four already mentioned plus *hosiotēs*, usually translated 'piety' or 'holiness', the virtue shown in dealings with the gods and what concerns them (rituals, sacrifice, taboos, etc.). It seems that Plato has decided, between the *Protagoras* and the *Republic*, that *hosiotēs* is not a distinct virtue from justice, dealings with the gods being merely a special case of dealings with others, so that examples of right dealings with the gods are cases of justice. This is not questioned and seems in fact to be a convincing claim (the Greek virtue of *hosiotēs* concerned one's institutionalized relations with the gods rather than any personal attitude of devotion). But in accepting it in the *Republic* without any protest at the idea that there are only four virtues and not five, Socrates' interlocutors are being pushed towards the kind of theory that Plato will produce. For the behaviour and actions that characterize piety are quite different from those that are the products of justice; piety involves sacrifices, vows, and priestly duties which are quite distinct from the kind of action displayed in other examples of justice. So in tacitly denying that these two virtues are distinct, and taking it that one state of city or person can account for these different kinds of behaviour, Plato is moving us away from the idea that different kinds of action are what determine distinctness of virtues. Virtue turns out to be more 'internal' than we had suspected.

Thirdly, Plato is confident (428a) that we can find justice by isolating the other three virtues and seeing what remains. This procedure has been much criticized on the grounds that it involves a fallacy; we do not know that what is left is what we are looking for unless we know that we have surveyed everything relevant, and Plato never tries to show this. However, his way of proceeding need not look so outrageous if we bear two things in mind. One is that there is a general presupposition of relevance in argument; Plato does not argue that the alternatives he mentions are the only ones there are, because he counts on his readers to assume that if there were any more relevant alternatives they would have been mentioned. Also, he does not have to claim that justice will turn out to be whatever is left over in the city when we have isolated the other three virtues, only that it is whatever is left over as a factor in the city's goodness, and we might expect to find the essential features of that laid out in the sketch we have been given.

Socrates now asks what makes the city wise, brave, moderate, and just. He is not satisfied in this search by finding merely that it contains wise, brave, moderate, and just people. The city's wisdom (and similarly its other virtues) belongs to it in its own right, and is not reducible to the wisdom of some or all of its citizens. It is not the mere presence of wise people that makes it wise, but their role – they rule. If there were wise people in the city but they did not rule (as is the case in most actual societies) then the city would not be wise merely because they were. The city is wise because it is so structured that the wise people rule; that it has this structure is a fact about it and not merely about the wise people.

It is important for Plato's extended parallel between city and person that the city's virtues, although they involve the virtues of the people in the city, are not reducible to these but belong to the city in its own right, because of its overall structure. For in the case of the person, likewise, he or she has virtues because of the condition and relation of his or her parts, but the virtue belongs properly not to the parts but to the person taken as an organized whole. Some have thought that this parallelism commits Plato to an 'organic theory of the state', the theory that the state is an organic entity over and above all the people in it. We shall see later that he does not hold this as a substantive point of political theory (pp. 179–80). But he is committed to the purely logical point that the city is an entity which has virtues in its own right and not in a way reducible to the existence of virtuous citizens in it.

All four of the city's virtues, as they appear, turn out to be somewhat odd, and not straightforwardly the Greek virtues of the time. Plato's account of the city's virtues partially revises our notions as to what these are. We end up, then, wondering whether he should present his account, as he seems to, as *confirming* our belief that the city is completely good. Something very similar will happen with the individual, and the question will occupy us more than once.

Wisdom (428b–429a)

There are many kinds of knowledge in the state, but none will account for the state's being clever or wise except that of the Guardians; and since this class is the smallest one in the state, the city owes its wisdom to that of the smallest part in it (428e–429a). It is crucial, though, that that group should be the *ruling* group (428e); the city is not made wise by the mere presence of the Guardians in it, but by their being in charge. If they did not rule, their wisdom would not make the city wise; this is connected to the fact that Plato is here concerned with wisdom in the sense of good judgement (428b) and the ability to *plan* and deliberate (428c–d).

Why should the Guardians be the ones with good judgement? Partly we are to accept this on the strength of the programme of education outlined, designed to produce intelligent and effective people. Plato adds another point when he claims that only the Guardians can reason on behalf of the city as a whole, rather than some part or group within it (428c–d). The people in the other classes can reason, but only to the extent of being intelligent about their own self-interest. Only the Guardians can reason in a way that will discover the interests of all in a way that goes beyond self-interest. Now this ability to plan for the common good rather than sectarian interest is what we would all like our politicians to have; but has Plato convinced us that only the Guardian class would have it – that people who spend their lives doing a job, rather than being educated in the way described, would be completely incapable of raising their sights beyond the interest of their own class? Plato will try to make his claim more plausible by his theory of the person's psychology, for it turns out that he thinks that people who spend their lives in productive activity have lives dominated by short-term objectives and desires. He never, though, argues that most people must be like this, and that the ability to use one's practical intelligence in a way that rises above one's own concerns must be limited to a few. He commits himself without argument to the anti-democratic thesis that the citizens with the wisdom that will make it well-governed will be the smallest class in the city.

It is worth noticing that Plato is throughout concerned with wisdom as practical overall planning; it is because of this that he insists, rather artificially, that other sorts of wisdom and knowledge, which have only limited and definite ends, will not count as making the city wise. This would perhaps have been found rather counter-intuitive by his contemporaries, who thought of wisdom (*sophia*) as intellectual excellence that could be shown in many different spheres. Plato restricts it, for his purposes, to practical wisdom, and in particular to the fair judgement shown in planning for a whole without favouring any of the parts. (There is no indication here that such practical reasoning might demand a great deal of very theoretical study.)

Courage (429a–430c)

The city is brave in virtue of the bravery of the Auxiliaries, who form the army; the behaviour of the other citizens is not relevant (429b). It is especially clear here that it is the role of the brave people in the state that makes the state brave, not just their presence. For the Guardians are presumably brave too, and for the same reasons; yet it is not their bravery that is said to make the state brave, and this is because they do not form the army, having other things to do. (Actually Plato has not said in so many words that the Guardians will not share in the warlike role of the Auxiliaries, but it is a fair inference from his insistence that one person do one job that the Guardians proper are thought of as having shared the education described but as thereafter leading a different kind of life suited to rulers.)

Plato expands here on the nature of courage, which he says is not just having the right beliefs about what should and should not be feared, but being able to stick to those beliefs in the face of temptations and coercions. He then claims that only products of an education such as he has described will have this ability, because they have gone through a total character-training and can therefore be guaranteed to hold on to the right beliefs. Anything not so produced is not really courage, including the behaviour of 'animals and slaves' (430b). Plato is giving us a 'persuasive definition' of courage; for (leaving animals out of it) slaves might well exhibit what we would be inclined to call courageous behaviour; but Plato wants us to call courageous only behaviour that results from a training of character such as he has described (430b). Once again we are being pushed away from looking for what is essential to a virtue in behaviour. Plato thinks that the same kind of behaviour (fighting off an attack, say) might be an example of courage or not, depending on whether it does or does not result from a habitual attitude and way of thinking and feeling, such as requires education to produce it. It is motivation that determines whether people are or are not courageous, not merely what they do.

The Auxiliaries' courage is said at 430c3 to be 'civic' or 'political' courage, in a way that suggests that this is a qualified way of being courageous. We shall see more clearly why Plato makes this qualification when we get to the discussion of parts of the soul. For the Auxiliaries' souls are not (as the Guardians' souls are) dominated by reason, and so although they have firmly internalized right beliefs about what is and is not to be feared, they lack the capacity for the critical reflection about the contents of their beliefs which Plato thinks is required for any virtue to be held in a genuine and unqualified way.

Moderation (430d–432b)

'Moderation' translates *sōphrosunē*, often translated 'temperance'. Neither English word is satisfactory, since *sōphrosunē* does not answer well to any one virtue that we recognize. It is discussed in the earlier dialogue *Charmides*, where the variety of characterizations offered (none of them satisfactory) show how hard it was even for the Greeks to pin down this virtue adequately. Suggestions offered there are that moderation is doing things in a slow and orderly way, or having a sense of shame, or minding your own business, or having self-knowledge, or 'doing one's own' (the definition of *justice* offered in the *Republic*). On the one hand moderation is connected with the avoidance of excess and vulgarity, and with polite and deferential behaviour. (It is sometimes thought of as the characteristic women's virtue, Greek women having to be deferential whereas men were brought up to be self-assertive.) On the other hand, moderation is also connected to the more intellectual idea of self-knowledge; it is thought of as knowing one's place, having a correct idea of who you are and what is due to and appropriate for your position. In earlier dialogues Plato stresses this element so much that moderation looks like the intellectual basis of all the virtues (*Charmides* 164d ff., *First Alcibiades* 131b, 133c ff., *Lovers* 138a ff.). But in the *Republic* he tries to deal with both these elements, that of deferential and self-controlled behaviour and that of self-knowledge.

Moderation in the city consists not of the role of any one class, where what the others do is indifferent (as with courage, 429b). It involves a relation of all three classes. It is the agreement and unanimity of all three classes as to who shall be in charge (432a) and is likened to harmony and concord (430e, 431e–432a). Moderation thus involves two elements. Firstly, all citizens, from whatever class, agree in their opinion that the right people are ruling. (In most states the rulers think this, but not the ruled; to this extent they are characterized by resentment.) And so Plato can say that moderation exists in both the rulers and the ruled (431e). This is the element of self-knowledge; the rulers know that they are the right people for the job, and the ruled know that they are not the right people for the job.

Secondly, there is the element of deference. For this agreement results in very different kinds of behaviour on the part of ruler and ruled. Each makes demands which are appropriate to their nature; so moderation requires the rulers to impose their own desires, and the ruled to acquiesce in the imposition of these desires on them. Plato claims (431b–c) that the ruled will characteristically exhibit a chaos of strong and uncoordinated desires, whereas the rulers who are more reasonable will impose desires that are rational and controlled by knowledge. If one is stressing this element it is no longer so plausible to say that moderation is found in *both* the rulers and the ruled. For only the ruled are called upon to show deference and self-control in restraining the urge for what they want. Moderation is in both rulers and ruled only in the sense that the behaviour of both is based on a shared view of what is appropriate to all classes. There is, then, a way in which moderation is displayed by all the citizens, but also a way in which it can be thought of as peculiarly the virtue of the productive class, because it is only from them that this common agreement demands restraint in the way they behave.

We are inclined to find Plato's demands repulsively autocratic; but we should remember that he is talking about a state supposed to be perfectly good. He is not saying that working classes in actual states should acquiesce in what their rulers demand; he is saying that *if* a state were ruled by people who were ideally wise and had the best judgement, then it would be right, in people that lacked that ability, to defer to their judgement. All the same, in making deference to the aims and values of their superiors the only way in which the bulk of the citizens contribute to the goodness of the city, Plato seems to be missing something. (We shall return to this, pp. 172–4.) And one thing is left unclear, which becomes no clearer later. Plato thinks that the members of the productive class have enough intelligence to recognize their own inferiority to the brave and wise Guardians. When their desires and pleasures are 'controlled' and dominated by the more austere desires and pleasures of the wise few, do they acquiesce willingly in this, freely abandoning what they themselves would prefer because they perceive the preferability of what is decided by those with better judgement? If so, the productive class are being thought of as naturally deferential, like working-class voters who choose to vote for the party of their 'betters' who oppose working-class interests. On the other hand, the productive class may be thought of as being able to recognize that the Guardians should rule, but as being all the same resentful of actual interference in the course of what they want to do. If so, they are being thought of as naturally unruly and having to be forced into deferential behaviour without naturally having the motivation. Now the first picture is what Plato most of the time wants, for he would hardly liken moderation to harmony if he thought that the behaviour it required was enforced and accompanied by resentment. Yet he goes out of his way to stress the unruly and unorganized nature of the productive class's aims, and the need for them to be *controlled* by the aims of the Guardians; they do not just naturally fit in without effort. The two pictures are hardly compatible, but Plato never clearly decides on one or the other. A similar problem runs through the parallel account of desire in the individual, which is controlled by reason. Plato's unclarity here is important. For it leaves us unsure how much force and coercion will be required even in the state run on ideal lines. If the productive class are naturally unruly and resentful, then to get them to act in an acquiescent way, as they recognize they should but do not want to, the Guardians will have to use force and fraud. We have already seen that they will freely use lies where these are in the true interest of the person lied to. So Plato does at times believe that moderation requires of the productive class behaviour that comes from fear or false beliefs. Whereas with the Guardians and Auxiliaries character and motivation were all-important, with the productive class Plato seems at least sometimes to give up, to admit that in their case all that matters is what they do, and not at all why they do it, what kind of characters they have.

One problem with the account of moderation is the role played in it by self-control. Socrates says (430e–431a) that strictly *self*-control is an incoherent notion, for *one* thing cannot both control and be controlled. What it must mean is that there are two parts or aspects of what is self-controlled, and that the better part controls the worse. This is then applied to the city; when desires of the best class control those of the worse, the city has self-control, and, if self-controlled, it is moderate.

Now in an earlier dialogue, the *Gorgias*, Socrates is asked what he means by 'self-mastery' (491d) and answers: nothing special, just what most people mean, being moderate and in control of oneself and master of one's passions and appetites. So it looks as though on the everyday level moderation is the clearer notion which is used to explain the notion of self-control or self-mastery. In the *Republic*, on the other hand, it is the notion of self-control that is used to explicate that of moderation. Is Plato explaining *A* via *B* in one context and *B* via *A* in another?

The answer is no. For in the *Gorgias* the moderation that was found so clear was the moderation of an individual person. But in the *Republic* Plato is out to explain the moderation of a city or state; that is why he finds it clearer to proceed by showing that what looks like the simple attribution of a characteristic to one thing must involve distinguishing the relation of its parts. And this account of moderation paves the way for that of justice; this likewise is shown to be a condition that holds of a whole in virtue of the relation of its parts.

Justice (432b–434d)

Justice as introduced is the strangest virtue of all, and Plato seems aware that his account is not obvious; at any rate, it is introduced with a lot of tiresomely winsome by-play on the part of Socrates. When he finally says what it is, it turns out to be 'some form of' the principle we have already seen, namely that all should 'do their own' and stick to what is appropriate for them (433a). Justice is not identical with the Principle of Specialization, for that assigned each person to one type of job, whereas here we are told that confusion or sharing of jobs does not matter so much, the really important thing being that the *classes* should be kept distinct (434a–b). None the less, justice presupposes and builds on the principle, for it would not be possible without it. It is clear that Plato thinks that a city cannot be just unless it recognizes and institutionalizes basic natural differences between people. Quite apart from the fact that Plato has a very harsh and pessimistic view of the extent to which people are naturally different, it is clearly already going well beyond any ordinary intuition to claim that this is what is required by justice.

Justice is introduced as something which 'rivals' the other three virtues for making the city excellent (433b–e). But if the state is just by virtue of the citizens' 'doing their own', that is, doing what is appropriate to their class, so that the classes do not conflict in their claims, we seem to get a problem. For justice might seem to be redundant, to be nothing over and above the presence of the other virtues. Justice, after all, requires no new range of actions other than what is required by the other virtues, only a refraining from certain things. However, we would be wrong to think of justice too negatively in this way. For the other three virtues on their own would not be virtues *of a whole*. Justice is a virtue of the city as a unity, for it requires of each citizen a recognition of his or her own role as contributing in some characteristic way to the common good. It might be thought that this role has already been performed by moderation, for that required each citizen to recognize his or her relation to the ruling class. But that was a recognition only of superiority and inferiority, not of the full scope of one's position in a particular class in a state which requires co-operation from all classes. Moderation requires knowledge of one's 'station and its duties', but more than that is relevant to justice. For to be just one has to 'do one's own', know what one's natural talents are and the ways these should be developed for the common good (cf. 433a, 435b, 443c, for references to the natural basis of justice).

Why, however, should doing one's own have anything to do with *justice*? It has little to do with what would normally be expected of an account of justice. For justice is normally taken to be concerned with one's relation with *others*. But now we find that the city is just, not because of its relations to other cities, but because of the relations of its own three parts. Plato has discussed relations with other cities (422b–e) and will do so again at 469e–471c, but does not regard them as central to the city's justice.

Further, justice has been brought in without any mention of other notions which are usually connected with it – equality, giving or receiving what is due, refraining from *pleonexia* (grabbing what is another's). Plato has cut justice out of its familiar context and introduced it in a new context of his own, and we might be led to wonder why he wants to claim that this fourth desirable state for a city to be in should be called *justice*.

Plato is aware of this, for he makes some attempt to show that what he is saying is not too outlandish. At 433a Socrates says that they have heard many people say, and have often said themselves, that justice is doing one's own. But who are these other people? They are not known outside Plato's works, and in those works the only other use of the phrase is in the *Charmides*, (161b ff.) where it is suggested as an account of moderation, not of justice. And repeating a thing yourself is hardly an argument for it. But Plato makes a better attempt at 433e to link his suggestion with more recognizable accounts of justice. Judges in the state will have as their sole concern that all shall have what is theirs and not have what is another's – that all shall in fact 'have their own'. And this is agreed to be just. 'In some way then possession of one's own and the performance of one's own task could be agreed to be justice' (433e12–434a1, Grube). However, why should a point about *having* one's own prove anything about *doing* one's own? Judges could justly make sure that all have their own in a city where the classes were not divided as they are in Plato's city, and where, therefore, people did not 'do their own' in Plato's sense. Plato has offered us no argument yet to show that these two notions of all having their own and all doing their own even cover the same cases, never mind being equivalent. By the time we get to the end of the *Republic*, we shall see why Plato takes the two notions to be connected. For he tries to show that in his state all have their own (that is, position, wealth, and honour are fairly and securely distributed) just because all do their own (that is, the basis of his society is one that reflects natural differences of endowment). But he cannot appeal to any of that here, for here he claims to be appealing to what we already find obvious to say.

So Plato does not succeed in showing that what he has introduced, in his own context of the 'doing one's own' principle, is what we all mean already by *justice*. However, does this matter? We know already that he is not out to codify the current usages of 'wisdom', 'justice', and so on. He wants to tell us what justice is, that is, to give an account of justice that is explanatory and enables us to see what is puzzling about the problems we found with it, and find the right answers to them. It is not surprising if a deep explanation of what justice is answers badly to our original intuitions about it; for these are not reasoned out, and they may be largely formed by inherited prejudice. So we may expect Plato's account of justice to be a revisionary one. We are not unfamiliar with revisionary accounts of justice, altruism, etc. that are based upon very general facts, or alleged facts, about society.

On the other hand, Plato cannot simply throw out of the window any considerations of what people ordinarily think that justice is. For, after all, the whole discussion started from problems that arose from the way ordinary, not very reflective people think about justice. If Plato has simply invented his own concept and decided to label it 'justice', then what he is doing is futile, not only because we might well ask why one should be interested in this, but because he is introducing his notion of justice in an explicit attempt to answer questions that arise from the accepted notion of justice.

Plato has in fact to do two things. One is to introduce a notion of justice which is not read off from ordinary usage and can serve to explain important facts about justice. This is what he does by means of the 'doing one's own' formula. The other is to show that in spite of its being introduced in an unfamiliar way, this is all the same the concept of *justice* that we are dealing with; we have not changed the subject. We can see from his attempt to show that 'doing one's own' answers to what we thought of as 'having one's own' that Plato does want to do the second as well as the first of these. In the present case the attempt is not very sophisticated (though he will return to the issues in Book 5). An analogous problem arises over justice in the individual, and we shall find that the same thing happens, except that there the attempt is more subtle and interesting, and also that the stakes are higher, for it was in terms of the individual's justice that Thrasymachus raised his challenge.

Plato is, then, trying to talk about the same concept of justice with which we began, and at the same time to revise it so that the account he offers does not merely reflect ordinary un-thinking usage but explains puzzles that would not be obvious if we had stuck to a close reflection of ordinary use.

His procedure here has recently been compared to that of scientists. Suppose we have a certain disease which we identify by its symptoms (say, a rash and a high temperature). We then try to find out more about the disease, and we do so by searching for the underlying causal structure of the pattern of symptoms. However, in the light of this we may find that the causal structure that explains the occurrence of most of the symptoms cannot explain a minority of cases (say where there is everything except the temperature). We are led to exclude some of the original cases that we set out to explain. However, we do not say that we have failed to find the disease, or that we have found not that disease but another one. What we say is that our intuitive methods gave us a wrong classification, and that cases without a high temperature never were cases of the original disease, however confidently we thought so. Scientific discoveries, by explaining phenomena we recognize already, sometimes lead us to correct our initial grounds for identification. But this is not to be construed as giving us a whole new set of concepts. Rather, the very same concepts that we always used have been refined and clarified for us. Now it is very tempting to take Plato as doing rather the same kind of thing. Rather than accepting the ordinary concept of justice, whatever that may be, he tries to provide his own explanatory clarification, by locating the explanatory basis of justice (taking this to be the 'doing one's own' principle). Accepting this will commit us to revising some of our beliefs about justice (for example, that it is possible in societies that are not organized on the 'doing one's own' principle). But still we are talking about the same thing, and are right to apply Plato's findings to solve our existing problems about justice.

The analogy is helpful up to a point, and may give us a vivid picture of what Plato is doing which will prevent our thinking, on the one hand, that he is inventing his own concept of justice in the context of the ideal state, or, on the other, that he wants to defend ordinary notions of justice exactly as they stand. In one respect, however, it may be misleading. For scientists make discoveries, and enlarge and alter our concepts, because they have special methods and tools of discovery. We accept what they say because they are authorities in their field by virtue of special training and competences. Hence we are prepared to let their discoveries alter our beliefs about substances that we learned about in a more primitive way to begin with. But justice and wisdom are not natural kinds or substances like those that scientists study; there is no uncontroversial scientific way of studying them. Anyone who, like Plato, undertakes to revise and improve our understanding of what they are cannot appeal to 'hard' facts established in an unquestionable way; he is appealing to facts about people and society which all are qualified to judge (though of course not everyone takes the trouble to do so, or is equally good at it). Plato has to appeal to considerations, some of them very general ones, which have claim on our acceptance anyway. Now it is true that he will go on to claim that philosophy, properly pursued by the properly qualified, will result in a complete and comprehensive understanding of disputed moral matters in a way that leaves no room for useful disagreement. But this is philosophy in the ideal state, not as it has ever been pursued; Plato never suggests that the *Republic* itself is an example of philosophical understanding of a completed and perfect kind. In the book he never tries to escape the test of seeing how his results square with the enlightened moral consciousness of most people.

From 434d–436a Socrates discusses the relation of justice in the state to justice in the individual; we shall return to this. At 436a he turns to the individual and begins by discussing parts of the soul.

So far I have talked about justice in the individual *person*, but Plato begins by asking 'whether we do everything with the same part of our soul, or one thing with one of the three parts, and another with another' (436a, Grube). We may think this question-begging, because 'soul' for us suggests an immaterial entity which is associated with, but separate from, the person, and the concept has religious suggestions. But the Greek word which is traditionally translated 'soul' (and there is no better single alternative to fill the exact grammatical slot) is *psuchē*, and talking of someone's *psuchē* need commit one to no more than talking about something as alive and functioning as a living thing. In many contexts *psuchē* is closer to 'life' than to 'soul'; it is, for example, normal to say that animals have a *psuchē* (and Aristotle claims that plants do too, since they are clearly alive, though this may have sounded slightly odd to a

Greek). So Plato's talk of 'soul' here is rather like our talk of someone's 'mind' to refer to certain mental phenomena without committing ourselves thereby to any particular theory about the mind, for example that it is something immaterial. Plato does in fact believe that the soul is eternal and distinct from the body, but when he comes to claim this in Book 10 (608d–612a) he is careful to say that so conceived the soul is simple and without parts, not just the composite soul minus the body. In talking about the parts of the individual's soul Plato is talking of the embodied soul, in a way that has remained accessible through the ages to people with the most diverse views on the metaphysical nature of the soul.

Talk of 'parts' of the soul has also been found a problem. But Plato never says that they are spatial or temporal parts, and in fact does not use the language of 'parts' himself very much. (The word for 'part', *meros*, is first used at 444b3; it is more common in English translations because Plato often uses more noncommittal prepositional phrases which are clumsy in English, like 'that by which we desire'.) Plato keeps his vocabulary here perhaps deliberately vague; he is insisting that there is complexity in a single person without saying too much about how that complexity might be realized. In another dialogue, the *Timaeus* (69b–72b), he does talk as though the soul's parts are located in parts of the body, but there is no hint of that in the *Republic*, where what is insisted on is the fact of complexity. The basic point is that the various kinds of complexity to be found in human behaviour cannot be adequately accounted for without allowing that the person is himself or herself complex. We will not understand an individual's actions unless we see that actions do not come from a single motivational source. There is more than one origin of behaviour within a person, and the way the person lives and acts indicates how these sources of behaviour are related. This basic idea has had a long history in psychology and has taken various forms. One of the more familiar is Freud's theory of the roles of the conscious and unconscious, and another is his later theory of ego, superego, and id.

The parts of the soul are distinguished by a long and elaborate argument in Book 4 (436a ff.) which is based on a principle implying that opposed states cannot hold of the same thing at the same time. It is usual to examine the parts of the soul as they are established by this argument. But there are two grave drawbacks to this procedure. Firstly, elaborate though the argument is, the parts it produces do not seem to be the same as the parts that Plato's account of the individual actually needs, and which he makes use of throughout the book. Hence, if we take it, as is usually done, that the parts are defined by the argument that introduces them, we find that Plato seems later to have changed his mind and to be illicitly smuggling in other elements. But if we proceed by assuming that the parts are defined by the use that is actually made of them in the *Republic*'s main argument, the theory appears much more unified and powerful, as well as more plausible, and Plato appears guilty only of an inadequate argument, rather than a fundamental change of idea. Secondly, there is something odd about the argument's status, for it establishes the distinctness of the parts on the basis of a necessary truth, whereas elsewhere (581b–c) he argues from experience that the distinctness of the parts can be seen in the different kinds of lives people lead. And Plato's main interest in the whole book in the theory of the parts of the soul is the idea that different kinds of actions and lives do as a matter of fact have their origin in the prominence of different parts of the soul. In order to present the theory as clearly and plausibly as possible I shall not turn to the initial argument that introduces it until I have given a rough account of each part of the soul as it figures in the *Republic* as a whole, not only in Book 4 but in the later arguments of Books 8 and 9.

There turn out to be three parts of the soul, corresponding to the three classes in the state.

(1) *Reason*

This is the part by virtue of which we learn (436a, 580d, 581b) and reason (439d). It is usually called 'the reasoning part' (*to logistikon*, 439d) though at 581b it is called 'the part that loves wisdom and loves learning' (*to philosophon, to philomathes,* cf. 376b). It has two main functions. One is that of searching for the truth and increasing one's knowledge; it is the only part of the soul that can do this, and so it is the part of us that desires to extend our knowledge of truths and finds pleasure in doing this (581b). It is important that for Plato reason is not conceived as aiming at academic, drily intellectual discoveries; it wants to find out all truth, in the practical as well as the intellectual sphere. At 440a–d, for example, it appears as the part by which we work out whether we have been wrongly made to suffer or are suffering justly. So it is what urges us on to intelligent practical choice as well as to the discovery of theorems.

Its other function is to rule in the soul (441e, 442c). (It corresponds to the Guardians who are to rule the other two classes.) There are two main reasons why it is appropriate for reason to rule in the soul, and we shall see that these are stressed in different parts of the *Republic* and it will not be altogether easy to reconcile them. One is that it is the only part that cares for the interests of the whole soul and not just itself, whereas the other two parts care only for themselves and not for the whole of which they are parts (441e). (The intended parallel is clear with the Guardians, who are the only class to care for the whole city including the other classes, and not just them-selves.) Reason, then, is the source of practical judgement about what is best for the person as a whole. The other ground for reason's rule over the whole soul is that a life which is shaped by devotion to the aim of reason, searching for truth, is a better life for the person to lead than a life shaped by devotion to the ends of the other parts. This second ground is not brought out in Book 4, where Plato puts more stress on reason's capacity to plan for the person as a whole.

(2) *Spirit*

'Spirit' is the traditional translation of *to thumoeides*, the name for this part at 441a. At 581b it is called 'the part that loves honour and winning' (*to philonikon, to philotimon*). This already brings out how hard it is to characterize this part in a way bringing out its character as a single source of motivation (indeed many have despaired and said that it has no real unity). Plato seems to be talking about two very different kinds of thing. One is a tendency to aggression and violence. Thus, spirit is said to be found in children and animals (441a–b, cf. 375a–b), and here Plato must mean assertiveness towards others in the pursuit of what one wants. However, at 581a–b it is the part that delights in victory and honours, that is, not just in pushiness but in getting what one can be proud of, what is sanctioned by

one's perception of what is right. And in Book 4 itself Plato tries
to identify it by describing the case of Leontius (439e–440a).
Leontius felt a desire to look at some corpses, and succumbed
to it, but in the process felt angry and ashamed of himself, and
rebuked his eyes, the seat of his enjoyment, in melodramatic
fashion. So there is something in Leontius which is capable of
opposing desire because of feelings of shame, feelings about
what is right and decent. These feelings are not to be identified
with reason, but they oppose a particular desire because of the
way the person feels about moral notions. The trouble is that
Leontius' feelings, and the desire for honour, don't seem to have
much in common with the impulses of children, or what goes
on in animals. Sometimes spirit seems to be quite crude, and
sometimes to be very like reason in demanding a perception of
what is acceptable to the person as a whole.

Plato thinks that these are manifestations of the same kind
of motivation because he is pointing to raw feelings which can
be trained into something more complex. What is displayed by
people who love honour is what results when the impulses of
young children are trained in the right way. Thus he says at
410d that the spirited part can become rough and harsh if it
does not get the right sort of training, whereas if it does it is
what makes people brave. It does so by enabling them, if
properly trained (441e–442a), to retain right beliefs about what
is fearful even under pressure of various kinds (442b–c). It is
hard for us to see a unity in what Plato is talking about because
he refers to spirit both in terms of the strength of the original
impulses and energy, and in terms of the submission to reason
which is the result of the character training that the Guardians
and Auxiliaries go through.

What, then, characterizes spirit? It is not just anger, nor
even emotion in general; this is too suggestive of a mere reaction
to the actions of others, whereas spirit is thought of as forming a
whole pattern of behaviour not dependent on what others do.
It is, however, thought of as emotive. It is more a matter of
how you feel about things, and tend to be affected by them, than
how you think about them. Spirit also, however, involves
reasons and reason-giving, in that it only motivates the person
when certain reasons are present. Leontius is not just feeling
bad; he can give reasons why he regrets what he did. Spirit is

thus different from wanting to get, or caring about, a particular object, for perhaps no particular reason. It is a motivation that can be educated, unlike mere desires to get certain things, which we may well be able to do nothing about. Spirit is perhaps best characterized by means of two notions which Plato does not himself stress (and has no very appropriate terminology for): it involves some reference to the self, and some reference to ideals. It involves the self in so far as one particular desire (like Leontius' desire to look at corpses) may be rejected because the person as a whole does not, as we put it, identify with that desire. Leontius felt shame at giving in to a desire which, in modern jargon, did not fit his self-image; he did not want to be the *kind of person* capable of doing such a thing. Ideals come in because a particular desire like Leontius' desire is not rejected because it is inconvenient, or imprudent, but because it is felt to offend against what is accepted as right and good by the person. Leontius feels shame, which is a reaction only intelligible in someone who has done what he feels to be *wrong*, not just imprudent or dangerous. In both these respects spirit is like reason, and may indeed seem to be doing the same job as reason (and Plato admits that they may seem too similar, 440e–441a). One key to the difference may lie in the comment at 441a that spirit is reason's ally 'unless it is corrupted by bad upbringing'. Spirit is thought of as educable and plastic; people can be trained to feel one way rather than another. (Spirit is analogous to the Auxiliaries in the state; their characters have been so trained that they repudiate aims that offend against their ideals, but they lack reasoned understanding of their way of life and its basis). Plato tends, on the other hand, to think of reason not as a disposition to be moulded, but as a gift which can be used or misused; it is not malleable, or attachable to different ends, without destroying its nature.

(3) *Desire*

The third part is called 'the desiring part' at 439d (*to epithumētikon*). Plato does not, however, think that this implies much in the way of a principle of unity, for he says at 580d–e, 'as for the third part, because of its manifold aspects we had no one special name to give it, but we have named it after the biggest and strongest thing in it and have called it the appetitive part [*epithumētikon*] because of the violence of the appetites for food, drink, sex and other things which follow from these.' (Grube.) That is, when Plato calls it the part that characteristically desires, it is not the *mode* of desiring that interests him, but rather the fact that desire is characteristically limited to its object without necessarily involving any further considerations. Desire is thought of as manifold and often chaotic because desire can fix on objects of just about any kind; there is nothing that unifies all cases of desiring except that some particular thing is sought for. (This is meant to be parallel to the productive class in the state, who do not have any unifying ideal but are each set on his or her own particular aim.)

The long discussion of desire in Book 4 concentrates on basic, easily recognizable examples of desire, especially bodily desires (those one has merely by virtue of having a body, desires for food, drink, sleep, and sex). These (except sleep, which Plato omits here, though he has plenty to say about it elsewhere) are mentioned at 436a, 437b, 439d, and said to be the clearest examples at 437d. Thirst is discussed at length, and in a way that makes it look like a simple craving, for it is emphasized that thirst is just for drink, not drink qualified in any way (437d–e, 438a–439b), that it drags the person to drink like a wild beast (439b) and is excitable (439d), and even said to be due to states affecting the body and diseases (439d). It fits with this that when this part is named after desire it is said to be 'unreasoning' (439d). All the emphasis on the basic and forceful nature of desires makes it look as though no cognitive performance at all should be ascribed to this part.

But in spite of Plato's vigorous language this cannot be the whole story. Even in Book 4, Leontius desires to see some corpses, a more complex desire than simple thirst (possibly, though, it is based upon a sexual desire, since we know from a fragment of contemporary comedy that Leontius was known for being attracted by young men as pale as corpses). And the desiring part is said to 'agree' to being ruled (442c, d) so it cannot be completely unreasoning. The later Books 8 and 9 make it quite clear that this part can indeed perform *some* reasoning about what it wants, and that bodily desires are thus only the clearest examples of the kind of desire Plato has in mind, not the only ones. At 580d–581a this part of the soul is called 'the part that loves money and gain' (*philochrēmaton* and *philokerdes*). Money comes in because it is the best way of obtaining one's gratifications; so this part is thought of as being able to reason out how to obtain its desires, and valuing means to this end. It is therefore capable of means–end reasoning, though not other kinds. At 571c–572b it is said to be responsible for creating wish-fulfilment dreams in order to gain its own gratification while the other parts are asleep and off-guard. Most significantly, we find that very different kinds of life can be said to be dominated by this part of the soul. Plato describes the oligarchic man, obsessively subordinating all other concerns to the getting and keeping of money; the democratic man, following any desire that happens to be uppermost and thus dividing his time between worthy and trivial pursuits; and the tyrannical man, dominated by unfulfilled lust. These are all lives dominated by the desiring part, and so it is clear that desire cannot be limited to simple bodily desires. Plato's concentration on these in Book 4 is somewhat misleading. Bodily desires are 'clear' examples of desires not because of their objects but because they display clearly the fact about desire which Plato takes to be the most important: desire is limited to its own fulfilment and has no motivational impact on the person's wider concerns. The person can desire something, and in so far as he or she desires it, try to get it, regardless of their estimate of the rightness, or prudence, of such a course. This is true of the thirsty man who drinks regardless of whether this is wise or not, and equally true of the avaricious man who subordinates his sense of good and evil to the getting of money. Desire is blind to any considerations beyond those of getting what it wants. (It is meant to be parallel to the members of the productive class, who are blind to any higher considerations than those of getting what they want.) It might in fact be better to think of desire as 'gratification', for this suggests both its self-contained nature, and the fact that it is not limited to immediate bodily desires but may involve quite a lot of calculating of the means to obtain gratification.

In Book 10 there is a discussion of art in which Plato makes further claims about reason and desire. Reason there enables us to correct visual impressions of a misleading kind by appeal to objective procedures of counting, measuring and weighing

(602c–603b); and it enables us to achieve distance from immediate misfortunes by placing them in a wider context (603c–605b). Desire appears as the part which unreflectively accepts visual appearances without checking up by objective standards; and also as the part which indulges in emotions, thereby both enjoying theatrical shows and providing material for them. It is not at all obvious why Plato thinks that reason and desire are fitted to fill these two new roles. We can see in an impressionistic way that desire is associated with what is 'subjective', that is, what appeals immediately to the person regardless of whether it is confirmed by intersubjective standards, and that reason is associated with what is objective, that is, distinct from immediate impressions and immediate gratifications and based on what can be judged to be the case after reflection. But Book 10 is hard to fit with the rest of what Plato says in many ways, and these extensions of the roles of reason and desire are best considered separately when we come to Book 10.

The language I have used to describe the parts of the soul has been patently anthropomorphic. Each part has its own desires and pleasures (580d–587e). They are aware of one other; desire can outwit the others; reason can control them; and they can conflict, producing 'civil war in the soul' (440e). Spirit and desire can try to usurp what is not their proper role (442a–b, 443d–e). Ideally they should agree (442d); spirit can be said to retain what reason declares (442c2). Reason has desires of its own; desire can carry out enough reasoning to attain its goals. All three parts have enough cognitive capacity to recognize one another, conflict or agree, and push their own interests. This has worried many people, who fear that the parts have been 'personified', that is, that they are just little replicas of the whole person. In fact they are not, but the point needs argument, and this will be offered after we have seen how the soul's virtues are defined in terms of its parts.

Once the soul's parts have been distinguished, the virtues follow in a way parallel to the virtues of the state (441c–442d). An individual is wise when reason rules, and makes decisions in the interests of the soul as a whole (442c). He or she is brave when spirit has been made the ally of reason as a result of training that ensures not only recognition of what is right but the power to stick to that recognition and feel motivated to act in accordance with it (442b–c). He or she is moderate by virtue of the recognition by all the soul's parts that particular gratifications should be subordinated to reason's overall planning, and by virtue of the desiring part's submission in accordance with this recognition (442c–d). The analogies with the city's virtues are clear. And, as with the city, the person is just because of the fact that each of his or her parts is functioning properly and 'doing its own' (441d). Again, this must not be taken too negatively: justice does not require anything further from any of the parts other than what is required by the other three virtues, but it is the virtue of the person as a whole, of all three virtues in so far as they are the virtues of a functioning unity.

A person is just, then, if each part is acting virtuously and as it should: if reason is ruling, spirit is ensuring that reason has adequate motivational backing and desire is acquiescing in control by the other two rather than pressing its own particular claims. Justice in the individual is the appropriate and harmonious flourishing of all aspects of him or her (443d). Because of this, justice as Plato defines it in Book 4 has been labelled 'psychic harmony', and this is apt, though strictly justice is the state that ensures psychic harmony rather than being identical with it. As well as describing the just person as unified and harmonious, Plato makes a comparison with health (444c–445b); he wants us to think of justice as a state where the person is completely fulfilled (or as we might say fully realized) because no aspect of him or her is being repressed or denied its proper expression. Plato's account of justice is thus importantly like modern notions of 'mental health' which likewise claim that the individual is in a bad state if important aspects of him or her are being frustrated, and that the good life is one in which this does not happen. We are not likely to agree with Plato's own diagnosis of what is important in human flourishing – in particular he is far too negative about the importance of fulfilling particular desires. But his basic idea of thinking of the best way of life as one in which the individual is 'healthy', 'functioning properly', and 'integrated', which establishes a notion of mental as well as physical health, is an ideal that is not only acceptable to us but part of our familiar way of thinking.

To define justice as an internal state of the person, rather than in terms of behaviour to others, raises quite grave problems which need a chapter to themselves. Before doing this it is helpful to consider in more detail exactly what is involved in the person's having a just soul. Here the key role is played by the role of reason, since the roles of spirit and desire have to be understood by reference to that of reason (they respectively back it up and acquiesce in its demands). So we have to ask, What is it for reason to rule in the soul?

In Book 4 what is most stressed about reason is its capacity to rule by virtue of knowing what is best for the soul as a whole and not just itself (441e, 442c). This suggests that reason rules in a way that we are ready to call 'rational' when a person acts in the light of their interests and aims over their life as a whole, not favouring present motivations, however strong, just because they are present ones. Reason weighs up past and future considerations as well as current pressures, and gives the current reasons importance corresponding to their long-term significance and not their present intensity. It thus enables us to act in a co-ordinated way over our life as a whole, without giving in to every short-term gratification. Reason in this role is what organizes and harmonizes other motives and makes it possible for us to attain all or most of our important ends without conflict. However, for reason to act in this role is not for it to have any motivational power of its own, as Hume clearly saw when he said that reason (so conceived) is and ought to be the slave of the passions. The faculty that enables us to attain our desires most rationally is not itself a desire, or a motivation with any particular end of its own.

Now when reason is said to judge for the soul as a whole, this suggests the limited, 'Humean' role of reason as rational co-ordinator of desires already given, with no motivational force of its own. But this cannot be all that Plato means. For a person planning their life rationally in this way would be a textbook case of self-interested prudence, rather than any kind of model of justice. Why should one be *just* by virtue simply of planning for one's life as a whole rather than satisfying one's desires just as they come? Plato does think that the just person in whom reason rules is prudent, but there is more to it than that. An unjust person might be perfectly prudent in the sense of being able to co-ordinate rationally the attainment of his or her desires.

We have seen that reason has another role (not much stressed in Book 4): to love and search for the truth in all its manifestations in theory and practice. This love of truth gives reason its own end, which it delights in pursuing (581b). So for reason to rule, it does not have to be limited to carrying out other ends efficiently; it will judge for the whole person in the light of the attainment of its own ends. Unlike 'Humean' reason, which takes the goals of the other parts of the soul as given and merely tries to achieve them in an efficient and organized way, reason as Plato conceives it will decide for the whole soul in a way that does not take the ends of the other parts as given but may involve suppressing or restraining them. We have already seen that desire will have to knuckle under to some extent, so reason will not just try to attain each object of desire but may suppress some desires in the interests of others. Reason, which is thought of as always *straining* towards the truth, is thought of as having considerable motivational force of its own. It is not inert, like Hume's slave of the passions, but does some things, and gets the whole person to do others.

We can see this more clearly from a brief look at the sketches of the various unjust men in Books 8–9. Plato there describes what happens when reason does not rule in the soul and the latter is dominated by spirit or desire. The 'timocratic' man, the first stage of decline, cares for honour and physical prowess above all (538–9). He defers to the powerful but is harsh to the defenceless, and has no internal restraint against caring too much for money. His successor, the 'oligarchic' man (553 ff.), thinks that money is all-important. He drives spirit from the throne in his soul and establishes there desire, with its demand for money. Reason and spirit are made to squat like slaves before the Persian king, and carry out the orders only of desire. The 'democratic' man rids himself of the authority and discipline of money-grubbing (559–561). He keeps open house among his desires, letting none dominate but yielding rule to whichever happens to be uppermost. Reason and spirit presumably help in gratifying whichever desire he happens to have. Finally the 'tyrannical' man (556–576) has a soul enslaved to one master desire, lust, which produces a chronic state of unsatisfied need, no part of the soul achieving its proper end.

Now in none of these men does reason rule, yet they are all 'rational' in the sense of being able to plan their life as a whole; only the tyrant fails in this to any extent. The democratic man leads a chaotic life, but there is no suggestion that the form his life takes is something out of his control. It is especially clear with the oligarchic man that reason is in control of his projects in the sense that he can plan and carry out his projects efficiently. Reason fails to rule in his soul because, although he is extremely prudent, his life is not shaped by the demands of reason; rather, he lets his life be run by the need to make money. Plato's account of the various unjust men makes no sense at all unless we are supposed to think that the rule of reason which is required for justice is more than the dominance of rational planning; the goals of reason must dominate the whole life.

We are still, however, entitled to ask what *this* has to do with *justice*. Why should straining after truth make a person just, any more than efficient planning?

Plato has no answer to this in Book 4, because the problem is not one that can be solved by appeal only to the moral psychology of Book 4. We shall not understand until the end of the central books what the connection is between justice and searching after truth. We can, however, exploit one hint that emerges from the contrast of 'Humean' and Platonic reason. 'Humean' reason is passive and leaves unquestioned the status of the desires which it efficiently fulfils, but Platonic reason does not. Reason is thus being thought of as *critical* of the other motivations in a way that they are not critical of themselves or of each other. In a soul ruled by reason, it is not just a matter of the strongest desire winning out – something which happens in the various unjust men sketched. Reason enables a person to make a critical and informed *decision*, rather than letting the strongest desire win the day. Because reason *chooses*, rather than mechanically following the strongest desire, we can see why later Plato will characterize the person ruled by reason as *free*, whereas the person ruled by another part of the soul is unfree and passive.

One more problem about the rule of reason in the soul should be mentioned at this point; it also will concern us further. The three classes in the state are thought of as made up of three different kinds of people: those whose souls are ruled by reason, the Guardians; those whose souls are ruled by spirit, the Auxiliaries; and those whose souls are ruled by desire, the productive class (581b–c). So far we have assumed, fairly naturally, that *all* the citizens will be just; there has been no suggestion that justice is only to be found in the Guardians. But if justice requires that the soul be ruled by reason, not just in the 'Humean' sense but in the stronger sense in which the person's life is shaped by pursuit of the ends of reason, can anybody be just except the Guardians, who alone have souls ruled by reason rather than by one of the other two parts? No doubt all the citizens have souls ruled by reason in the 'Humean' sense, but we have seen that this is compatible with injustice. What about the Auxiliaries, whose souls are dominated by the aims of spirit? How can they be just, lacking the strong rule of reason?

As the *Republic* proceeds, Plato in fact loses interest in anyone but the Guardians, and there is some truth in the charge, often made, that he identifies the just person with the Guardian type and does not care if the other citizens in his city are not strictly speaking just. On the other hand, it is surely intolerable for all the citizens except 'the smallest class' not to be just, or to be just in some reduced sense. Perhaps we can take a cue from the fact that even the Auxiliaries' courage was qualified as being 'civic' or 'political' courage (430c3). Plato possibly means us to understand that only the Guardians, whose souls are ruled by reason in the strong sense, are *self-motivated* to be just. The other classes are just *only* in a city where the Guardians' justice is imposed on them and thus counteracts the natural tendency of their souls to go wrong because they are led by goals that do not on their own ensure justice. The Guardians too require a political context to be just, but not because they would otherwise go wrong without external direction, rather because they would otherwise be ineffective and not able to exercise their justice. So in a sense they *are* the only class that is just – that is, they are the only class that can be just from their own resources, without having to be controlled from outside. And Plato drifts into proceeding as though the other two classes were not really just, and loses interest in them, because he is not very interested in justice that requires external sanctions to exist. He is only interested in people who can be freely and autonomously just – the Guardians, whose souls are ruled by reason.

Let us return to the argument that introduces the parts of the soul at 436a ff. Plato begins by bringing in, with some fanfare, a general principle 'that one thing cannot act in opposite ways or be in opposite states at the same time and in the same part of itself in relation to the same other thing' (436b, Grube). Sometimes this is referred to as the Principle of Non-contradiction, but this is misleading; that principle concerns propositions and their logical relations, whereas Plato is here concerned not with propositions but with whether a certain thing can have certain properties. Furthermore, he is concerned with opposites in a very broad sense, not just contradictories. He picks out those that are apparent in the individual – agreeing and disagreeing, wanting something and refusing it, making towards and pushing away (437b). He is concerned not with *any* conflict but with the conflict that results when we observe both of these opposed states in a person at the same time. The Principle of Conflict, as it is best named, shows that if there is such a conflict, then the person is not a unity, but is in a way two. (This point has been used before, in the discussion of 'self-mastery', but has not before been generalized and stated explicitly.) Plato gives an extended example which serves to distinguish reason and desire. A man may desire to drink, yet control this urge. Thus there is a conflict: he both accepts and rejects the same thing at the same time. This can only be explained by saying that he is not a unity, but contains distinct parts: distinct in that there can be no common motivational root of the urge to drink and the urge to refrain. If they were not distinct, they would not have created the appearance of conflict in the person as a whole.

So the Principle of Conflict is used to show that despite our everyday assumption that a person is a unity (after all, he or she comes in a single body) none the less the facts of human behaviour compel us to treat a person as containing more than one motivational source. Plato thinks that he needs an elaborate argument because the point he is making clashes to some extent with common sense.

There are grave problems with the argument, however, which we can bring out initially by asking whether every conflict in motivation shows that there are really distinct parts of the soul. If wanting to drink while at the same time wanting to restrain the urge shows that there are distinct parts of the soul, what of the case where I want to write a paper, but also want to watch the late night movie on TV? These two motivational urges lead to a conflict – both can't be followed by the same person at the same time – but do they create separate parts of the soul? It is absurd if every case of conflicting urges creates such parts, for then there will be infinitely many such parts. Clearly Plato does not mean this.

It may be said that there are not separate parts for the desires to write a paper and to watch TV because it is only contingent that these desires *conflict* – it just is a part of my situation (having left insufficient time to do the writing) that both cannot be done, and there is nothing in their nature which makes them necessarily conflict. On its own this will not quite do, for how are we to draw the line between desires which do and those which do not conflict necessarily? But the suggestion points to a more satisfactory solution. Plato does not have in mind conflicts which are created by facts about the *objects* of the motivations, only conflicts created by the nature of the motivations themselves. The fact that I cannot both write a paper and watch TV shows something about the nature of these activities (they exclude each other in limited time) rather than about the nature of my desire for either. Our lives are full of conflicts because we want objects that are not jointly attainable, but these do not all show that there are parts of the soul, because the problem may come simply from the character of what we want.

Conflict located in the motivations themselves, rather than their objects, seems to be what Plato has in mind in the long argument to distinguish reason from desire. For he stresses constantly that the desire that concerns him is *just* desire. Desire is *only* for drink (437d–439b). Desire on its own is not for cold drink or hot drink, for good drink or for a lot of drink. It is presented as simply the urge to drink, which pulls the person like a beast (439b) and is due to 'emotive states and diseases' (439d). It is called 'unreasoning' (439d) and looks like a simple craving, with no cognitive content. We might think that desire must have some content, at least enough to recognize its object as being the desired object, but Plato is not concerned to make this point. For it is said that desire is incapable of wanting its object as being good (438 ff.); and this comes as part of a larger argument to show that desire is incapable of wanting things of a certain kind at all. Desire for an object of a certain kind, whatever kind that might be (e.g. good) is itself desire of a certain, qualified kind, not just simple desire. Desire itself looks like a blind craving; any content it might have would apparently be the work of reason, for there is nothing in the nature of desire itself to account for the cognitive element when, for example, it is good drink, and not just drink, that is desired.

Plato takes such pains to separate reason from desire in this way because he wants to stress, in accordance with the Principle of Conflict, that they are utterly *distinct* kinds of motivation. By harping on the incompetence of desire to characterize its objects in any way, he makes it clear that the conflict is not due to the nature of the object of desire, but lies in the way that the person relates to that object – with attraction on the one hand, and repulsion on the other.

Unfortunately the result is that Plato has divided the soul into a totally irrational, craving part and a rational, cognitive part. And this is not what he wants in the *Republic* as a whole, for three reasons.

(i) The argument here gives us a wrong conception of desire. By making it look contentless, reduced to the level of animal drive, Plato is apparently limiting desire to the basic biological desires which arise from having a body, and are independent of one's beliefs. But though this fits the example, and though in Book 4 such desires are stressed (see p. 129), this is inadequate for desire in general. Even in Book 4 the bodily desires are only the 'clearest' examples. Later the part of the soul is characterized as 'money-loving' (580e) because money is a means of gratifying desires, and it is described in ways implying that it is capable of beliefs about how to attain fairly complex and long-range desires. Even in Book 4 it not only fights the other parts but can agree with them. Throughout, desire is treated as capable of much more in the way of beliefs and reasoning than this argument seems to allow.

(ii) The argument here gives an inadequate and potentially misleading characterization of reason. This emerges if we ask *why* reason opposes the desire to drink. We are not told, but we are probably right to infer that it is for reasons of health (the desire being due to 'diseases'). The person is thirsty, but should not drink because he is about to exercise, or perhaps has dropsy; that is, it is in his interests to refrain from drinking. Now to do this reason does not need anything more than the limited 'Humean' role of organizing desires so that they form a harmoniously attainable whole; it does not have to have any aims peculiar to itself which might conflict with particular desires. This comes out clearly if we reflect that the example shows a use of reason which would be compatible with various kinds of injustices that result from reason's not ruling in the soul in the stronger sense. All the types of unjust men described in Books 8 and 9 do not have reason ruling in their souls in that their characteristic aims are contrary to those of reason; yet they are all perfectly capable of restraining the urge to drink when it is not in their interests to do so. They all retain reason in the limited role of prudence. So if the argument were meant to show us what reason is, it would be most misleading; we would have to conclude that Plato had, consciously or not, changed his mind when he connected reason's rule not with prudence but with justice.

(iii) Because the argument divides the soul so definitely into rational and irrational parts, it makes the place of spirit questionable. For spirit shares features of both desire and reason – it motivates the person to feel, rather than think, but it is rational in that these feelings rest on certain kinds of reason and would not be felt in their absence. The argument separating reason from desire so sharply seems to leave no conceptual room for spirit; spirit turns out to be like reason in so far as reasons are appealed to, and like desire in so far as impulses come in, but seems not to be a unity in its own right. And in fact spirit is established rather awkwardly in Book 4, after the long passage distinguishing reason from desire. The Principle of Conflict is invoked to show that spirit must be separate from desire, because it can oppose it (the story of Leontius, 439e–440a). But then it is simply claimed that spirit can be found in children and animals, where reason is absent (441a–b); there is no application of the Principle of Conflict, and hence no satisfactory argument to show that spirit is really distinct from reason, and so a distinct part of the soul. Many interpreters who have been struck by this awkwardness have concluded that Plato did not really think that there was a convincing third part of the soul, and that spirit is only brought in to correspond with the Auxiliary class in the city. But the Book 4 argument is not only troublesome for the status of spirit; it raises problems for all three of the parts.

All the soul's parts, then, are at least underdescribed by the way they are introduced in the Book 4 argument. If we take that argument as establishing what they are meant to be, then we have to conclude that, as he goes along, Plato without explicit warning expands the parts; reason comes to have aims of its own instead of serving as a 'Humean' co-ordinator of given desires, spirit comes to have a unity not established by the argument, and desire comes to have belief-content rather than being a craving incapable of perceiving its object as qualified in any way whatever. If this is right, however, Plato is not just careless, but is putting forward an incoherent theory: first he establishes that desire is the kind of thing that *cannot* have any cognitive content, then he proceeds on the assumption that it can, and the other parts are juggled to match.

We have to conclude that Plato's actual argument for the distinctness of the soul's parts does not establish what the parts are which he needs and uses. But we can see why he uses this argument; his immediate concern is to establish, against disbelieving common sense, that the soul does have separate parts, and this is what the argument does show, though in a way that does not adequately indicate their natures. The trouble is that Plato's parts really *are* distinguished as much by their objects as by the nature of their operation in the individual. That is how they are introduced at 580–581, where the basis for distinguishing them is to be found in experience and not in any principle put forward as a necessary truth. (Although Plato does not discuss the matter explicitly, he does seem to regard the Principle of Conflict as necessarily true; certainly his use of it would be inept if it were the kind of truth that just *happened* to be true.) So his argument distinguishing the parts by a conflict which is not due to their objects, while it succeeds in showing that they are distinct, is almost bound to fail to show adequately what they are. And in fact Plato drops the example of the thirsty man, and his examples to show conflict in the soul thereafter are all (more interesting) cases where the parts conflict because they urge the person to seek incompatible goals. (The oligarchic man, for example, avoids conflict between reason and desire by subordinating reason to the ends of desire, particularly money-making. If reason were not so subordinated, it would urge him to do actions which would be fair and just, but would conflict with making money.)

This leads us, however, straight to another problem. Each part has desires and pleasures, and tries to gain them, sometimes at the expense of the other two; they conflict, agree, and so on. That is, they are freely described in terms that are normally used only of the person as a whole. But the theory was introduced to explain certain behaviour on the part of the whole person showing that he or she is not a real unity. The parts are explanatory entities, parts needed to explain the behaviour of the whole. If they themselves, however, can be described in the way the whole person is, have we not reproduced the problems that led to the need for the theory in the first place? The desiring part is introduced to explain why sometimes I reach for a drink even when there is countervailing motivation. But then it turns out that we can say that the desiring part *wants* a drink, and tries to promote this aim even when the other parts do not concur. How have we advanced from saying that *I* want a drink though I realize that there is something to be said against it? How is my desire to work out the truth explained by saying that I contain a little reasoning part whose main desire is to know the truth? The parts lead to a regress of explanation if they reproduce, as they seem to, the features of the whole person that needed the explanation in the first place. Let us call this the Homunculus Problem: is the theory not worthless if it explains the behaviour of a person by introducing in the person homunculi, little people to bring about the behaviour?

The Homunculus Problem has led many interpreters to conclude that Plato's theory of the soul's parts is a mistake, and that it cannot ever get off the ground. But if one sees the Homunculus Problem as a real *problem*, it may well be because of certain assumptions about what form a psychological theory ought to take. We cannot write off Plato's theory without first asking *why* it is supposed to be wrong to explain the behaviour of a person as a whole in terms of the behaviour of his or her 'parts'.

Plato's theory is the first sustained attempt to explain intentional human behaviour illuminatingly, to explain why we act as we do. Now until fairly recently it has been widely assumed that to be scientifically illuminating – to have any prospect of bringing us new knowledge – a psychological theory must explain intentional behaviour in terms of entities which cannot themselves be characterized in the way that human behaviour can be. Intentional actions, for example, have been explained in terms of 'colourless' pieces of behaviour, or movements described in such a way as to leave out anything characteristic of human behaviour. Or else actions have been explained by citing the firing of neurons, or other physiological happenings, which, again, are not themselves examples of human behaviour or anything analogous to it. This kind of approach is sometimes called the 'bottom-up' strategy because the assumption is that we have a firm foundation in our knowledge of bodily movements or neurophysiology, and that human behaviour can only be explained by citing such events, and so reducing it to something quite unlike human behaviour.

But another approach is just as viable, one which is sometimes called 'top-down'. Examples of it (of very different kinds) are Freud's analytical theories, much work in cognitive psychology, and some related work in Artificial Intelligence. What is to be explained is some phenomenon of intentional behaviour – perhaps the behaviour of the whole person, as in Plato's theory. Explanation proceeds by breaking down this phenomenon into smaller parts or functions, which are more specific, so that we can use them to explain the whole performance, but which are still characterized in ways appropriate to human behaviour. This strategy can be applied on a smaller scale. Thus, the fact that humans remember things in charac- teristically long-term or short-term ways is explained by postulating a short-term and a long-term memory; items for recall go into the short-term memory and this hands over some of them to the long-term memory, which stores them. (Of course this is a crude oversimplification; most theories of memory involve many more than two kinds of memory.) These two kinds of memory are simpler than the original pheno-menon of 'human memory' which covered all our recalling in an undifferentiated way, because they are precisely specified and limited to a single function; they do not display the parti-cular complexity which characterized the phenomenon to be explained, and thus they can help to explain it. However, they are still characterized in some ways that are appropriate to the original phenomenon of remembering.

It is easy to think of such an explanatory entity as being itself a homunculus – a little person within the big one, doing things. *But* this is not necessarily objectionable, as long as one is clear that the item in question is *meant* to be something that is both simpler than the whole person with all their other functions, and also something that shares features with the whole person. If one is applying the 'top-down' strategy, there is no need for the explanatory items to be things like neurons which belong to a different science. And so there is nothing wrong with talking of the explanatory parts of a whole person as though they were themselves people of a very simple kind. Talking of them as homunculi is very natural and unavoidable. One 'specifies a homunculus by prescribing a function *without saying how it is to be accomplished* (one says, in effect: put a little man in there to do the job)'. (The quotation, and the ones following, are from D. Dennett (see note at end of chapter).) But this need lead to no regress of explanation, just because the homunculi are simpler than the whole person: they are precisely limited to a single function. 'Homunculi are *bogeymen* only if they duplicate *entire* the talents they are rung in to explain.' That is, we are in trouble if the homunculus reproduces the features that were found puzzling about the whole person. But 'if one can get a team or committee of *relatively* ignorant, narrow-minded, blind homunculi to produce the intelligent behaviour of the whole, this is progress'.

Plato's parts of the soul are, I think, best thought of as just such a committee of relatively ignorant and narrow-minded homunculi (though Plato would not have thought of them *all* that way). They are not meant to be items to which human behaviour can be *reduced*, items like neurons that belong to a different science. They are, precisely, homunculi, reproducing some but not all of the functions of the whole. Desire, for example, is what gets the person to gratify particular wants. It includes the ability to figure out how to do this; this is how it gets us to gratify a want. So it is cleverer than mere animal craving. But it is much less clever than the whole person, and less clever even than the reasoning abilities. It is the same kind of theoretical item as the short-term memory, and, like it, it appears pretty stupid in isolation.

There is one snag in this picture. It is clear that desire and spirit are limited functions, whose tendencies and beliefs do not replicate those of the whole person. But what about reason? It is stressed that this can reason things out for the person as a whole; and if so, there is some danger that it is reproducing the capacities of the whole person. This suspicion is deepened by a passage in Book 9, where the person is compared to a man who contains within himself a little man, a lion, and a many-headed and protean monster (588b–589b). These conflict in the unjust man, whereas the just man has brought it about that the little man can control the beast with the help of the lion. The image unfortunately makes clear that while desire and spirit do not reproduce the characteristics of the whole person, reason seems to; why else would it be a little man inside the big one? The more Plato insists that reason is responsible for the welfare of the soul as a whole, the more he expands its capacities until it threatens to become not just a homunculus but a bogeyman. However, there is no necessary identity between the interests and desires of the little man and those of the big one; the whole person can be in a state where he 'starves and weakens' the little man (589a). The interests and desires of reason are not a reduplication of the interests and desires of the whole person. Only in the case of the perfectly just person do they coincide; but this is an ideal, not an example of ordinary human behaviour that the theory serves to explain. In describing reason as a little man Plato is being picturesque but somewhat misleading.

I conclude that as the parts of the soul are used to explain the condition and behaviour of different types of person, there is no need to be worried by the Homunculus Problem. We do not have to choose between, on the one hand, thinking of the soul's parts as 'personified', reproducing the whole person in a regressive way, or, on the other hand, thinking of them as entities that cannot themselves have beliefs and desires or be characterized in ways appropriate to the whole person. Rather, the parts have some, but not all, of the features of the whole person whose behaviour they are introduced to explain. We find, then, a richly suggestive use of the 'top-down' kind of strategy for explaining puzzling facts about human behaviour. Plato's theory is crude and unspecific by modern standards; but all the same, it would today be considered a more fruitful *kind* of theory than 'bottom-up' attempts to explain human behaviour by reducing it to items that have none of the features of human behaviour.

But while there are no problems with the theory as a theory of the soul, or person, there are problems when we turn to the relation of soul and state, and the way their parts and virtues correspond.

What is the relation of justice in the soul and justice in the state? This problem is often approached by asking, Which is prior in Plato's thought, the state or the individual? Some have thought that he worked out his theory of the state first and then applied it, with some strain, to the individual, treating the person as a mini-city. Others have thought that a theory of the individual is mechanically transferred to the state, making that into a super-individual.

There are two passages which seem to put the individual definitely first. One is 435e–436a. 'Well, then . . . we are surely compelled to agree that each of us has within himself the same parts and characteristics as the city? Where else would they come from? It would be ridiculous for anyone to think that spiritedness has not come to be in the city from individuals who are held to possess it, like the inhabitants of Thrace and Scythia . . .' Likewise Greece is held to be intellectual because Greeks are, and Egypt and Phoenicia are money-loving because Egyptians and Phoenicians are. Plato is saying that a city has a virtue *V* because the individual citizens have *V*. It is not clear, however, how the 'because' is to be taken, and anyway his examples are extraordinarily bad ones to make any point about a *city*, for they are all examples of ethnic groups with no political unity, not of groups of individuals united by civic and political relations. The other passage is 544d: 'You realize . . . that there are of necessity as many ways of life for men as there are types of cities? Or do you think that governments are born "from oak or rock" and not from the characters of the men who live in the cities, which characters tip the scales and drag other things after them?' (Both quotations from Grube.)

Do these passages show that for Plato the individual is prior as a subject of justice and other virtues, that a city is *V*, for any virtue *V*, if and only if the people in it are *V*, and that it is *V* *because* they are *V*? Hardly. The two passages seem to be claiming no more than that in actual states, the nature of the government (or the way of life, in the case of politically dis-organized ethnic groups like the ones he cites) will come to reflect the preferences of the individuals – something compatible with many interpretations of the state–soul parallel. And in his actual account of the city's virtues, we have seen that the city's being *V* does not just come down to there being *V* people in it, but is a fact about the city and the role it gives to the *V* people. And finally, just before the first of the above passages, Plato puts forward at length another suggestion, a most important one by the side of which the two quoted passages are marginal. Socrates begins by repeating that they began by looking for justice in a city, because there it would appear in larger form. He proposes to transfer the account to the individual to see if the results there agree. If it doesn't, they must return to the city and see what adjustments are needed there. 'By thus comparing and testing the two, we might make justice light up like fire from the rubbing of firesticks.' (435a, Grube.)

For this procedure to work, it must be the case that *neither* soul nor state is prior, but that both have the same status in the discovery of what justice is. What follows, at 435b, makes this explicit:

Well now, when you apply the same name to a thing whether it is big or small, are these two instances of it like or unlike with regard to that to which the same name applies? – They are alike in that, he said.

So the just man and the just city will be no different but alike as regards the very form of justice? – Yes, they will be.

Now the city was thought to be just when the three kinds of

men within it performed their own task, and it was moderate and brave and wise because of some other qualities and attitudes of the same groups. – True.

And we shall therefore deem it right, my friend, that the individual have the same parts in his own soul, and through the same qualities in those parts will correctly be given the same names. – That must be so. (Grube.)

Plato is claiming here that justice in person and city is exactly the same kind of thing, that, as we might put it, 'just' has the same sense when applied to a city and to a person. Why does he believe this?

The references in the passage to 'applying the same name' might suggest that Plato is assuming that cities and people are just in the same way simply because we use the word 'just' of both. That is, he would be assuming that if two things (however dissimilar in other ways) are both called '*F*', then they must both be *F* in exactly the same way. It would be strange, however, if Plato were on such an important point following ordinary usage without argument as a guide to the truth, something he is elsewhere very disinclined to do. And later in the *Republic* he recognizes that 'just' can apply in a primary and a derived way; actions are just in so far as they foster a just state of soul (443e).

Plato's precise claim is that just people and just cities will be alike 'as regards the very form of justice'. The Greek word translated 'very form' (*eidos*) is prominent in later contexts where Plato discusses Forms, and while it would be wrong to read these into the text here, we do find one point of contact with the later passages: Plato is bringing in a metaphysical assumption from outside the immediate discussion. Rather than arguing from our use of words to the nature of things, he is making a direct claim about the real nature of things. Justice, he thinks, must be single in form; if cities and people are truly just, then they cannot be just in radically different ways, even if they are very different kinds of thing. What makes a person just cannot be something quite different from what makes a city just; otherwise there would be two distinct kinds of justice, and Plato cannot accept this.

Person and city, then, are just in the same way; the facts about their constitution which have been discussed at length show that they must be thought of as structurally identical. This assumption, however, leads to a difficulty. It seems irreconcilable with the earlier suggestion that in some sense a city is V because the citizens in it are V. For we get an infinite regress. Why is the city V? Because the citizens in it are V. But if they are V in the same sense that the city is, the same question can be asked about the sense in which *they* are V; and so on. We can avoid this by saying that the citizens are V in a way that prevents the further question from arising; but then we have given up the idea that citizens and city are V in exactly the same sense. So we cannot have both: either we have to give up the idea that city and person are just in the same sense, or we have to give up the idea that there is any way in which we can explain the city's V-ness by appeal to the V-ness of individuals. Clearly it is the second which has to go; Plato's remarks that suggest this cannot be taken in a way that would establish a principle which could conflict with his explicit principle that city and person are V in exactly the same sense.

Even so, Plato still has to face an insuperable problem. The difficulty can be brought out in many ways. If city and person are just in exactly the same sense, then their justice will have a common structure which is discernible in each. But if we follow this up, we get unacceptable results whether we begin with the state's justice and try to find it in the soul, or begin with the soul's justice and try to find it in the state. Trying to do either must be legitimate if state and soul are exactly alike in their justice; but in neither case does it work out right.

Let us take the theory of the parts of the soul, as we have seen it sketched. Justice is the condition where each part performs its own job rightly. But if we understand the state's justice in terms of this, then justice in the whole state is the condition where each class does its job, the classes being made up of people who correspond to the parts of the soul that is dominant in them. The productive class, for example, correspond to desire, desire being the part that is dominant in the souls of the members of the productive class. Now desire can reason, but only in the limited means-end way required for it to gratify a particular desire. If the productive class functions in the state like this, then they will be thought of as primitive examples of humanity, limited in their reasoning capacities to particular and short-term gratifications. Now while Plato does sometimes think of them this way (see pp. 116–17) he more often wants to think of them as having enough reasoning capacity to appreciate their role in the city's functioning and its goodness. And, more importantly, if each class corresponds exactly to some limited function in the soul, then in an important way the citizens of the state will not share a common human nature. The reasoning that the productive class do will be a quite different kind of reasoning from that done by the Guardians. And, in spite of the extent to which he thinks people do differ, Plato does not want to deny a common human nature to all his citizens. The differences between members of the different classes are extreme, but they are not as extreme as the differences between the different parts of the soul.

So let us begin from the state; all the citizens are alike in some way (in the myth they are all children of the earth) as well as being different (containing different 'metals'). The state is just when each of the classes so conceived is performing its own task – that is, when members of the classes do not do what members of the other classes are supposed to be doing. Let us see what results from the structure of justice so conceived in the soul. The parts of the soul will then be analogous to the members of the different classes, that is, to people who have souls containing these elements, different ones dominating in members of different classes. Unfortunately, the parts of the soul will then all contain reason, spirit, and desire, and so they all become tripartite. Each part will contain its own reason, spirit, and desire, and the differences between them will be like the differences between the members of the three classes – that is, reason will have more, and more dominant reason than the other two, spirit will be dominated by spirit, and desire will have reason and spirit just like the other two, but be dominated by desire. So the soul corresponds to the state; but each part is now tripartite in a way exactly analogous to the whole person, and the homunculi have become bogeymen. Why is one person dominated by reason? Because his reasoning part is dominated by *its* reason. Why can another person not resist immediate gratification? Because her desiring part is dominated by desire. In each case we can ask about the part *exactly* what we asked about the person. So we do get a regress of explanation. This is clearly a hopeless way to understand the justice of the soul – and one not required by the way Plato regards his theory of the soul.

So if we understand justice in the soul as this is required by the way Plato characteristically regards the soul, we get objectionable results for the state. And if we understand it in a way best for the account of the state, we spoil the theory of the soul – the homunculi do replicate entire the talents they were rung in to explain. Plato cannot sustain the claim that soul and state are just in exactly the same way.

Does this matter? The claim that they are just in precisely the same way does not spring inevitably from the needs of the *Republic*'s main argument. Could Plato not claim instead that city and soul are just in illuminatingly similar ways, without committing himself to the claim of their structural identity that ruins his argument?

Plato *could* make this concession, and it would make the Book 4 argument more plausible; but from his point of view the concession would be very damaging. For the claim that justice is single in form turns out to be part of a larger claim, that goodness in whatever kind of manifestation is single in form. To admit that there is an ultimate distinction of type between the kind of goodness that makes a city excellent and the kind that makes a person excellent is to admit that not only justice, but goodness itself is not unitary; and we shall see that it is crucial for Plato to claim that there cannot be ultimately different kinds of goodness.

Throughout the *Republic* Plato treats his claim that justice benefits the individual agent as part of the same project as his political proposals; it is the same justice that is shown in both. We have seen that city and soul are not just in the same way; Plato's argument has split down the middle. But though for Plato there is a failure here, for us the argument becomes more digestible when issues of individual and of social justice are divided. I shall turn first to justice in the individual soul, asking whether Plato has answered Thrasymachus' problem; and then, separately, to the *Republic*'s account of justice in the state.

FURTHER READING

Parts and virtues of the state are well discussed in J. Wilson,

'The Argument of *Republic* 4' in *Philosophical Quarterly* 1976.
An excellent discussion of the soul's parts is J. Moline, 'Plato
on the Complexity of the Psyche', *Archiv für Geschichte der
Philosophie* 1978. Spirit is discussed in J. Gosling's *Plato*, ch. 3.

The argument in Book 4 has been the subject of several
detailed articles, including R. Robinson, 'Plato's Separation of
Reason from Desire', *Phronesis* 1971, J. Stalley, 'Plato's
Arguments for the Division of the Reasoning and Appetitive
Elements Within the Soul', *Phronesis* 1975, and (controversially)
T. Penner, 'Thought and Desire in Plato', Vlastos (ed.),
Plato 2.

The analogy of state and soul is lucidly discussed in B.
Williams, 'The Analogy of City and Soul in Plato's *Republic*',
in *Exegesis and Argument, Phronesis* Supplement 1.

The quotations from Dennett are from 'Artificial Intelligence
as Philosophy and as Psychology' in D. Dennett, *Brainstorms*.
He himself concludes that the 'top-down' strategy can be used
to eliminate intentionality from psychological explanations (in
a non-reductive way). However, I take his remarks on
homunculi to have wider application and to illuminate a theory
like Plato's that sees no need to eliminate intentionality at any
stage.

Chapter 6

The Defence of Justice

By the end of Book 4 we know that justice is what produces inner
harmony in a person (443d–e) and is to the soul what health is
to the body (444c–445b). It is clear what the benefits of justice
so conceived are: who want to be in a state analogous to
confusion and illness? Once you see the difference between a
life that gives all the elements in a person's make-up proper
scope, and one that frustrates and misdirects them, you cannot
seriously doubt that it is valuable to have the state that ensures
the former.

But even if Plato is right about what the elements in our
make-up are, and what their proper scope is, a step seems to be
missing. What it is obviously worthwhile to have is 'psychic
harmony', that is, justice as a state of the soul that ensures
psychic harmony. But is Thrasymachus countered by the claim
that it doesn't pay to be unjust in the sense of having a disordered soul? He claimed that it paid to be unjust in the
common or garden sense of doing various actions usually
regarded as unjust. And Glaucon and Adeimantus wanted
Socrates to show that it paid to be just in the sense of not doing
those actions, even if one could get away with it. What is the
relevance to this of psychic harmony?

Plato has been widely accused of a fallacy in his reasoning
here – the fallacy of equivocation, proving something different
from what one is asked to prove. For the answer offered here (in
terms of psychic harmony) to Thrasymachus' defence of
ordinary injustice does look to be irrelevant. Psychic harmony
is a condition of your *own* soul – that is why having it benefits
you – whereas ordinary justice concerns behaviour to *other*
people. Why should having a rightly ordered soul make you

keep your hands off other people's property? Plato surely has
to show that there is some connection between Platonic justice
(the state of a rightly ordered soul that leads to psychic
harmony) and ordinary justice, characterized by not doing
things which exploit and wrong others. And surely it has to be a
strong connection; the argument will fall apart unless Platonic
justice entails ordinary justice and vice versa – that is, unless if
you have the one you are bound to have the other. But Plato
nowhere seems to believe that ordinary justice entails Platonic
justice. Cephalus is ordinarily just, but Plato thinks very little
of his complacency and devotion to money-making. Plato does
believe that Platonic justice entails ordinary justice; for after
characterizing justice as the right ordering of the soul he goes
on to claim that a person just in this way would never perform
any of a variety of commonly recognized unjust actions –
embezzlement, theft, public and private betrayals, promise-
breaking, adultery, neglect of parents and the gods (442d–
443b). But he simply *asserts* this, without producing an
argument, and there seems no obvious ground either for his
further claim that the Platonically just agent would not do any
of these things *because* he is Platonically just (443b).

Does the main line of the *Republic*'s defence of justice then
collapse as soon as it is introduced? We are naturally loath to
think so, and many interpreters have claimed that while there
is no explicit argument to link Platonic and ordinary justice,
none the less the materials for such a link are there in the book
and merely have to be brought out. If so, then there is no fallacy
and Book 4 is a cogent answer to Thrasymachus.

How far can this line of defence get?

It is implausible right from the start to claim that Plato thinks
that ordinary justice entails Platonic justice. If he had thought
this, he would have argued like a conservative for the status
quo; he would have defended the likes of Cephalus and
Polemarchus and tried to show that their views are defensible
either as they stand or without basic adjustment. But in fact he
seems to go out of his way to show us how inadequate such a
notion of justice is, both as personified in Cephalus and as
articulated by Polemarchus. Instead of shoring up anything
they represent, Plato begins again with an entirely different
line of defence, one that involves the detour through the

structure and virtues of the city. It is not clear how any of this is relevant to the traditional views of ordinarily just people. So from the start we see that Plato's defence of justice is not going to be a defence of any actions that people like Polemarchus regard as just, or actually do themselves. It is possible to be ordinarily just without being Platonically just – and an ordinarily just person is not covered by Plato's defence of justice against Thrasymachus. On any account, then, Plato is at least restricting the area of what 'justice' covers in order to defend justice.

However, it will still be significant if there is an entailment from Platonic to ordinary justice. For in that case, Plato will be claiming that it is worth while being Platonically just, because this is a state which is clearly valuable; and also claiming that this is an answer to Thrasymachus, because the Platonically just person will necessarily be ordinarily just (the point that concerned Thrasymachus). If there is an entailment, then Plato will have defended ordinary justice, because he will have shown that it is worthwhile having a state that has to lead to ordinary justice. So we should examine attempts to show that Platonic justice does entail ordinary justice.

One important point is that it is a mistake to take the analogies of health and harmony to suggest that justice, conceived of as psychic harmony, is being thought of as a static state of feeling good. Reason does not just organize the various desires into a harmoniously attainable whole; it also has aims of its own, and the person in whose soul reason rules will be a person led to do certain things and choose certain alternatives. Plato's own analogy of health makes clear the benefits of justice, but on any view it is limited and misleading. However, the problem is not solved; for even if reason's rule makes me act in certain ways, still there is the problem that it seems to be a beneficial state of *me*; why should it lead me to do things which are commonly recognized as just, like refraining from exploiting others?

A later passage at 485d–e is relevant here. Strong inclinations in one direction, says Plato, weaken those in other directions; so the just man, who is set on the intellectual goals of philosophical discovery, will have no interest in the pleasures of the body, or the money needed to obtain them. Concentration on the aims of reason makes one lose interest in other things. So, even without knowing much yet about what precisely is involved in concentrating on the aims of reason (and nothing Plato says in Book 4 shows why this should entail doing philosophy) we can see that the Platonically just man would lack most discernible reasons that lead people to be ordinarily unjust. Why would he be unjust if he is not interested in power or money?

But all this shows is that the Platonically just person will not be ordinarily unjust through the motivations of spirit or desire. But while this may exclude quite a lot of temptations to injustice, does it exclude them all? Could reason itself, in pursuit of its ends, not prompt the agent to do an act ordinarily considered unjust? If this happened, then, since reason's rule would not have been threatened, psychic harmony would not have been threatened, yet an ordinarily unjust act would have been committed. And why should the rational thing to do not be something offensive to our ordinary sense of justice? We are especially sensitive to this in the context of the ideal city, where the Guardians, who embody reason most fully, are in charge of the communal life of all the citizens. Rational planning for a community, even done with the interests of all in view, is quite likely to outrage the moral feeling of those community members who are not predominantly rational. It may be urged that this is an idle worry, for in the ideal state things are so organized that all 'do their own' and recognize their due position; the rule of the Guardians means that things have been organized in such a way that each gets what is appropriate. The Guardians will not be offending against ordinary justice because in the ideally just state conditions are such that there is no occasion for ordinary injustice.

But would this satisfy Thrasymachus? Surely not; and rightly. For he wanted a defence of justice in the world as it is, not in utopian conditions. Even if (implausibly) he agreed with Plato over everything about the just state, he could complain that Plato cannot appeal to it in order to show that the rule of reason will necessarily result in what ordinary morality would prescribe. Thrasymachus was impressed by certain facts about the world as it is: the things most wanted are usually in short supply and people are usually in competition for them. That is why he thought that the unjust man was the intelligent man who made the most of a situation of natural conflict. It is no answer to this to say that everything would be different in the ideal state. No doubt it would, even without any theory of Platonic justice. So we cannot make any appeal to the idealizing conditions of the perfectly just state to show that Platonic justice *must* lead to ordinary justice, that reason's rule in the soul will always lead to the agent's doing the commonly just thing. The problem of the alleged fallacy has not gone away. There is no convincing entailment from Platonic to ordinary justice, any more than from ordinary to Platonic justice. Has Plato then simply changed the subject?

As long as we look at the problem in the way we have done so far, asking, 'Does Book 4 with its definition of Platonic justice answer Thrasymachus' challenge?' it will indeed appear that Plato has changed the subject. To appreciate what Plato is doing, we must first make an important distinction.

Ethical theories can be distinguished, in a broad but clear way, into two types: *act-centred* and *agent-centred*. Act-centred theories are the kind most familiar in recent traditions of moral philosophy. They begin from a focus on the notion of *the right act*: the primary question is taken to be, 'What is the right thing to do?' and the primary notions are taken to be those of *duty*, *obligation*, and *morally ought* – for the acceptable answers to the question, what is the right thing to do, will be taken to be those giving lists of duties and obligations. If we go on to ask what a good person is like, we will be told that the good person is the person who does what he or she ought to do, that is, the person disposed to perform the right action on all or most occasions. We identify the good person as the person who can be relied on to do his or her duty, and their virtue lies in conscientiousness about doing the right thing.

By contrast, an agent-centred theory begins in a different place. It focusses on the notion of the *good agent* or *good person*. It takes the primary questions to be, 'What kind of person should I be?' 'What is the good life?' 'What kind of life is admirable?' We find out what is the right thing to do, by asking what kind of thing the good person would do in these circumstances. The right thing to do is identified as the kind of thing done by the good person. For the agent-centred approach, the primary notions are not duty and obligation, but *goodness* and *virtue*.

Of course, most moral theories have something to say about both actions and agent; what distinguishes the two kinds is not that the one deals only with acts and the other only with agents, but that for the one sort acts come first as moral subjects, and for the other, agents do. Both Kantianism and utilitarianism are act-centred theories, because, although they talk about moral appraisal of agents, they make it secondary to that of the appraisal of acts, which is thought of as the fundamental moral problem.

Now already in Book 1 we saw Plato bringing out the deficiencies of people who think that justice is a matter of knowing lists of duties. This approach was seen to be essentially shallow, because it made justice a matter of the performance of acts that were imposed without springing from the agent's own deepest concerns. It could provide no answer to genuine questions whose pressure was felt: Why act like this at all? Is acting like this appropriate to the kind of person I admire and would like to be? We can now see that the whole progress of Books 2 through 4 has been an attempt to build up a notion of the just *agent*. (This process began even in Glaucon's speech, where he made the high point of his case against justice the comparison of the lives of just and unjust men (360e–362c) – indeed, they were compared to three-dimensional portraits (361d). But Glaucon concentrates on the two lives (360e1, 361e1, 362c7) entirely in terms of what the people do and what happens to them – the just man is tortured, the unjust man does all right. It is left to Socrates to turn our attention to the just man's inner life rather than his external fate, and ask what kind of person he is.) Plato has, in Books 2–4, through the extended soul–state comparison, concentrated on the individual's soul, goodness, and virtues. He has set aside the question of just acts to consider at length the environment that would produce and reinforce good people, the education that would bring them about, the proper artistic surroundings that they should have, and the psychological basis for all this. The whole development of the argument is summed up vividly at 443c–d, where Plato says that the sphere of justice is not external actions but a person's own inward self. He has made the just *agent* primary, not the question of just *actions* which dominated the concerns of Thrasymachus, and of Glaucon and Adeimantus.

There are two important corollaries of explaining what justice is by describing the just person rather than by saying what actions are just.

Firstly, we have to have some *independent* way of saying what the good person is like. It is clearly unhelpful to say that just acts are those the just person would do, if all you can say then about the just person is that he or she is the kind of person who would likely to do just acts. You have to be able to say independently what kind of person the just person is. (This is the kind of consideration which makes some people despair of the agent-centred approach, for we suspect very general claims about what people ought to be like. But though Plato's ideas are certainly unacceptable as they stand, we tend to do something rather similar when we characterize people in terms that presuppose the truth of a general theory of human nature – as, say, 'repressed', 'bourgeois', 'macho'.) Plato's moral psychology, his theory of the parts and virtues of the soul, aims to do precisely this. The just person, we are told, is the person who is integrated and morally healthy. This account makes no appeal at all to just *acts*. It tells us in some detail what a just person is without reference to the way he or she acts. We have been prepared for this by the extended account of the education that will produce good people. It was an education of character, not of academic accomplishments. Plato has given us a full picture of the development of the just agent before turning to the matter of just actions. And his so doing is an important basis for his claim that justice is something that is worth having for the agent. For justice is in this way shown to answer to what is important in one's human nature; it is the fulfilment of one's basic needs. (Though, as we have seen, this does not mean that it answers to the desires one has at a particular time.)

Secondly, and crucially: if just acts are to be specified by what the just agent will do, then we cannot lay down *in advance* what acts are just acts. To do this is to return to the rigid and external attitude to justice which has been found wanting. If we take seriously the primacy of being a certain kind of person, we cannot draw up lists of rules or maxims which will settle the question of which actions are the just ones – for this will depend

to a great extent on the circumstances. Because the conditions
of just people's lives differ greatly, justice will express itself in a
great variety of ways and types of behaviour, and no lists of
rules can capture ahead of time all the complexities of action
that will face the just agent. Of course we know *something* here;
we can in fact predict with a fair degree of accuracy what kinds
of cases are likely to occur, and so we can lay down rules as useful
guidelines. It is, however, hopeless simply to *begin* by citing
various duties and lay it down that whatever the just person is
like, he or she will do these. Plato touches on this point explicitly, though not very clearly, at 443e5: the just man, he
says, will think and name the just action to be that which
preserves and creates psychic harmony. This is an idea which is
to become much more developed in Aristotle's ethics (and
those of the Stoics): the good man is the norm for just action;
he can tell you what the right thing to do is, because he is just.
It is clear from what Plato says here that the just man identifies
the just action by reference to the state of psychic harmony
which is Platonic justice, not by reference to lists of duties
accepted from any external source.

    We can now see why there is no simple answer to whether
Plato changes the subject and commits the fallacy of equivocation when he answers a question posed in terms of just actions
in terms of the just agent. Plato wants to defend justice, not
some invention of his own, and to keep in touch with, and add
to our understanding of, the problems that emerged with the
notion in the first place. He does, that is, want to answer
Thrasymachus. On the other hand, it is clear that he cannot
answer these questions precisely as they were posed, for the
problems were raised over just *acts*, and Plato thinks that the
basic questions about justice have to be posed and answered in
terms of the just *agent*. As we have seen, a theory about the just
agent will have implications about just actions, but these will
no longer be the primary concern. Plato has not, then, changed
the subject, but he *has* changed the method of approach. He is
trying to replace the inadequate act-centred concept of justice,
held by people like Cephalus and Polemarchus, by a more
adequate theory, and he thinks that such a theory must be
agent-centred. In Book 1 we saw that Plato's targets are not
only moral sceptics like Thrasymachus who question the value

of justice, but also conventionally moral people like Polemarchus and his father. At the time it was not clear why these very different kinds of people should be attacked together. This is now rather clearer. Plato wants to replace the act-centred conception of justice precisely because it cannot provide a convincing answer to the obvious problems which leave people unsatisfied and lead them to moral scepticism. He cannot answer Thrasymachus properly without in the process showing what is wrong with the kind of view held by Cephalus and Polemarchus – and, indeed, by Glaucon and Adeimantus, whose particular moral conclusions are unimpeachable, but who lack any understanding of why they are, or why it is better to be this way rather than another.

Plato is thus trying to improve our understanding of justice in a way that involves throwing out, or at least drastically modifying, some of our beliefs about justice. We have seen something very similar in the case of justice in the state (see pp. 120–3); there too the focus is turned from outward behaviour to inner regulation, and there too Plato wants both to do justice to what is problematic about justice as we conceive it, and to show us that our conception is at many points importantly wrong. It is to some extent a matter of taste whether we say that he has changed the subject, or say that he has retained the subject but drastically changed the method of treating it.

We saw that in the case of justice in the state, the analogy sometimes drawn with scientific method and the way it revises our beliefs about the subjects of its discoveries, is useful up to a point but cannot be pressed. Plato's picture of the just agent is built on his account of character education and his moral psychology, which are, perhaps deliberately, quite untechnical; they involve only considerations which are accessible to all morally serious people. Plato is not claiming to revise our notion of justice because he has special expertise; he is revising it by pointing out to us facts which we see have a rational claim on us, though we may not have been aware of them, or their importance, before.

However, we should not be misled into thinking that the account offered is aimed at answering to everyday beliefs. For the account of justice is meant to be *explanatory*: Plato is trying to find a state which non-trivially explains its manifestations in just behaviour. A passage where this is clear is 590a–c, where he claims that various undesirable states, like licentiousness, obstinacy, weakness and baseness of spirit, 'have long been condemned' because they involve a forcible and unnatural ordering of the soul's parts. He does not mean that most people have been adopting his theory of the soul's parts and using it to condemn certain behaviour, rather that his theory explains why behaviour that is condemned is, in fact, rightly condemned.

Interpreters of the *Republic* have often stressed one side of Plato's account of justice at the expense of the other. Those who emphasize that Plato is trying to answer the moral scepticism of Thrasymachus often present him as a conservative trying to drag people back to the past and forcibly re-establish a moral consensus that had broken up. This ignores the great shift brought about by moving from an act- to an agent-centred approach; the attitude of the past, seen in people like Polemarchus, will no longer do. Others have stressed the revolutionary nature of some of Plato's proposals, and have presented him as totally changing the subject; but this obscures the fact that he does try to answer a challenge posed in traditional terms – 'Why should I refrain from unjust actions if I can get away with them?' Of course we may not think that Plato in fact succeeds. We may think that his proposals are either too conservative or too revisionary. But the *Republic* is best viewed as a magnificent balancing-act, an attempt to answer troubling problems about justice by providing an improved account of what justice is.

Let us try to apply this point more closely to the alleged fallacy of equivocation threatening the success of Plato's argument. Plato, it was said, was asked to defend ordinary justice, i.e. doing just acts and refraining from unjust ones, but what he did was to justify Platonic justice, i.e. having a rightly ordered soul; but this misses the point unless Platonic and ordinary justice are mutually entailing. Now we have seen that because Plato shifts from an act-centred to an agent-centred concept of justice, we cannot expect anything like an entailment between the two notions. We have to reject the idea that Socrates is either answering Thrasymachus in the latter's own terms, or changing the subject entirely. Rather, he wants to retain what he takes to be the central beliefs about justice and alter only the peripheral beliefs and the ones he takes to be false or misleading. This may seem a disappointingly messy way to proceed; it is tidier to hold that Plato has either committed a fallacy or not, either changed the subject or not. But the kind of account I have suggested answers much better to what Plato actually does in the first four books; they end with a revisionary account of justice as psychic harmony, which is then checked against our ordinary intuitions about justice. We shall see that the central books introduce new factors into the account of justice, but it is in the first four books that Plato makes the shift from justice as a matter of acts to justice as a state of the agent.

In the light of this shift, how does Plato regard ordinary justice? We have seen that it cannot be sufficient for Platonic justice; a conscientious performer of the acts required by justice may be a shallow conventional person with no inner harmony. Someone like Cephalus does his duty because he sees that, on the whole, it pays; but it is unintegrated with his deepest concerns, and regarded as compatible with a life dominated by the part of the soul which according to the account of Platonic justice is the lowest one, the one that should be most kept under control.

But if it is not sufficient, what role does it play? There are two respects in which ordinary justice plays a role in constraining the account of Platonic justice.

Firstly, Plato claims, emphatically, that the condition of having a just soul is created, fostered, and maintained by the doing of just actions – see 485d ff., 443d–444e, and 588e–591e. The analogue here is health: as healthy actions produce health, so doing just actions produces justice, and doing unjust actions produces injustice.

But there are two distinct issues here. One is the point that we become just by doing just actions. This is, in a way, a truism, though one that act-centred theories tend to ignore, and it is only stressed in agent-centred theories (like Aristotle's, for example). The other is the point of justification: will doing actions recognized as ordinarily just make you a Platonically just agent? But here the answer is no: for the question of what acts are ordinarily just, what duties one ought to do, is settled by society's moral consensus quite apart from considerations of what makes an agent Platonically just. Not only does following society's rules not suffice to make you a just agent; it might turn you into a cramped and rigid person incapable of the freely chosen and reasoned life that Plato will present as the just person's life. Not only does conscientiousness not guarantee virtue; it might fail to promote virtue, since virtue requires harmony and appropriate development of all the soul's parts, and that might well be stunted by a rigid adherence to rules, and a strong sense of their importance.

Secondly, Plato does appeal at the end of Book 4 to 'commonplace' judgements of what is ordinarily just, and claim that Platonic justice will meet them (442d–e). So he does think that ordinary justice constrains the content of Platonic justice. But it provides only a constraint, and of a rather negative kind at that; common beliefs are appealed to only on what is absolutely ruled out, not on what is either permissible or desirable. Plato trusts our intuitions only on clear-cut cases of what the just person will *never* do. We have seen already in Book 1 that they are likely to be untrustworthy on subtle or controversial cases. Ordinary justice, that is, not only is not sufficient for Platonic justice, but is not a good positive guide to its content, only a negative check on what the boundaries are.

It is interesting that Plato never argues for his assumption that beliefs about just acts can so much as provide a constraint on a theory about just agents. He takes it for granted that even the unenlightened do *know* that there are some things which it is *always* unjust to do, which even a product of Platonic education would never do. Now in a way this assumption is a very natural one to make. For an agent-centred theory that held that the right thing to do was what the good person would do, with no constraints at all on what kind of action this might be, would seem to be uncontrollably revisionary. Stoic moral theory is of this kind; it accepts the implication that there is then *no* kind of action ruled out from being the right thing to do if the good person sees reason to do it. Thus, even cannibalism and parricide might be the right thing to do. This leaves us feeling slightly dizzy – surely there must be *some* things that the good person would never do? Plato is not prepared to be as revisionary here as the Stoics were later to be. He allows that the just person would never do some kinds of thing which for a Greek represented utter wickedness (our examples would no doubt be different).

However, again there are two issues here. We can see why Plato thinks that there must be some constraints on an agent-centred theory, that we would feel lost if we thought that *any* kind of act whatsoever could be the right thing to do. But why is he so sure that the moral consensus of his own time is right about the examples he cites? How does he know that it really is unjust to commit adultery, merely because most people of his time feel strongly that it is? If there must be some constraints, why these?

Plato gives us no help here; he just assumes that these examples of moral consensus are all right to build on. He seems to be using here, without articulating it or being aware of the need for defence, an idea which we find much more developed in Aristotle. This is the idea that when constructing a moral theory about, say, justice, we have to begin with the most central judgements of the moral consensus we have grown up to accept; otherwise we have no ground to stand on. Morality is a matter of practical judgement, and a moral theory is not an abstract structure like a mathematical proof; it rests on people's acceptance of certain beliefs and their capacity to live with certain attitudes. Abstract considerations give us insufficient reason to throw out our most basic moral assumptions, because these are what we live by. This does not mean that a moral theory must end up justifying what we thought already; only that it cannot ignore our most central intuitions on important topics – a theory that does, like the Stoics', is likely to seem crazy. We can see from this that when Plato assumes the rightness of central points in existing moral consensus as a constraint on his own ideas about justice, there is nothing in this strategy guaranteeing that his theory will be conservative (it is far from that), only that it will have some claim to be realistic.

It may seem surprising that Plato is ready to allow empirical constraints on his theory of justice. Aristotle is quite happy to do so, but his approach is usually contrasted with Plato's very sharply. And in the central books we shall see that Plato puts forward an account of the procedures of philosophy, including moral philosophy, which sharply rejects any such appeal to experience as probative, or as a real constraint on the search for truth by pure reason. He talks there as though the true philosopher will attain complete truth about moral matters without relying on experience at all. He recommends a way of doing moral philosophy which has no interest in being realistic, or in answering to what people believe already.

But we must be careful not to confuse the ideal moral philosophy which Plato puts forward as the method of ideal philosophers in the ideal state, with the actual moral philosophy which he does in the *Republic*. Plato never claims that the *Republic* itself is an example of the perfect method of philosophy which he praises so highly. And so we must not underestimate the extent to which, in trying to change our way of looking at justice, he also wants to answer to what makes these problems real in people's experience. It is of course confusing that Plato uses one method while extolling another, even though he makes it clear that the method he extols is an ideal one which nobody has ever yet succeeded in putting into practice. (Aristotle is more consistent here; he rejects Plato's claims for the ideal method and defends the one he uses as the only legitimate method.) Many interpreters have been misled into thinking that because Plato recommends what looks like a purely *a priori* method of moral philosophy, therefore in his practice he is ready to ride roughshod over any existing intuitions however central. But we have seen that this is not so; his method steers between the extremes of conservatively justifying the status quo and boldly revising our basic ideas.

We have already seen one respect in which Platonic justice will revise our ideas about which actions are just: the Guardians' attitude to truth. We can see clearly from this that although Plato thinks that consensus about just actions shows that the ideally good person would never steal or commit adultery, he does not think that it shows that he or she would always tell the truth. The importance of truth in the Guardians' upbringing has been stressed. To be deceived is terrible; God hates falsehood and loves truth (382e). Later passages stress at length the Guardians' almost fanatical devotion to truth: 485c–d and 490a–d describe raptly how their souls will strive tirelessly for communion with what is true. And yet we have seen that they lie to the other citizens quite straightforwardly (see pp. 107–8, and 459c–460a). 389b–d states explicitly that the Guardians may lie to the others in their interests although it would be wrong for the others to lie to them. But there is not meant to be a contrast here; rather, it is because they are so keen on the truth, because they have natures that love it, that they can lie on occasion – for then it would be the right thing to do in the light of the whole of the truth. Plato is not urging the Guardians cynically to lie for the public good. Rather, he thinks that it is right for them to perform certain actions because of the kind of people they are. Because they are just, what they see fit to do will be right, even if it is also a case of lying. We are not to worry about their breaking the rules, because, when just people do this, the rules ought to be broken.

This example brings us to an aspect of agent-centred theories that may worry us. In allowing the Guardians to perform lying acts because they are truth-loving agents, Plato is licensing them to manipulate other people. The account of justice as a state of the agent seems to lead to violations of the dignity and perhaps rights of others. Now Plato holds the views he does about lying partly because of his beliefs about the inferiority of the others to the Guardians in intelligence. But even if we abstract from this, we are left wondering how an agent-centred account of justice can answer questions about the rights of others. If psychic harmony is deemed compatible with manipulative lying to others, then, even if consensus about ordinary morality provides some constraints on how the just person may treat others, we are left at the end of the day wondering whether after all Plato is on the right lines in his answer to Thrasymachus.

The Book 4 account of justice, then, will not do on its own as an answer to Thrasymachus. It has deepened our understanding of justice by insisting that what matters is not observance of external demands but the kind of person the just person is; what really matters is not what he or she does but why it is done, what the person's motivation is. But so far too much is left open; the more justice is presented as a state of the agent, an achievement of the individual, the less it seems to have to do with the rights of others and constraints on our behaviour towards them. In the central books Plato tries to provide what is missing in the Book 4 account – with what success we shall see.

The Book 4 account does, however, meet the first part of Glaucon's challenge: justice has been shown to be a state that is worth having for itself and not only its consequences. Health has good consequences, but we do not want to be healthy merely because of these: the difference between really being healthy and merely appearing to be is important to us because it is the difference between being in a stably functioning physical state and being in an upset and unstable state in which the various organs are interfering with one other's proper functioning and the whole person feels insecure. Justice is supposed to be analogous to health in these ways. Plato has at the very least shown that this kind of defence is possible. For as long as one tries to show that it benefits me to perform various duties, the task may seem hopeless: what do these various duties have to do with *me* and what *I* want out of life? The various actions commanded by conscience may seem to have no hold on me at all. But Plato has tried to show that justice is not a matter of external demands but answers to what I cannot help recognizing as my needs as a human being. Someone might perversely want a disordered soul, but they could hardly claim that this was a rational claim for a human being to make. If we disagree with Plato's claim that justice is the fulfilment of our human nature, it may turn out to be not so much that we think that this is the wrong way to recommend justice, as that we find his theory of human nature too unsubtle and monolithic, too insistent that the general claims of reason are always of more worth in a human life than the satisfaction of particular desires and attachments.

Plato will try to show, in Books 8 and 9, that justice also has good consequences, in particular that it makes the agent happy. The notion of happiness has not figured in the Book 4 argument at all; justice has not been presented as a state which is good to have because it will produce happiness, but simply as a state which is good to have. Health is worth having whether you are happy or not; for all we have seen so far, justice might be like that. In fact, while justice brings happiness (so the later books claim) its value to the agent is not dependent on this. This claim may sound strange to us, because we are used to utilitarian theories that try to make plausible the idea that people cannot but want their own happiness as their only final end, so that any condition, like that of being just, can only be of value to the agent as a means to his or her happiness. Even if we reject the cruder forms of utilitarianism, it is hard to shake off the assumption that if something is valuable to an agent, the agent's happiness must have something to do with it. But for him to be doing what he wants to do, Plato has to show first of all that justice is valuable to the agent without reference to the agent's happiness. What Plato is saying is less familiar to us from modern moral theories than from certain religions, which claim that it is valuable for an agent, not just to do or believe certain things, but to be a certain kind of person, and that this state has a kind of value ('spiritual value') which is independent of the agent's happiness. Such a state may be supposed to have good consequences, for example, in leading to eternal happiness, but these consequences are not what makes the state valuable to the agent; they are, for example, the wrong reason for pursuing it. But while this analogy is useful, it should not lead us to think of psychic harmony as static, or a state of rest and contentment. We shall see in the central books that the rule of reason in the soul is thought of as a state of hard intellectual work and effort: being just turns out to require being a philosopher.

FURTHER READING

The problem of Plato's 'fallacy of equivocation' was first posed sharply in D. Sachs, 'A Fallacy in Plato's *Republic*', *Philosophical Review* 1963. Many articles have since been written in reply, including: Demos, 'A Fallacy in Plato's *Republic*?' *Philosophical Review* 1964; Vlastos, 'Justice and Happiness in the *Republic*', in Vlastos (ed.), *Plato* 2; Kraut, 'Reason and Justice in Plato's *Republic*', in *Exegesis and Argument, Phronesis* Supplement 1; Sartorius, 'Fallacy and Political Radicalism in Plato's *Republic*', *Canadian Journal of Philosophy* 1974. My own article, 'Plato and Common Morality', *Classical Quarterly* 1978, gives an overview of the main lines on which the problem has been approached. See also Irwin, *Plato's Moral Theory*, ch. 7, sections 9–11.

Chapter 7

Plato's State

After having shown that justice is worth having for its own sake, Socrates is about to proceed to the demonstration that justice is worth having for its consequences too. But we do not get this till Books 8 and 9, for he is interrupted by Thrasymachus and Polemarchus, who reappear unconvincingly from Book 1 to demand a justification of the community of wives and children that had been casually mentioned at 423e–424a. Socrates obliges; what starts as a comparatively minor digression brings to the fore the ideal, impractical-seeming side of many of Plato's provisions for the state; and this raises the question of the feasibility of any of these provisions. This question is given a lengthy answer which leads to the claim that justice involves philosophical insight, a claim made in some of the *Republic*'s most famous passages. Before broaching these matters it is helpful to give an overall look at Plato's treatment of social, as well as individual, justice.

Books 5 to 7 are formally a digression from the main argument; Plato makes this point very insistently and we would be wrong to ignore it. But at once we run up against a problem, obscured by the fact that we are formally turning aside from the main argument. After trying to show that his account of justice in the individual person can meet the constraint of ordinary moral intuitions, Plato goes right ahead to discuss without warning proposals for communism of property and destruction of the nuclear family – proposals that he knew would outrage all his contemporaries. The contrast is very great; at 443 Socrates reassured his hearers that the Platonically just man would not do the commonly unjust act of committing adultery; but now we abruptly find that justice requires a communal way of life where 'adultery' has no application because there is no monogamous marriage. Why does Plato move so fast from honouring to flouting moral consensus? One answer is that the conclusion of Book 4 gave an account of justice in the individual, and that there Plato is concerned with human nature as it is; he wants his proposed account to be such as plausibly to have application in people's lives; whereas in Book 5, in talking of the state, he feels free to talk of idealized conditions where human nature is likewise idealized. He is not interested in 'partial compliance theory' or in adjusting actual difficulties and conflicts of interest. Several times in Book 5 he makes clear that in discussing various proposals he is simply skipping the matter of their practicability. He assumes that what is for the best is possible, this being the *ideal* state; and then considers all in one go the question of whether such a state is feasible at all (at 471c ff.).

Plato's political proposals are often misunderstood through being inflated. He is not trying to put forward a whole 'political philosophy' dealing with all matters important for the relation of individual and state. We have only a sketch of the ideally just city, presented in an unsystematic way; the bitty passage from 412b–427d gives us a basis for the account of the virtues, and the Book 5 passage (449a–471c) takes up only some of the points in it. Plato says so little about the city except in so far as concerns its justice, that we know virtually nothing about the citizens' way of life (a lack that has been filled in by different scholars in very different ways). One indication of this is that it is only from a single, very off-hand reference (433d) that we know that there are slaves. It seems extraordinary that Plato should not treat this as a matter even worth discussion; he assumes it as an economic fact of life not relevant to justice, the conditions for which only exist among free people who can shape their own lives. Plato presumably thinks this way because he is assuming normal Greek life as his background (a life in which the need for slaves was not questioned); Plato's ideally just state is not a full detailed picture of a Perfect City, but an implementation of what would be needed, in his view, to make existing cities just.

If we are cautious, and avoid the romantic and polemical embellishments that often mark discussions of 'Plato's political philosophy', the *Republic* can be seen to contain seminal (and very controversial) opening moves in many important political debates.

EQUALITY AND RIGHTS

Plato's society has offended and continues to offend many, because he is frankly and unapologetically inegalitarian. But there is no one simple way in which it is clearly true that all citizens either are or should be equal; so we have to look with some care at the ways in which people are unequal in Plato's state before pronouncing generally on his attitude to inequality.

The three classes, Guardians, Auxiliaries, and the productive class, live different kinds of life and have different education and upbringing. (Plato, though, is so uninterested in detail for its own sake that it is not really clear how much, if any, public education as he describes it is available for the producers.) Two things about this class system even in the abstract strike us as offensive.

Firstly, it is a difference not only in status but in an entire way of life. The producers presumably live normal family lives; the Guardians live communally without nuclear families or children. (For these purposes 'Guardians' includes Auxiliaries; the politically crucial divide is between the producers and those who control them.) The Guardians' education, being a total character-training, separates them in attitude, interests, tastes, and pursuits at every point from the producers. The latter are left within bounds to go their own way, whilst all the Guardians' activities, public and private, are focussed on a single end (519b–c; cf. 424a–425c). In spite of Plato's emphasis on the city's unity there is no common culture. The values of 'the city' are the values of the Guardians, and the producers, whose work supports them, do not share them; in fairness, they are not expected to make sacrifices for them or fight for them.

Secondly, the divide is one of absolute power. Right at the start the producers were forbidden to follow their desires against the city's interests (374b) and since then there have been references to the rulers using force and lying to maintain control. The producers can change jobs, but if they try to claim any kind of political power this is suppressed (434a–b). Plato is at least honest here; he says openly that the producers will lack freedom, *not* that they will be free in some 'higher' sense in which higher, perfect freedom is service to some higher, more informed will.

Now for a Greek the paradigm of lacking power while another has it, is being his slave, and Plato actually says that *in this respect* the producing class are slaves of the Guardians. A long later passage makes this clear (590c–d): We should be ruled by reason, and a man whose own reason is weak must be ruled by another's:

'Therefore, in order that such a man be ruled by a principle similar to that which rules the best man, we say he must be enslaved to the best man, who has a divine ruler within himself. It is not to harm the slave that we believe he must be ruled, as Thrasymachus thought subjects should be, but because it is better for everyone to be ruled by divine intelligence. It is best that he should have this within himself, but if he has not, then it must be imposed from outside, so that, as far as possible, we should all be alike and friendly and governed by the same principle.' (Grube.)

Plato says openly that the producers will, like slaves, lack all autonomy over their own lives. A slave cannot decide what to be or how to live or what goals are appropriate. Here we must refrain from thinking that this implies that the producers will be humiliated in melodramatic fashion, or interfered with in the details of day-to-day life. The Guardians are not interested in playing Big Brother. The producers' private thoughts and actions are of least, not most, importance in the state. We should think perhaps of an Athenian slave living apart from his master, who might well be comfortably off and run his own business without interference, indistinguishable on the surface from a free man. The crucial point was that he was not free to change his way of life, or to take important decisions that would displease his master.

Plato does, then, insist on the most extreme inequality of power that there could be. (In so doing, we should note, he has entirely divorced power from wealth; the powerless Productive Class own all the property and have all the money; cf. 416d–417b, 419e–420a.) But it is wrong to conclude right away that he is a monstrous totalitarian, or is justifying tyranny. His ideas are more interesting than that.

Firstly, the passage quoted shows that according to Plato even this extreme of being in another's power does not mean that the people cannot be 'friends'. (The Greek word *philoi* does not imply, as 'friends' does, personal liking, only a certain solidarity such as is normally felt in a common enterprise.) Why should the person powerless in Plato's state resent it? He or she is not capable of exercising political power and the rulers are; furthermore, they are so constituted that, trained as they are, they will never misuse their power. It is to the slaves' advantage to be ruled by someone who knows their own best interests, since they are incapable of recognizing what these are.

The obvious answer to this is that it is not in human nature not to resent being in another's power, regardless of whether this is recognized as being prudentially or morally the best thing. A person who did not so resent it would be lacking in a sense of self-respect and self-worth, and however well-off they were we would despise them, just as we despise Uncle Tom however sincere his lack of resentment at his position. Plato, although writing in a society that was highly conscious of the importance to the individual of self-assertion, still seems to think that those who are dominated because they are lacking in intelligence will be in a good state if they are 'friends' with the people who control the shape of their lives. He is not sensitive to the idea that all people, whatever their intellectual repertoire, have a capacity for self-respect and autonomy which is lost if they are so totally in someone else's power as to be their 'slave'. He does not see this loss on the part of the productive class as a degradation of something that potentially has worth – and to that extent he is writing off, as of no value, the capacity of the members of the productive class to run their own lives. He writes it off because they might not do it very rationally; they might make a mess of it, and others would do it for them in a more co-ordinated and effective way. He sees nothing to be gained in their doing it for themselves. He cannot see that anything of worth is lost when the highest moral attainment of the majority of his citizens – the only virtue that is distinctively theirs – is deference to their betters. Plato has been accused of treating the producers as 'human cattle', and this is not true; but they are in an important sense an oppressed class, because their lives are so structured that, while they contain variety of activity and no local interference, they contain no basis for self-respect.

This point leads us to the second. Plato has been accused of planning a 'caste state' and sanctifying privilege and oppression. But he does not think that any actual people should have the power that his Guardians have. Rather, the Guardians are to have power because they are wise, and the producers are to lack it because they are weak in reason. No-one is to have power merely by virtue of birth, only because of their aptitude. So Plato's endorsement of the Guardians' absolute power is conditional on there being any people who are wise – and he means *ideally* wise, the people who are both naturally fitted to rule and are the products of a long education such as he has described. 'Those who are wise should have absolute power over those who are not' does not imply that anyone should have absolute power, unless they really are ideally wise people, given that the world is as it is. So he is not advocating drastic in-equalities of power in the real world, only saying that the ideally just society demands them.

Plato has muddied his own argument here, and called forth much unnecessary polemic, by his further claim that the qualities on the basis of which power should be unequally distributed are mostly inherited, and by his elaboration of eugenic proposals. This is unfortunate in many ways. It makes the class system look like a simple-minded practical proposal, rather than a claim about what the ideal society would require; and it leads people (including Aristotle) to ask unanswerable questions about how it is to work. The questions are unanswer-able because there is not enough background to settle them, and because Plato is unsure what to ascribe to heredity and what to environment and training. Sometimes the system looks meritocratic: children are to be brought up according to aptitude regardless of their class of origin (415b–c, 423c–d). But it is obvious that Plato believes that on the whole the classes will 'breed true'. Unfortunately this is partly based on the false belief that acquired characteristics can be inherited, since he thinks each generation's upbringing will improve the natures of the next (424a). Book 5 contains a down-to-earth (not to say brutal) eugenic programme; but it is very odd. What the breeders' aim ought to be, surely, is intelligence, since it is reason that makes for the gulf between Guardians and others. But in fact Plato breeds for brawn, not brains; it is courage in battle, not proving theorems, that wins extra sex so that 'good specimens' will improve the 'herd'. The repellent stock-breeding talk is irrelevant to the basis of the class system. We do best to ignore the confused eugenics and regard the class system as an abstract expression of the idea that social justice requires that the wise have absolute power over the less gifted. It is not a blueprint for existing societies to use to justify existing inequalities, or bring about related inequalities by making the existing system more meritocratic. It has application only in the idealized conditions of the perfectly just society.

It is easy to see why Plato thinks that such extreme inequalities of power are justified: unless the Guardians had control over the others, they could not run the city as they saw best; so reason would not rule in the city and it would not be just. But even allowing for the sake of argument that this is true, can these inequalities allow the citizens to be happy? And do they not violate the rights of the majority?

Plato thinks that the inequalities are compatible with all being 'friends' – so life is not to be soured by invidious privileges. But he gives the citizens' happiness little thought. If all goes well in the whole city, then 'we must leave it to nature to provide each group with its share of happiness' (421c). He sees a problem only with the happiness of the *rulers*; one to which we shall return. He does not concentrate, as we would, on individual happiness; he thinks instead of the happiness appropriate to one as a member of a certain class.

But if some are the slaves of others do they not lack any rights? Plato has no word corresponding to 'rights'; so though we can ask the question we must do so carefully.

Quite generally, if I have a right to something, then I am protected in having it, or doing it, by some moral or legal sanction; no-one may interfere with my freedom to do or have it, even if such interference would promote some desirable end. Some rights are uncontroversially created by legal or social convention; interesting and disputed questions arise about rights when they are not backed up by existing sanction but are held to belong to people whether this is recognized or not. Such rights are typically connected with *equality*: they belong equally to all, unlike rights created by legal or social convention which apply only to those recognizing that convention. Are there any rights which all people equally have? More narrowly: in Plato's state, are there any rights which all the citizens equally have simply because they are citizens? (This is more manageable than the former question, since Plato does not think that there are rights which all have merely by virtue of being human; cf. 470c–471b.) By now it is clear that the answer is: in a sense, yes, and in a sense, no. All have equal rights in that there is no arbitrary discrimination, no unfairness due to lack of impartiality. The Guardians are not exploiters; the producers have a right to those benefits from the common workings of society which are needed for them to function best in making their contribution to the common good. If any class is exploited it is the Guardians, for it turns out that they would find greatest fulfilment in doing things which they do not have a right to spend their time doing. It should be stressed, because it is often implicitly denied, that all classes are protected in freely having and doing what is necessary for them best to fill their social role – and this by no means implies uniformity of individual needs and tastes.

But there is no substantive equality in the *Republic* over and beyond impartiality. Most of the citizens, because they are taken to lack the rational capacity to organize their lives in their own and society's best interests, are put totally under the control of those who do have this capacity. The Guardians are not constrained by a constitution, bill of rights, or code of laws – the function of laws is to put the Guardians' plans into practical operation, not to serve as checks on them. The only constraint on the Guardians' treatment of others is their disinterested moral character; when the character-training fails, the result is that the majority are enslaved in the worst fashion (547b–c), the process not being hindered by any institutional check. We are likely to think that Plato is both too pessimistic in thinking that human nature is so unequally gifted in reason, and too optimistic in thinking that those who are so gifted could be so disinterested as to rule well with no external sanctions on their rule. But even if we agreed with him on both of these points, we would still miss any sense that all are equal in respect of human worth, whatever their intellectual or practical attainment. Most of the citizens in Plato's state have no rights if that is taken to mean that there are constraints on people's behaviour based on common humanity, not contributions to the common good. Theories of equality and human rights are grounded on the claim that there are some rights which all have equally, just because we are all equally human, and which are not gained or lost by virtue of rationality or moral goodness or social contribution. There are some things that cannot be done to people, however wicked or useless, because humans are 'ends in themselves', in Kant's phrase, and not things to manipulate. Human beings have a special kind of value which all have equally just because it does not vary with talent or excellence. Such ideas are no doubt vague, but we have a clear enough notion of them and their import to worry at their total absence in Plato's state. Even if we believed, with Plato, that there is no need to worry about what the Guardians will do to the others, still it is disturbing that in the state there are no rights which *antecedently* limit what may be done to people in the interests of producing either efficiency or morality.

FRATERNITY AND UNITY

Plato offends us by the extreme divisions in the state; ironically, he also offends us by his insistence on the degree of unity the state must have. The difficulty here is resolved by the fact that, especially in Book 5, the extraordinary measures to create unity apply only to the Guardian class; the state's unity depends on the unity of this class (465b, 545d–e).

Unity has already been stressed (pp. 103–5); in Book 5 unity is stressed, not as a contingent advantage, nor, explicitly, as constitutive of what a state is, but as a city's greatest good (462a–b). In fact, it is so great a good that to ensure it the Guardians are denied nuclear families and private lives. They live, eat, and train communally; at intervals they mate (this seems the best word for it) and the children are brought up in communal crèches and nurseries. These measures do not spring from modern preoccupations with the tensions of the nuclear family (though cf. 465b–c). With optimism about the possibilities of human nature so extreme as to be impressive, Plato justifies them as increasing the whole state's unity. Guardians will regard all contemporaries as siblings, and all of an age to be fathers and mothers as parents. Emotions now tied to individuals will be spread over society; time and energy will not be uselessly spent in petty competition and duplicating effort (cf. 464c–d). 'Privatization' of feelings of pleasure and pain breaks up the city's unity, whereas if all think of the same things as 'mine' all will be happy or sad together (462c, 463c–464a). The best city is the one most closely resembling an individual, which suffers when one of its members does, just as the whole person suffers pain when his or her finger hurts. (462c–d).

These statements, especially the last, have led many to ascribe to Plato an 'organic theory of the state': the idea that the state is itself a kind of organic entity, a super-individual, while individual people are merely its parts with no genuine separate life of their own. This often goes with claims that Plato's state foreshadows certain kinds of totalitarianism and fascism which regard individuals as incomplete parts of a higher unity, the state, in serving which they find their only true self-fulfilment.

But again we must make distinctions before rushing into condemnation. Plato does undeniably subordinate individual interests to the common good; but this is not an entity over and above the varying kinds of goodness of the varying kinds of people. The state is nothing over and above the people making it up, or rather it is the context in which different kinds of people can attain the excellence appropriate to them. Similarly the city's happiness is just the happiness of all the citizens. When Plato contrasts the happiness of the whole city with other happiness, the contrast is always the happiness of one class in it, not the happiness of all the citizens (419e–421c). Indeed, he thinks that *if* all the citizens were made happy in an inappropriate way, then so would the city be (420e). Later (519e–520a) it is repeated that the happiness of the city (as opposed to that of one class) precisely consists in all the citizens' mutually sharing the benefits they can bring.

But has not Plato's whole argument in the long parallel treatment of state and soul assumed that the city has its characteristics and virtues in its own right – that 'the city is brave' precisely does not reduce to 'there are brave citizens in it', but is a fact about *the city* and its internal structure?

Two points are relevant here. Firstly, even if the state is a brave, wise, etc. entity, this does not make it an *organic* entity. City and person are structurally similar, which is why it is illuminating to *compare* the city to a person (cf. 462c–d). We may fault the comparison and think that it misleads Plato (as Aristotle does, at *Politics* II, 1–6, in complaining that Plato aims at a degree of unity inappropriate for a state and proper only to an individual). But a state that can be effectively compared to a person is not being thought of as itself a kind of person; the comparison would fall through for lack of two different kinds of thing to compare.

Secondly, although Plato does insist that the state is brave, wise, etc. in its own right, and can legitimately be a subject for such predications, this commits him neither to the substantive metaphysical claim that the state is an entity *distinct from* the citizens making it up, nor to the substantive political claim that the city as a whole has interests that take precedence over the interests of the citizens. Modern political theories have debated both these issues extensively, but Plato does not raise them, and does not even seem aware of them. He clearly subordinates individual desires and interests to the common good, but the common good is just the collective harmonization of the desires and interests that individuals ought to have, those they would have if they were 'doing their own'. There is no *further* common good imposed on the citizens once all are doing their own. And, while he raises questions about whether there are entities distinct from anything we can experience (the Forms), he does not suggest anywhere that the city might be such an entity. There is no room in Plato's metaphysics for the city as an entity distinct from all the citizens.

We may well find a gap here. If the state's moral qualities belong to it in its own right, and are not reducible to those of its citizens, then there surely is a genuine problem about its metaphysical status. Plato does not want the state to be a Form, that is, one of the entities he does think are distinct from what we experience. But if it is not a Form, and yet not just a collection of individuals (since it has qualities in its own right), what *is* the state? We can easily see how the *Republic* suggests a theory of the state as an entity distinct from the citizens, and perhaps an organic entity. All the same, it does not contain such a theory.

Plato does not sacrifice individuals to a reified State. But we have seen that he does not hesitate to sacrifice the needs and interests of actual people to those of the ideal individuals of his theory of human nature. He began by setting up the state as a mechanism for bringing it about that all the natural needs of human nature, in its different forms, would be harmoniously fulfilled. But he ends up imposing on people demands that most of them will see as externally sanctioned and not fulfilling their nature as they see it. We have gone from an attractive picture of the co-operative fulfilment of joint needs to a much darker picture in which all are compelled to join in fulfilling needs which most of them do not recognize as their actual needs. The villain here seems to be Plato's belief that only a few have the qualities necessary for excellence, so that rational attainment of excellence will involve forcing most people to go along whether they like it or not.

WOMEN'S PLACE

The most shocking suggestion in Book 5 to Plato's contemporaries (and to Plato scholars until very recently) is the proposal that women should be Guardians. This is not just a product of the 'community of wives and children', which would have been entirely possible without making the women Guardians; and it is often thought to be a feminist proposal ahead of its time, an affirmation of women's rights, and a protest against their subordination, not to be taken up until Mill's *The Subjection of Women*. In fact it is not: if we look at the proposals we see illustrations of the points discussed above, for Plato's interest is neither in women's rights nor in their preferences as they see them, but rather with production of the common good, and a state where all contribute the best they can according to their aptitude. This, he thinks, will best fulfil women's natures – but not their natures as *they* perceive them.

Athenian women in Plato's day led suppressed and powerless lives. They were not legal persons; an heiress, for example, passed with the property to her nearest male relative, who was expected to marry her to preserve the family estate. Respectable women were kept in a separate part of the house, and never went out (even shopping was done by men) except on festivals. They saw no men other than their nearest male relatives, and husbands; they had virtually no interaction with the social, political, and romantic life of men. Women were not even men's primary sex-objects; what we think of as a man's 'love-life' and 'sex-life' centred on young boys, whose social and psychological life he could share, whereas he would share virtually no interests with his wife. Seldom have the sexes been so segregated in every aspect of life, or women relegated to such a marginal and passive role. Plato's proposal that the sexes share the same way of life is truly revolutionary. It is the point at which he goes furthest in claiming that ideal justice would require society to be unimaginably different from the existing society. Yet Plato's proposals are not aimed at relieving the misery and humiliation of women forced to live such an appalling life. The present set-up is said to be 'contrary to nature' not because it is thought of as intolerably warping people's lives, but because women could, in Plato's view, contribute to the common good as men do, even though as things are they achieve little. Plato's whole argument depends on the claim that the nature of women does not demand that women have different occupations from men (453e–455a). Socrates reminds his hearers that they had accepted that each person should do the job they are fitted for by nature. But the only natural differences between men and women are biological (454d–e): the male begets, the female gives birth. And this is not a relevant difference for determining occupation, any more than baldness is relevant to whether someone should become a cobbler.

This is an admirable argument as far as it goes; for Plato has removed any possibility of treating women as inferior *as a class*, and for disregarding the merits of an individual just because she is a woman. But the argument suffers from being too generally stated. What *does* count as a relevant difference in nature? We are entitled to ask this, since so much hangs on it, and since biological differences have been honestly thought relevant to aptitude for doing some jobs. But it is not clear what Plato would answer; he is relying on a very general and *a priori* theory of human nature rather than respecting actual facts about people. He never points to the unhappiness caused by the low status of women in his day (he thinks of the effect of freeing women from seclusion as liberating the *man*, 465b–c).

It is obvious from the references to women in his writings that he has a low opinion of women as they are, and thinks them capable neither of liberating themselves nor of having opinions worth considering.

Nor is Plato concerned with women's rights; as we have seen, he lacks the notions of equal human worth and dignity that stand behind theories of human rights. He sees women merely as a huge untapped pool of resources: here are half the citizens sitting at home wasting effort doing identical trivial jobs! The state will benefit if women do public, not private jobs (if this does not flout nature, as it does not). Benefit to the state is the sole, frequently repeated ground for the proposals (456c, 457a,b,c, 452d–e).

This is important, since it means that the proposals have nothing to do with women's freedom to choose their own way of life. Plato would feel justified in compelling them to serve the state, rather than their families, even against their will (the issue does not arise in the *Republic*, but it is admitted at *Laws* 780a–c). And if the state could for any reason no longer be benefited by the contribution of women, there would be no reason not to push them back into the home. (Again, this does not arise in the *Republic*, but later, in the *Laws*, where Plato no longer thinks that *anyone* can serve the common good disinterestedly, as is demanded of the Guardians, he shows no compunction in submitting women to all but a few contemporary modes of repression; see *Laws* 780–781, 804–6, 813–14.) Moreover, we should notice that even in the *Republic* the proposals are limited to Guardian women; Plato sees no need to improve the lives of the producer-class women, who can make no distinctively useful contribution to the common good. And he sneers at the prospect of equality between the sexes in any actual society as corrupting the natural hierarchy (563b). He does not, then, think that it is wrong in itself for women to be subjected to men, only that under ideal conditions it constitutes an irrational waste of resources. No feminist could be happy with an argument implying that there is nothing wrong with any actual society that oppresses women.

And the proposals have two further defects.

Firstly, Plato combines his argument with a belief that even under ideal conditions women are not as good as men. At

455a–d he argues that there are no occupations for which only women are fitted, because men are better at them all, even women's traditional preserves like cooking. Men are better equipped mentally and physically, and can beat women in all fields (455a). (He does allow that not all men are better than all women.) This is an insulting way to claim that there are no specifically female competences. And Plato never even argues that there are no specifically *male* competences, though he claims this (455d). The argument is incomplete: it is left open for an opponent to claim that even if men and women can naturally do the same things, men are always better at them, so that in a state with such a premium on excellence men will still take all the front-rank positions, and women, while they will not always come bottom, will bring up the rear. This is not an argument that springs from serious consideration of women's talents and capacities.

If we take into account the previous argument against judging all women inferior as a class just because they are women, then Plato might be envisaging a few exceptional females even if most women are inferior to men in intelligence, character, and tastes (and Plato believes this; he accepts and even exaggerates offensive contemporary sexist stereotypes. Cf. 469d, 431b–c, 563b, 557c; *Cratylus* 392b–d; *Timaeus* 42b–e, 90–91a.) But in fact Plato does not stress this possibility. He does once later (540c) include women amongst the front rank of Guardians, and twice (454d, 455e) suggests that they could be doctors. Otherwise he envisages them only in traditional nurturing roles (460b) and as soldiers. By far the bulk of his references to women Guardians concern fighting and athletic training (452a–b, 453a, 458d, 466c–d, 467a, 468d–e). In this he is following the initial metaphor of watchdogs that introduced the discussion (451d): female dogs live like the males, except for breaks for giving birth; why is this not the case with humans? Aristotle objects in the *Politics* that the analogy is not apt because animals don't have to do housework; but we need not go that far to find something unsatisfactory with the metaphor (see pp. 80–2). Plato is confused. As with the eugenic proposals, he argues vigorously, but for the wrong thing. Physical training is not what distinguishes the Guardians (in the *Laws* women train, but this makes no impact on their low status). What Plato should be arguing for is what he once recognizes at 540c: sex is irrelevant to the highest intellectual and moral studies, and women can take their rightful place as equals with men in a society where virtue and all excellence is attained in challenging and co-operative study and there is no premium on aggression and pushiness. In most of Book 5 Plato disappointingly forgets this, and spends his time claiming, irrelevantly and grotesquely, that women can engage in fighting and other 'macho' pursuits nearly as well as men.

IS THE IDEAL STATE POSSIBLE?

The discussion of the more outrageous proposals brings to the surface, at 471e, the issue that can no longer be postponed: can the ideal state be realized in practice? Opinions differ about this perhaps more violently than about any other issue. The *Republic* was 'meant by its author not so much as a theoretical treatise, but as a topical manifesto' – Popper, *The Open Society and its Enemies*, vol i, p. 153. 'These are not so much the machinations of a totalitarian monster as the dreams of an impractical theorist.' – Guthrie, *History of Greek Philosophy*, vol. iv, p. 469.

Plato does waver on this issue; but that is because the *Republic* does not have a single aim. It answers the question, whether justice is worth *my* while; but it also pictures the ideally just state. Doing the latter seems pointless if it is avowedly impracticable; but an ideal of justice is none the worse for being non-realizable in practice if its purpose is to inspire the individual person to be as just as he or she can be. At 472a–e, and right at the end of Book 9, the end of the main argument, Socrates says that it does not matter if the just society is an unattainable ideal, as long as it does serve as an ideal for the just person to try to realize in his or her life. None the less, throughout Books 5 and 6, he argues at length that the just society *could* come about – cf. 502c: it is hard but not impossible. Evidently he thinks that his political ideal is discredited, whatever its value for personal virtue, if it can be shown to be hopelessly impracticable. Plato wants us to read the *Republic* not as an enjoyable fantasy, but as something to affect how we live, and for this he has to show that the just city, the society of good people, is not impossible *in principle*. He does not have to show more than that; it is not, for example, necessary for him to have detailed advice as to how to go about it.

The task is all the same hard, for the just state is not brought about by progressive legal reform, but only by a total change in people's hearts and minds, such as needs a long training to produce. Because Plato downgrades so much the role of institutions in producing a just state, and emphasises exclusively the need for the rulers to have characters of a certain kind, he is in a bind. The just state can only be brought about by just people, but just people are the products only of a just state, such as nowhere actually exists. (This is brought out even more by the insistence that the just ruler must be a philosopher, even though we have yet to see quite how unusual a philosopher would be.)

One reasonable response to this would be gradualism: *we*, being products of an imperfect state, cannot produce a *perfectly* just state, but we can try to improve what we have and hand on our reforms to a progressively better educated generation. Plato rejects this move entirely. The just man in a bad society, he thinks, can *only* save his own soul (496a–497a); he is not called on to improve the lot of others. Plato never argues for this. Presumably he thinks that his reforms are so drastic that tinkering will never produce them, and might produce more harm than good. He rests his hope on breaking into the circle: perhaps somewhere, some time, a just man *might* arise even in an unjust society (502a–c) and have the power to stop tinkering and start afresh (500e–501c), even if this means the desperate step of taking over only the under-tens, to bring them up under an education that will make them just (541a). It is sometimes thought that Plato had in mind, in his picture of the miraculously virtuous tyrant, a particular ruler who decided to become a philosopher, Dionysius II of Syracuse (at least in the very tainted tradition that comes to us in the pseudo-Platonic *Letters*). But this is highly unlikely, and would spoil the point: Plato has at most to show that the philosopher ruler is *possible* in principle, not that one will shortly come along. In fact he does not think it likely that any will come along in the foreseeable future, since the truly just and intelligent person is the most likely to be corrupted by society (494a–495b; again Plato is talking about what is likely, and nothing at all is gained by supposing him to have an actual person like Alcibiades in mind, as some romantically suppose).

The more Plato stresses (as he does in Book 6) the philosopher ruler's unique blend of all possible intellectual and moral gifts, developed to their fullest pitch (484–487), the less plausible it is that he or she could exist anywhere but as a result of upbringing in the ideal state. Plato can show only that it is possible in principle, though practically unlikely, to break into the circle. The just state remains more effective as an ideal to stimulate virtue in individuals than as a blueprint for any real society. We find here, unnoticed explicitly by Plato, a divergence between justice in the state and justice in the individual – a respect in which the uniform account he wants breaks down. For while perfectly just people can exist only in the ideally just state, and the ideally just state can exist only when people are perfectly just, the effect of this is not the same on social and individual justice. Plato seems on the whole reconciled to leaving the just state as an ideal, whereas he wants individuals actually to improve by reading the *Republic* and using it as an ideal to which to conform themselves. This suggests that while for him justice in the state is an all-or-nothing affair, individual justice *is* a matter of degree: one can be more or less just, and can improve gradually. In allowing this Plato is making another concession to common sense, which holds that justice, and goodness, in people is a matter of degree. It was left for the Stoics, bolder than Plato, to insist that justice in the person too is an all-or-nothing affair: either you are perfectly just or you are not just at all.

One final important point. The knowledge required in the philosopher ruler, absence of which makes existing states go badly, is *practical* knowledge. The ruler is like a skilled pilot (488a–489a) or a doctor (489b–c; cf. 382c–d; 389b–d) as opposed to current rulers who are like an animal-keeper who has learned only through experience how to cope with his animal's moods (493a–e). Now a pilot or doctor needs intelligence and rationality, but theirs are practical skills developed in experience. The analogies suggest (plausibly enough) that the rulers will be people with practical wisdom and experience. When we turn to Plato's account of what their knowledge is, we are in for a surprise.

FURTHER READING

Much has been written on Plato's political theory, often intemperately.

The earliest criticism is Aristotle, *Politics* II, 1–6 (often surprisingly crass and literal-minded, much below Aristotle's best).

In the twentieth century Plato has often been attacked as a precursor of totalitarianism. Cf. Russell, 'Plato and Politics'; Crossman, *Plato Today*; and Popper, *The Open Society and its Enemies*, vol i. These 'liberal-democrats' are attacked, sometimes effectively, by R. Barrow in *Plato, Utilitarianism and Education*, a vigorous but philosophically undisciplined defence of some of Plato's ideas. Bambrough (ed.), *Plato, Popper and Politics* is a collection of articles relevant to the Popper controversy.

A brief article by Versenyi, 'Plato and his Liberal Opponents', *Philosophy* 1971, distinguishes substantive issues of moral philosophy from disputes about cognitivism in ethics; the issues are confused in much of the above literature.

The issue of Plato's alleged 'organic theory of the state' is excellently discussed in J. Neu, 'Plato's Analogy of State and Individual: The *Republic* and the Organic Theory of the State', *Philosophy* 1971.

Much the best discussion of Plato's theory of justice (to which this chapter is very indebted) is Vlastos, 'The Theory of Social Justice in the *Republic*', in H. North (ed.), *Interpretations of Plato*, and forthcoming as part of a larger work on Plato's theory of justice.

Specific issues

Plato's proposals about women have produced much good recent work, including Wender, 'Plato: Misogynist, Paedophile and Feminist', *Arethusa* 1973; Calvert, 'Plato on Women', *Phoenix* 1975; Okin, 'Philosopher Queens and Private Wives', *Philosophy and Public Affairs* 1977. My article, 'Plato's *Republic* and Feminism', *Philosophy* 1976, is helpfully criticized in Lesser, 'Plato's Feminism', *Philosophy* 1979. My account of the position of women in ancient Athens may be found controversial, but there can be no doubt that, although working-class women (perforce) led free lives, the ideal of female behaviour was a life sharing virtually no activities with men. See Dover, *Greek Popular Morality in the time of Plato and Aristotle*, and his excellent *Greek Homosexuality*, which gives a chilling picture of what we would call 'gender roles' in ancient Athens.

Issues of eugenics and population policy are discussed in a special issue of *Arethusa*, vol. 8, no. 2, Fall 1975, including Mulhern, 'Population and Plato's *Republic*', and Fortenbaugh, 'Plato: Temperament and Eugenic Policy'.

Plato's readiness to sacrifice actual individuals' wants to their ideal, enlightened wants is illuminated by three excellent discussions of a related topic, Plato's conception of the individual as object of certain attitudes of love and attachment: Vlastos, 'The Individual as Object of Love in Plato', *Platonic Studies*; Kosman, 'Platonic Love' in Werkmeister (ed.), *Facets of Plato's Philosophy*, *Phronesis* Supplement 2; Nakhnikian, 'Love in Human Reason' in *Midwest Studies in Philosophy*, vol. iii.

Chapter 8

Belief, Knowledge, and Understanding

After having claimed that the ideally just state will only come about when a ruler arises who is (through being a philosopher) just in the actual world (473c–d), Plato gives a long argument to show that it is knowledge that marks off philosophers from other people: this ends Book 5. For most of Book 6 he argues that philosophers are the best equipped, by nature and achievements, to rule: the fact that the proposal strikes most people as ludicrous is due to the fact that the influences of society make existing philosophic natures either ineffective or warped. Then Plato takes up again the issue of what it is about the philosophers' knowledge that makes it suitable to guide the state (504a ff.). Only they have the understanding that comes from knowing the nature of the good; Socrates himself does not claim to know this, but indicates its nature by the famous figures of Sun, Line, and Cave (which run over the division between Books 6 and 7). The rest of Book 7 discusses the kind of further education necessary for those who are to attain this understanding. When we return, in Book 8, to the main argument about justice, we have learnt much that we would not otherwise have suspected from Book 4 about the rule of reason in the soul that is required by psychic harmony. Reason's functions derive from its capacity to *know* what is right; and Books 5–7 show us that this knowledge is harder to come by, and less tied to the agent's own interests, than we might have thought.

The three central books contain some of the most famous and difficult passages in Plato, and we will have to separate and discuss four important issues (in this and the next three chapters): (1) What is it to have knowledge, and how does it differ from merely being right? (2) What are the 'Forms' that

Plato mentions in his argument? (3) What is the understanding of the good that is depicted in Sun, Line, and Cave? And (4) what is 'dialectic', the philosopher's kind of reasoning that according to Plato is required by the search for truth? It is vital, in considering these issues, not to tear passages out of context; for while they are fascinating in their own right, they are there as parts of the attempt to answer the overall question, what kind of knowledge must one have to be truly just?

Reason's rule in the soul has been characterized by its judging on behalf of the whole soul, and its impelling the person to search for truth. Now we find that it involves *knowing* what is right, for the just person, who to be a just ruler must be a philosopher, is distinguished from non-philosophers by knowledge. However, a little thought shows that reason would be ineffective at its two other tasks if it did not know what was the case, and the right thing to do; so this is not surprising. What, however, is *knowing*? It is more than just being right, or having a true belief, though what this difference is, is one of the recurring puzzles of philosophy. In the *Republic* there are two attempts at solving it.

In Book 10, 601b–602b, the difference is elucidated by reference to *use*. In the case of anything that can be made and used, the skill of making it will be different from the skill of using it. (Plato assumes here that they will be found in different people, but this is not necessary.) The maker has true beliefs about the making of flutes or bridles, but only the flute-player or horseman has knowledge about them, because only he has experience of the qualities that make a thing good or bad for its appropriate use (601d–e). The user's knowledge of what makes a thing good or bad for use is the source of the true beliefs that the maker has about how to construct it.

This passage does not pretend to give a general characterization of knowledge: the distinction is made *en passant* in an argument about something else. But we can see more general principles on which Plato is relying. Knowledge involves an experience which is, in some sense, direct, by contrast with which belief is, or can be, second-hand. (But there is nothing mysterious about this directness; it comes from close 'acquaintance' with the subject-matter in a quite ordinary sense.) Knowledge also involves the articulate ability to say what the known item is, and why it is the way it is; and this involves knowing what makes for its goodness or badness. True belief need involve none of this. This is, Plato claims (601d) not only the case with artefacts but is true of 'living things and actions', though it is not clear how 'use' is to be extended to these.

Knowledge, then, is *an improvement on true belief*. Similar accounts are given elsewhere in Plato, at *Theaetetus* 200–201 and *Meno* 97–8, though in both of them the notion of goodness is not explicitly mentioned. The *Theaetetus* suggests that knowledge may be 'true belief with an account' and the *Meno* suggests that having 'reasoning about the cause' may render true belief stable enough to amount to knowledge: both make prominent notions that we should render by something like 'explanation'. (In neither dialogue does Plato come up with a successful account of knowledge, but he does not conclude that an account of a totally different form must be offered.) Such suggestions are in two respects like modern theories that represent knowledge as true belief plus justification, or plus the right causal route to the object of knowledge. They take it that we have a going conception of true belief, and ask what improvement to this would constitute knowledge. And they also take it that the improved state will be a state improved with regard to the very same things that the unimproved state is concerned with: flutes, bridles, or whatever. (The *Theaetetus* mentions the witnessing of a crime, and the *Meno* mentions the road to Larisa.)

There are, however, important disanalogies with modern theories. Plato does not regard as being at all important some distinctions that bear much weight in modern analyses: the differences between *knowing that*, *knowing how*, and *knowing an object*. For him, knowing (and applying) certain truths about flute-playing is just part of knowing how to play the flute, the whole being regarded as 'having knowledge of the flute'. If his concerns answer to a stress on any one of our 'knowing' idioms, it is *knowing what*: for we shall see that he associates knowledge with knowing what a thing is, knowing its essential properties. Most important, the kind of improvement over true belief that knowledge constitutes is not one familiar from the post-Cartesian tradition. It is not an increase in certainty, or a relief from doubt. Knowledge is not opposed to scepticism. The craftsman's beliefs are true, and fine as far as they go; Plato never suggests that they might be false, or that we should try doubting them. The user's state is better than the maker's, not because he is more sure of anything, but because he has understanding of the subject-matter and its point in a way that the maker lacks. The maker's beliefs are inferior, not because they are or might be false, but because they proceed from a state that lacks any understanding of *why* they are true, and can give no explanation of them; indeed, some of them might be false for all the maker knows, even if they are not such that either he or we could doubt them.

So it is understanding, and not certainty, that is the mark of knowledge, and the person with knowledge is contrasted not with the sceptic but with the person who, for practical purposes, takes over true beliefs in an unreflective and second-hand way. It is important to bear this in mind in the analysis of Plato's longer, complex distinction of knowledge from belief in Book 5 (474b–480a). Plato's approach to knowledge here differs from the Book 10 account in two respects.

Firstly, whereas in Book 10 it was assumed that we found comprehensible already what true belief was, and then looked for the improvement on this that would give us knowledge, in Book 5 we begin with our intuitions about knowledge, and it is belief that is the problematic item. This means that here Plato avoids the persistent problems that dog attempts to define knowledge as improved true belief. For these tend to founder on the fact that examples can systematically be constructed which fit the definitions but conflict with our intuitions about knowledge – which seem more trustworthy than the definitions.

Secondly, whereas the improvement-on-true-belief kind of account tries to improve the knower's relation to the objects of his or her true belief, Book 5 argues that the objects of true belief are *distinct* from those of knowledge. Perhaps no other Platonic thesis has caused such controversy. For if items of knowledge can never be objects of belief, and vice versa, then the philosopher will live in a different cognitive world from other people. This is sometimes called Plato's 'two-worlds' view about the objects of knowledge: those who have knowledge are not in a better state than the rest of us about the world we share, but have moved on to something different, and the world of people and actions that we experience can never be *known*.

Now even before looking at the argument we find it *prima facie* odd that an object of belief can never be an object of knowledge. For a start, it violates our intuition that the same thing can be first believed and then known, that coming to know is not changing the subject. (In fact Socrates is made to say that he has mere beliefs about the Forms, which are 'officially' objects only of knowledge; 506b–c; cf. 505b–c.) More importantly, it runs up against what we expect, given the main moral argument of the *Republic*. The Guardians are the truly just people who are able to direct others who lack knowledge of what is right and best for them. How can the Guardians' knowledge be relevant to doing this, if its objects belong to a different world from the world of objects of belief? On many interpretations of the Book 5 argument, Plato's epistemology comes out conflicting uncomfortably with his ethical theory: if the just person's search for knowledge is to lead to a different cognitive world from that inhabited by the likes of us, then that search becomes an exercise in glorious self-frustration; knowledge turns out to be irrelevant to the problems that inspired the search for knowledge in the first place. We shall see, however, that, carefully interpreted, Book 5's thesis that knowledge and belief have distinct objects does not in itself commit Plato to thinking that there can be no knowledge, only belief, of people and actions. Even though we shall also see that Plato sometimes does endorse this idea, it does not come from the requirements of knowledge; Plato does not *characterize* knowledge in such a way as to create a host of problems for everything he has said about the just person so far.

Socrates begins (474b) by getting Glaucon to agree that philosophers, who are literally 'lovers of wisdom', are distinguished by loving *all* wisdom of whatever kind. (Reason is the part of the soul by which we learn everything that we learn.) Glaucon misinterprets this to mean that the philosopher will be a sort of omnivore of learning (475d), as though he were someone who wants to know all about physics *and* entomology *and* the history of the Holy Roman Empire. If so, he says, philosophers will be like the 'sight-lovers' (*philotheamones*) who rush round seeing plays and spectacles of all kinds. Socrates corrects him (475e–476d): the sight-lovers are concerned with many beautiful things, he says, whereas the philosopher is distinguished by his concern only with beauty itself, and likewise the one thing that is just or unjust, good or bad (476a). This is the true object of knowledge (476d), whereas the apparent multiplicity of these single Forms in our experience (476a) is the object only of belief.

Thus abruptly is introduced what is often called Plato's 'theory' of Forms; the word 'Form' is used at 476a for the objects of the philosopher's study, and the distinction between the *one* Form and the *many* things that partake of it (476d) is supposed to be familiar already to both Socrates and Glaucon. This is an odd way to proceed, and more will be said in the next chapter about this 'theory'. Meanwhile we should notice that the structure of the whole argument is very careful:

(1) Socrates and Glaucon agree that the philosopher has knowledge and others, including 'sight-lovers' have only belief, because the philosopher is concerned with the one Form in each case, and these are objects of knowledge, whereas the other people are concerned with the many things that partake in Forms (another term not explained so far), and these are objects of belief (474b–476d).

(2) But this is not convincing to those who do not accept the distinctness of Forms and things that partake in Forms (476a). This, of course, includes the average reader.

(3) So Socrates argues on ground that they will accept (476d–478e):

(i) Knowledge is only of what is; belief is of what is and is not (476d–478e).

(ii) The many beautiful things that concern the sight-lovers are cases of things that are and are not; so they are objects only of belief. A Form, however, is a case of what is; so it is an object of knowledge (478e–480a).

To understand this we must look separately at (3 i) and (3 ii).

(i) *Knowledge and what is* (476d–478e)

What does it even mean to say that knowledge is of what is? Here Plato's Greek makes things difficult for us. In English we have different expressions for 'to exist', 'to be true', and 'to be (something or other)'. Plato has only one word, *einai*, which covers all three. In Greek, to say that a thing *esti* may be to say that (a) it exists, (b) it is true, or (c) it is *F* for some *F* – it is brave, or three feet tall, or just. It is best to keep ourselves aware of Plato's conceptual assumptions by using the artificial English '*x* is', or by talking of *x being*, remembering that to us this can be understood in various ways; in particular 'is' has (a) the existential use ('*x* exists'), (b) the veridical use ('*x* is true') or (c) the predicative use ('*x* is brave (just, three feet tall, etc.)'). (There is also the 'is' of identity, but I shall ignore this since it is irrelevant to the present argument.) Plato's assumptions here are quite different from those that we would be inclined to make; in particular, we would assume that to say of some *x* that it exists is to be talking of an object, whereas to say of some x that it is true is to be talking of some statement or proposition, a quite different kind of thing. Here again, though, it is more fruitful to lay aside our point of view in trying to understand the terms of Plato's argument, to make sense of what he is saying without imposing our assumptions on him.

Socrates is meant to be arguing from uncontroversial premises (476d). Now two points are granted him by Glaucon right at the start, and are clearly taken to be acceptable without prejudging the issue. These are: knowledge is of what is, since what is not cannot be known (476e). (Later (477b) knowledge is said to be 'of what is, to know it as it is'.) And: what fully is, is fully knowable, whereas what is not in any way, is not knowable (477a). (This second point sounds bizarre to us, but Socrates presents it as something agreed on whichever way one looks at the matter, so it is something that our interpretation of 'is' had better make sense of.) Which of the uses of 'is' just distinguished has Plato in mind here?

(a) Clearly he is not concerned with being in the sense of *existence*. Firstly, it is hardly uncontroversial that only what exists can be known. (Surely we can know a lot about the ancient Greeks' gods, which don't exist.) Secondly, this would involve making Plato argue about what is 'fully existent' and 'in no way existent', but the notion of *degrees* of existence does not make sense; whatever Plato means by talking of degrees of being, it can't be degrees of existence. Everything that exists does so to the same extent, as it were; one thing cannot exist more than another. Some interpreters are unfazed by this difficulty: they urge that since Plato does talk of degrees of being, we should try to make sense of the notion of degrees of existence. But this overlooks two facts. Firstly existence, as a distinct notion, is *our* concept; if we are to use it to interpret Plato we must show that we can *already* make sense of the notion of degrees of existence *before* claiming to find it in Plato's metaphysics. Secondly, even if Plato did have a deep metaphysical theory of degrees of existence, the notion would appear at the end of some argument, rather than as a common-sense point that Socrates and Glaucon share before the argument begins. The interpretation in terms of the existential use of 'is' has another disadvantage; it makes the whole argument rest on a rather childish fallacy, for Plato will be arguing, from the fact that particular things are *F* and not-*F*, that therefore they both exist and do not exist. This gives Plato a very silly argument, and we should try to do better if possible.

This does not, of course, mean that Plato is *excluding* the existential use of 'is'; indeed, since he does not possess a distinct word for 'exists', it is very likely that he takes his conclusions about the 'being' of Forms to have bearing on what we would call their existence. What is important to get clear is that the notion of existence plays no role in the *argument*. It is important to stress this, because some translations of this passage foist the existential interpretation on this argument by actually *translating* 'is' as 'exists'. This is wrong; we should read the neutral 'is' throughout before attempting interpretation.

   (b) It is initially plausible to take the veridical use to be in play here. For it *is* uncontroversial that knowledge is of what *is true*, and that what is false cannot be known. So Plato would be making Socrates put forward a truism, as he says he is. Further, this reading makes the argument's conclusion sound more attractive, for in saying that knowledge is of what is, whereas belief is of what is and what is not, Plato would be saying that knowledge puts us in touch only with truths, whereas belief can relate us to falsehoods as well as truths; something that has the advantage of sounding true as well as intelligible. And right at the end of the argument there is a passage that seems to demand the veridical reading: the opinions of the many, says Socrates, roll around between being and non-being (479d). Whatever the force of 'roll around', this makes good sense if what is being said is that they contain falsehoods as well as truths. Even if we adopt another overall reading, we have to admit that at these two points Plato does employ the veridical use.

But the veridical use will not account for the whole argument. Firstly, at 477a–b and 478b–c, belief is distinguished from something else, namely ignorance, whose object is 'what is not'; and here 'what is not' cannot mean 'what is not true', since falsehoods can also be the object of belief (cf. 479d). (Plato does elsewhere show himself exercised over the possibility of false belief, but the question does not arise here.) Secondly, the second point supposed to be truistic at the beginning of the argument was that what fully is, is fully knowable; but the notion of degrees of truth does not make any more sense than that of degrees of existence. Nothing can be 'fully' true; so that cannot be the right way to interpret Plato here. 'Degrees of truth' does figure as a theoretical term in some philosophical theories of truth, but it can hardly be appealed to, any more than degrees of existence, as something that all would agree to without controversy.

Again, this is not to say that the notion of truth is irrelevant to the argument; Plato's claims about *being* can sometimes be harmlessly reformulated in terms of *being true*. But we cannot interpret the crucial moves in the argument adequately by means only of the veridical use of *be*.

(c) Our best bet, then, is the predicative reading: 'is' should be read elliptically, as 'is F' where 'F' is some predicate. Something is, if it is F – tall, four feet wide, green, and so on. (We shall see that Plato is not concerned with all predicates, only a limited range of them.) The two truisms on this reading make good sense. Only what is can be known – because you can only know of something that it has a property if it does have that property. I can only know of something that it is long, if it *is* long. If it isn't long, I can't know that it is long. And what fully is, is fully knowable, because only what is fully F – for example completely just – can be known without qualification to be just. I can only know completely, without qualification, that something is just, if it is completely and without qualification just. (This sounds to us much less like a truism, and we shall examine it forthwith.) The predicative reading copes well with the interpretation of the initial premises, and gives a good rendering of the argument as a whole.

Plato, then, begins from what he takes to be established by our intuitions about knowledge. It is significant that he begins this way, for it underlines the fact that he is not arguing to a conclusion about the nature of knowledge. He assumes that we know pretty well what the nature of knowledge is already; the worry comes when we try to say coherently what belief is. His first truism seems acceptable: knowledge is of what is. That is, I can't know something that is not the case: if I think that something is F, then I only *know* this if the thing *is* F. This does seem to be a rock-bottom intuition about knowledge. But the second truism is less obvious: what fully is, is fully knowable, while what in no way is, is quite unknowable. Degrees of knowledge vary with degrees of being. So I only know fully, without qualification, that something is F – that a particular action, say, is just – if it is fully F – that is, completely and fully, just, just without qualification.

This point is underlined later at 477e, where Glaucon confirms that knowledge is *infallible* whereas belief is not. That is, if I know about something, I can't possibly be wrong about it. Knowledge excludes the possibility of error. Now if Plato thinks this, we can see why he thinks that unqualified knowledge must have as its objects things or actions that are unqualifiedly what they are. For only something that has a property unqualifiedly has it in a way that excludes the possibility of being wrong about it. If something has a quality, but only in certain circumstances or from certain points of view, or in some similarly qualified way, then in predicating that quality of it we might possibly go wrong; so we could not have unqualified knowledge of it. For if knowledge is 'infallible', it precludes not just actual error but the very possibility of error; so unqualified knowledge could not have as its object anything which could, as it were, let the aspiring knower down – it must have the quality predicated of it 'fully' and unqualifiedly.

Plato finds this a truism: that he does so is crucial for the structure of the argument. To us it seems far from obvious – indeed, not even true. Why can't I know, fully and without qualification, that a particular thing is F even where it is not fully F but only partially or defectively F? Plato thinks that I can only know without qualification that an action, say, is just if it is just without qualification. But why could I not recognize and take into account the defects and qualifications that any action's justice is bound to have, and thus know that it is qualifiedly just? Plato excludes this: I cannot know that an action is just from one point of view and unjust from another; I can only know, properly and without qualification, what is just without qualification. But why should an account of knowing imply this?

Here again we see how different are Plato's requirements on knowledge from our post-Cartesian ones. He finds it natural to think of knowledge as coming in degrees which vary with the intelligibility of its object; and this is because he is not thinking of knowledge as the result of excluding sceptical doubt. If knowledge is thought of as a state that is incorrigible, there seems no reason at all for its object to be limited to what has the appropriate quality fully or unqualifiedly; what matters rather is the relation between knower and known that guarantees certain freedom from error in the particular case. But Plato is not concerned with whether or not I am right to be sure in this case; for him the advance to knowledge is a progress to increased understanding, and this comes about not by focussing ever more sceptically on one's grounds for a particular belief, but by setting the belief in a wider context of one's other beliefs and their mutually explanatory relationships. It is because knowledge comes with an increase of explanation and of understanding that Plato finds it natural to think of it as a matter of degree, rather than as an all-or-nothing matter of sheer certainty. And because of this we can find less puzzling his assumption that we will agree without argument that what is fully knowable, fully is. For while it is not plausible that one can only be certain about what is unqualifiedly what it is, it is more convincing to claim that we can have full, systematic and unqualified understanding only of what has fully and un-qualifiedly the character it is thought to have.

It is worth noting that these assumptions, which Plato feels entitled to take for granted, make more palatable to him the conclusion of this argument, which has been found so scandalous: that knowledge and belief have different objects. For if knowledge requires a systematic set of grounds, we may well be reluctant to identify the isolated object of belief with the object of knowledge which is known in a whole explanatory context. (Whether Plato produces convincing grounds in this argument for the distinction is, of course, another matter.)

Knowledge, then, is of what really is whatever it is. Knowledge without qualification is of what is what it is without qualification. Ignorance, the opposed state, is of what is not in any way – that is, completely lacks the feature ascribed to it. Something is the object of my ignorance if it totally lacks the quality I predicate of it, just as it is the object of my knowledge if it has that quality in a way excluding error about it. Knowledge and ignorance are taken to be intuitively clear, and the problem is to give a coherent account of belief as something 'between' them, with an object which both is F and is not F.

To provide such a coherent account Plato appeals to the concept of a *dunamis* – a word variously translated as 'faculty', 'capacity', or 'ability' (477b–d). Capacities can be distinguished only in two ways – by their objects and by what they effect (477c–d). Knowledge and belief are agreed to be capacities. This is meant to be obvious, indeed trivial – knowledge is our capacity to know, belief our capacity to believe. Are they in fact distinct? Capacities must differ in their objects and effects. But knowledge does differ from belief, being infallible while belief is not (477e). So belief cannot have the same object as knowledge; so it is not of what is – that is, it is not of what is completely and unqualifiedly F. But its object is not that of ignorance – for to be ignorant of something is to miss the mark completely, lack any true belief, whereas belief involves having something right about its object. And belief falls between knowledge and ignorance rather than being an extreme beyond either of them. (Plato seems to mean that belief must be defined in terms derivative from those used to define knowledge and ignorance, rather than introducing totally new terms.) So belief is of what both is and is not – i.e. what is F and also not F. The object of belief is what has a quality and also its opposite. Plato does not just mean that an object of belief, e.g. a particular action, *is* in the sense of being, e.g. just, and *is not* in the sense of not being, e.g. generous, kind, etc. For its not being generous would not qualify its being just; it might not be generous and still be unqualifiedly *just* – but then its justice would be an object of knowledge and not belief. An object of belief 'is and is not' in the sense of being *F and not-F*; hence, it must be the bearer of *opposite* predicates.

This part of the argument has been criticized because of the use made of the notion of capacity. Firstly, Plato uses sight and hearing as examples of capacities (477c), and it is sometimes thought that this misleads him into thinking of knowledge and belief as if they were analogous to perceiving an object. This view is encouraged by the fact that Plato talks of objects of knowledge in an undifferentiated way, instead of thinking in terms of *knowing that* and talking of propositions or statements. However, sight and hearing are only analogies, and play no part in the argument. Plato does tend to use perceptual metaphors for cognition (as we talk of 'seeing the truth', 'grasping the point' and so on), but it is a mistake to see them as dominating his account of knowledge. The second criticism is more serious. Plato carefully distinguishes two criteria for something's being a capacity, only to run them together. Since capacities are distinguished by their effects and their objects, why can't knowledge and belief be distinguished by their effects, but have the same objects? Plato never takes note of this possibility, yet it is essential for the claim that knowledge and belief have distinct objects. He thus leaves a gap in the argument, which is to that extent weakened. We can explain the omission if he is assuming that his two criteria – the capacity's effects and its objects – are logically distinct but not in fact separable. Knowledge produces a state that is distinctively *knowing* because its objects are of a certain kind (being what they are without qualification), and belief produces a state which is distinctively *believing* because *its* objects are of a certain kind (being what they are and also the opposite). So capacities distinguished by their effects are also thereby distinguished by their objects. This assumption seems plausible enough; we may feel that it loads the dice in favour of the conclusion that knowledge and belief have distinct objects; but whether this matters remains to be seen.

To sum up a stretch of argument which is difficult both because it is so abstract and because of Plato's undifferentiated notion of *being*. Plato has not proved anything about knowledge. He has made assumptions about knowledge which his hearers share, and proved a conclusion about belief. He has assumed of knowledge not just that it is of what is the case, but that it is infallible: it is of what is the case in such a way as to exclude the possibility of error about it. Ignorance, in contrast, is such that having it excludes the possibility of being right. Belief is distinct from both of these: its object is such that it both *is and is not*: that is, it is *F* and also not-*F*. This seems to us a weird claim about belief. But we have seen that Plato requires the object of belief to be both *F* and not-*F* (and not merely *F* and not-*G*, not-*H*, etc.). For only if the object of belief is not-*F* is its being *F* debarred from being an object of knowledge; its being not-*F* shows conclusively that it cannot be fully, unqualifiedly *F*, as is required of an object of knowledge. Its merely being not-*G* would not show this. We have seen that the requirement that the object of knowledge be unqualifiedly *F* arises naturally for Plato from his linking knowledge with increased understanding, rather than with refuge from doubt. His conclusions about belief seem less weird if we give due weight to the assumptions he takes the reader to share with him about knowledge.

(ii) *Forms and what is* (478e–480a)

Socrates now returns to the distinction between the 'sight-lover' who maintains that there are 'many beautiful things' and the person who thinks that there is really only one thing that is beautiful, the Form. The many beautiful things turn out to be mere objects of belief, since each of them equally well appears ugly; and similarly the many just, pious, etc. things equally well can be said to be the opposite (479a–d). Only the Form of Beauty is unqualifiedly beautiful, always beautiful and never the opposite of beautiful (479e). So only the Forms are objects of knowledge, being the only things that truly and unqualifiedly are (480a). So only the person accepting that there are Forms has knowledge and is a true philosopher.

Plato argues rapidly because the moves are familiar to him; we need some background.

We have already seen in Book I that there and in earlier dialogues Plato presents Socrates as concerned with the inadequacy of certain kinds of attempt to define ethical terms (pp. 21–2). Unreflective people say that justice is giving back what you owe, or that piety is prosecuting for murder. They fail to appreciate that their examples of just or pious behaviour could equally well, in other circumstances, be examples of the opposite. It is hopeless to try to define F by citing examples of F that could equally well be not-F.

The present passage takes up and expands on this concern: there is a distinction between the many Fs, which can just as well be not-F as F, and 'the F itself', which is completely and fully F and never the opposite. There are, however, two new notes struck.

Firstly, while Plato here mentions just/unjust and pious/impious, he also introduces other terms: beautiful/ugly, double/half, big/small, and heavy/light. He is concerned with a wider range of qualities than ethical ones: the fact that alleged examples of justice or piety can also in some circumstances display the opposite is now seen as part of a wider phenomenon: terms whose application is unsatisfactory because their instances can also be seen to be instances of the opposite.

Secondly, Polemarchus and Euthyphro and their like offered unsatisfactory *kinds* of action to account for justice and piety, not particular instances. The present passage concerns the 'many beautifuls', etc.; and while these *can* be read as being many different accounts of beauty, justice, doubleness, etc., the passage does suggest to most readers that Plato is contrasting the many *instances* of beauty, justice, etc. with the one Form in each case. It is only fair to add that this is a matter of great controversy. One problem is that the 'sight-lovers' as first characterized seemed to be experts of some kind rather than people who just observe instances, and it seems ludicrous if their claim that there are many beautifuls, not one, merely comes down to the claim that beauty has many instances. But in spite of this the passage as a whole makes most sense if what are being contrasted with the one thing that is fully F are the many inadequate instances of F.

Why does Plato think that particular instances of beauty, smallness and justice are also instances of ugliness, largeness and injustice? (For this is what he is claiming, in spite of making

Socrates claim at 479a that the many beautifuls, etc. will also *appear* ugly, etc. This has been taken as weakening Plato's argument to the claim that the many beautiful things will also *appear* ugly, without claiming that they will also *be* ugly. But in Greek using 'appears' does not imply, or always suggest, 'but isn't, really'. 508d makes it clear that 'appears to be *F*' is perfectly consistent with 'and really is *F*, too' – something rather strange in English. So Plato's claim is that the many beautifuls *are*, not just appear, both *F* and not-*F*.)

Plato, rather to our surprise, does neither of two things that we might expect him to do. Firstly, he never indicates why he picks on the terms he does – why both *just* and *heavy* but not, say, *round* or *red*? We shall come back to this point more than once. Secondly, he never indicates why, even for the terms he puts forward, we should accept it as *true* that where each applies to a 'many', so does its opposite. At first the idea sounds ludicrous. We can say that Helen of Troy is beautiful; why must we also say that she is ugly? Plato is evidently relying on the principle that whenever we can apply one of his terms to a particular – to one of a 'many' – then it will always be possible to apply the opposite of that term to the same particular, by considering it in different circumstances, or from a different point of view. Of course we can say that Helen is beautiful, but we can also say truly of her that she is ugly if we compare her earthly beauty with that of a goddess, or look at her from a peculiar perspective, or wait until she is very old. In the *Republic* Plato does not say much to defend the idea, but we can usefully compare a passage from another dialogue, the *Symposium*, where the speaker, Diotima, talks of all the ways that particular beautiful things can also be said to be the opposite of beautiful (211a). They may be beautiful in one way only, not in another. They may be beautiful at one time but not another, losing or changing their features through time. They may be beautiful only relative to one thing, and ugly relative to others. They may be beautiful only in one place or context and ugly in another. Plato is appealing to a very wide range of considerations. One is the fact of change, but more stressed is the fact that particulars, in their contexts, can be considered from many points of view, and our ascription of qualities to them often relies on features that are relative to some context. The

Symposium passage makes it clearer why Plato here includes terms like *double* and *big*, for these are *relative* terms: our ascription of them is relative to some standard, since what is, e.g. a small animal may be a large mouse, and double 2 may be half 8; so from different points of view the same thing is both large and small, both double and half.

So for a range of terms their application to particulars, the instances of them in our experience, is unsatisfactory because, for a variety of reasons, these terms apply, but so do their opposites. The particulars both are *F* and are not-*F*. Are we then to conclude that particulars are somehow self-contradictory and incoherent? That would be a bizarre conclusion, and anyway we know already that Plato is committed to thinking that 'one thing cannot act in opposite ways or be in opposite states at the same time and in the same part of itself in relation to some other thing' (436b), since this is the Principle of Conflict in his argument to distinguish the soul's parts. Plato thinks, rather, that the fact that particular things can be said to be beautiful and also ugly shows that the terms 'beautiful' and 'ugly' are not being applied unqualifiedly when they are used of particulars. Helen is beautiful, but because she can also be called ugly when she grows old, she cannot be *unqualifiedly* beautiful. Giving back what you owe is not *unqualifiedly* just, because an action of that kind could from another point of view be seen as unjust. Twice two is double, but it is not *unqualifiedly* double, because it is also half, namely half eight. (In the case of relative terms we are likely to find this point obvious, since nobody is likely to think that twice two is unqualifiedly double, or that a mouse is unqualifiedly large; but we have seen that it never entered Polemarchus' head to think that there was any qualification to be made about saying that returning what one owes is just.) There *are*, however, unqualified applications of the terms whose application to particulars is always qualified, and so unsatisfactory. This is something Plato does not argue for here, but just assumes. We might well think that even if we accept what has been suggested about the unsatisfactoriness of our use of terms like 'just' and 'double' to particulars, this is not sufficient to show that such terms *do* have unqualified application. Nothing is ever unqualifiedly big: but why should this worry us? Surely this merely shows that 'big' and terms like it are irredeemably relative, their application being always relative to some standard, so that they have no unqualified application. We are not inclined to think that the fact that anything that can be called large (relatively to something) can be called small (relatively to something else) shows that 'large' *must* have an absolutely unqualified application to *something*. So we are inclined to find argument lacking when Plato proceeds, as he does here, to claim that the terms he mentions do have unqualified application to something – namely, to what he calls a Form. We shall return in the next chapter to the question of why Plato does not provide anything here in the way of argument for the existence of Forms. It is clear, however, that he does take there to be Forms – a Form being the unqualified bearer of a predicate which is applied to particulars only qualifiedly, in such a way that not only can it be applied, but so can its opposite. The Form of Beauty contrasts with the 'many beautifuls' in that while each of them is only qualifiedly beautiful, as is shown by the fact that from some point of view it can also be called ugly, it is unqualifiedly beautiful, beautiful in such a way as to exclude the possibility of ascribing ugliness to it in any way. As Forms are introduced, then, a Form is an unqualified bearer of its predicate, precluding its opposite. The Form of Beauty is 'the beautiful itself', the thing which is beautiful in such an unqualified way as never to be ugly, unlike particular beautiful things which are always ugly in some way, from some point of view or in relation to something else.

If we turn back to Socrates' initial characterization of the lover of Forms (474b–476d) we can see that Forms there play exactly this role. The Form of Beauty is 'the beautiful itself' (476c–d), that which is completely and only beautiful. Each Form is only *one*, but appears many in our experience (476a): the world presents us with many things which we call beautiful, not realizing that only the Form is really, unqualifiedly beautiful. And (475e) the beautiful is distinct from the ugly because they are *opposites*. What is really beautiful is precisely what can never coexist with its opposite; hence particular things, which are always in some way ugly as well as beautiful, are different from what is really beautiful, the Form. Particular things were said there to 'partake in' the Form (476d); the term is not explained, but we can take a partaker in a Form to be a particular thing in so far as it has qualifiedly the quality that the Form has unqualifiedly.

We can now see why Plato moves so rapidly to saying that the 'many beautifuls' are and are not, while only the Form is (and, hence, are objects of belief and knowledge respectively). Particular things are and are not beautiful because they can all with equal right be said to be (in some way, from some point of view) ugly. Only the Form is completely, fully, beautiful and nothing else, because only the ascription to the Form of beauty precludes ascription of the opposite. Hence only the Form *is*, while particulars both *are and are not*. For, as we have seen, we must interpret Plato's talk of *being* here as the predicative use of 'be': the Form fully and unqualifiedly is *F*, while particular *F*s both are *F* and are not-*F*. Hence, since Plato has shown that knowledge is of what is, while belief is of what is and is not, Forms are obvious candidates for being objects of knowledge, and particular instances of Forms are obvious candidates for being objects of belief. We have been persuaded that our intuitions about knowledge are such that as knowledge and belief are characterized, their objects are distinct; and also that Forms and instances of Forms are plausible candidates for being objects of knowledge and belief respectively.

Forms have been discussed only briefly, and not argued for, but a few points have emerged about them which are important.

Firstly, while Plato concentrates on the 'positive' members of his pairs – beauty, justice, etc. – 476a makes it clear that the argument equally well produces Forms like Ugliness and Injustice. This point is dropped; later Plato apparently forgets it, for he links knowledge of Forms to goodness, never to badness.

Secondly, the person who recognizes that there are Forms is said to be 'awake' while the person who does not is 'dreaming' (476c). This idea will become prominent in later passages, but the present argument does not indicate how we are to understand it.

Thirdly, in arguing against the 'sight-lovers' Plato betrays a tendency to oppose Forms to the world of sense-experience. But the argument at no point depends on inadequacies of the senses, since it involves terms like 'just' and 'pious' whose application is not straightforwardly a matter of describing what one senses.

Most important, however, is the fact that the considerations on which Plato draws here to distinguish Forms apply only to a restricted range of terms. The Book 5 argument is often called 'the Argument from Opposites', for the excellent reason that it concerns the application of terms that have opposites, and has no application to terms that don't have opposites. The terms that Plato picks out as having only qualified application to particular things are a mixed bag – just, pious, beautiful, double, big, heavy – but they are united in all having opposites: what shows us that this thing or action is only qualifiedly F is precisely the fact that it can also be said to be (from some point of view, etc.) not-F. There is a contrast here with a term like 'man'. We apply it to many particulars, and take it that there are 'many men'. But this assumption of ours is not faulty in the way that the assumption that there are 'many beautifuls' can be faulted. For each of the many beautiful things turned out also to be (from some point of view, etc.) ugly. But we cannot appeal to the same kind of considerations – change, context, relativity to standard or interest – to show that each particular man is also (from some point of view, etc.) a not-man. Nothing can be, even qualifiedly, both a man and a not-man. (The reasons for this are deep ones. Very roughly, 'man' picks out an essential property of whatever it applies to, that is, a property such that the particular thing that has it could not have lacked it. Hence no sense attaches to supposing that the same particular thing could have both that property and its opposite.) So in the case of terms like 'man' the line of thought we have seen Plato develop gives us no reason to say there is a Form. The argument distinguishes Forms only for terms with opposites, because only they set up the needed contrast between qualifiedly and unqualifiedly being F. So the argument has shown that there are Forms for terms with opposites, though so far we have no idea of whether this is meant to apply to all terms with opposites, or just Plato's own examples, relative terms and moral terms.

This bears crucially on the question, what are the 'two worlds' of knowledge and belief distinguished in Book 5? The objects of knowledge are distinct from those of belief, and they are Forms. But two points are very important here.

Firstly, Plato has not argued, and the argument does not imply, that *only* Forms can be objects of knowledge. Plato has argued that knowledge is of 'what is', and belief is not; and he has then claimed, separately, that Forms are examples of 'what is', Forms being unqualified bearers of their predicates; but he has not said or shown that *only* Forms can be cases of 'what is', and so objects of knowledge. For he has not shown that knowledge must be of a special kind of entity – that it can only have as its objects items that are universals or abstract entities or any special kind of thing. Knowledge is of what is F and cannot be not-F. This consideration would let me *know* that Socrates is a man; for, as indicated, it is never possible to say that he is a not-man as well as that he is a man. So nothing that Plato has said has excluded our having knowledge of things that are not Forms – e.g. that Socrates is a man, and many other things about the world around us. As long as the alleged object of knowledge does not fail the point about application of opposites, it will be a case of knowledge, for all Plato has said about knowledge. Plato has not set out to show that every case of knowledge is a case of knowing a Form. He has been concerned to show that we do *not* know some things about the world around us that we thought we did know. We thought, for example, that we knew that a particular action was just; but, by the Argument from Opposites, we did not know this. In the case of some terms, their application to particulars can never be a matter of knowledge; only their application to Forms can. But it does *not* follow from the way Plato has characterized knowledge that this is the case with *all* terms.

Secondly, Plato has contrasted Forms, which are objects of knowledge, with particular instances of Forms (things that 'partake in' Forms), which are objects of belief. But this contrast cannot be identified with the contrast between universals and particulars. Theories of universals are theories about the application of *every* general term, whereas this argument produces Forms for only a restricted range. Analogously, objects of belief are not simply particulars; as we have seen, Plato's considerations about knowledge would allow particulars to be objects of knowledge in some respects.

Objects of belief are particulars as qualified instances of some terms, namely, those terms that have unqualified application to Forms. Plato has not argued that particular things and actions cannot be known just because of their sheer particularity. Nor has he argued that there is anything about the fact that they are experienced – seen, touched, etc. – which debars them from being known. (There has been an implicit contrast with people who rely on their experience, but nothing more.) So he has not excluded particular objects of experience from being known just because they are particular objects of experience. For all he has said, I can know that Socrates is a man, and that this action is a killing. What I cannot know is whether Socrates is tall, or whether this killing is just. In *these* respects we lack understanding of the world around us.

So we can say, if we like, that Plato has a distinction between the 'two worlds' of knowledge and belief, with their distinct objects. But this does *not* imply that only Forms are objects of knowledge, or that particular things and actions cannot be known. What can be known is 'what is'; in some respects, e.g. whether this is a man, we can get answers from experience which tell us 'what is', but in some, crucial respects, e.g. whether an action is just, we cannot, and in these cases what we know must be a Form, because in these cases 'what is' must be a Form, not any particular. Particulars are objects of belief or knowledge, according to this argument, depending on the kind of claim being made about them. And because Plato does not tell us what the range is of the terms he is considering, we don't yet have much idea of what the respects are in which particulars cannot be known.

Later, Plato does make some more drastic assumptions about knowledge and belief, and in some passages in Books 6 and 7 he is clearly thinking that only Forms can be known, while the world of particular things and actions can only be the object of belief. But it is important to be clear that this is *not* implied by the way he characterizes what knowledge is. It has another source.

Opinions differ sharply over this very difficult argument in Book 5, and it is fair to say that while my interpretation is hardly original it is a minority view, and that most interpreters would hold that in this argument as well as later Plato is consigning all particulars to the realm of mere belief, holding that only Forms can be known. It should be by now abundantly clear why I do not think that this is a plausible reading of the argument; but it would at least give Plato a consistent position on the relation of Forms and knowledge. For he does later talk, in the figurative passages (especially the Cave) as though particular things can only be objects of belief in all respects, and only Forms can be objects of knowledge. So on the interpretation I have given, Plato is in Book 5 arguing for something weaker than what he will sometimes claim later. This seems an obvious defect in an interpretation. I shall indicate when we get to the later passages why I think that Plato says things, in figurative language, that go beyond what he has argued for. But is is worth pointing out now some advantages of the weaker interpretation of this argument in making sense of Plato's overall concerns in the whole *Republic*.

We have already seen that Plato's search for knowledge is not the post-Cartesian search for a state immune to sceptical doubt. Rather it is a search for understanding. This means that he has no reason to think that knowledge will be achieved by a negative, corrosive doubting of all our previous beliefs. Rather than undercutting the beliefs we have, we advance to understanding their significance and finding them intelligible. Of course, when we have knowledge, we may find that some of the beliefs that we accepted are in fact false. But we do not *begin* by trying to doubt the truth of particular beliefs in a wholesale way, as Descartes recommends that we do. Take a particular belief, e.g. that this particular action is just. For Plato, the trouble with this is not that it is not true. It *is* true (let us suppose that it is Socrates' refusal to escape from prison). It is not that particulars are never just, or that they have the quality that the Form has only in some drastically second-rate way. Rather, the problem is that not only is it true that the action is just, but unfortunately something else is true too, namely that it is also unjust (from some point of view). The person who simply thought that it was just was not wrong as far as he or she went, but was missing something – something that might not be at all obvious in a case like the one I have suggested. What matters is not to reject any truth in the beliefs we have, to go round trying to convince ourselves that this is not really a just action. Rather, what is required is imaginative widening of one's horizons to take in contexts in which even this action could be considered unjust, and to see that besides the unsatisfactory ascription of justice to particular actions there is also the possibility that there might be something that is unqualifiedly just, freed from all the contexts and limitations inevitable with an action's justice – the Form of Justice, the only thing that really and unqualifiedly is just. This has already been likened to waking up from a dream, rather than to finding relief from doubt.

It may be objected that Plato's view of knowledge is not after all so dissimilar from the Cartesian one, since both are revisionary: both result in our finding that most people turn out not to have knowledge about lots of matters on which they thought that they did. However, Cartesian conceptions of knowledge are revisionary in a wholesale way: we turn out to know *nothing* of what we thought we did, except the results of the Cogito (or whatever else is favoured as the foundation of knowledge). Plato's conception of knowledge, on the other hand, is constrained in two ways from downgrading all or most of our knowledge-claims to the status of mere belief.

In the first place, the *Republic* is answering a philosophical question that is posed in ordinary terms: Thrasymachus' challenge arose from comprehensible doubts about the worth of justice as ordinarily pursued. So Plato's answer must keep in touch with the original concept. We have seen in Chapter 6 that while the account of Platonic justice was very different from the original notion of justice that people in Book 1 began with, still Plato sees the need to let his account be constrained by our central intuitions about the ordinary concept; otherwise he will have missed the point. Plato's account of justice shows that some of our ordinary beliefs about justice are false, according to him – for example, the belief that the just man will never lie. But he does not do this by urging us to doubt that lying is always wrong, or by getting us to throw out all our beliefs about justice. He tries to get us to accept this as part of what flows from a deepened understanding of justice that comes from learning about the parts of the soul and psychic harmony. It is one of the ways in which he wants us to correct our concept, but we do so on the basis of an understanding that we have attained of our concept and our beliefs about it. We have seen at length that Plato's entire method of approach precludes a wholesale throwing out of our beliefs about justice.

There are two ways in which Plato's approach to justice is relevant to his approach to knowledge. One is that it would simply be very odd if his treatment of justice were quite different from his treatment of knowledge, if after giving a subtle and complex account of justice and its relation to what we already believe about it, he were to put forward, baldly, the idea that knowledge is such that, extraordinary though it seems, we have no knowledge of particular things and people. But knowledge is more closely connected with justice than that, because, as we have seen, justice requires reason's rule in the soul, and this requires knowledge. So if Plato is giving a very revisionary account of knowledge, he is committed by it to giving a much more revisionary account of justice than he has given in the first four books. If a person's justice is based on his or her knowledge, and there turns out to be no knowledge of particular matters of fact, then justice, strangely, turns out not to be concerned with particular matters of fact. (We shall see that something like this does seem to be implied in the figurative passages like the Cave, but we shall also see that this leads to conflict with the main argument about justice.)

This leads to the second constraint: whatever the discussion of knowledge is like, it has to form a comprehensible part of the *Republic*'s main moral argument. We are to be shown that justice is worth having for the agent; in the process Plato has claimed that, because it is only in the just person's soul that reason rules, only the just person has knowledge, the kind of practical knowledge missing in actual rulers but desired in the ideal ruler (as claimed in the long Book 6 discussion). To get us to accept this, and its implication that the wise should rule the unwise, Plato has to show plausibly that some people do have knowledge of moral and political matters, where all agree that knowledge would be desirable but seems to be lacking. He is urging us to accept rule by those who have knowledge in areas where we have only belief. But while we may accept that we lack knowledge about justice (why else the need for the *Republic*?), why should Plato ruin his case by presenting this as part of an overall position claiming that anyway we lack knowledge about everything, including the simplest matters of fact? In Book 1 Socrates showed Polemarchus that he was wrong in thinking that he knew about justice. He did this not by undermining his belief that he knew about everyday matters – horses, dogs, and skills – but precisely by relying on his having this knowledge. Similarly with justice and knowledge itself. Plato begins from our intuitions about knowledge, but it would outrage these if it turned out that we lacked any knowledge about particular things and actions just because they are particulars. We are not urged to go in for sceptical doubts. We *are* encouraged to be humble about our claims about justice and other such matters (as the morally complacent are not). And we are supposed to see that we lack knowledge in these areas. This was, indeed, what the moral sceptic claimed. But Plato also assures us that knowledge can be found. And this is not a matter of certainty or confidence. (Moral sceptics are unmoved by claims that one is confident about moral truths.) Plato's claim is rather that in moral matters a kind of understanding and clarity is possible and attainable, and should guide our actions if we are to lead a good life. It is just not part of this enterprise to cast doubt on whether we really know particular matters of simple fact.

FURTHER READING

Interpretation of the Book 5 argument is very controversial: the interested reader should follow up some alternative views.

For the problems surrounding Plato's undifferentiated use of 'be', see C. Kahn, *The Greek Verb 'Be' and the Concept of Being*.

An interpretation based on the existential use of 'be' can be found in Cross and Woozley, ch. 8 of *Plato's Republic, A Philosophical Introduction*, 'Knowledge, Belief and the Forms' (reprinted in Vlastos (ed.), *Plato* 1). G. Fine, 'Knowledge and Belief in *Republic* V', *Archiv für Geschichte der Philosophie* 1978, interprets the argument in terms of the veridical use. The predicative use is the basis of the interpretation of two well-known articles by Vlastos, 'A Metaphysical Paradox', in *Platonic Studies*, and 'Degrees of Reality in Plato', *Platonic Studies*, and Bambrough (ed.), *New Essays On Plato and Aristotle*.

The question of whether the 'many' are particulars or types, and its importance, are discussed in J. Gosling, 'Ta Polla Kala',

Phronesis 1960; F. C. White, 'J. Gosling on Ta Polla Kala', *Phronesis* 1978; also 'The "Many" in *Republic* 475a–480a', with the rejoinder by Gosling, in *Canadian Journal of Philosophy* 1977. The notion of capacity or faculty involved is discussed in J. Gosling, 'Doxa and Dunamis', *Phronesis* 1968, and J. Hintikka, 'Knowledge and its Objects in Plato', with comments by G. Santas, in J. Moravcsik, *Patterns in Plato's Thought.*

A good example of a more traditional interpretation than mine is R. Allen, 'The Argument from Opposites in *Republic* V', in Anton and Kustas (eds.), *Essays in Ancient Greek Philosophy.*

There is not much written on Plato's notion of knowledge and its general differences from modern concepts; the best available article is J. Moravcsik, 'Understanding and Knowledge in Plato's Philosophy', *Neue Hefte für Philosophie* 1978. See also S. Scolnicov, 'Three Aspects of Plato's Philosophy of Learning and Instruction' in *Paideia*, Special Plato Issue, 1976.

Chapter 9

The 'Theory' of Forms

Knowledge, then, has Forms as objects, though nothing so far implies that knowledge is *only* of Forms. In the next two chapters we shall follow up the kind of understanding that knowledge involves, but first we need to follow up the introduction of Forms. This is especially necessary since Forms were not argued for as part of the *Republic*'s argument. The idea that there are Forms was brought in from outside the discussion – a very odd procedure which turns Glaucon suddenly into an experienced philosopher. We have to look at Forms in the whole dialogue, and the roles they play, to see how dependent the *Republic*'s main argument is on the claim that there are Forms, and also to understand the claim, which is often made, that the *Republic* contains Plato's 'Theory of Forms'.

Books on Plato often refer to Plato's 'Theory of Forms', but this has to be handled with caution. Plato not only has no word for 'theory'; he nowhere in the dialogues has an extended discussion of Forms in which he pulls together the different lines of thought about them and tries to assess the needs they meet and whether they succeed in meeting them. The *Republic* is often treated as a major source for the 'Theory of Forms', but even here there is no open treatment of what they contribute to the argument. Explicit discussion of them is not very prominent: there are only three passages where we find it, though the long figurative passages of Sun, Line, and Cave, as well as some more casual references, obviously have Forms in view.

One of the three passages has already been discussed – the Book 5 passage where Forms are introduced as suitable objects of knowledge because they are examples of 'what is': only a

Form bears its predicate unqualifiedly, as opposed to particular instances which are not only F but also not-F. This consideration only applies to terms that have opposites, and Plato was concerned with two groups of these, moral terms like 'just' and relative terms like 'double'.

In Book 7, 521–525, Socrates discusses at length the kind of study suitable for the Guardians' further education. There are problems on the adequacy of this passage for what it claims to support (see pp. 273–4), but what concerns us now is the stretch of argument from 523a–525b. Some of our sense-perceptions, Socrates says, do not stir up any use of the mind, because perception on its own settles them adequately; but some do, because perception plays dirty tricks (523b). Glaucon thinks that he is referring to perceptual illusions, but Socrates reaffirms that he is talking about standard cases. He illustrates this by a down-to-earth example. If we look at one of our hands, we can distinguish the three end fingers by sight with no trouble; each is a finger and we can tell this adequately by looking. Sight is never the source of anything that leads us to say that any of the fingers is also not a finger. But it is different with certain qualities of a finger, e.g. its size; here we get 'contradictions in perception'. What we see enables us to say that the finger is large, but also, and equally well, to say that it is small. So in these cases the mind is forced to reflect, and to come in to settle the problem. Plato is appealing to the same kind of consideration as in Book 5: what is large (compared with one thing) can with equal right be called small (in comparison with something else, from a different point of view, etc.). Here this is blamed on the senses, because when the mind comes in to reason things out (524b) it declares that the contradiction is only an apparent one: 'large' and 'small' cannot *really* apply to the same thing, since what is really large is distinct from what is really small (524c). Thus we are moved to ask questions about what sort of thing it could be that could be really large or small, and to grasp that it cannot be the same as the largeness or smallness that we perceive with no effort in something like a finger. Rather, it is something 'intelligible', something that has to be worked out and grasped by the mind; we will only get to realizing that there is such a thing if we think about the matter rather than being content with what we can experience with no particular effort on our part. We see here an idea which will be further developed, that in thinking we are *doing* something, actively reacting to a phenomenon, whereas in perceiving we are just passively taking it in.

The word 'Form' is not used in this argument, but the objects of thought that are distinguished from what we perceive must be Forms: apart from their role in the overall argument and the similarities with the Book 5 passage, it is said at 524c that the mind is moved to ask about what really is large and really is small, terms used for Forms as examples of 'what is'. As well as the similarities with Book 5, however, there are two major differences:

Firstly, the argument is not about knowledge and belief; in modern jargon, it is about ontology, not epistemology. This difference is not of great consequence, however. In Book 5 Plato did not argue that knowledge by its nature required Forms as objects: knowledge was argued to be of 'what is', and Forms were brought in as examples of 'what is'. In Book 7 Forms appear as 'what is', but the further move about knowledge is not made. Book 7 contrasts thought and the senses, and this should not be assimilated to the contrast between knowledge and belief; it does not result from the Book 7 passage any more than from the Book 5 one that everything we experience through the senses can only be an object of belief.

Secondly, Book 7 seems to argue for a more restricted range of Forms, since it talks of what we learn from our use of the senses, whereas Book 5 included moral qualities and mathematical qualities like doubleness. But again there is less difference than first appears. The argument is not limited by appeal to 'the senses' to strictly observable, sensed qualities. Admittedly the example of the finger illustrates observation. But it is essential to the argument in its context that one of the problematic notions that call out the mind is *oneness*: the same thing can be both one and many – that is, one finger and many joints, etc. – and so oneness or unity must be one of the qualities which by producing contradictions in perception show us vividly that there is only one thing that has the quality un-qualifiedly, and is distinct from any instance of the quality in our experience. Now Plato's treatment of oneness is a mistake (for reasons too complex to enlarge on here). But on any account it commits him to thinking of oneness as something that can be encountered by the senses; otherwise the argument would not prove what he wants it to prove. And if oneness can be so perceived, why not doubleness, from the Book 5 list? So the Book 7 passage does not restrict the Book 5 list much, if at all – though admittedly the status of the moral qualities remains obscure in Book 7. Plato does not have in mind a narrow biological definition of the senses, but rather the broader notion of encountering something in one's experience, passively interacting with the world rather than being moved to think and ask questions about it. (As I use 'experience' in discussing these passages it covers not just perception but also the more everyday notion of 'experience' in which the experienced person has picked up a lot of beliefs about the just and the beautiful as well as about the large and the small. For Plato the important contrast is between unreflective acceptance of perceptual or moral impressions, and critical thinking about those impressions. 'Experience', while perhaps not the most natural English for the former state, at least avoids putting a false emphasis on the role of perception.)

Not only does concentration on the senses not significantly restrict the range of what this argument proves: it introduces an unnecessary confusion. Plato talks of 'what the senses tell us' and 'what the mind tells us', as though these were two mutually independent sources of information; and a correspondingly sharp distinction is drawn at the end between what is intelligible, the object of the mind, and what is visible, the object of the senses. This suggests that the senses on their own are competent to pronounce on anything observable, whereas the mind takes over when it comes to objects that are not observable. But the operative distinction in the argument is not that between observable qualities reported by the senses and unobservable qualities reported by the mind. Rather it is the distinction between two kinds of concept: those, like 'finger', that can be ascribed adequately on the basis of experience, and those, like 'large', whose ascription is problematic, raising puzzles that cannot be solved as long as we confine ourselves to experience, and which therefore have to be reasoned through. What makes these concepts disputable is that they give rise to

'contradictions in perception' – they make an intelligent person
see that there is something rationally offensive about a state of
affairs which most people happily accept – rather than that it is
the *senses*, as such, which are doing the reporting. So Plato's
language here, which makes the senses and the mind sound like
two independent agencies, is seriously misleading. It obscures
the contrast that is important for the argument, and it tends to
make us overlook the fact that both the senses and the mind are
involved in our ascriptions of both kinds of concept. You need
the senses as well as the mind to ascribe 'large' correctly, as well
as to ascribe 'finger' correctly. The difference is that in the one
case matters end there, whereas in the other intelligent people
feel that there is a puzzle and that matters do *not* end there.
Later, in the *Theaetetus*, Plato in a passage (184–6) about the
mind and the senses implicitly improves on the account he
gives here. He there makes it clear that both mind and senses
are involved in judgements about the observable world, and
that they work interdependently, not like two separate faculties
fortuitously operating in the same person.

So the differences between Books 5 and 7 are not as great as
might appear at first, and the similarities are striking. In both
passages Forms appear as 'what is' – that is, as unqualified
bearers of predicates which in their application to particular
instances apply only qualifiedly. The Form of *F* is what really,
completely, and unqualifiedly is *F*, whereas particulars manage
to be *F* only with qualifications. The most striking similarity,
however, lies in the reliance both of them put on *opposition* in our
judgements; it is because perceptual experience turns up
'opposites' (523c, 524d) that we are led to realize that there
are Forms that are what they are without qualification or the
possibility of applying the opposite term. In both passages we
find the same line of thought, namely, the Argument from
Opposites.

Book 7, however, makes clearer than Book 5 the way that it is
essential to the argument to produce only a limited range of
Forms. For we can only recognize the inadequacy of the senses'
reports on largeness and the like by contrast with the adequacy
of our application of concepts like *finger* to what we experience.
We are only stirred up to think by realizing that experience has
its limits, and can result in intellectual discomfort. If every

concept were like *finger*, such that it could be applied to what we experience in an unqualified way with no possibility of applying the opposite, then we would never feel the intellectual discomfort that leads us to recognize that there are Forms. And if every concept were like *large*, so that application of it in our experience always led to ascribing both it and its opposite to the same thing in different contexts, then we would still feel no intellectual discomfort, because there would be nothing to compare our unsatisfactory performance with, no reason to think that unqualified application of any concept was ever possible. As it is, Plato's argument requires us to have the ability to characterize some things in the world adequately, in order to realize what the problems are that lead us to go on and find other adequately characterizable things, which, to the surprise of the unreflective, are not to be found in experience but can only be grasped by thought.

Some may object that Plato's argument here does not require there to be a limited range of Forms. All that it needs is that there be a contrast within our experience between the ways in which two kinds of term apply, a contrast sharp enough for us to realize that there are Forms in the first place. Once we have realized that *some* terms, like 'large', cannot be applied adequately to what we encounter in experience, but can only be applied adequately to items that we cannot experience, we have realized that there are Forms; but it is not necessary that Forms be limited to the range that led us to that realization. For all Plato has argued, there might be a Form for *every* term, and terms that have opposites might only be the most *obvious* examples, and therefore the examples with which we begin.

Now this is certainly possible; nothing Plato has said explicitly demands that Forms be limited to the range of terms that have opposites. On the other hand, nothing he has said encourages us to think that the argument can be generalized, either. As far as the present passage is concerned, it is more plausible that it has a limited range of Forms in view. For the argument is *not* generalizable, as we have seen: it *depends* on the contrast between terms that do, and those that do not, have satisfactory application in our experience. So, if Plato does not have a limited range of Forms in view, then either he means us to generalize the argument, although we cannot coherently do this; or he thinks that the question, what Forms there are, is quite independent of the question, what Forms the human mind is capable of coming to recognize. While the latter is a possible view, it is too sophisticated to be ascribed to Plato merely because the argument is for a limited range of Forms whereas some interpreters want Plato to be arguing for more.

This is not the end of the story, though. For while the Argument from Opposites, which is the nerve of the two longest and most careful passages that concern Forms, only produces Forms for a limited range of terms, those with opposites, Plato never explicitly says this, and some of the things he says elsewhere seem to go against it. There are in fact three sources of difficulty here. One is that the passages of argument that concern Forms greatly underdetermine what 'theory of Forms' we are to ascribe to Plato. I shall come back to this at greater length shortly. The second is that outside the passages of argument Plato often refers to Forms in ways that have no obvious connections with the Argument from Opposites. In the central books and later he sometimes talks of the objects of the philosopher's knowledge as though what essentially characterized them was being stable and changeless, in contrast to the objects of less satisfactory cognitive states, which are liable to change. (Cf. 484b, 485a–b, 508d, 521d, 527b, 534a, 585a–586b (esp. 585c–d).) Now Forms, as produced by the Argument from Opposites, will be changeless: that which is beautiful in such a way as never to be ugly will, *a fortiori*, never be ugly through change. But one can contrast objects of knowledge that never change with other objects that do change, without reference to opposites. And again, while one way in which particulars can have opposites predicated of them is by changing, it is not the only way; in the case of most of Plato's examples it is more plausible to think of the thing not as changing but as being characterizable in different ways at the same time, from different points of view or different contexts. Plato's move from using the Argument from Opposites to talking of Forms as changeless would have more support if it were the case that he thought of all particulars as always changing; for if an object is always changing that is a ground for saying that for all or most of its qualities it has not only them but their opposites at some point. But Plato nowhere in the

Republic commits himself to thinking that particulars are always changing (although in some other dialogues he shows interest in certain 'theories of flux' that claim that there is nothing stable about the world we experience). In any case, even if Plato had relied on the assumption that particular things are in flux, this would not have sufficed to show why all particulars should be considered to be changing by contrast with the unchanging Forms; for he is as concerned with particular *actions* as with particular things, and while he was familiar with theories that all particular objects are in flux, it makes no sense to think of a particular just action, say, as itself being in flux. So there remains no obvious connection between Plato's employment of the Argument from Opposites and his tendency to contrast changeless Forms with the mutability of the world of particulars that we experience.

The third source of difficulty is that even in the passages of argument themselves we cannot say firmly what the range of Forms is to be. Plato clearly has a going intuitive idea of what terms he wants Forms for, and these include relative terms, mathematical terms, and moral terms. But he never tells us explicitly what the range is to be; his examples do not settle matters, since they differ in the two passages; one might wonder whether there are examples of the kind of term he wants that do not fit the Argument from Opposites, and vice versa; and his procedure raises a number of problems which he is not aware of, but which make it very hard to say with certainty exactly what he takes the argument to apply to. Two of these problems are very important. One is that it is not clear whether Forms are opposed to particular instances, or to types of instance. The Book 7 argument contrasts Forms with a particular thing, a finger, and its largeness. And the Book 5 argument makes most sense taken this way too. But, as mentioned (pp. 194–5) the lover of Forms is contrasted with the 'sight-lovers', who seem to be people who do not just consider instances of beauty and justice, but have views as to what kind of thing beauty is. And it is said at one point that what roll round between fully being and not being at all are the opinions of the many about beauty and the like (479d). This suggests that knowledge of a Form is being opposed not to recognizing a particular instance, but to giving an account of, say, beauty; and the person who insists that there are *many* 'beautifuls' and not just the one Form will be insisting, not that beauty has many instances, but that there are many different *kinds* of beauty, many different ways of being beautiful. If so, Plato is thinking of the Form of Beauty as contrasted not (as on the interpretation given) with a particular beautiful thing in so far as it is beautiful, but with a type or kind of beautiful thing. Now on the one hand it is hard to explain away these indications in Book 5 that Plato is thinking of types, not tokens, of beauty. But Book 7, using the same argument, is clearly about particulars, and the Argument from Opposites gets what plausibility it has from its application to particulars; it is highly unconvincing to claim that opposites always hold of any *type* of beautiful thing. These brief remarks hardly do justice to the issue; for one thing, there are different ways in which the claim about opposites can be taken when it is applied to types. But at any rate it is clear that Plato has not faced and lucidly sorted out the difference between kinds of particular instances, and the instances themselves, in so far as this is relevant to his arguments for Forms.

The other difficulty arises from the fact that Plato lumps together relative and mathematical terms with moral terms. For when we apply terms like 'large', 'one', 'half', or 'soft', it is characteristically to particular *things*, material objects. But the moral terms, like 'just', 'pious', 'beautiful' and the like, apply to *actions*. (They also, of course, apply to people – indeed, if Plato's account of justice is anything to go by, this would be their primary use. But the problems with Socratic definition, out of which Plato's concerns grow, come from being able to say that the same kind of *action* can be both just and unjust, etc.) Since Plato treats all the kinds of term he mentions on a par, we naturally assume that he is thinking of actions as being particulars, like the objects such as fingers to which we apply 'large' and the like. The question, whether actions are particulars like material objects, is a deep and complex issue, over which philosophers disagree very strongly. Plato, however, shows no awareness even of there being any problem with treating objects and actions on a par. In the same way as he lumps 'large' and 'just' together without further explanation, he lumps together the many large things and the many just 'things' without further ado. But the cases are not at all similar.

For one thing, particular objects change through time, and can be thought of as unstable and therefore admitting opposite characterizations; but it is not at all intuitive to think of particular actions themselves as changing over time. (This is one reason why many resist the assimilation of actions to the status of particular objects.) A child may be small now and become large later, but a particular action cannot be just now and then become unjust later. (At least, if one maintains that it can, it is for theoretical reasons, none of which Plato shows the slightest sense of noticing.) Plato seems rather to be concerned with the point that a particular action can be both just and unjust at the same time, from different points of view.

These two difficulties cut across each other, so that if we ask, to what is the Form of Beauty being opposed on a particular occasion, there might be four answers: a particular beautiful object, a kind of beautiful object, a particular beautiful action or a kind of beautiful action. With terms that apply only to objects or only to actions there are only two possibilities. But it is never clear exactly what Plato has in mind. In these arguments we get the impression that Forms are being opposed on the one hand to particular *objects* (like the finger) but on the other hand to kinds of *action* (when people have opinions about the 'many justs', surely it is different kinds of action that might be just).

So, while it is clear that Plato in these passages wants a limited range of Forms, he does not make it easy for us to say what that range is. The Argument from Opposites does not generalize, but neither is it quite clear what exactly is the restricted range of terms it is to apply to. The Argument from Opposites, although it is presented as if it were a simple and bold line of thought, in fact contains different strands which raise different problems. Plato sometimes follows one strand, like the mutability of particular objects, which has no obvious application to other strands, like the problems in saying what kinds of action are just. He is overimpressed by the boldness of his argument; he does not see that he is holding together a number of very different considerations. Later, when we find him apparently thinking of Forms in ways that do not correspond well to the Argument from Opposites, he is probably not trying explicitly to generalize the results of a restricted argument (which anyway is not generalizable). It is more likely that he is unawares following up one strand further than he can consistently go.

There is a third passage in the *Republic* where Forms are discussed: Book 10, 596a–597e. It is brief and problematic, and conflicts in many puzzling ways with the treatment of Forms in the body of the *Republic*. (This is not the only way in which Book 10 is an odd-man-out in the book; see Chapter 14.) The passage comes in a context where Plato is claiming that art is trivial and worthless. He begins by claiming that painters have no knowledge of what they paint, and tries to show this by downgrading the status of what they produce. To this end, Forms are brought in, rather unexpectedly. At 596a Socrates says, 'Do you want us to start looking in our usual way? We are accustomed to assuming a Form in each case for the many particulars to which we give the same name.' (Grube.) Since, he goes on, there are many beds and many tables, i.e. many particular items which we call 'bed' and 'table', there must be a single Form of Bed, and Form of Table. The Form is what the craftsman 'looks towards' and tries to embody in his work when he makes beds, whereas the painter, more superficial, copies only the way particular beds appear. The painter's product is thus of low status, 'three removes from nature'; the craftsman's bed, make looking towards the Form, is of higher status, though still lowly compared with the Form. The Form of Bed is made by God, and there is only one (597c). God made only one, either because he chose to or because he had to. There can't be more than one Form; if there were two, then these two would have the same form, and so there would (*per impossible*) be a further Form of Bed in which they both partook.

This is all that is said about Forms in this short passage where they are introduced *en passant*; but in many ways their introduction makes for trouble if we think back to the central books.

Firstly, the claim at 596a is the claim that there is a Form for every general term applicable to a plurality of things. This is the only passage in Plato where he says this, though the reference to 'usual way' and 'we are accustomed' suggests some background of which we have no further notice. (It has been questioned whether 596a does in fact make this claim, or can be interpreted in a weaker way compatible with the other passages about Forms. I shall accept the stronger claim since, besides being more generally accepted, it is more in tune with the other oddities of Book 10.)

This passage is dear to the hearts of those who think that the 'theory of Forms' is a theory of universals. For 596a seems very like an allusion to the 'problem of universals'. How is it that we can apply the same word to a number of different things and call them all tables or beds? We do this, and we do it success-fully – but with what justification? Perhaps there is no further justification (the 'nominalist' response); perhaps we do, in fact, use the same word for a number of particular things, but there is nothing other than the fact that we do have this practice to justify our so grouping them. Perhaps, however, there *is* a further justification (the 'realist' response): quite apart from our decisions so to use the word, it does in fact name, or pick out, or correspond to, something in the nature of things, something real distinct from particular things, a universal. 596a looks very like a 'realist' claim: we call all beds beds because the word 'bed' names the Form of Bed, and particular beds are so called because of their relation to the Form of Bed; it is the existence of the Form of Bed that justifies our practice of calling all beds beds.

Now quite apart from the merits of this line of thought, it is odd to find Plato arguing this way. It is not that he shows no concern elsewhere for the problems of how we use general terms – he does, at e.g. *Meno* 72–74. And he sometimes claims that particulars are 'named after' Forms (e.g. *Phaedo* 78e, *Timaeus* 52a, *Parmenides* 130e, 133d). And in 435b of the *Republic* he showed himself aware of the issue that arises over calling very different kinds of thing by the same word. Even given these concerns, however, there are problems with the Book 10 passage. For one thing, Plato shows himself apparently clear that the Form is to be a universal distinct from particular things, whereas elsewhere he is not so clear whether it is particulars, or rather types of particulars which are defective as compared to the Form (cf. pp. 224–5). More important, the earlier passages argued for a restricted range of Forms, whereas the present passage would seem to churn out a Form for every general term, with no restrictions. The Argument from Opposites cannot be generalized to cover every term; but the

Book 10 argument, which following Aristotle we can call the One Over Many, applies with no inbuilt restrictions to all terms. But this creates a serious difficulty. It is not just that the One Over Many produces, at the very last moment, *more* Forms than we were expecting. It produces them in a way that alters their role. For, if we consider the Argument from Opposites, Forms are produced by hard thought about some concepts, and can be grasped only by those that see the intellectual deficiencies of relying unthinkingly on experience in all cases. Grasping the existence of Forms is part of the ascent to knowledge, which is difficult and not open to all; and those that fail, while they lack understanding, are in a state which is adequate as far as it goes. But if we consider the One Over Many, it looks as though particulars are all defective just because they are particulars; as though Forms are grasped not by hard thinking about problematic concepts but by a trivial application of the One Over Many in every single case; and as though grasping that there are Forms is not a gaining of understanding in some cases but a simple recognition of what everybody does all the time, namely apply general terms.

Plato does not seem to realize it, but we cannot just combine the Argument from Opposites with the One Over Many; the latter produces Forms in a different way that does not let them play their role in the gaining of understanding that develops by recognizing that some problems must be thought through because they are not settled by experience.

Secondly, it is odd (and unique in Plato) for a Form to be made by God; Forms are eternal and uncreated. It might be said that we should not make too heavy weather of the talk of Forms being created by God: this is just introduced so as to produce a parallel with the craftsman and painter, so that we have God making the Form of Bed, the craftsman making the bed, and the painter making the representation of the bed. That is, the language here comes from the nature of the example, which is an artefact. But this in turn faces us with another difficulty. Firstly, the passage does not rely entirely on artefacts, since at 598b–c the painter is said to paint a cobbler and other craftsmen, so presumably the same line of thought would produce a Form of Cobbler, though the obvious absurdity of this makes one think that Plato has not seen this implication. Secondly, even if we restrict ourselves to artefacts, we are in difficulties over there being Forms of artefacts if Forms are to be *separate* from the particular things that partake in them, as is required by the Books 5 and 7 arguments. It is part of the line of thought in those passages that we come to see that what we can grasp only by exerting our minds is not the same as the quality that we can recognize just by looking. But how can this apply to beds? When the craftsman makes beds 'looking towards the Form' (596b) we can understand this without too much difficulty: to make a bed is not to copy any particular bed (for this could be done without understanding what beds are and what they are for) but rather to bring it about that particular pieces of wood embody certain general principles about comfort, use, and so on, which constitute the function of a bed. This account of the making of artefacts is given also at *Cratylus* 388 ff., where Socrates says that a carpenter making a shuttle does not copy the old broken shuttle, but rather considers exactly what type of shuttle is required, asks himself precisely what each type is for, and then brings it about that the particular piece of wood embodies the functional principles required to achieve this. Aristotle adopts this account of making things: to make an artefact is to embody a form in some materials. However, Aristotle also (in *Nicomachean Ethics* I, 6) ridicules Plato for holding this when his Forms are so sharply separated from particular instances. How can anyone be helped to make a bed by 'looking towards' a Form that is utterly distinct from the characteristics that are to be found in any actual beds? Aristotle is happy to say that the form of bed is something that we can all see in particular beds; it is just the way the materials are organized. But Plato cannot say this.

Thirdly, the role of Forms in Book 10 is not only not consistent with that of Books 5 and 7; it introduces the possibility of an infinite regress.

The Form of F is what is, unqualifiedly, F, and for this it must be F in the same sense as the particulars that are only qualifiedly F. Particulars are not F in a different sense from that in which the Form is F; nor are they F in some radically defective or lower sense. The arguments that have been laid out would not work if the Form were not F in the same sense as that in which the particulars are F; the difference is rather that the Form is, and they are not, unqualifiedly F. So the Form of Justice will be just, the Form of Beauty will be beautiful, and so on. This feature of the Forms is often labelled 'self-predication'. (This name has become standard, but is perhaps unfortunate, for it suggests that, just as we first identify some object, say Helen, and then say of her that she is beautiful, so we first identify the Form of Beauty and say of it, oddly, that *it* is beautiful. In fact the Form of Beauty is not identified independently of being what is beautiful: it is the only un-qualified bearer of the predicate 'beautiful', not one more object that might or might not have been beautiful.)

If, however, Forms are universals, as in Book 10, then the Form F will be what makes particulars F, in the sense that it is the item, not identical with any of them, which legitimizes our calling them all F. This is often called the 'non-identity' assumption; the Form of F can't be identical with any particular F thing, or it couldn't be what makes it right to call them all F.

But this raises the possibility of a regress. For if the Form is F in the same sense as the particulars (by self-predication), then it is (by non-identity) another F thing to add to the F things. So won't there have to be another Form, call it F', which is what makes Form and particulars all F? And then we can make the same move about the new Form. F': if it is F in the same sense as all the other F things, Form and particulars, and it is not identical with any of them, then the same questions arise. The regress is vicious, because we cannot have even one Form without having infinitely many.

Now in Book 10, at 597c, Plato seems to deny this. There is only one Form of Bed, he says, because if there were even two there would have to be another one whose Form they would both have, and *this* would be the Form of Bed. The problem Plato envisages is just the one sketched: the Form of Bed is distinct from particular beds, but it is a bed in the same sense that they are (597b), and this raises the possibility of the Third Bed, over and above Form and particulars. Plato flatly denies this: it is ruled out by the Form's uniqueness. But is this an adequate reply? We know the Form is *meant* to be unique: but surely the threatened regress shows that it *can't* be.

Plato gives this matter more thought in *Parmenides* part 1 (especially 132a–b). Scholars are very divided over the question of what exactly was the problem Plato saw, and whether or not he thought that his blocking move in *Republic* 10 could be any kind of answer. The matter cannot be confidently settled, nor adequately discussed in a brief space. (Nor can the interesting issue, why Forms as produced by the Argument from Opposites are not liable to this difficulty.) But one thing is clear: the role of Forms in Book 10 does land Plato in a difficulty, whether he recognizes this or not. And this is only the most severe of many difficulties produced by the Book 10 Forms. Without Book 10 Forms would have had a comprehensible and relevant role as objects of the kind of knowledge that demands hard thinking and is thus found only in those with the questioning intelligence Plato demands of his Guardians; Forms are relevant chiefly to moral and mathematical studies, those suitable for training wise rulers. (We shall come back to this role of mathematics.) Book 10 injects, as an afterthought, confusion and conflict over what looked a relatively clear point. It is significant that in part 1 of the *Parmenides* Socrates is made to say that he is sure that there are Forms for moral and mathematical Forms, less sure about ones for 'man' and other terms for natural kinds, and very unwilling to have them for hair, mud, and dirt. Opposites are not mentioned, but in fact he is happy with the results of the kind of application that we have seen of the Argument from Opposites, and he is unhappy with terms that have no opposites. We see perhaps an indication that Plato is unhappy about generalizing the Argument from Opposites, without seeing exactly what has gone wrong. It is surprising that he is not more tentative about Book 10. For the role of Forms there conflicts with the results of the Argument from Opposites, and with its role: it is hard to see what on earth Forms so produced have to do with the understanding that distinguishes the wise and the just.

This problem of reconciling different passages raises the question, In what sense does Plato have, in the *Republic*, an overall 'theory' of Forms? Immense amounts have been written about Forms, and the reader will do best to make his or her own judgement on the various conflicting views; there is here no substitute for reading all sides and deciding for oneself who gives the best account. What follows is only one view among many. I make no claim to deal with Forms in general, only with Forms as they appear in the *Republic*, which I treat as complete and self-contained; although we may get useful help in understanding Forms from passages in other dialogues, I do not think that an account of the role of Forms in one dialogue should essentially depend on passages from outside that dialogue.

We are in no doubt that Plato believes that there are Forms. But what is it for there to be a *theory* of Forms? It is often understood this way: Plato had a full-scale, worked-out, overall theory that introduced Forms as entities that solve problems that worried people but had not been adequately solved. Forms are thus theoretical entities, brought in for their explanatory value. Many writers on Plato have, explicitly or implicitly, taken 'theory' this way, analogous to a scientific theory that explains phenomena in a way removing puzzles about them. They have commended Plato for the economy of his theory because it is supposed to solve so many problems. Plato is thought to have proceeded somewhat as follows. He was worried by certain problems, like the break-up of moral consensus and the prevalence of change in the world, and was upset by the conclusions that people tended to draw from them. The 'theory of Forms' introduces entities that account for the phenomena suggesting the worrying conclusions and account for them in such a way that those conclusions are seen not to be warranted. For example, once we are assured of the existence of the Form of Justice as well as particular just actions, and grasp that it is not subject to the deficiencies that they are subjected to, we see that we should not be worried by those deficiencies or be led by them to be relativists or sceptics about justice.

If this *is* what Plato is doing, then we can reasonably expect him to do three things. One is, to argue for Forms from the phenomena whose adequate explanation is supposed to require them. Another is, to show that the explanatory roles they fill in different contexts are all consistent. Another is, to show that Forms offer *good* explanations, that they are not just *an* answer to certain worries but a better answer, with more explanatory value, than any alternative.

Plato does none of these things. Nor is this just a question of lack of sophistication about theories and explanation; he does nothing that could be seen as even a first move towards these requirements. This is clearer in the case of the last two requirements than in that of the first. Plato never argues that Forms can be independently shown to have explanatory value, or that they can be shown independently to provide better answers than other kinds of explanation. This is why many people have criticized the theory for being vacuous and offering no real explanations. Nor does he ever try to show that the Forms' roles are consistent. In the *Republic* we find the unexplained gulf between Book 10 and the other passages about Forms, a gulf that cannot be bridged and gets not the slightest explanation. We find, moreover, that although the Argument from Opposites is presented in a form that cannot be generalized, none the less Plato does sometimes talk about Forms as though one or other of the considerations that that argument rests on had general application – as, for example, when he contrasts Forms as stable by comparison with particulars as liable to change. Plato is very casual about which characteristics of Forms he stresses in a given context. (This is certainly true of the *Republic*; the above claims need more backing in so far as they touch on other dialogues.)

More surprising is the fact that Plato never offers an argument for Forms that would establish them as entities suitable for a theory of the kind envisioned. In Books 5 and 10 Forms are quite explicitly brought in as being already accepted by all the interlocutors, though they are new to the reader. The same happens at 505a with the Form of Good. And neither of the extended passages in Books 5 and 7 sets out to argue that there are Forms in a way that would convince someone who did not already accept this. The Book 5 passage establishes conclusions about knowledge and belief and then applies claims about Forms to these. The Book 7 passage sets out to show that there are certain studies that are suitable for getting people to think in an abstract way, and Forms are brought in to show this. It is not the object of either passage to prove that there are Forms.

This may seem a perverse thing to say. For if Plato does not try to show us that there are Forms in *these* passages, then there is virtually nowhere where he *does* try to show us that there are Forms. For these are among the passages that people have always taken as the heart of Plato's thinking about Forms. Now it would be perverse to deny that there is *any* sense in which these passages 'argue for Forms', just as it would be perverse to deny that Plato had a 'theory of Forms' in *any* sense of the word 'theory'. Certainly these passages are meant to have some effect on the way we are to think of Forms. But what is important here is that although they are passages of argument, and introduce Forms, and are passages of argument about Forms, they do not argue for Forms from premises that we could be expected to accept already. Plato does not argue from the phenomena (in a way that Aristotle certainly does). He does not point to the existence of puzzles that we recognize, or truths that we are all prepared to accept, and try to show that giving an adequate explanation of these commits us to accepting Forms. He is not unaware of this kind of argument. In a work by Aristotle, *On the Forms*, certain arguments are retailed which were offered in the Academy by Plato for the existence of Forms. (It can, I think, be shown, though not here, that there is good reason to ascribe these arguments to Plato and not just to 'Platonists'.) These arguments *do* argue from the phenomena to Forms. They argue that if we accept the existence of well-defined branches of knowledge, or the existence of thinking about things that have perished, or the existence of memory, or the existence of predicating general terms, than we are committed to thinking that there are Forms. But in the dialogues Plato never argues like this. His arguments always involve Forms without arguing to them from the phenomena. The dialogues contain no convincing argument with which to face the person who does not yet accept that there are Forms, but is worried by certain existing puzzles, or accepts certain obvious truths. There is no argument to get us from premises that we accept to the existence of Forms as a conclusion.

None of this means that Plato had no 'theory' of Forms at all. He certainly has beliefs about Forms which are not just isolated but form some kind of interconnected whole (though, as we have seen, the degree and kind of interconnection is not very obvious). But the 'theory' cannot be treated as resembling in any way a theory that offers explanations that we desired, and can be expected to find convincing, quite independently of any prior commitment to Forms. The theory is not a theory to solve our problems or explain the phenomena to us in a way that everyone will find convincing whether or not he or she already believes that there are Forms. It is not 'economical' in its explanatory power because Plato is not trying to hoard explanatory resources at all.

Why does Plato proceed in this way? In the *Republic* the answer (to the extent that we can find an answer) is less clear from the passages about Forms than it is from Book 6 and its discussion of the philosophical nature and how it gets corrupted in the world as it is. Plato thinks that usually the world, especially the political world, goes badly, but not because people are stupid; there are many people around who are all too intelligent, and what goes wrong is that their cleverness is corrupted, so that they pursue mean and devious ends and become proud of their skill in attaining goals that are petty and despicable (518d–519b; he is thinking of the kind of thing to which Watergate provides a good modern parallel). There are plenty of people sharp enough to be good at arguments. What is lacking, and what Plato sees as requiring an overturning of society's values so that philosophers rule, is what can only be described in very general terms as an appreciation of true values. Most people, Plato thinks, do not prize or even understand what is truly worthwhile, because their experience narrows their vision and concentrates their thoughts on self-interest and short-term gratifications. The truly just person, on the other hand, is someone capable of becoming a philosopher and rising above the partial viewpoint of his or her own situation to appreciate and live by truths that are not qualified by reference to particular interests or points of view. The understanding that the wise and just person achieves (of which of course more remains to be said) involves Forms: the first step is to see that knowledge extends beyond what is merely given in experience, and to appreciate that there are notions that can only be understood by hard thinking. Recognition that there are Forms is thus the first step towards the kind of understanding that distinguishes the wise from the unreflective.

Forms are not presented as something to be argued for from

premises that all would accept, or to explain the phenomena that we all appreciate, because the ability to reason to such entities would not distinguish the wise from the merely sharp whose intellect might be put to bad use. Plato always connects Forms with recognizing and valuing what is good, not just with having the capacity to follow an argument.

Forms are thus more than theoretical entities in a theory that explains the phenomena; a knowledge of them is part of the *good* person's understanding. Plato sometimes (though not in the *Republic*) talks of the ascent to the Forms as being one of love and desire, as though the Forms had an attractive force. But this should not be misunderstood: the Forms are not equally attractive to the philosopher and to the clever ruthless exploiter. Rather, Plato thinks that no amount of intelligence will grasp the Forms if it is directed to self-interested and narrow ends.

It is thus a change of heart more than a mere sharpening of the wits that is needed to make one realize that there are Forms. Of course one can argue about them, as Plato does; but the first move is not a purely intellectual one. (That is why Plato is so pessimistic about the possibility of a philosopher ruler arising in the world as it is now; he would have to have, not just brains, but the kind of just character unlikely in anyone not brought up in a just society.) Hence Plato does not make it appear that our acceptance of Forms hangs entirely on our accepting certain arguments. For we might go through the proof perfectly and still fail to grasp the point of it. This is a very important point for Plato, and one to bear in mind, because here he differs considerably from modern philosophers. We should be careful not to rush to the other extreme and confuse Plato's procedure with an easy anti-intellectualism which claims that profound truths are grasped only by direct vision or intuition, and that mere reasoning is impotent. No-one has more respect for reasoning and argument than Plato. But he is still convinced that on its own it will not produce a philosopher. Although it creates difficulties for him, Plato insists that the philosopher is the *just* person, that grasp of Forms is part of a *moral* understanding of the world. In a way uncongenial to modern philosophy, he holds that moral considerations determine what it is that counts as knowledge, rather than mere cleverness and sophistry. So Forms (in the *Republic*; this is *not* a general claim about all the dialogues) form the basis of the *good* person's understanding, not part of a detachable 'metaphysics'. This is one reason why the role of Forms in Book 10 is so intrusive; Forms there seem unconnected to the understanding that is comprehensibly part of virtue.

It has often been stressed that Plato shows sometimes towards the Forms the kind of attitude that is best described as 'mystical', talking of them in the central books in the language of religious faith and conversion. And knowledge of Forms is often described in perceptual metaphors – Forms are 'grasped', or 'seen', as though by vision. These points are distinct, but there is an obvious connection; for the perceptual metaphors make it more natural to think of the Forms as revealed to an intuition that somehow transcends or replaces thought. These ways of talking about Forms are indeed prominent, so prominent that they cannot be swept away as 'mere' metaphor; and they are understandable if we recall that Forms are not just the kind of explanatory entities that anybody, even a clever sophist, could grasp and see the point of. However, there are limits to the helpfulness of stressing the perceptual metaphors, and of thinking of knowledge of the Forms as being, or being like, intuition and faith. Admittedly the realization that there are Forms is described in terms that make it sound more like a conversion than like finding a proof (521c – it is the soul's turning-round from darkness to light). But it turns out to be the start of a rigorously intellectual training based on mathematics, very unlike any kind of faith. Too much stress on the idea of vision and intuition may suggest a kind of passive acceptance that underplays the positive mental effort and hard work required for progress in Platonic understanding. And it is a mistake to stress the language of vision too much at the level of individual Forms. Some scholars write as though Plato thought that we turn from distress at the deficiencies of particular just actions to a wholly satisfying view of the Form of Justice, this being the end of the story, or at any rate the end of the story about justice. But this suggests that the role of Forms is to be satisfying explanatory entities that solve our existing problems and convince the uncommitted; and we have seen that this account of Forms is not adequate. It also suggests that knowledge of Forms provides certainty; but we have seen that for Plato the point of having knowledge is not to find security from doubting whether our beliefs are true; rather, it is to understand the significance of the truths we have. It is better to apply the metaphor of vision to the whole thesis that there are Forms, rather than to any concern with individual Forms. The claim that there are Forms is rather like the claim that there are objective ethical values. There can be plenty of argument about and concerning such a claim, but whether or not one accepts it is not likely to hang on the convincingness of particular arguments. Conviction is more likely to build up slowly, as one comes to follow arguments, the use of certain key notions, the prominence given to certain ideas by those that uphold the thesis and those that deny it. If one comes to be convinced that the thesis is true, one is less likely to say, 'Now I have finally figured it out' than 'Now I see the point' or 'can look at things in the right way'. Similarly, if someone fails to realize that there are Forms, this failure is not to be assimilated to sheer stupidity, incapacity to work through a proof. It is a failure to *see* that knowledge is not limited by our everyday experience and interests (and indeed may result in some revisions in the opinions we had) but requires thinking on our part and following through concepts that are not grasped adequately on the basis of our experience alone.

People might deny that there are Forms for two kinds of reason. They might never have thought about it before and simply find the idea odd and unnecessary. Or they might deny the thesis on various philosophical grounds. They might, for example, claim that the Argument from Opposites does not prove that there *are* any unqualified bearers of the relevant terms, but rather that it merely shows that there can be no such thing as an unqualified application of 'just', 'large', and so on. Plato makes no attempt to meet the objection of such a sophisticated relativist. As we have seen, there are no 'arguments for Forms' to convince us that Plato's claims are more convincing that an opponent's. Despite Thrasymachus in Book 1, Plato's main concern in the central books is not with the hostile sceptical or relativist opponent, but with the apathetic and indifferent many. It needs effort to achieve even the beginnings of understanding, and most people, Plato thinks, are too sunk in their own concerns to make that effort. Even if they had the intellectual ability, it would not occur to them to think of anything larger than their career or family or personal affections. So people who do not realize that there are Forms are not necessarily believing anything false, but they are missing something. It is a natural metaphor to say that they are 'blind to' things that really matter. Plato uses this way of talking (cf. 484d–e), but his favourite metaphor is the dream: most people (493e–494a) are asleep and dreaming, whereas the philosopher has 'woken up to' the Forms. It does not matter what metaphor we use, as long as we realize that Forms are not the end of a journey of faith, beaming out certainty and security to a passive audience. They are the beginning of an intellectual quest, calling on all one's resources to search for the truth, a journey that Plato will describe in the Cave figure as a breaking out of passive conformity to intellectual liberation.

FURTHER READING

Enormous amounts have been written on the 'theory of Forms'; the following is only a selection.

The traditional view of the 'theory' is lucidly set out in Cherniss, 'The Philosophical Economy of the Theory of Ideas' in Allen (ed.), *Studies in Plato's Metaphysics* and Vlastos (ed.) *Plato* 1. Another overall view is collected from passages in different dialogues by A. Wedberg, 'The Theory of Ideas', ch. 3 of *Plato's Philosophy of Mathematics* and in *Plato* 1. A thoughtful and much less 'unitarian' view can be found in Moravcsik, 'Recollecting the Theory of Forms' in *Facets of Plato's Philosophy*, *Phronesis* Supplement 2 (1976).

Particularly relevant to the Argument from Opposites are: Kirwan, 'Plato and Relativity', *Phronesis* 1974; Nehamas, 'Plato on the Imperfection on the Sensible World', *American Philosophical Quarterly* 1975; Irwin, 'Plato's Heracleiteanism', *Philosophical Quarterly* 1977.

The claim that Forms and particulars are *F* in different senses is defended clearly in R. Allen, 'Participation and Predication in Plato's Middle Dialogues', in Allen (ed.), *Studies in Plato's Metaphysics* and Vlastos (ed.), *Plato* 1, and criticized effectively by F. C. White, 'Plato's Middle Dialogues and the Independence of Particulars', *Philosophical Quarterly* 1977. White, in 'The *Phaedo* and *Republic* V on Essences', *Journal of*

Hellenic Studies 1978, discusses clearly the different implications of different arguments about the Forms.

On the threatened infinite regress, see (out of the copious secondary literature): Vlastos, 'The Third Man Argument in the *Parmenides*', *Philosophical Review* 1954 and in Allen (ed.); Vlastos, 'Plato's Third Man Argument: Text and Logic' in *Philosophical Studies*; Strang, 'Plato and the Third Man', *Proceedings of the Aristotelian Society Supplementary Volume* 1963 and in Vlastos (ed.), *Plato* 1. On Book 10 see also Cherniss, pp. 360–74 of 'The Relation of the *Timaeus* to Plato's Later Dialogues' in Allen (ed.).

Chapter 10

Understanding and the Good: Sun, Line, and Cave

The person with knowledge, then, is the person who thinks things through where others remain unreflective, and who realizes that there are objects of knowledge that are not to be found in experience, the Forms. From Plato's discussion of knowledge, and from the passages of argument that serve to introduce Forms, it does not follow that knowledge is *only* of Forms; and because Plato links knowledge with understanding rather than with certainty he has no obvious reason to demand a wholesale critical rejection of our previously held beliefs. Indeed, given his account of justice he has reason not to introduce a concept of knowledge that requires such wholesale rejection. (Cf. pp. 212–15). In Books 6 and 7, however, Plato gives a long and detailed account of the requirements of knowledge, in the form of the three figures of Sun, Line, and Cave and a description of the further education needed to train the Guardians who are to achieve the highest kinds of knowledge. And we find that the upshot of these famous passages is a much more revisionary account of knowledge (and, with it, of justice) than has emerged so far.

Knowledge, for Plato, requires understanding; but what does understanding require? Two things emerge from Plato's discussion. One is that understanding is *systematic* because it involves explanation. The person with mere 'true belief' is in possession of various truths, and so has what we are prepared to call knowledge of various matters of fact. But these truths are isolated, or hang together for arbitrary reasons; knowledge, by contrast, forms an explanatory whole. The user of bridles is in a better state than the maker (pp. 191–2) because, although the maker may have a perfectly good grasp of certain facts about bridles, he has no unified grasp of the function and use of bridles such as enables the expert to say why the various requirements for a good bridle are as they are. Understanding is connected with explanation, with being able to say why things are the way they are; and to be able to explain things is to be able to relate them systematically and show what is basic and what dependent, and how they are interrelated. Modern theories of explanation often claim that to explain a particular occurrence – to be able to say *why* it happened rather than just *that* it happened – we must show that it falls under a law relating kinds of occurrence. Plato does not talk of laws or generalizations, since his model is not any kind of science, but he shares the general idea that a particular claim may be true, but is not explanatory in isolation. For it to be a case of knowledge – something we understand, as opposed to mere belief – something that is held to be true in isolation – it must be shown to fit comprehensibly into an explanatory system of truths. His model for such an explanatory system is mathematics. This side of Plato's concern with understanding will be followed up in the next chapter.

The other requirement for understanding is that it must crucially involve reference to goodness. This claim is more startling than the other, and not just because of its abstractness. If our paradigm of systematic explanation is scientific or mathematical, reference to goodness seems out of place. We tend to think of goodness as something that defies systematic explanation; statements about goodness are often interpreted as being arbitrary expressions of personal taste, rather than objective claims about something that can be systematically explained. Plato, however, is far from thinking that goodness is subjective, or marginal, something that cannot be part of an organized explanation. Indeed, he makes it fundamental to all real explanation, and hence all understanding.

At 505a Socrates says that the greatest of the philosopher-rulers' studies is the Form of Good, from which just actions and the like derive their usefulness and beneficial qualities. But, while all agree on the importance of knowing the nature of the good, and in this matter alone are not satisfied with appearance, wanting what is really good, there is little agreement over what the good is – though suggestions that it is knowledge or pleasure are obviously not adequate (505a–506b). Socrates himself says that he does not know what the Good is, and has only feeble beliefs (506b–e), but consents to point out its nature by an analogy. He gives, in fact, three: Sun, Line, and Cave, all of which explicate the place of the Good in the just person's knowledge, and the form that knowledge takes.

Before going on to the Sun, it is worth noticing some points of interest in Socrates' procedure. Firstly, a Form is again brought in from outside the discussion as something the interlocutor has 'often' heard about. Socrates does not argue for it, and he refuses to discuss it except indirectly. Plato is helping himself to the claim that the Good, the object of all human strivings, is the Form of Good. We can see by now why he finds this obvious (though recognizing that others do not). Everyone, he says, wants what is really good; their behaviour is not otherwise explicable (505d–e). But then the Good that all seek must be what is really and unqualifiedly good; and what is unqualifiedly good and never evil is just what Plato calls a Form, the only unqualified bearer of the predicate 'good'.

All the same, we, if not Plato, should pause. For Forms are crucially *distinct* from particular things to which the same predicate applies. The Form of Good is not in the world of our experience, since it is not the same as anything we call good. But is it not then odd, that when people seek what is good they are looking for something which is *ex hypothesi* different from anything to be found in people and actions? Aristotle criticizes Plato sharply, clearly with his passage in mind, at *Nicomachean Ethics* I, 6: it is absurd, he says, for the object of people's strivings to be something unattainable in the world of particular actions, a Form separate from particular good things. This is a serious problem, because the Good is what is studied by those who are to rule: if they learn about something that is never to be found in experience, how can their knowledge of it be the *practical* wisdom they are to have? Right at the very beginning of Plato's discussion of the Good and its role for knowledge we find him making an assumption about the nature of the Good that seems to turn it into an object of detached, rather than practical, knowledge.

But even if we waive the special problems arising from Plato's

Good being a separated Form, is it legitimate in any case to talk of *the* Good? Aristotle makes this criticism too in the same chapter. There is, he says, nothing which is just good, good without qualification, as *the* Good would have to be. 'Good' is a term that has no such absolute, unqualified employment. Its use is always relative to some set of criteria. What makes for a good man is essentially different from what makes for a good action. Aristotle distinguishes senses or uses of 'good' according to what it is that is said to be good. (Modern discussions concentrate more on the fact that what is good from one point of view may not be good from another.) Plato produces no arguments against this position, one which is often simply taken for granted in modern discussions. For him to have done so would have been tantamount to arguing for the existence of the Form of Good, which is something he chooses not to do. So right at the start of the discussion Plato parts company with someone who believes that for something to be good is always for it to be good *for X*, or *from Y's point of view*, or *a good Z*. He clearly thinks that an ethical discussion cannot get off the ground with someone who rejects the starting premise that besides particular goods that are relative to various interests and criteria, there is also *the* Good, which is, objectively, just good, not good relative to anything. As with Forms generally, Plato offers no direct argument. Presumably we are to become convinced of the truth of his claim more indirectly, by the whole long passage which follows.

The first figure, the Sun, begins from the distinction between Forms and 'the many', Forms being objects of thought as opposed to the many things and actions that are instances of Forms, which we know through experience. Sight is the most prominent of the senses that inform us about the world of experience, and it is also distinguished from the other senses by the fact that it needs a medium – light. Light is provided by the sun, which thus makes sight possible, since we can only see things clearly to the extent that they are illuminated for us by the sun.

The sun, supreme in the visible realm, corresponds to the Good, supreme in the realm of thought. It enables the objects of knowledge to be known by the mind, as the objects of sight are seen by the eye. Further, just as the sun causes things not only to be seen but to grow and come into being, so the Good gives the objects of knowledge not just their knowability but their reality, though it is itself 'beyond reality' (or 'beyond being').

'Plato's Good', which he refuses to clarify here, became a byword for obscurity. How can the Good make things known, still less make them be what they are, in a way comparable to the workings of the sun? Plato is putting forward two thoughts, though he leaves them deliberately schematic. Presumably he believes that they are true, but has no idea how to argue for them, and perhaps thinks that they are not the kind of truth that can be argued for, but must be accepted in the light of other considerations and arguments taken as a whole. The first thought, that the Good makes things known, is what we might perhaps express by saying that goodness is fundamental in any explanation. This is a perfectly comprehensible idea, though one that the majority of modern philosophers would reject. Many philosophers draw a sharp distinction between matters of fact and matters of value, and hold that, since a thing's goodness is a matter of value, it cannot enter into the same kind of explanation as matters of fact about it. But Plato holds not only that facts and values are not radically different kinds of thing, known in different ways, but that values are fundamental to explaining facts. He willingly commits himself to the claim that values can be *better* known than facts, that they are *more* fundamental to our understanding. Many modern philosophers would find such an idea extraordinary; but it is not clear at this level of generality where the truth lies. We can understand Plato's very programmatic claims only when we see the use he puts them to, in all three of the figures and not just one.

The second thought is that the Good makes things not just knowable, but actually makes them what they are. This, and the enigmatic claim that the Good is itself 'beyond being', have led to many complex metaphysical interpretations, particularly by the Neo-Platonists. But it is possible to take the thought fairly simply, as being just the correlate of the claim about knowledge. If goodness is fundamental for our understanding of the nature of things, then it must be fundamental in the nature of things, else our understanding would not reflect the world as it is. For Plato, not only is there no gap between our knowledge of facts and our knowledge of values, there is no difference of ultimate nature between facts and values in the world. And if goodness is basic for our understanding of things, then in the world goodness and other values are not peculiar or derivative entities; they are just as real as other things, indeed in some obscure way *more* real. Without going into the metaphysics of this claim, which he leaves hanging, we can see that Plato commits himself to the very general claim that goodness is supreme in the order of things, and hence basic to any attempt to make the world intelligible. We must be careful not to confuse these beliefs about the sovereignty of good with shallow optimism about Providence and all being for the best. Plato's enthusiasm for what is absolutely good, the separated Form, coexists with extreme pessimism about the amount of goodness to be found in the actual world.

One thing clear about the Sun figure is that it is an analogy: *as* the sun is in the visible realm, *so* the Good is in the intelligible realm. The distinction between visible and intelligible is now further explicated by the figure of the Line (509d). The difference is illustrated by the ratio of an unequally divided line, its parts divided in the same ratio. The result is:

where BD:DC and CE:EA as BC:CA. (Plato does not himself remark that this results in DC and CE being equal.) These sections represent levels of clarity. BD contains 'images' (*eikones*) of which examples are shadows and reflections of objects. These are later (511d–e) said to have as the corresponding mental state *eikasia*. I leave this untranslated because it is very disputed what the correct translation should be.

DC contains the originals of these images; examples are living things and natural or manufactured objects. The corresponding mental state is *pistis* or 'belief' (the word suggests confident belief).

CE and EA are harder. Plato is referring very elliptically to issues that are later made clearer in Book 7. In CE the mind uses the contents of DC in turn as images and thus is forced to seek on the basis of hypotheses – for example, students of mathematics reason on the basis of certain mathematical assumptions or hypotheses, and are forced to use visible illustrations, although they are reasoning about intelligible objects, not the contents of DC. This is *dianoia* or 'thinking'.

In EA the mind proceeds entirely by means of Forms, reasoning not from hypotheses but rather *to* an unhypothetical first principle. This is *noēsis* or 'intellect'.

Since BD:DC as CE:EA, the contents of BD should stand to those of DC as those of CE stand to those of EA. The contents of BD are images or reflections of those of DC; but with CE and EA Plato does not say this straightforwardly, but presents the difference between the sections as being one of method.

Is the Line an analogy, like the Sun? In that case, the lower part is merely illustrating facts about belief and its objects which illuminate knowledge and its objects in the upper part. Some features of the Line suggest that this is indeed the case.

Firstly, the Line is introduced as classifying the intelligible and *visible* world, carrying on from the Sun; and the language of vision is sustained throughout. But this is weak, for at 510a (and 534a in a passage that refers back to this one) the lower part is said to represent the whole world of *belief*, not just of vision.

Secondly, the equality of DC and CE suggests that Plato is not interested in having each section of the Line illustrate an increase in clarity over the one before; his interest lies rather in the ratio BC:CA and the light cast on CA by BC and the internal structure of each, not in the whole line that results.

Thirdly, the lowest stage of the Line, *eikasia*, is not a significant state in its own right. How much time do we spend looking at images and reflections, and how interesting is this?

It has a point only as illustrating the relation of imaging holding between the contents of BD and DC (which in turn illuminate the upper part of the line).

So it does look as though the relation between BD and DC is an easy one (literal imaging) to aid us in understanding the very obscure relation between CE and EA. And so we have the visible illustrating the intelligible, just as in the Sun figure, the only new feature being the use of the contrast between image and original to express the relation between the visible and intelligible realms (as well as the relation within the visible realm which illuminates that within the intelligible).

However, as often happens with Plato, his eagerness to use analogy and images to illustrate a point leads him into intellectual unclarity. For there are also convincing signs that the Line is not just an extended analogy, but is also meant to be in its own right an ambitious classification of the different states a person may be in with regard to knowledge, from the lowest to the highest.

Firstly, we do have one line, not two, whereas in the Sun the two terms of the analogy were quite distinct. And the stages of the continuous line are said to correspond to degrees of clarity (509d, 511d–e), suggesting that the Line is not merely a device to let the bottom part provide an analogy for the top part.

Secondly, the passage stresses something which is odd if all that is going on is an analogy of visible and intelligible realms. Mathematicians, we are told, use the contents of DC as images, though the DC inhabitants are originals of the images in BD. This point is made three times (510b, 510e, 511a) in a very brief passage, and it precisely links the perceptible and intelligible worlds that have to be held in contrast if the Line is only an analogy.

Thirdly, the passage at the end of the Line (511d) has Socrates listing four mental states which differ in clarity as do the objects to which they correspond; the mental states are said to be clear in so far as their objects partake of truth or reality. This seems to be an explicit attempt to present the Line as a classification of cognitive states and their objects, not just a limited analogy.

So the Line, uncomfortably, both distinguishes the visible and intelligible realms to compare them, and also puts them on a continuous scale of epistemological achievement. Undoubtedly one function of the Line is to grade our cognitive states according to their distance from full knowledge with understanding. We learn from the Line various important points about knowledge. One is that the prominence of the image/original relation shows that Plato puts a premium on knowing a thing directly, rather than indirectly via reflections or images. Another is that in the crucial stage of moving from objects adequately apprehended by experience to Forms, an important role is played by mathematics. Another is that mathematics is nevertheless inadequate, for two reasons: it relies on visible illustrations, and it depends on hypotheses, whereas the true 'intellect' of the philosopher is free from these defects and operates only with reference to Forms (511b–c). We already know why mathematics is specially useful; it more than other subjects forces one to think out problems rather than being satisfied with what we can see; and this is the beginning of wisdom. But what these defects of mathematics are, and whether they are linked, and how philosophical reasoning avoids them, are matters not clarified until Book 7.

There are some oddities with the Line's classification of cognitive states and their objects. For one thing, the lowest stage, *eikasia*, seems not to correspond to anything significant in our lives, and appears to be there only for the sake of the analogy to be made between visible and intelligible worlds. Everyday beliefs mostly fall under 'belief', and the important stage is the one where the person is forced (by mathematical reasoning or whatever) to think things through and realize that there are Forms as well as particulars. Another, related point is that 'thinking' (*dianoia*), the all-important stage of forcing oneself to think things out, is confined to mathematical thinking. This seems too restrictive. In the Book 7 passage at 523–5 mathematical concepts are only some among those that make the mind work out what experience does not satisfactorily settle. Further, where in the Line is the Good, so stressed in the figure of the Sun? Reading the Line after the Sun we are naturally led to think that the Good is identical with the 'unhypothetical first principle' grasped by the person with *noēsis* or 'intellect'. But it does not fit into the scheme of the Line very happily. It cannot be just one of the contents of EA;

but if not, where can it go? Worst of all, however, the Line's uncertainty of purpose makes it unclear how the cognitive states are being classified – by their objects or by their methods. In the lower part it seems clearly to be by object – one moves from *eikasia* to 'belief' by looking at trees rather than at reflections of trees. Does the same, though, hold in the upper part?

Pressing this question creates unexpectedly annoying difficulties; no answer seems quite right. Unless we are content to say that the contrast between BD and DC is of a quite different kind from that between CE and EA (which would be an admission that Plato's analogy is inept) we have to choose one of two unsatisfactory alternatives.

(1) The analogy does carry over; the logic of the passage demands different objects for the mind in CE and in EA. But since EA contains Forms, what does CE contain? Now we know from Aristotle that Plato at some point held that mathematics studies not Forms but 'intermediate' objects, which are different from the objects of sense-experience but distinct also from Forms, since they are 'many but eternal'. A little reflection shows the plausibility of this: mathematicians talk about *circles* and *lines*, not about the physical diagrams that illustrate them, nor about the unique Form of Circle and Form of Line. But while this idea makes most sense of the passage and its reference to mathematics, nothing in the *Republic* has prepared us for it. And it conflicts directly with what is said in the passage at 510d, that mathematicians talk about the 'the square itself' and 'the diagonal itself' (surely Forms) as well as the stress throughout the central books on mathematics as the best introduction to the kind of thinking that recognizes Forms.

(2) But if 'thinking', especially mathematical thinking, leads us on to Forms, then the contrast between it and 'intellect' or purely philosophical thought must be a difference of method as regards the same object. Such a difference is not hard to find, especially in the light of Book 7: 'thinking' studies Forms in isolation, for the purpose of special subjects like mathematics, whereas 'intellect' studies them for their own sake, and in systematic connection, as being dependent on the Form of Good for their nature and intelligibility. However, if this is the case, then the scheme of the Line breaks down – the structure of the bottom part has no real analogy in the top part – and Plato is

misleading when he concludes the passage by listing four states (each with its own object) that are stages of progressive cognitive improvement.

The insolubility of this problem is a good illustration of the difficulties that Plato runs into by using images to make a philosophical point. The imagery is apt to get overloaded, as happens with the Line, because Plato is trying to do two things at once with it. And the detail of the imagery tempts us to ask questions that cannot be satisfactorily answered within the terms of the imagery; if we treat it with philosophical serious-ness the image turns out incoherent. As Iris Murdoch says (*The Fire and the Sun*, p. 68), 'The Theory of Forms, when read in conjunction with the explanatory tropes of the Line and the Cave . . . can certainly produce some blazingly strong imagery in the mind which may well in the long run obstruct under-standing.' Plato might well agree; he certainly warns us that he is providing *only* images.

The Cave is Plato's most famous image, dominating many people's interpretation of what Plato's most important ideas are. This is a pity, because, as with the Line, severe problems arise over interpreting the imagery philosophically, and there are persistent disagreements.

Imagine, says Socrates, prisoners in an underground cave with a fire behind them, bound so they can only see the shadows on the wall in front of them, cast by puppets manipulated on a wall behind them. They think that this is all there is to see; if released from their bonds and forced to turn round to the fire and the puppets they become bewildered and are happier left in their original state. They are even angry with anyone who tries to tell them how pitiful their position is. Only a few can bear to realize that the shadows are only shadows cast by the puppets; and they begin the journey of liberation that leads past the fire and right out of the cave to the real world. At first they are dazzled here, and can bear to see real objects only in reflections and indirectly, but then they look at them directly in the light of the sun, and can even look at the sun itself.

The prisoners are 'like us', says Socrates (515a). The Cave is, then, not just the degraded state of a bad society. It is the human condition. Even in the ideally just society, we all start in the Cave. We don't all end there, though; at least in the ideally just society some, who are the Guardians, journey upwards to achieve knowledge and wisdom.

The Cave is Plato's most optimistic and beautiful picture of the power of philosophy to free and enlighten. Abstract thinking, which leads to philosophical insight, is boldly portrayed as something liberating. The person who starts to think is shown as someone who breaks the bonds of conformity to ordinary experience and received opinion, and the progress of enlightenment is portrayed as a journey from darkness into light. Unlike the passive majority, people who start to use their minds are doing something for themselves; after the first (admittedly mysterious) release from bonds it requires the person's own utmost effort to toil upwards out of the Cave. Few thinkers in philosophy or fiction have given a more striking, and moving, picture of philosophical thinking as a releasing of the self from undifferentiated conformity to a developing and enriching struggle for the attainment of truth.

With this picture, and necessary as the other term of the contrast, goes Plato's darkest and most pessimistic picture of the state of those *not* enlightened by philosophy. They are helpless and passive, manipulated by others. Worse, they are used to their state and *like* it, resisting efforts to free them from it. Their satisfaction is a kind of false consciousness about their state; they cannot even recognize and respond to the truth about their terrible condition. This picture notably puts *all* the ordinary person's beliefs on the same level; it does not fit the picture we have had so far, namely that most of the beliefs people have are all right as long as they are about unproblematic matters of experience, and that knowledge is only lacking about difficult and disputed matters like justice. In the imagery of the Cave Plato presses so far his antipathy to the passive and acquiescent state of the unreflective that the unenlightened state is presented as being totally substandard. We shall see that this blanket condemnation leads to a problem of interpretation, but even without this it is clear that to liken all our ordinary beliefs to the seeing of shadows creates a sharp cut-off between the state of the enlightened and that of the unenlightened. They do not inhabit the same cognitive world. The Cave has always provided the main support for those who interpret Plato as holding that the philosopher has knowledge which has nothing to do with experience, and as consigning everyone else to a mental state no better than that of illusion, one quite cut off from knowledge and pathetic by comparison with the real thing.

At 517a Socrates tells Glaucon that the image must be applied as a whole to what has gone before. Clearly the cave and fire correspond to the visible world, and the world outside the cave to the realm of thought. But how detailed is the correspondence? This is a subject of great dispute. Traditionally the Cave has been taken to fill out the scheme of the Line; and it is very plausible that something like this is meant – what else could Plato be referring to? If we do this, then the state of the bound prisoners will be that of *eikasia*, and when they are turned around painfully to see the puppets and fire they get to the stage of 'belief'. The ascent out of the Cave is the ascent from the world of the senses and what they tell us to the world of thought; seeing reflections is the stage of 'thinking', *dianoia*, while seeing the real things is 'intellect' or *noēsis*, and the sun is the Form of Good.

We would perhaps be tempted to harmonize Line and Cave even without Plato's encouragement, since there is an obvious continuity of interest in the relation of image to original. But apart from the fact that the Cave does not divide neatly into four sections, there are two problems of harmonization which both point up the problems latent in the Cave.

Firstly, while the Line stresses the passage from the world of sense to that of thought, and by making this a case of the image/original relation stresses its continuity with what happens within those worlds, the Cave stresses the sharp division between them. The journey out of the Cave is unlike anything that happens *in* the Cave or out of it; there are, as in the Sun figure, two worlds, contrasted and not continuous. This is pointed up by the Cave's insistence on the inexplicable nature of the conversion to enlightenment; the prisoner's release from bonds is an unexplained intervention, not an extension of anything done before. The Line, on the other hand, presents each move to more clarity as a comprehensible example of something done before: a move from image to original.

Secondly, how can the prisoners be in a state of *eikasia*, as they must be if correspondence with the Line is to be maintained? *Eikasia* in the Line was literal looking at shadows and reflections. But the prisoners represent the ordinary person's beliefs in general. Of course, Plato wants us to see everyday beliefs as no better than seeing shadows and reflections. But what are we to do about the state of 'belief'? In the Line this is the normal state of seeing trees and people. In the Cave it is painful, requires effort, and induces bewilderment.

There are two obvious ways to remove the problem. One is to inflate *eikasia* in the Line, claiming that Plato means it there to cover all ordinary beliefs. He introduces the class by means of the easy examples of literal reflection only to prepare us for the idea that *all* everyday beliefs are, properly considered, really about mere shadows and reflections. But this interpretation cannot survive a careful reading of the Line; the contrast there drawn between *eikasia* and belief is quite straightforward, gives us a clear literal case of the image/original relation, and would never have suggested further inflation to anyone not aware of the problem with the Cave.

The other response is to admit that *eikasia* in both Line and Cave means simply looking at shadows, and to urge that what needs expansion is the notion of *looking at shadows*. The prisoners in the Cave are described as looking at the shadows of puppets, but what this signifies is the taking over, in unreflective fashion, of second-hand opinions and beliefs. If the prisoners are 'like us' when bound and not when turned round, then their state must, surely, include more than literally looking at shadows of objects. But both moves fail to avoid the problem that if, on the natural way of making Line and Cave correspond, the prisoners are in a state of *eikasia*, then *eikasia* has a different range in Line and Cave. In the Line, it covers looking at reflections, something we spend a fraction of our time doing. In the Cave, it covers what we spend nearly all our time doing.

This shift can be partly explained by the fact that the whole tenor of the Cave is to downgrade our ordinary beliefs, to urge us to regard them as being no better than looking at shadows. The Cave is more pessimistic than the Line about even the best of our everyday beliefs. There is also, though, a more precisely specifiable cause of the problem. The whole Cave is an image, an extended metaphor. Within the metaphor, the prisoners are literally looking at shadows cast by physical objects (a state which looks like that of *eikasia* in the Line). But then we find that within the metaphor another layer of metaphor has been added: the puppets are within the whole image literally puppets, but they also stand for moral qualities – the prisoners dispute about shadows of justice and the like (517d–e). So within the whole image the shadows are literally shadows and metaphorically are any ordinary opinions about things like justice, taken over unreflectively and based on acquiescence in the way things appear rather than effort to find out how they really are. No wonder it is tempting both to compare and to contrast the prisoners' state with the state of *eikasia* in the Line. Given the logic of the whole image of the Cave, the states do correspond, but Plato has, once again, overloaded his imagery, and, in order to make the low state of the prisoners a plausible picture of the human condition, has got us to think of their state not just as part of the whole image, but on a further level of metaphor; this makes his point graphically but wrecks correspondence with the Line. Once more he has himself illustrated the dangers in the philosophical use of images, dangers which he warns against without seeming strikingly alive to. For if Line and Cave are to be interpreted consistently, then the Cave cannot be a picture of the universal human need for enlightenment, which it is clearly meant to be. Plato has got so carried away by his desire to stress the utterly contemptible nature of the state unenlightened by philosophical thought that the imagery, memorable though it is, has no consistent overall interpretation.

Sun, Line, and Cave are philosophically frustrating; they point us in too many directions at once. Their power has always lain in their appeal to the imagination, and the harsh forceful contrast they draw between the life content with appearance and superficiality, and the richly rewarding life dedicated to finding out the truth. Their appeal is so strong that interpreters are perennially tempted to try to harmonize them in a consistent philosophical interpretation, despite Plato's own warnings on the limits of the kind of thinking that is guided by images and illustrations.

All three images stress vision and sight, and two of them use light as a metaphor for the truth. The Cave is especially rich in visual detail. However, it and the Sun resist visual representation; only the schematic Line can be successfully turned into a visual aid, while attempts to picture Sun and Cave, for all their pictorial suggestiveness, render them merely bizarre. The only successful visual translation of the Cave's terms of metaphor that I am aware of is Bernardo Bertolucci's movie *The Conformist*. (This is based on a novel of the same title by Alberto Moravia, but the use of the Cave imagery to interpret the story is entirely Bertolucci's idea, and indeed is something that can only be done in cinematic terms.) It has often been pointed out that the Cave is a 'dynamic' image whereas the other two are 'static', and no doubt this is why we have had to wait for the availability of movie techniques for Plato's image to be successfully interpreted in other than philosophical terms. It is worth considering the movie briefly, because it brings out in two very interesting ways points which we are likely to forget if we concentrate on the Cave solely for its significance for the 'theory of Forms'.

One point is that, although the Cave represents the general condition of 'people like us', it has features that suggest a particularly bad society. The human condition is not a social vacuum; there are people in the Cave manipulating the prisoners, as well as the prisoners themselves. The prisoners are prisoners within a given political system; they are political conformists. The protagonist of Bertolucci's film, Marcello, is a conformist in Mussolini's Italy. Fascist Italy is portrayed cinematically in terms of images, reflections, and fragmented appearances. Such a society models for us particularly well the kind of society that Plato saw in contemporary Athens: a society interested in surface and *bella figura*, impressed by showy and unsound schemes and grandiose buildings, a society where what matters is not truth but presenting a good 'public image' and manipulating public opinion. (Cf. *Gorgias* 517a–519d.) A society like this has no interest in encouraging its citizens to develop their own moral views. It has every interest in encouraging conformity to received opinion by dominating 'the media' (as we put it) and getting people to care only about the images presented to them, seeing no need for a positive moral response of their own. Bertolucci's development of

Plato's Cave brings out how much an individual is encouraged to make false choices, and to do things he can recognize to be unworthy of him, if he lives in a society that positively rewards false and superficial values and encourages intelligent people to make only a cynical use of their abilities. This is a point which it is easy to miss in the Cave if we are concentrating on the philosopher's struggle for enlightenment; Plato, though, does not forget the importance of society and the formative power it has over the kind of lives people lead. He is so concerned with reforming education to produce good people that we are justified in seeing in the Cave not only a general point about humanity but a picture of false education and the wrong kind of society.

The Conformist is also interesting for one important way in which Plato's image is put to a characteristically twentieth-century use which reveals itself as highly un-Platonic. For Marcello does in the end make the painful turn towards the fire, and we are left in no doubt that he will, even at considerable outward cost, no longer live by what he can see to be factitious values. But even a film so aware of society makes the start of Marcello's intellectual liberation come from his realizing and facing the implications of particular facts about himself. His failure to make genuine moral choices comes from his failure to face truths about himself which he is unwilling to recognize because of their implications. The knowledge represented in the movie by the turning to the fire is *self*-knowledge, and we are given to understand that it is the denial of truths about the self that leads people to live unauthentic lives, lives that are fragmented, unintegrated, and spent pursuing false and superficial values. To us this seems the natural place to begin. We tend to think that wisdom is built on self-knowledge, and that the beginnings of wisdom are found in facing facts about oneself. We find it natural to think that the false consciousness of the prisoners, their failure to recognize the state they are in, is due to ignorance of the ways in which their lives are deformed by the manipulations of others. They are ignorant of themselves. It is important to see that Plato does not think in this way. The prisoners *are* ignorant of their real nature and real needs, but no role at all is played in the intellectual awakening to these needs and natures by particular facts about individuals.

The knowledge that the prisoners wake up to is impersonal; individual scrutiny of self plays no role at all. Plato sees no intellectual value in particular facts about particular individuals. The prisoner's mysterious release from bonds is to be achieved by abstract and impersonal studies like mathematics. The ascent out of the Cave offers no personal interest or fulfilment, not even the satisfaction of having shed inauthentic roles. Plato is at pains to stress how much at odds the ascent puts you with other people, and how peculiar they think you (516e–517a, 517b–d). The culmination of the whole journey is comprehension of the Form of the Good – and this is precisely not what is good for the seeker, or good for others, or good in relation to anything or anyone, but simply and un-qualifiedly good, in a way that is completely impersonal and indifferent between individuals.

One result of this is that it is indeed mysterious why anybody would be impelled to start the journey. In the *Symposium*, Plato stresses the force of personal love in turning us from the unthinkingness of everyday life to the eternal and impersonal Forms, and in the *Phaedrus* (250b–d) says that Beauty is the Form that is first and most easily found attractive. (These themes are pursued in many of the novels of Iris Murdoch.) But the *Republic* is more austere. The philosophers turn towards the impersonal Good because that is where they are led by impersonal disciplines like mathematics. Although Plato does elsewhere say that philosophers will feel desire for the truth (cf. 485b, d, 486a), the message of Sun, Line, and Cave is that it is mathematics that leads to the Forms. But why should future philosophers ever in the first place see the importance of studies of such an abstract kind, not directed to any self-promoting end? Plato has no answer, and in making the prisoner be freed and forced to turn round by someone else, is perhaps admitting that he has no answer, other than the fact that some people just are by nature dissatisfied with materialistic self-seeking and conformity, and are 'impelled', as we put it, by their own intellectual bent to see the value in studies that everyone else regards as a waste of time.

Sun, Line, and Cave all in different ways stress the im-personal nature of the knowledge of the Good that is the basis of the just person's understanding and grounds all explanation of matters of fact. The Line tells us that the disciplines that first lead us to real knowledge are not concerned directly with moral aspects of the world, but are, surprisingly, abstract and mathematical (and this at a point where such a claim has not been at all filled out). The Sun and Cave have stressed the extreme difference between any of our ordinary thinking about personal concerns and the thinking that can amount to knowledge. We are left in no doubt about the difficulty of being a philosopher and turning through abstract studies to the Form of Good, the good which is absolute and in no way relative to anybody's or anything's interests or needs. We would not have expected these developments just from the actual discussions of Forms, but they are unmistakeably there.

But these developments ought to worry us. For if we recall the main argument, Socrates showed that justice was the harmonious state of a person's soul, as part of an argument to show that justice was worth having *for the person*. Justice in the soul is like health in the body. It is the state controlled by knowledge of what is best for all the factors concerned. Reason in the soul knows what is best for *all* the soul's parts, including personal aspirations and particular desires. Now we find, however, that this knowledge requires an abandonment of one's personal concerns. The Good that is the supreme object of knowledge has nothing to do with one's *own* good; it is the purely impersonal Form of Good. But how can the knowledge that produces harmony in my soul, caring for all my concerns, require me to turn away from the world I share with others and concentrate on what is simply just and good, not just or good *for me*? How can the knowledge developed by mathematics, the kind of understanding it engenders, make my soul harmonious? And if not, why should it be something that I would obviously want to have? But the whole argument of the *Republic* was meant to show that justice, and the knowledge it involves, was something that I should want to have. Something seems to have gone very wrong.

This problem can be restated in terms of a distinction between two conceptions of what the philosopher is like. For the developments of Sun, Line, and Cave have made the philosopher's knowledge appear to be no longer practical, but rather theoretical, and we can distinguish two conceptions of the philosopher that correspond to this: the *practical* one, and what (following Irwin) I shall call the *contemplative* one.

Plato has claimed that to be truly just one needs to be a philosopher – that is, not simply be right by accident or luck in one's upbringing, but have full and properly based articulate understanding. But all the same, the philosopher's knowledge should, if the argument is to work, be of a practical kind. That is, even if knowledge requires grasp of Forms, it must be applicable to experience in such a way as to guide the person to make good particular choices; it must enlighten the process of moral development that he or she actually goes through, and be of use in particular cases. (Plato himself makes the point at 484c–d, 520c.) The just person's knowledge, however much it may require theoretical grounding and the ability to give reasons of a highly abstract kind, must be practical in the sense that having it makes a difference in experience and particular decisions. Practical knowledge is what makes the just person *just*, when he or she might not have been. This is the point of comparing the ideally just rulers to skilled pilots or doctors, who make the right decisions in practice because they know what they are doing; they do not just have a happy knack, but understand their subject. Plato has claimed that this kind of knowledge is worth having because it is a condition of having psychic harmony, that is, a fulfilled and integrated personality rather than a confused and frustrated one. If this is what the just person's knowledge is, then while it may require grasping Forms it cannot be limited to them but must be displayed in experience; one's understanding of Forms and the Good is shown in the making of rational and grounded decisions instead of unreflective and prejudiced ones.

On this way of looking at the philosopher's knowledge, we do not need to squeeze out of the discussions of Forms more than the obvious results of them: namely, that in some important matters we need thought, and not just the ordinary course of experience, to attain understanding, and that the wise person's claim to make others' decisions better than they do lies in superior understanding of disputed and difficult matters, something that requires study not necessary in unproblematic matters of fact.

We have seen, however, that Sun, Line, and Cave suggest a

different picture of the philosopher – the contemplative picture, where what characterizes him or her is the desire to escape entirely from the world of practical affairs. Philosophical knowledge is associated with impersonal disciplines like mathematics rather than with the desire to sort out actual tangled moral problems. The knowledge that involves understanding of the Forms is represented as so infinitely worthwhile in itself that everything else – everything typical of the human condition – is mere trash by comparison. It is completely unclear how such knowledge could ever have application to matters concerning the two lower parts of the soul, which are concerned with particular and personal things; and these parts are downplayed in these passages in favour of a stress on reason and mathematical thinking as being the capacity in virtue of which a philosopher rises above his or her fellows.

The idea that study of Forms is an end in itself and is to be contrasted with the lowly status of practical concerns goes naturally with the view that knowledge not only begins but ends with Forms, that there is properly speaking no knowledge of particulars, only an inferior state of belief; if Forms are the only objects of knowledge, then particular people, things, and actions are not capable of being known, just because they are particulars. The Sun begins with a wholesale contrast between objects of thought and objects of perception (507b); the Line suggests that different cognitive states are correlated with different objects; and the philosopher emerges from the Cave into another world, leaving the original environment behind. If knowledge is only of Forms, then it does require a wholesale downgrading of our originally accepted beliefs. The people who advance to understanding will not check their discoveries against our intuitions, or beliefs about matters of fact; they will resolutely turn away from consideration of any particular matters of fact – from the 'darkness' into the 'light' of Forms.

These are very different ways of looking at the rule of reason and what it requires in the soul. Why does Plato not see that they are very different? How can the just rulers be compared to doctors and pilots when the beginning of wisdom is to turn away from mortal trash? Plato seems to have drifted away from what the argument needs, the philosopher as practically wise, the good person who is the norm for moral judgements because judging rationally and from understanding. We now find the philosopher raptly contemplating Forms and only Forms, dismissing the world we experience as being on the level of a shadow or a dream.

The practical conception of the philosopher, though it does not entail that there be Forms only for a restricted range of terms, fits much more happily with that idea; and the contemplative conception likewise, though it does not entail that there are Forms for every term, fits more happily with that view. For if knowledge requires grasp of Forms, and also requires a wholesale rejection or downgrading of our beliefs about everything, there seems absolutely no point in limiting Forms to a restricted range of terms. It is therefore all the more frustrating that Plato's position on this issue is not unambiguously clear in the *Republic*. The actual passages of argument that involve Forms depend on a restricted range of Forms, but Plato is not explicit or clear about this, and the considerations that produce this range seem to be of diverse kinds. Further, Plato sometimes talks of Forms as though what characterized them was changelessness (p. 223), and in Sun, Line, and Cave talks as though there were something inherently defective about the whole world of experienced particulars just as such. And in Book 10 (admittedly an odd production as a whole) he brings in Forms in a way guaranteed to cause conflict with the accounts in Books 5 and 7. This means, unfortunately, that we cannot rely on what is claimed about Forms to settle the question, whether Plato is confused about shifting from the practical to the theoretical conception of the philosopher. For Plato gives us no independent way of getting clear precisely what his claims about Forms are; and the apparent move of generalizing from a restricted range of Forms is just part of the shift from the practical to the theoretical conception of the philosopher, not something that can independently explain it.

One thing that is clear is that nothing *compels* Plato to the contemplative conception of the philosopher. Certainly it is not merely the recognition of Forms. Plato could have stressed as much as he liked the value of studying the Forms and the perspective from which all worldly concerns seem infinitely little, and still have held the practical conception. The philosopher would then be a person in whom this knowledge grounds and directs his or her practical judgements and makes them good ones, that display understanding and promote justice in the world. This would make plausible, if anything could, the just person's claim to rule those who are not just. Plato does not need to stress those features of the philosopher's knowledge, which surface in Books 6 and 7 – the stress on mathematics, the Cave's insistence on wholesale rejection of everyday beliefs and downgrading of everyday concerns. These seem to spring from the contemplative conception of the philosopher, not just from recognition of Forms and the need to grasp them.

Further, the two views are destined for conflict. For the contemplative view makes the philosopher's detached study of Forms infinitely more valuable than anything he or she could achieve in the practical sphere. There is no comparison: everything but the studies that lead one out of the Cave are mere rubbish. So on the political level we are moved to ask what it is about this knowledge that fits philosophers to *rule* themselves and others. And on the individual level we have to ask whether this incomparable supremacy of the aims of reason allows reason to function as the best arbiter of the interests of *all* the soul's parts. How can it allow any weight at all to the claims of the other parts, when these are compared with the claims of reason? The objects of every faculty but reason have already been judged to be, in comparison with its objects, worthless trash. But if reason's claims are so incomparably superior, how can its rule produce harmony and unity in the whole soul, as was so much stressed (p. 126)? The practical conception of the philosopher is a comprehensible development of the main argument; the contemplative conception undermines it. Why should exclusive study of Forms lead to psychic harmony?

Plato may simply be confused here in letting the contemplative conception develop without warning from the practical one. He may just be so predisposed to think that study of Forms is all-valuable that he does not notice the problems that this causes for his argument. However, before ascribing simple muddle to him, we should look for a better explanation. The problem, after all, should be as obvious to Plato as to us; and it is Plato who both spends pages of Book 6 discussing the need for philosophers to have a knowledge which is practical and directive, and then from the very beginning of the Sun figure makes the Good that they seek into a separate Form. The problem comes because Plato is being over-ambitious and treats two very different things as parts of a single project. (We have seen something analogous already in his desire to show that soul and state are both just in exactly the same way.) Plato does not want to allow that practical and theoretical reasoning (the notions of reason uppermost in the practical and contemplative conceptions of the philosopher) ever *could* conflict. He thinks of reason as a *single* faculty that can be displayed either in practical contexts or in theoretical contemplation and reasoning; and so no matter how much he stresses the disinterested and detached nature of contemplation of the Forms, he wants this to be an exercise of the *same* reason as is shown in good practical judgement. He would reject any distinction of practical and theoretical reasoning, and hence of the 'practical' and 'contemplative' conceptions of the philosopher; he would say that there was only one conception, that of the person in whom reason is supreme *both* in contemplating the Forms *and* in making good practical decisions.

But we have seen that this will not do; this idea is inherently unstable, because the claims of contemplation as they are presented deny the value to practical and individual concerns that is required for good practical judgement. Plato is led by his desire to see reason as a unity to give unsatisfactory answers as to how it operates. Aristotle, in his *Nicomachean Ethics* (especially the sixth book) reacts sharply against Plato in a way we find sympathetic; he clearly distinguishes practical reasoning from theoretical, and insists that a person outstanding in one may be undistinguished in the other. Young men, he says, can be excellent mathematicians but morally immature, for sound moral judgement comes with experience. (This is undoubtedly a hit at the *Republic*'s mathematically-based programme for pure moral understanding.) Theoretical reasoning concerns universals, whereas action and practical choice are inevitably concerned with particulars; so the two are quite distinct in form and operation. (However, in spite of his clarity on this point Aristotle himself sometimes succumbs to the temptation to assimilate the form of practical reasoning to that of theoretical, and he also fails to reconcile the claims of both forms of reasoning in a single life. Plato's ambitious idea is not a *gratuitous* one; it is one that has appealed to many.)

It is in terms of the distinction between the practical and contemplative conceptions of the philosopher, and his assimilation of them, that we can best understand a famous problem that besets Plato in the *Republic*. The Guardians' progress is the journey out of the Cave; so if they are to rule others they must leave the studies that they excel in and find pleasant and rewarding, and go back down into the Cave. Plato makes it clear that they will not want to do this (519c–521b) and that it will be a matter of 'persuasion and compulsion'. (He does not specify how much compulsion, or how it will work.) Now given the practical conception of the philosopher, there is no obvious reason why he or she should be unwilling to rule: previous training will have developed those capacities and that knowledge which (even if unobviously) best fit a person to decide better than others. The Guardians' reluctance comes from the contemplative conception of the philosopher (significantly it arises within the Cave imagery). Someone engrossed in the study of impersonal Forms, someone who has rejected as trash the claims of the world we experience, can hardly be keen to conduct interviews and sit on boring committees. Once the Guardians are thought of as finding their natural fulfilment in detached intellectual study, there is an obvious problem, why they should return to the Cave. Plato offers several reasons for why they will none the less go. Some are bad or obviously inadequate: thus, they owe it to the city for their privileged upbringing (520a–c); rulers who don't want to rule are better than those who do (520d). The real ground is stated at 519e–520a, and is repeated at 520e in the claim that we are making a 'just order to just people'. The Guardians know what is just because they have the knowledge that is based on the Form of Good. Their return is demanded by the justice that prescribes disinterestedly what is best for all (519e–520a). They do not go down because it is better for them; they would be happier and better off doing philosophy. Nor do they sacrifice themselves altruistically for the others; the others do benefit by their rule, but so do they, for under any other rule they would suffer, deprived of their appropriate role of organizing society for the best. They go down because they realize that that is best – simply *best*, not best *for* any particular group of people. They know what is really good, not good relative to the interests or situation of anyone. And it demands their return; so they go. Their motivation is thus very abstract. They are not seeking their own happiness. Nor are they seeking that of others. They are simply doing what is impersonally best; they make an impersonal response to an impersonal demand. They are not swayed by considerations of their own happiness or their own interests; they consider these merely as part of the workings of the whole, and give them their due place and value along with everybody else's. They take a wholly impersonal attitude to their own happiness, along with everybody else's; and this is because their judgements are made in the light of the impersonal Good, the separated Form which is what is simply *good*, not good relative to anything. They can act in the light of what justice requires because they can detach themselves from their own personal standpoint; for they have experienced the enlightenment which the Cave portrayed as a turning away from one's own personal concerns towards the light of abstract studies and the separated Forms.

But this throws us right back on the problem already raised: why should *I* do what justice requires? The *Republic* began from the inadequacy of act-centred theories, which presented justice as a set of arbitrary and external demands. The discussion of the state, and of the soul's parts and virtues, allowed Plato to show that justice is not this, but is a state of the person that is clearly in their interests, because it is the condition for psychic health and unity. But the central books seem to have undermined this claim, by showing that the knowledge required to be just is knowledge of what is *impersonally* just. Now this does give us an answer to something that worried us before: why should just people not act against the interests of others? Now we have seen that they will not do this. But in the process we have ruled out their acting in their own interests either. For it has turned out that they do not act in, or against, *anybody's* interests, but in accordance with the impersonal prescriptions of what is absolutely just and good. However, Plato made Socrates accept the strongest form of Glaucon's challenge: show me that it is in my interests really to be, rather than only to seem, just. If this was accepted as legitimate, why is it not legitimate to ask, why *should* a Guardian go down to the Cave, when it is so clearly not in his or her interests? Why should a Guardian be, rather than seem, just? Why not, for example, try to get out of the descent by faking some incapacity for practical affairs?

Many people try to rescue Plato from this problem by pointing out that the Guardians themselves do not perceive the requirements of justice as conflicting with their interests. For, although they are (given the contemplative conception of the philosopher) happiest doing their abstract studies, they have attained a complete understanding of themselves and their role in the light of the impersonal Good, and so they can think of their own happiness impersonally and accept without resentment its sacrifice to the requirements of impersonal goodness. They accept a personal loss; but they have been trained to think impersonally about themselves as well as the rest of the world. For if knowledge, and the attainment of understanding in the light of the Good, require one to reject the importance of particular claims and individual interests, why should one's attitude to oneself be any exception? The Guardians can abstract from the personal viewpoint, from which one cares about one's own happiness and interests in a specially intimate way, and come to see themselves externally, as being merely parts of the whole, citizens with a part to play (and a specially vital part at that). And because they can take this viewpoint, and indeed do so in so far as they are thinking as wise and enlightened beings, they judge, and act, from a point of view from which sacrifice of mere personal happiness is not really a sacrifice that matters, or causes grief or resentment. We have seen that their treatment of the others in the state was done from a point of view that abstracted from the importance of individual concerns and values and thought of people entirely rationally, purely in the light of their objective social contribution (pp. 92–4). Now we see that they are quite consistent; they extend this attitude to themselves. And so we can see that they do not see the sacrifice of going down into the Cave as a real sacrifice, really against their interests; the loss it entails is one that they regard in a detached and impersonal way. There is no reason for a Guardian to care more about the loss of his or her personal happiness than to care about such a loss on the part of another person; it is not something that is judged to have any real value by comparison with the claims of what is rationally and impersonally required.

But this only raises the more urgently the question, why in that case *I* should want to be a Guardian? This matters, because the Guardians are not just a fanciful idea; they are what just people in a perfectly just society are supposed to be like. But now we see that justice demands that I retreat to a point of view from which I can judge my own happiness and interests in exactly the same impersonal way as everybody else's. I must come to cease to care about my own happiness in a specially intimate way. But why ever should it be in *my* interests to want to do that? Plato did not undertake to show that you have a reason to be, rather than seem, just if you are intellectually gifted and capable of taking an entirely rational and impersonal attitude to your own interests. This would have been totally irrelevant to Thrasymachus' challenge. What he undertook to show was that *anyone* has a reason to be, rather than seem, just. But it is far from clear that anyone has a reason to be just if that implies taking the viewpoint on one's own interests that the Guardians do. Justice was to have been shown to be in *my* interests. But now it requires that I abstract completely from my interests. But this seems no less external a demand on *me* than the rules of justice as put forward by Polemarchus. We seem to be right back at the beginning.

The Guardians' return to the Cave has always been recognized as a major problem in the *Republic*. For the results are very ugly whether the Guardians suffer real loss by doing it or not. If they suffer real loss, because their own prospects of happiness are sacrificed, then justice is not in their interests – and yet they are the paradigms of justice in a just society, and Plato set out to show that justice was in the agent's interests. But if they do not suffer real loss, because they view their own happiness as rationally and impersonally as they do everybody else's, then justice seems to demand an ideal, impersonal viewpoint which it is not in the interests of any actual people to adopt. We thought that Plato's account had the virtue of taking seriously the claims of justice on us as we are; now justice demands that we positively stop being human. The more the Guardians' justice requires that they conform their own viewpoints to that of impersonal reason and impersonal goodness, the more any actual person is driven to ask why, if this is what justice requires, there is any reason for *him*, or *her*, to be just. Plato cannot have it both ways. Justice cannot be shown to be good for me *and also* good in a way that has no reference to anybody or anything particular at all.

Why *should* I be just? By demanding that the just person be a philosopher and by then turning the philosopher into a contemplator only of eternal Forms who abstracts from everything individual and personal, Plato has forced us to ask this question all over again.

In fact, the main argument, resumed in Books 8 and 9, does remain alive to the question that was posed at the beginning and answered in Book 4. The central books are not forgotten, and sometimes the philosopher appears in the contemplative role, but the main thrust of the following books follows through the attempt to show that justice is worth my while, is something that it benefits the individual agent to have. The glorious impersonality of the just person's viewpoint disappears from the main argument. The central books, for all their striking effect, have sent the moral argument in a new, and disturbing, direction. We shall return to this question when we have followed through Book 9 to the end of the main moral argument.

We have seen that the most obvious source of Plato's difficulties is his shift from the practical to the theoretical conception of the philosopher. This is *not* due simply to the introduction of Forms, which is quite compatible with the practical view. It stems partly from Plato's own predilection for contemplation and theoretical study as the activity that has highest worth, and his tendency to contrast everything else with this as paltry and perishable. But it stems also from his refusal to allow that in developing the contemplative picture of the rule of reason in the soul he is doing anything *new*. He will not allow that the functions of reason might ever be divided; he does not think that intellectual absorption will make claims on a person that cannot be reconciled with the claims of practical judgement. Hence the reason that made just decisions for me and for others becomes identified with the reason that studies what is absolutely just, just unqualifiedly and not just for me or for anyone. Plato does not see that such a notion of reason is bound to split, and to threaten the coherence of his argument for the worthwhileness of justice. This is not, however, a simple mistake. There is a grandeur in the way that Plato makes the wise ruler be an intellectual genius *as well*, refusing to allow that the detached study of eternal truths is not an extension of the same thing as the just person's powers of practical judgement, but is something entirely different.

FURTHER READING

The philosophical implications of the Guardians' understanding of the Good are best and most lucidly brought out in J. Cooper, 'The Psychology of Justice in Plato', *American Philosophical Quarterly* 1977. N. White's *Companion to Plato's Republic* is also helpful on these passages.

Sun, Line and Cave are the subject of an enormous literature. Discussions which highlight the very different possible interpretations of their details are, Cross and Woozley, *Plato's Republic, A Philosophical Interpretation*, ch. 9; Raven, 'Sun, Line and Cave' in *Plato's Thought in the Making*; Robinson, *Plato's Earlier Dialectic* chs. 11 and 12; Malcolm, 'The Line and the Cave', *Phronesis* 1962; Wilson, 'The Contents of the Cave', *Canadian Journal of Philosophy* Supplement II, 1976; Morrison, 'Two Unresolved Difficulties in the Line and the Cave', *Phronesis* 1977.

Chapter 11
Philosophy and Mathematics

At 521c ff. Socrates turns to the kind of education that will produce Guardians who can achieve the highest kind of understanding, and this occupies the rest of Book 7: first the propaedeutic studies and then 'dialectic' or philosophical reasoning. *Prima facie* this might appear unnecessary for the argument, since we have already seen in outline what the Guardians' knowledge is like in so far as this is relevant for justice. But the further discussion is needed if we are to understand how knowledge of goodness needs to be developed through mathematics; and Plato is anyway clearly interested in discussing the nature of philosophical knowledge for its own sake.

THE PROPAEDEUTIC STUDIES (521c–532d)

The Guardians are not to begin studying philosophy at once; Plato thinks that this would have destructive effects (537e–539d). Because philosophy makes one question what has hitherto been taken for granted, if it is begun too young it can produce too negative an attitude: old truths are thrown out with nothing to replace them. Plato cautiously concludes that philosophy should be studied only by the comparatively old. They must have spent many years studying abstract and formal disciplines; they must also have seen active service, and be experienced and mature. They are to follow rigorous thinking through fearlessly to its conclusion, but they must be realistic about the implications, neither romantically idealistic nor prematurely cynical. But all the demands here are made in very general terms; a curriculum is sketched, but it is clear that we are not to take very seriously the precise number of years allotted to each subject. (Cf. 539e. It is entirely fanciful to suppose, as some do, that we can read off from this passage anything at all about actual or projected studies in the Academy.)

First comes arithmetic (521d–526c), then plane geometry (526c–528b), solid geometry (528b–e), astronomy (528e–530d), and harmonics (530d–531c). These are all to be studied from a purely mathematical point of view. It is made very clear that the chief point of these studies is to encourage the mind in non-empirical and highly abstract reasoning. Plato is not so concerned to produce experts in these subjects as he is to produce people who are accustomed to *a priori* reasoning about subjects where most people comprehend only an empirical approach. (Cf. 526d–e.)

The detail of these studies is of mainly scholarly interest, but there are three general points worth making about the nature of the 'course'.

(i) The curriculum is introduced by the argument at 521 ff. (which we have already examined, pp. 218–22) that some concepts provoke the mind into recognizing Forms, and among these is that of *oneness* or *unity*. Plato is impressed by the way that even a beginner learns that a unit in arithmetic is treated as indivisible in the way that units met with in our experience are not: one book is also many pages, but an arithmetical one or unit is just one, and not many of anything. Plato is here treating 'one' as a predicate that applies to its object in the same way as 'long' or 'thick', and is duly impressed by the way that mathematicians add and subtract with *ones* that are just one and not many of anything. Unfortunately, this makes these units look rather like Forms, and if the same is true of other mathematical concepts then Plato is well on the way to introducing mathematical objects as being like Forms but 'between' them and particular things. He has clearly not thought out this problem (cf. pp. 251–2). Unfortunately, too, this way of thinking of number terms is quite wrong, though for reasons too complex to discuss here; they were first brought out clearly by Frege.

However, that 'one' is like 'long' or 'thick' in provoking the mind, by its use, to recognize Forms, hardly suffices to show that counting and arithmetic are the best studies to lead one

274 *Philosophy and Mathematics*

on to the highest level of understanding, still less that they must
be followed by years of geometry and astronomy. What about
the other concepts that the argument used (e.g. big and small,
soft and hard (523e–524a)? It soon becomes clear that Plato is
independently impressed by the techniques and methodology of
the mathematical sciences, and that their role is not based on
this argument alone.

(ii) Plato's insistence on a purely mathematical approach to
studies like astronomy and harmonics has often led to accusa-
tions that he is 'anti-scientific'. Particularly notorious is his
insistence at 530b–d: 'Let us then study astronomy by means of
problems as we do geometry, and let the things in the sky go, if
the study of astronomy is to make the naturally intelligent part
the soul useful instead of useless.' (Grube.) However perfect
the heavens, they are a material thing subject to change and
decay, and therefore can at best serve as a model for the true
study. This seems to downgrade what we would regard as
intellectually serious science.

If Plato is charged with being anti-scientific, this must be
against the background of some theory as to what 'science' is.
What is usually meant in this connection is that he is anti-
empiricist, and more precisely anti-inductive. He opposes the
idea that we look at the facts of experience and inductively work
out hypotheses to explain them. This is merely what we would
expect given all he has said about the need to turn to thought
rather than experience to gain understanding. Experience does
not point the way; we only understand empirical facts to the
extent that we bring our own thought to bear on them. This
attitude is compatible with some views as to how science should
proceed – particularly those that recommend not forming
hypotheses inductively from the data but rather the
'hypothetico-deductive' procedure of putting forward a
hypothesis and then testing its application to observed facts.
This actually sounds rather like the advice reputedly offered by
Plato to astronomers in the Academy; he told them to find out
what uniform and orderly motion can be postulated to 'save the
appearances' of the motions of the planets.

We should remember, however, that at least here Plato is not
interested in what we call science. Though one probably could
construct some 'philosophy of science' from his views overall,

he writes in this passage as though he does not regard empirical observations as being in any way the arbiter of a theory. And this suggests lack of interest rather than a view one way or the other. Some people have indeed wondered whether he is entirely serious in his claims here. How could there be a purely non-observational astronomy? What would make a problem in such a study be a problem in *astronomy*, rather than geometry? Plato has not thought his position through. But it is clear that he *does* want us to stop at an *a priori* level regardless of the subject-matter. Once again we see a strong and unargued prejudice in favour of theoretical and purely contemplative knowledge, refusing any significance to particular matters of fact and the application of theory to them.

(iii) Because these studies are so pure, and do not claim legitimacy from their applications, Plato insists several times rather defensively that they are worthwhile although practically not useful; they serve to develop the intellect, and we have already seen that this is in itself infinitely valuable. Again we see the influence of the contemplative conception of philosophy and wisdom. (Cf. 525d, 526a–b, d–e, 527a, d–e, 529b–c, 530e, 531c.) But, as if uneasy about this, Plato also insists that these studies are *not* in fact useless, but are of the highest practical value. (Cf. 521d, 522e, 525b–c, 526d, 527c.) These latter claims, however, strike an odd note. Plato does not claim that they are of practical value because they lead to rational and informed decisions on practical and ethical matters. They are practical in a much cruder sense – useful for counting and measuring armies. In modern jargon they are useful for technology; and Plato's enthusiasm here strikes us as the keenness of the aggressive technocrat. Arithmetic is to be studied 'both for the sake of war and to attain ease in turning the soul itself from the world of becoming to truth and reality' (525c, Grube). This utterly grotesque statement may sum up quite well the philosophy behind a lot of NATO research funding, but it is a sad fall from the idea that knowledge of the highest kind has the practical force of making one just in action and decision. An informed and rational practical judgement would operate on all practical matters, not excluding the buying and selling which here is rejected with such contempt (525c), as not being a fit subject for the philosopher's attention (as though rulers never needed to descend to consider the just regulation of buying and selling). We see here one pernicious result of the shift from the practical to the contemplative conception of the philosopher. Instead of the wisdom that unites theory and practice, we find theory so exalted that practice is dragged in at the end and in a degraded role; pure theory proceeds in contempt of the practical world, but with occasional spinoffs that improve war technology. Here we have a relatively concrete example of the way in which the contemplative conception of wisdom distorts the agent's relation to the world of particular concerns.

Dialectic (532d–535a)

After the mathematical studies comes the 'coping stone' (534e) of dialectic, the kind of purely philosophical reasoning which is the Guardians' highest achievement and provides the justification for their ruling in the state; only after becoming thoroughly versed in dialectic do they go down into the Cave to see better than the people there (520c).

What is dialectic? Robinson, in his careful and comprehensive book *Plato's Earlier Dialectic*, emphasizes that for Plato, 'the word "dialectic" had a strong tendency . . . to mean "the ideal method, *whatever that may be*." In so far as it was thus merely an honorific title, Plato applied it at every stage of his life to whatever seemed to him at the moment the most hopeful procedure.' (P. 70.) The *Republic*'s discussion has similarities to the treatments of dialectic in the *Meno* and *Phaedo*, but also differences which warn us that dialectic in the *Republic* must be interpreted as making sense primarily of the *Republic*'s concerns.

Plato says virtually nothing positive and direct about dialectic; he makes Socrates warn Glaucon that this cannot be done (532e–533a). Partly this may be because Plato is not sure how to define philosophical thinking. (Very few people, after all, have been sure that they could.) But Plato's procedure also makes the point that the true nature of philosophy is apparent only to those who have spent some time doing it. You do not find out what philosophy is by reading books on 'What Philosophy Is', but only by doing some. This is one of the few points on which one can be sure that Plato thought consistently throughout his life. All the same, one can give some helpful indications as to the nature of philosophical thinking, if not a definition, and this is what Plato does, mainly by contrasting dialectic with something else – the way in which mathematics proceeds.

There are two passages which tell us essentially all we know about dialectic. One is the Line. Here 'intellect', *noēsis*, the highest kind of thought, is contrasted with a lower kind, *dianoia* or 'thinking', which is displayed characteristically by mathematicians. (Cf. pp. 248, 250.) Two things emerge as limited about the way mathematicians reason. They are 'compelled' by the nature of their activity to use physical objects as images; they use diagrams and models, even though they are talking not about these but about objects of thought, 'the square itself' and 'the diagonal itself' (there are some problems about this; cf. pp. 251–2). They are also limited by using *hypotheses*. A hypothesis is an assumption, something taken to be true or clear for purposes of argument. Plato is not saying that mathematicians are at fault in regarding their starting-points as merely provisional. His complaint is that they proceed from starting-points which are in fact merely provisional but do *not* question them; they have a dogmatic attitude to what they should, but do not, regard as hypothetical. Plato, writing from the philosopher's viewpoint, calls these starting-points 'hypotheses', although that is not the word that the mathematicians would use. Mathematicians, he is saying, are complacent even if they do not admit it. They 'assume the existence of the odd and the even, of figures, of three kinds of angles, and of kindred things in each of their studies, as if they were known to them. These they make their hypotheses and do not deem it necessary to give any account of them either to themselves or to others, as if they were clear to all.' (510c, Grube.)

What happens in true 'intellection' or *noēsis*? Here reason treats the hypotheses as literally hypothetical (511b), as things laid down, to be treated as steps to reach the first principle which is unhypothetical. Having reached this it comes down again to a conclusion, 'without making use of anything visible at all, but proceeding by means of Forms and through Forms to its conclusions which are Forms.' (511c, Grube.) *Noēsis* renders intelligible, via the first principle, the objects of mathematical thought, which are not, as studied in mathematics, really understood.

The other passage is 531–4, where the imagery of the Cave is used. Dialectic presupposes the mathematical sciences, but these are useless without an overall comprehensive and synoptic account and overview (531d). Dialectic can give an account of what it knows (531e) and also defend it (534c); it is the only study which demands knowledge of what each thing really is, rather than petty details of doing or making (533b). The mathematical sciences are also concerned with what has real and unqualified being, but by comparison they are only dreaming (533b–c): their methodology leaves their starting points unquestioned, although they are only hypotheses. It is only dialectic that 'destroys the hypotheses' and reaches the stage of giving an account of each thing, rather than being satisfied with getting consistent results from unexamined premises (533c). It lifts the soul's eye out of the mud (533c–d, one of Plato's more revolting mixed metaphors) and starts the mind on the journey described in the Cave, ending only with the grasp of the most fundamental notion, that of the Good (532b, 534b–c).

Nearly everything about dialectic is disputable – not surprisingly given Plato's indirect approach. For clarity I shall deal with various problems separately.

(1) Mathematics has two defects compared with dialectic. It relies on visible diagrams, and it does not question its assumptions. Plato never indicates that, or how, these two defects are connected, but a very plausible connection can be made. Like most Greeks of his time, Plato, when he talks of 'mathematics', is thinking primarily of geometry – the geometry that was being furthered by people whom he knew in the Academy, and would eventually be given its canonical form by Euclid. This geometry, as is well known, relies at various points on our intuitions about space. Plato is criticizing geometers for taking for granted various basic truths and key concepts just because they seem to be so clearly given in experience. A diagram of a geometrical demonstration makes it seem obvious in a way that Plato distrusts: the clarity is given to the senses rather than deriving from a rigorous process of

thinking through the matter. But whereas geometry leaves its assumptions ungrounded because their truth seems to be clearly given in experience, dialectic relies on experience at no point (511c): it is concerned only with Forms, with what can be grasped only by thought. So it must produce its clarity the hard way, not by examples but by intellectual rigour.

Philosophical thinking, then, is entirely non-empirical. Its truths do not depend on experience and they are known *a priori*, without reference to experience. This, of course, fits only the contemplative picture of the philosopher. Although Plato has not given up the practical picture – he says that the philosophers will see better than the others when they return to the Cave (520c) – still nothing in these passages shows why people who have spent years in studies of these *a priori* truths would have any aptitude or liking for making the practical judgements about particular situations that ruling would require. It is all too likely that those who are suited to dialectic would find ruling a painful bore. For it could not be more heavily stressed that dialectic's conclusions are entirely general; whereas action and decision are about particulars.

Plato's claim that philosophical thinking is entirely *a priori* will not meet with much sympathy nowadays, but before dismissing it we should bear some points in mind. Plato does not think that the fact that philosophical truths are insulated from empirical discussion or refutation renders them trivial. On the contrary, they are to be of more significance than the truths of the special sciences. Even if we reject this claim, we should at least not confuse it with the fairly recent idea that philosophical truths are *a priori* because philosophers cannot make substantive factual discoveries themselves and are not required to take them into account. Relatedly, Plato has no thought that philosophical truths, because they are not established or refuted by particular facts, are therefore to be discovered by examining the meanings of words, or are in any way dependent on the way we use language. He lays no philosophical weight on the distinction between what a word means and what makes it truly applicable. In terms made familiar by Kant, he takes philosophical truths to be *a priori* but synthetic, not established or refuted by our experience but all the same substantive theses of great generality, with important implications for all the special sciences.

(2) Plato contrasts dialectic with the mathematical sciences by putting heavy stress on two metaphors: image/original and dreaming/waking. In the Line, the relation of image to original within the lower part is reproduced in the upper part, so that mathematics stands to dialectic as *eikasia* stands to *pistis*, 'belief'. The relation is, of course, hard to interpret (pp. 248–52). In the latter passage (531–4) the imagery of the Cave is deliberately recalled and so mathematicians are thought of as studying the reflections of the objects outside the cave whereas dialectic studies the actual objects (533b–d). More prominent, however, is the idea that mathematicians are only dreaming whereas the philosopher is awake (533b–c, 534b–d). The two metaphors are related, for the dreamer is thought of as taking an image for a reality; he thinks that he sees Mount Everest whereas he is really only seeing a dream-image that represents Mount Everest to him. (It is very questionable whether this is what dreaming really is, but it is tempting to think of dreaming as a state of viewing images that represent real things, and this is the way of regarding dreams that has made them of most interest to philosophers.) Mathematicians are 'dreaming' because they passively accept the nature of their subject-matter as it appears to them, and so do not ask the questions that would reveal its real nature.

What is the force of these metaphors? Obviously we are meant to think that the object of philosophy is superior to that of mathematics – it really is whatever it is in a way not achieved by mathematical objects, it is the reality and not the mere image or appearance. But there is another implication running through Plato's use of this figurative language. Philosophy knows its subject-matter *directly*, whereas mathematics, even if it does have the same kind of subject-matter, does so indirectly. Looking at a reflection of a tree gives you some knowledge of the tree, but of an indirect kind. Similarly, mathematics, though it has the great advantage, for Plato, of studying objects of thought and not particular things in the world (that is why it is such a good introduction to philosophy) does not study that subject-matter in the most revealing and important way. Only philosophy studies its subject-matter in such a direct way that it knows it for what it is. We see from the Line that we begin with images and shadows, and that at every stage but the last the originals of the images become in turn images themselves for the next stage of cognitive advance. Only at the highest stage, of philosophical thinking, do we have a direct and wholly unmediated view of reality.

This point is often misinterpreted as being the idea that dialectic produces at the end an intellectual intuition which infallibly guarantees the certain truth of what is untuited. On this view, dialectic culminates in a direct vision of the Good, and of everything else in the light of the Good, a vision that guarantees the certain truth of what is revealed, because the knowledge it gives is direct and leaves no room for any mediating process where error could enter.

Now clearly dialectic does culminate in knowledge, which is infallible. But Plato is not saying that knowledge is produced by a faculty that guarantees its own infallibility. If he were presenting dialectic as such a foolproof method, his view would be absurd. But we have already seen that he is not interested in certainty as opposed to doubt. For him, directness of knowledge is associated not with an obsessive concern with whether what one believes could be false, but rather with an understanding of the subject-matter which makes it wholly clear what the thing in question is. Indirect knowing is associated with shadows and images, which are suggestive and often highly useful, but which do not give us exact or complete knowledge of the originals, and may let us down because we think of the originals in terms which are appropriate only to the images. (As, for example, Sun, Line, and Cave are suggestive about the nature of the Good, but let us down if we seek in the imagery for philosophical rigour suitable only to direct investigation of the Good itself.) The direct knowledge of the Good produced by dialectic is the kind of insight that results from comprehending a whole subject and seeing particular truths from the perspective of a complete understanding. Someone who has reached this stage will have gone through and tested the most important truths and the moves that can be made with them, and will be long past the stage of doubting whether any particular step is true. Philosophers who think that knowledge must be direct in order to exclude sceptical doubt pick on rather different items to be objects of certain knowledge. They tend to claim that we have direct knowledge of sense-data and the like, items that are given to us in experience so directly that there is logically no room for error. Plato puts our objects of direct knowledge at the other end of the cognitive scale; they are Forms separated entirely from the world of particulars. This is a strong indication that he is not interested in the kind of directness that precludes scepticism about the truth of particular claims. It is significant that philosophy has direct knowledge of what *mathematics* has indirect knowledge of; and what is inferior about mathematics is not that the statements it makes might be false or that we can't feel sure about them. Mathematics is for Plato the paradigm of a study that gets nearest the truth. He has no doubts of a modern kind about the status of mathematical truths in general. Nor does he seem to worry about whether particular mathematical claims might be false (after all, mathematics has better built-in ways of checking for errors than any other body of knowledge that Plato would be likely to compare it with, like medicine). What is wrong with mathematics is that it lacks the grounds for complete understanding; its objects are not transparently intelligible, because they are approached through empirical techniques that do not provide us with full understanding, and may even mislead, by suggesting that there is such understanding where there is not. Only Forms can be directly known, not because we have a direct, error-excluding intuition that for some reason picks out only Forms, but because Plato thinks that only Forms are in principle completely intelligible, and that dialectic, the philosopher's reasoning, is capable of a comprehensive understanding, using no methods or terms which are potentially misleading because they have primarily an empirical application.

(3) A related point: Plato describes the process of dialectic in two kinds of way which at first glance do not go very happily together. On the one hand, dialectic involves being able to 'give and receive an account' of its objects; one must be able to say what each object of study really is. Whatever this amounts to it is something articulate; and 'dialectic' derives from *dialegesthai*, to converse. On this view, dialectic looks like a development of the Socratic conversations of which we have

had a sample in Book 1; it demands verbal articulateness and interpersonal exchange. (Cf. especially 534b.) On the other hand, there is constant use of the imagery of vision and grasping, and a deliberate recalling of Sun, Line, and Cave where the metaphor for knowledge is turning towards the light. But this makes knowledge look like something non-verbal and non-articulate that each person has to do for himself or herself. How can arguing with somebody else help you to see?

These two modes of describing dialectic only come into conflict if we think of the knowledge produced by dialectic, in too post-Cartesian a way, as being a state of certainty that excludes being wrong. For if the intuitive vision of Forms (especially the Form of Good) is such a direct knowledge that guarantees certain truth, then the verbal and argumentative side of dialectic looks at best redundant. If one has direct certainty, what can possibly be added by arguing about it? The obvious way of resolving this problem, one adopted by most interpreters, is to say that the two descriptions of dialectic refer to two stages of it. One argues with other people, and *then* one has, oneself, a vision of the truth which is direct and guarantees certainty. The trouble with this is that it is an obviously crazy method for attaining knowledge. However much one tests out one's ideas against others' responses, seeking in every way to find and exclude errors, one can never guarantee that this will result in truth; one may *feel*, overwhelmingly strongly, that one knows what one has thus tested, but why should this *guarantee* that one has knowledge? Many have been driven to think that Plato thinks of dialectic as a method for attaining truth through co-operative inquiry and search, which is then, in a totally mysterious manner, crowned with individual visions of self-guaranteeing certainty; they then have to explain why he held such a silly idea.

The remedy is surely to realize that the vision of Forms, and of the Form of the Good, does not guarantee truth – we already know by that stage that we have the truth – nor provides any certainty that was not already present. It is not something extra that happens at the end of the argument, like a prize. It is just the state of understanding that has come about by the time the person concerned has attained complete mastery of the subject-matter and through familiarity with it and its structure has insight into what was formerly seen to be true but without understanding of its significance. The visual metaphors stress the directness of the knowledge concerned; but this is the directness not of certainty but of complete and unmediated understanding of the subject-matter in its own terms, and there is no reason why *this* should exclude argument and discussion. One can articulate one's understanding of a subject. So the verbal and visual descriptions of dialectic do not clash; and Plato uses both because both are necessary for his conception of what true philosophy requires. Knowledge is both something shared and impartible (as is stressed in earlier dialogues where teachability is the main mark of knowledge) and also a matter of personal achievement – I must see the truth for myself before I have knowledge, rather than mere rote learning. The most rigorous and articulate reasoning on its own will not amount to certainty; it will only guarantee consistency (533c). Knowledge results only when reasoning and argument lead to insight. Hence the merely clever will never become philosophers, for insight requires a certain kind of vision, the ability to appreciate values and their importance. On the other hand, knowledge is not achieved by someone, however morally sensitive, who is not bright enough to follow an argument. (No wonder Plato thinks that only a few can achieve real knowledge, and that even this requires the total restructuring of society.)

(4) Dialectic leads up to the Form of Good; for all his stress on mathematics Plato thinks that knowledge requires and depends on an appreciation of values, and that goodness is fundamental to our full understanding of any matter, even the most abstract. He would presumably be unmoved by objections that goodness does not seem relevant to any proof in Euclid, and that mathematics is a modern paradigm of a value-free subject. He does not argue the case especially for mathematics, and it is not clear how he would go about it. But it is clear that in making the Form of Good supreme he is claiming that goodness is, however unobviously, fundamental to making *any* subject intelligible. This is a crucial claim, but it is left vague, and it is a legitimate complaint that for all the grand language we are left without any idea of how to go about taking the first step. Exactly how does goodness render things understandable?

Plato is no help here. Sometimes it is said that in modern terms he is claiming that the basic kinds of explanation will be teleological and functional, making ineliminable reference to goals and purposes which things have and by reference to which they are said to be good or bad specimens of their kind. But perhaps even this amount of precision is wrong, for Plato says nothing about the particular forms of reasoning that dialectic will employ to show 'what each thing is'.

(5) Dialectic is *synoptic* (531d): it takes an overview above the special sciences and is 'the study of their association and kinship with one another . . . to show how closely related they are.' (Grube.) The dialectician will not necessarily be an expert in every discipline, but he or she will have enough grasp of the important features of each branch of study to be able to see what the proper form is for each, and how it should best proceed, and will know the proper status of truths in all sciences and their relative dependencies.

This is a very bold claim for philosophy, which appears as no less than the queen of the sciences, putting each in its proper place. But, grandiose as Plato's language is, it does not necessarily, as often thought, make philosophy into a 'super-science'. Philosophy is, precisely, *different* from the sciences; they are concerned with particular pieces of knowledge, whereas only philosophy seeks understanding in general. Since understanding is connected with being able to provide explanations, in systematic fashion, for what is known, we could say that dialectic is concerned, not with particular explanations, but with the conditions for explanation in general.

What Plato means here is made obscure by the difficulty in interpreting the Line (pp. 251–2) which leaves it unclear whether the different kinds of thinking displayed in mathematics and philosophy have different objects, or whether philosophy is distinguished rather by its characteristic approach to subject-matter studied already by the mathematical sciences. If the highest kind of thinking does have its own objects, then philosophy is not wholly characterized by its special kind of concern with the structure and concepts of other sciences. And some of Plato's language does suggest that philosophy has its own, specially exalted, subject-matter. But surprisingly little is made of this; Plato's words here (which are notoriously capable of differing interpretations) can quite well be taken as claiming that philosophy's task is, in modern terms, essentially 'second-order'; what it studies are not objects proprietary to it, but rather the methods and concepts of other sciences. It studies these not in the way that is internal to the sciences – it does not, for example, prove theorems in mathematics – but rather in a 'topic-neutral' way that tests and establishes the coherence, usefulness and application to the phenomena of such concepts, and their mutual dependencies. This is certainly what Aristotle takes the job of dialectic to be. In the *Physics*, for example, he does not directly investigate the natural world – he is not 'doing physics' – but investigates, in a distinctively philosophical way, the concepts needed for investigating the natural world, such as time, place, motion, the infinite. What is distinctively 'dialectical' about these investigations is that they use no presuppositions or methods that are confined to the special sciences. This is the task that the philosopher characteristically does, and the justification for his doing it is that without it the sciences proceed in a haphazard and probably muddled way. Here we see one recognizable development of Plato's claim that dialectic should 'crown' the study of all the other sciences. Of course Aristotle differs from Plato on important issues, notably that he thinks that dialectic depends on assumptions that anyone would grant, and thus is a kind of extension of common sense, whereas Plato keeps it as the prerogative of a highly trained few. But Plato's insistence that in dialectic one must defend one's thesis 'as if in a battle' (534b–c) suggests the way Aristotle develops an argument by putting forward the pros and cons of a view. And in the Academy 'dialectic' did develop into a generally available mode of argument, taking as its subject-matter various theses which one had to attack or defend in a skilful way. The argumentative side of dialectic easily let it develop into a kind of competition. Aristotle wrote a kind of handbook for these competitions, the *Topics*, and we can possibly hear echoes of them in Plato's *Parmenides* part 2. Reading a few pages of these works helps to keep in focus the very general things said about dialectic in *Republic* 7.

In the *Republic* Plato is sure that dialectic is supreme over all the other sciences. But he has not clearly made up his mind whether this is because of the superior and exalted nature of its subject-matter, or because of its distinctive way of treating the areas covered by the various sciences. Partly this hesitation may come from his reluctance, for other reasons, to give mathematics its own subject-matter (cf. the Line). But what he says about dialectic's synoptic view of the other sciences can all be perfectly well interpreted in terms of the latter idea; and this is not only the more attractive, but more consonant with the way dialectic developed both in the Academy and in Aristotle.

(6) Dialectic proceeds by 'destroying the hypotheses'. We have seen that this means destroying their hypothetical nature; dialectic 'gives an account' of them, without which they should be accepted merely provisionally (not dogmatically, as happens), and with which their truth and importance is properly understood, so that they can be accepted in the way appropriate for them.

What are hypotheses? And what is it to give an account?

There are two lines of interpretation here: very roughly, one takes the hypotheses to be concepts, and giving an account to be producing a clarifying definition, whereas the other takes hypotheses to be propositions, and giving an account to be giving a proof. Both interpretations answer very plausibly to some of the evidence.

Plato's use of the expression 'give an account' has more links to defining, and to saying what a thing is, than it has to proving. Moreover, the hypotheses actually mentioned at 510c seem to be mathematical concepts rather than mathematical propositions. And dialectic is concerned with 'saying what a thing is' (533b) whereas proving is never explicitly mentioned. On this line of interpretation, Plato is recommending that philosophers do something like conceptual analysis, clarifying concepts which are used in the special sciences in an unreflective and perhaps confused way. This is not as low-key as we might think if we assume that conceptual analysis must be trivial; Plato does not think of it as trivial, or to be done by scrutinizing meanings of words from an armchair. Aristotle's treatment of time in the *Physics* would be an example of the kind of 'conceptual analysis' in question, and that is hardly trivial.

On the other (more traditional) interpretation, hypotheses

are propositions, and to 'give an account' of a hypothesis is to remove its hypothetical character by giving a proof of it. On this interpretation, two things are explained which remain unexplained on the other. One is, why Plato thinks that mathematicians' hypotheses are specially in need of attention from dialectic. For we can see how someone might be moved to replace appeal to intuition in mathematics by appeal to rigorous reasoning and proof. (Modern interpretations are frequently indebted to the attempts by Frege and Russell to 'reduce arithmetic to logic' when they describe what Plato has in mind. But there are so many disanalogies that this is a dangerous parallel. Plato is thinking mainly of geometry, not arithmetic; he does not have a developed formal logic in mind; and he is trying to overcome the deficiencies of mathematical practice by dialectic, not by improving mathematics.)

The other advantage of this interpretation is that we can see why dialectic is in all Plato's images consistently higher than mathematics. For, if dialectic 'gives an account' of the basic propositions of mathematics by providing proofs of them, we are given a picture in which, just as theorems are derived from more basic propositions within mathematics, so the basic propositions of mathematics itself are derived, having as it were the status of theorems, from even more fundamental propositions that the philosopher has shown to be basic. The task of philosophy is to produce, perfect and defend a deductive system of propositions in which particular pieces of knowledge about mathematics (or some other special science) are grounded by being shown to be derivable from propositions higher in the system. The entire system, in which each proposition is first treated as a hypothesis, then proved, ultimately depends on the 'unhypothetical first principle', the Form of Good.

This interpretation, which in varying forms is very common, depends heavily on the suggestion in the Line and Cave that knowledge forms a body which is not only structured, but hierarchically structured. Plato, however, actually says little in non-figurative language that implies that knowledge forms a body of truths in which the lower depend on the higher and can be shown to be derivable from them. And this view involves two serious problems. One is that, in a world where Aristotle has not yet begun to codify the forms of valid argument and formalize logic, Plato has no precise terms for 'proposition', 'imply', 'derive', and no explicit distinctions between premises, conclusions, and rules of inference. Vague talk of ascent to and descent from a first principle does not warrant ascribing to Plato the notion of a 'deductive system'. And, secondly, on this view the 'unhypothetical first principle' ought to be a proposition, indeed a super-proposition from which all the basic propositions of the special sciences can be derived. But not only is it hard to conceive what such a proposition could possibly be like: everything else in these passages suggests that this 'first principle' is not a proposition at all but is the Form of Good, and it is not clear how anything could be derived from that, never mind the basic propositions of mathematics. The very fact that the Good is basic to all explanation suggests that explanation cannot be correctly thought of as deductive in form.

However, the deductive model of dialectic does do justice to something which, while not on the surface of the Republic, is not far below it. Plato is clearly impressed by mathematics more than by any other intellectual discipline. And we have enough historical background to conjecture why. Mathematics, and in particular geometry, was the only branch of knowledge familiar to Plato which had advanced not only in making particular discoveries but also in organizing its material into a form which clearly conveyed the structure of the subject in intelligible form. Euclid's Elements were based on earlier Elements, and we know that two members of the Academy produced similar works. What impressed Plato was clearly the fact that mathematics had surpassed other fields in producing not just strings of results but orderly presentation of those results in a way displaying their systematic and intelligible dependence on the basic axioms and rules of inference. Geometry was Plato's only model of a science where one could achieve not just bits of information but an understanding of the whole rationally organized system, and see what was basic, what derived, and how each result depended on what had gone before.

It is clear that Plato's concept of philosophical understanding is much in debt to what he knew of geometry. He associated knowledge with understanding of a system in which it is clear what is derivative from what, and where grasp of the basic truths (which may, of course, be the last things one learns) produces insight into the whole system and its constituents. Dialectic is not a method for finding out truths, but a way of rendering the truths we already know transparently intelligible. Philosophical understanding is, as it were, geometrical understanding writ large: there is the same insistence that knowledge requires a rational hierarchy of truths to be grasped by the intelligent person with insight – only in the case of philosophy the truths are about the whole of practical and theoretical knowledge, not just about triangles and squares.

The deductive interpretation does justice to these aspects of Plato's demands on understanding – demands which Aristotle takes up, though he insists against Plato that the separate sciences are all autonomous, and depend each on their own first principles, not on a set of common overarching ones. But although these considerations show that there is some reason to think of dialectic on the model of a geometry like Euclid's, they do not nullify the problems with that view, such as Plato's lack of precise logical vocabulary, and the way in which some passages do suggest that dialectic clarifies concepts rather than proving propositions. In fact we cannot reasonably ascribe to Plato an awareness of a sharp distinction between the two alternatives. There are reasons for this, of a very general nature which are too broad to discuss here, going back to the fact that Greek philosophical terminology does not naturally suggest distinctions that we find obvious between concepts and propositions. Even Aristotle, who discusses similar issues in the *Posterior Analytics* in a much more sophisticated way, does not distinguish as sharply as we would wish between the basic concepts and the basic propositions in a science. But while we cannot ascribe to Plato a precise notion of a deductive system of knowledge, it is clear that he is influenced by the model of geometry into thinking that understanding requires that knowledge form a system in which it is clear what is basic and what derived, and in which grasp of the basic is necessary for insight into the significance of the derived. When any subject is transparently intelligible, there will be nothing in it merely hypothetically entertained, for all the underlying assumptions will have been thoroughly examined and their grounds will be clear and explicit.

(7) The Line clearly suggests (511b–c) that there is not only a 'way up' to the unhypothetical first principle, but also a 'way down' involving only Forms. What is the difference between them? So far we have indicated what the way up is. It treats the assumptions of each science, particularly mathematics, as literally hypothetical; it examines their status and position in the science, and gives them their appropriate position, their truth and their significance now understood and no longer taken for granted. (A good analogy is again offered by Aristotle's procedure in the *Physics*: instead of unreflectively assuming that there is, for example, such a thing as time with the properties we intuitively take it to have, we investigate the concept philosophically, find that our intuitions clash rather badly and that the nature of time is very unclear, argue the matter out and then proceed with a better understanding of time and how temporal concepts work, and particularly how they are dependent on the concepts of motion and place.) Every step 'upwards' is an extension of our understanding of first the problem, then the concept, then the subject, and finally and ideally, the whole of human knowledge; and to achieve this is no less than to understand the nature of goodness. But then there is the way down. What is left for the way down?

Interpretations that make dialectic a method for achieving certain knowledge, though defective in other ways, do not have so much trouble here. The way up is there the way *to* knowledge, and once we are securely certain we can secure all individual bits of knowledge on the way down by providing a proof for them. However, if the way up is a way to progressively greater understanding, then the final stage has already been achieved when one attains the insight that comes from complete mastery of the subject. There seems no room for any further downward stages that could add to understanding.

Plato does not make the way down very prominent, and if it has no role in adding to understanding we might regard it as a mistake, or an oversight. But we can see from the way that Aristotle picks up the idea and proceeds in the *Posterior Analytics* that the downward path does have a role – as a way of presenting and expounding what has become intelligible. Aristotle insists that a science begins with the simplest, most basic notions and proceeds to the more complex – not because

292 Philosophy and Mathematics

that is how we *discover* truths, or even how we first learn them, but because that is the method of rational presentation that will best facilitate understanding of the subject-matter. So if Plato does intend to make anything of the way down, he must be thinking of a transparently intelligible presentation of the subjects that have been gradually understood on the way up and so form a systematic and intelligible body of knowledge.

There is one hitch to this solution, however. Such stress on a rationally clear presentation of knowledge, developed by Aristotle in the *Posterior Analytics*, goes with an Aristotelian view of the relation of philosophy and the special sciences. For Aristotle, philosophy is continuous with science and like it in being a growing and cumulative body of knowledge, to which individuals make their contribution, relying on what has gone before. So for him a philosophically perspicuous presentation of a body of knowledge is something which can be achieved and handed on; philosophy is a co-operative and developing venture.

But Plato does not believe in such fixity of philosophical achievement. It runs up against his repeated insistence that philosophical truth is something that each individual has to discover for himself or herself, not something that can be handed on without difficulty. All education does, he has stressed, is turn the eye to the sun (518d); each person has to make his or her own effort to see for themselves, and from this point of view the achievements of others are not to the point. It is because he is always alive to this that Plato downgrades books; for him no book, however full of philosophical truths perspicuously displayed to promote understanding, will guarantee that *you* get the point, and he prefers to think that live argument, rather than the reading of books, is the real doing of philosophy. That is, presumably, why he chooses to write in the detached and literary dialogue form, instead of baldly laying his ideas on the table: ideas are only given *point* when set in a context which reminds the reader of the need for a positive personal response, and provokes him or her into making it.

So if Plato is serious about the way down, and does mean it to be the kind of explanatorily perspicuous exposition pioneered by Aristotle, he has not thought his way clearly between two alternatives. He does want philosophy to be of lasting, indeed eternal, value, and so he wants dialectic to have a more than ephemeral result. But he also does not want to lose sight of the fact that dialectic is always personal: it is always aimed at *you*, and what matters is that *you* are moved to stir yourself and reach out for the truth instead of passively taking in the opinions even of the wisest.

FURTHER READING

Robinson's classic book, *Plato's Earlier Dialectic*, deals with these topics in chapters 6, 7, 10. There are stimulating discussions in Crombie, *An Examination of Plato's Doctrines*, vol. ii, pp. 171–97, 548–62; Gosling, *Plato*, chs. 7 and 17; N. White, *Plato on Knowledge and Reality*, ch. 4. Hypotheses are discussed in Hare, 'Plato and the Mathematicians' in Bambrough (ed.), *New Essays on Plato and Aristotle*, and C. C. W. Taylor, 'Plato and the Mathematicians: an Examination of Professor Hare's Views', *Philosophical Quarterly* 1967. Frege's discussion of number-terms is to be found in his stimulating and untechnical *The Foundations of Arithmetic* (trans. J. L. Austin).

Chapter 12

The Benefits of Justice

At the beginning of Book 8 Socrates and Glaucon explicitly refer back to the discussion of Book 4, before the 'digression' of Books 5–7. We return to the use of the larger letters of justice in the state to illuminate justice in the individual (545b), via the observation that the characteristics of states depend on the characteristics of the individuals in them (544d–e; cf. pp. 146–7). But the focus in these books is on the individual rather than the state: we are told that we are to examine justice and injustice and what they do to the individual (544a, 545b) so as to meet Thrasymachus' challenge (545a–b), and the discussion of states and individuals is followed by a series of arguments to show that justice brings the individual a happier and more pleasant life (580–592). Books 8 and 9 form an integral part of the answer to Glaucon's challenge: justice has been shown to be worth having for itself, like health, and now we move beyond the health analogy and show that justice has good consequences, for it benefits the individual and makes his or her life more pleasant. Book 4 showed that justice was worth having for itself; now we see its results, what it does for its possessor (cf. 367b, d).

THE TYPES OF UNJUST STATE AND INDIVIDUAL (543–580)

Plato traces the decline of the just state and individual through four stages: timocracy, oligarchy, democracy, and tyranny. The resulting eight vignettes of state and individual have been admired for their literary power, but they leave a reader who is intent on the main argument unsatisfied and irritated. Plato's procedure is both confusing and confused.

Firstly, he is not merely describing what exists in experience, any more than in his account of justice and the just person. While claiming that there are four kinds of unjust state, he admits that there are many existing kinds that do not fit neatly into this classification (544c–d), so the classification is an *a priori* one: these are the four essential forms that injustice is bound to take, apparent counterexamples being regarded as mere eccentricities. But on the other hand Plato thinks that the forms he identifies are found in experience; he calls his 'timocracy' the 'Cretan or Spartan kind praised by many' (544c) and some details of his picture of democracy are obviously taken from contemporary Athens. Now, obviously there is nothing wrong with appealing to experience to confirm one's theories about how political developments ought to go. But Plato never makes it clear where he is theorizing and where he is describing contemporary facts, and this leads to confusion (especially in his account of the democratic state).

A second, more important problem comes from the tidy pairing of kinds of city and kinds of person. The just person was parallel to the just city because both were unified and harmonized by the right relation of their parts. It emerges that Plato thinks of injustice as a progressive disruption and breakdown of this harmony. But why should there be precisely four kinds of breakdown that are exactly parallel in city and person? Plato is making a large and unwarranted assumption in taking it that the parallel between unified city and unified person will be followed by precise parallels between four kinds of differently disunified cities and persons. This assumption makes much of Books 8 and 9 artificial, and at many points the parallel of unjust city and person breaks down in a way not true of the parallel of just city and person.

The degenerate forms of state and individual are presented as historical progressions one from another. But this raises an awkward question right at the start. How can the ideal state ever *degenerate* in the first place? It was presented as an ideal, perhaps attainable but certainly not actual. Surely the ideally just state is something that the deficient states fall short of, not something that they result from.

The matter is complicated by the fact that right at the beginning of Book 8 Glaucon recapitulates the Book 4 discussion and says that the person and city there described were just, 'although it seems that you still had a finer city and man about which to tell us'. (543d–544a; Grube.) On the face of it, this implies that the philosopher rulers of Books 5–7, and their city, are different from the just person and city of Books 2–4; and some have drawn the conclusion that the 'digression' of the central books is not meant to be part of the main moral argument. But, though this would get us out of some problems, it will not do. It is the philosophers' state that is the starting-point for the various kinds of falling-off – at 543a the rulers are those excelling in 'philosophy and the waging of war', a clear if grotesque reference to the central books. And the arguments about pleasure at the end of Book 9 rely on the equation of justice with philosophically based wisdom. So Glaucon's phrase that suggests otherwise is an (unexplained) oddity.

However, how *does* the philosophically ruled state degenerate? Plato says only that because the rulers' reasoning is 'involved with sense-perception' (546b) they will inevitably go wrong on the elaborate numerical calculations required to ensure that the right sexual unions are promoted (546a–d). Plato is symbolically expressing the idea that no ideal can ever fully be realized; the world we experience can never exemplify what is perfectly, unqualifiedly, and stably just. The Form of Justice is *separate* from the experienced world. (This fits rather awkwardly with the earlier insistence that the ideal state could possibly be realized – pp. 185–7).

It *is* clear what form the degeneration takes: there is a break-down of unity in the Guardian class (545c–d). Plato repeats the point that it does not matter so much if members of the other classes do not stick to their jobs: it is a breakdown of the Principle of Specialization in the Guardian class that leads to disaster for the entire state. Once the whole state's priorities are determined by ambition and search for glory and victory, its internal structure is upset. The Principle of Specialization does not totally break down; although the Guardians lose their function of ruling (presumably the truly philosophical types survive ineffectually or are corrupted) there is still a sharp distinction between producers and rulers – the feature in which this state is still closest to the ideal state. But there is no longer fraternal feeling or perceived unity of the common good, since the rulers have private property and families and rule in their own interests, while the producers are openly exploited and enslaved (547b–c; contrast 463a–b). This kind of state is called 'timocracy', a name indicating that what the rulers value most is *timē* or 'honour'; Plato thinks that something like this is found in Crete and Sparta in his time. It is unfamiliar to us as any kind of state, but some of its features are suggestive of what we call imperialism. The rulers in fact exploit the ruled, and use their power for their own private profit, but avowedly they pursue high-sounding ideals of honour and glory that for them legitimize their aggression and exploitation. This is not because of individual hypocrisy on the part of the rulers, who are genuinely idealistic, but lack the insight to see that their limited and jingoistic ideals are bound to end up in the enslavement of the weaker for the profit of the stronger. We see here, as in the descriptions of all the degenerate states, that what matters for Plato is not the nature of the formal institutions – laws, constitutions and so on – but the character and education of the people in charge (546d, 548b–c, 549b).

The timocratic man also shows a kind of inner instability in that he does not live up to his ideals, because they are inadequate. He is idealistic and initially sensitive to the arts, but his behaviour conforms to the realities of power: he is deferential to the more powerful and harsh to those under his control. As he grows older the appeal of ideals fades and he sinks to a concentration on gaining money (549a–b). This kind of person is dominated by the spirited element in the soul, and the picture of him fits what we know of this: he recognizes the claims of reason and the appeal of rational consideration of what is good for all, but on his own is unable to live up to those ideals; if pursuit of the common good is not forced on him, he cannot from his own resources sustain the motivation to pursue it, but will lapse into self-interested behaviour. It is no accident that he degenerates into money-grubbing and brutality towards the helpless, since his ideals are inadequate to produce just action; a life devoted to the pursuit of glory has a built-in tendency to dislocation between what is seen as admirable and what one is actually motivated to do.

Two points of difficulty stand out. Firstly, Plato does not only want us to see the disharmony of the timocratic man's soul as the result of his allowing prominence to the wrong part of the soul; he wants it to be precisely parallel to the disharmony in the timocratic state. This claim is not plausible. For a dis- unified state corresponds better to conflict between two or more kinds of person than to one kind of internally conflicting person. This problem will recur through all the sketches. The parallel with the state is less convincing than the claim that can be independently made about the individual in terms of the soul's parts, and the present case is no exception; we find it all too plausible that devotion to militaristic ideals contains in itself a tendency to selfish dominance and ex- ploitation.

Secondly, Plato chooses to tell a temporal story about the types of degenerate individual also: the timocratic man is the father of the oligarchic man, and so on. But how do people become unjust, especially after the happy state of being just has been described so amply? Here Plato does not even offer us numerology. The timocratic man is the son of an ineffective intellectual in an unjust city, with a nagging wife (549c–550b). This can hardly be the ideal state, where the just rule, and there is no such coarse misogyny. The timocrat is the person who reacts against the position of the just man *in the world as it is* (cf. 496b–e). This would not matter did it not bring out a contrast with the degeneration of states, which go downhill not from the actual but from the ideal, thus undermining the extended parallel between individual and city.

Next comes oligarchy, which is literally rule by the few, but is thought of by Plato as rule by the rich. It is presented as disillusioned timocracy: people become cynical about glory and openly competitive in self-aggrandizement. Money is made a condition of office, so that the Principle of Specialization is overthrown (551a–b); hence jobs are in the hands of people not suited for them, and some have no social task at all (552a). This is inefficient, and also leads to breakdown not just of fraternal feelings but of any conception of the common good: poor and rich form in effect two cities in what is only nominally a single city (551d). The poor, with nothing to spend, are obviously not contributing to any common good; but, Plato insists acutely, neither are the rich (552b–d), who do spend, but only for themselves and on what they want, not in accordance with any public policy. So in the oligarchic city ideal unity has further broken up, and any unity it has is fragile and precarious.

The oligarchic man is dominated by the desire for money, and his reason and spirit are forced to work only in its interests (553c–d). Plato represents this condition as resulting from disillusion with higher ideals (553a–b); he cannot even imagine anyone admiring self-made millionaires for qualities like enterprise or energy. The oligarch suppresses all his desires that interfere with money-making, squalidly concentrating on profit (554a). Such a life is controlled, very firmly, by a single aim, but for Plato it does not amount to a unity – the oligarch's life is not really a harmonious and unified whole, for it is given direction not by the part that knows about and allows for the interests of all, but by a part that is intent only on achieving its own ends regardless of the rest, and hence represses much of his character because allowing it scope would interfere with the chief preoccupation. So far this is pretty convincing: life and literature give us many examples of how love of money even more than love of honour leads to a life which is unsatisfying as a whole because it is shaped by obsession with gain, and characterized by frustrated desires. The 'company man' intent on nothing but making ever more money, and indifferent to larger ends, is the very type of a repressed and deformed personality. However, Plato unfortunately is so concerned with the parallel with the city that he insists that the oligarch is 'not one man but two' (554d), dividing his desires into two kinds, those that he feels free to indulge while concentrating on money-making, and those he does not. These presumably correspond to rich and poor in the city. This is over-schematic: the oligarch lacks internal harmony not because he is neatly split into a rich part and a poor part, but because the specious unity imposed on a life by an obsession with money does violence to the person's development in all kinds of ways, which may vary very much and have quite different results in different cases.

Plato now gives a long, complicated, and largely unconvincing account of how oligarchy becomes democracy (555b–557a), which has little to do with his account of democracy itself. In a democracy the breakdown of unity is complete; there is not only no universally recognized common good, but no universally respected common government (557e–

558a). The hold not just of the common government, but (to Plato's horror, 558b) of common culture and education are comparatively weak, and individuals are encouraged to develop divergent life-styles. Plato calls democracy a society-shop (557d) because of the citizens' lack of conformity to one way of life. Such a tolerant society permits and encourages weakenings of what Plato sees as the natural hierarchies in actually existing societies: old and young, male and female, free and slave (563a–b).

It has often been thought, and with reason, that Plato has contemporary Athens in view: the exchange at 563d–e suggests this, as well as 563b where he mentions the free behaviour of slaves which we know was noticed in Athens; and the general impression of personal rancour suggests some settling of scores on Plato's part. But if parts of his description *are* aimed at contemporary Athens, they miss. Plato presents democracy as defined by tolerant pluralism, but Athens was a populist democracy, with a clearly defined way of life separating those with power from those without, and about as tolerant of openly expressed nonconformity as McCarthyite America. Plato knew that Athenians were not free to disobey the law (Socrates could hardly ignore his death-sentence!); that Athens was one of the worst cities in the Greek world as far as concerned equal freedoms for men and women (563b is absurd if Athens is in view); and that not only were foreigners like Protagoras and Anaxagoras driven out for expressing unpopular views, but even citizens who, like Euripides, publicly held unorthodox opinions had life made so miserable for them by public vilification that they often left Athens to escape the pressures. What Plato presents as the tolerant indifference of democracy could not be further from the state of affairs at Athens, the chief example of ancient democracy, and by suggesting otherwise Plato only muddies his case. Democracy has to be, for Plato, a permissive free-for-all with no, or weak, sense of overall unity, because it is a further stage of breakdown of the ideal state's unity. His obvious hostility to democracy so conceived illustrates the depth of his opposition to any form of pluralism. A pluralist state that accepts the fact that its citizens' primary loyalties and cultural commitments will be to different and conflicting groups within the state is, in Plato's eyes, not doing what a state should do. For he thinks that the point of a state is to make its members part of a political and cultural unity that brings out the best in everyone, because everyone will be guaranteed the place that best fits his or her talents. Plato does not have the reasons, drawn from experience, that we have for being suspicious of this view of the state's functions, and hence for being ready to accept various forms of pluralism. Indeed, since Athenian democracy was so far from any kind of pluralism, Plato is pouring scorn on the idea without ever having experienced it, or anything remotely like it.

There is a puzzle in the introduction of the democratic man. Socrates distinguishes carefully (558d–e) between two kinds of desires: the necessary ones, which we have just by virtue of being human and whose satisfaction benefits us, and the unnecessary ones, whose satisfaction is not beneficial, or is harmful. It is implied that the oligarch's son becomes a democrat by ceasing to discriminate between necessary and unnecessary desires, giving them all free rein (cf. 559c–d). But the oligarch does not limit himself to desires that are necessary in this sense: the desires whose satisfaction he allows are those compatible with making money, and these might well be both artificially acquired and harmful in their satisfaction. Why does Plato overlook this? He has shifted in his view of the oligarch: he is no longer thinking of him as a person trying desperately to *make* money (as at 554d) but has moved to thinking of him as a miser who tries only to *save* money – and the democrat is correspondingly thought of as the person with no inhibitions about spending on what is not necessary.

No doubt there are people like Plato's democratic man, who elevate spontaneity into a principle and reject any long-term plan of life; but are they the most characteristic of the democratic city? Plato's democracy is made up of divergent types of people, but why should these people not have individually strong and coherent characters? Plato is confusing a city made up of a variety of kinds of people with a city made up of people each of whom is an individual variety. He wants the former, to give a coherent account of the democratic city, but the insistence that city and soul are parallel leads him to the latter. But the kind of person he depicts has no obvious connection with democracy. The city–soul parallel has not just led to artificiality; it has broken down completely.

This makes another important point prominent. Running through all the descriptions so far is the idea that degeneration is a dissolution of unity. Thus the timocratic state is incompletely just because its ideals do not guarantee its unity, which is undermined by the rulers' selfishness. The oligarchic state has only a fragile unity because rich and poor identify more closely with the interests of their own group than with the state as a whole. The democratic state has no significant unity at all, since the state's demands have less force for individuals than personal or group interests. Analogously, the timocrat is not completely at harmony with himself because self-interest diverts him from impartial ideals. The oligarch is internally conflicted because he has to suppress some parts of himself to the overriding search for money. The democrat does not see his life as being any kind of unity, living always in the short term.

This line of thought expands intelligibly on what was said about the Guardians as ruling in the interests of the whole city, and reason as caring for the whole soul. Deterioration sets in when reason is dethroned and either serves another end or collapses completely. This is what we would expect from Book 4's emphasis on reason as alone capable of caring appropriately for all the soul's parts. But unfortunately it implies that the worst state is pluralist democracy, and the worst man the democrat, who lacks reason as a ruling force even in the shape of common prudence or foresight. But 'worst' here is 'most unjust'; and the contrast to the just man has since Thrasymachus been not the democrat but the *tyrant*. The challenge Socrates is trying to meet is that of showing that it pays to be just rather than wielding complete power unjustly. In this argument the democratic man, and his current absorption in whatever turns him on, is not to the point.

And in fact Plato adds the 'tyrannical state' and tyrannical man as being the last and most unjust state and person, as is needed by the overall argument. But neither emerges convincingly from what has gone before. Plato tells a long story about how democracy leads to complete anarchy, and anarchy to domination by a tyrant (562a–569c), and how similar anarchy among a person's desires leads to domination by one of them, namely lust (571b–575a). However convincing or not we find either account, they are hardly a natural extension of what we have discovered so far about the virtues of state and soul. As far as the state goes, Plato's claim that anarchy results in tyranny may have some historical support, and so may the claim that a state under a tyrant is wretched even when superficially glamorous; but neither is an integral part of the illustrated decline from the just state's ideal unity. Similarly the claim that when all desires are tolerated equally the result is domination by lust may or may not be true, but has no visible connection with what we have learned so far about the soul and its parts.

Plato spends much time and imaginative effort on his pictures of tyrannical state and man, and reasonably so, since they are crucial to the main argument. But logically they are excrescences on a line of thought complete already with the democratic man. The relentlessly long, overwritten, and emotionally charged pictures only make clear the complete breakdown of the city–soul parallel that Plato has laboured to establish. The picture of the city under the heel of a dictator is graphic, and little need be said about it. But the 'tyrannical man' is hardly a parallel to it; and he is hardly a picture of a *tyrant*.

The city is 'tyrannical' in the sense of being tyran*nized*; it is run by someone who has no conception of the city's welfare, but is merely out for his own gain. But the individual tyrant is not naturally thought of as someone who is in himself tyrannized in this sense. The tyrant, at least the successful kind admired by Thrasymachus, is self-possessed and successful at attaining his goals – not just petty goals but the ultimate goal of ruling other men and whole cities. Plato insists that the tyrant reproduces in himself the important feature of the tyrannized state: his whole soul is run by a part that has no conception of its own good or that of the whole soul with all its parts. The candidate for this is lust (573a–575a). At first this seems a quite extraordinary idea – what has lust to do with tyranny? Plato is pressing the idea that the tyrant's soul must be dominated by a kind of motivation that has not only no conception of the good of the whole, but no real notion of the whole self. He chooses lust, presumably, as being the archetypical motivation that is wholly fixed on getting its object and is in itself indifferent to the other factors in the soul and their interdependent satisfactions. For the soul to be controlled by lust produces the paradox, which Plato exploits, that what looks like the person getting what he wants is actually a case of the opposite. The person is subject to a blind fixation on a particular object to such an extent that his other desires are so disrupted that his personality is effectively destroyed; the notion of his getting what *he* wants has collapsed. The ideal is for the whole person's life to be shaped according to a rational pattern which determines what particular desires are to be satisfied. But here the satisfaction of a particular desire takes over the whole soul, and any overall pattern is wrecked. Plato details the obsessive and unfulfilled nature of a life dominated by such a motivation; and we can hardly fail to agree that we would hate to be like that – incapable of sustaining friendship, trust, or most forms of activity that make up a coherent human life.

But is it convincing that this is what a tyrant is like? Plato's tyrant would not last a week. It has sometimes been thought that Plato is recounting personally observed details of a tyrant he had encountered, Dionysius I of Syracuse. But this is absurd. Plato's description is suited to a Caligula, someone effortlessly presented with absolute power who finds that with the removal of all normal inhibitions reality and fantasy merge until sanity is lost. (Plato's description of the encroaching of fantasy-life at 571b–572b stresses a theme found continually fascinating in literature and life.) But what Plato says has no application to a tough-minded dictator like Dionysius I, clever and effective in gaining and keeping power. Plato's vivid portrayal of the riot of the id is irrelevant to the fact of power over others, the most important thing in a dictator's life. Most real successful dictators have in fact been (like Lenin and Stalin) tireless bureaucrats with conventional opinions and unimaginative private lives. Plato would have been nearer the mark if he had portrayed the dictator as being someone impoverished by his concentration on power and narrowed by his rejection of other claims on his soul. The claim that a tyrant is always a psycho-pathically dissolving personality misses the point. The problem shows up rather painfully when he compares the tyrant to a sick man who is forced continually to exercise and fight (579c). Glaucon, oddly, comments on the aptness of the comparison, but it is utterly inept. For of course a sick man would *lose* his fights; whereas Socrates accepted the challenge to show that the extreme of *successful* injustice is even so not worth having. His reply has taken the form of showing that, however successful, injustice will bring inner misery. But the inner misery he has portrayed is that of a person who would thereby be incapacitated from being successfully unjust.

So as a part of the main argument this whole section is very weak. The descent to injustice does not follow one consistent principle, for its climax, the picture of the tyrant, is disturbingly irrelevant to the needed conclusion. We carry away only the point that the tyrant is innerly insecure; his power can be snatched from him like that of the slave owner suddenly at his slaves' mercy (578d–579b) and thus depends on externals, not inner resources. But this does not answer the question, what is wrong with being a dictator when one *is* successful? and Plato's claim that one's sense of self will dissolve does not convince.

Beneath the formalist city–soul parallels, and misguided notion of the tyrant, this passage contains some deep and interesting points about what happens when the soul is dominated by parts other than reason, which cares for the whole soul. What is convincing in the passage are these claims; and these are what are carried on in the rest of Book 9, where we find arguments that appeal directly to the theory of the soul's parts to show that justice ensures happiness and injustice the opposite. The valuable points in Books 8–9 come out with their proper force only when the hampering city–soul parallel is dropped. Once more we see that Plato's insistence that city and individual person are just and unjust in exactly the same way not only does not help, but actually hinders, his argument.

JUSTICE AND HAPPINESS IN THE INDIVIDUAL (580–592)

Glaucon has agreed that the cities and individuals become progressively more unhappy as they become unjust (580b–d). This is called the 'first proof' that the just person is the happiest, since, despite the lack of argument, it is taken to be obvious that a unified condition, comparable to health, in which all the soul's parts are directed by the part, reason, that can plan for them all, is preferable to the various kinds of obsessive and disrupted lives that result when any other part imposes its priorities on the soul as a whole.

Plato now gives two more proofs that the just person is the happiest (580d–583b, 583b–588b) and the rest of Book 9 draws out the implications of this and concludes the *Republic*'s main moral argument. This section has been much criticized, and it does at least *prima facie* raise some troubling problems.

Firstly, we return to the tripartite soul from Book 4 (580d–581c). The three parts are: the part that learns and loves wisdom, the part that gets angry and loves honour, and the part made up of manifold desires, which loves money. The parts are characterized as much by their distinct objects as by the way they operate, but this is not inconsistent with Book 4 (pp. 141–2). These three parts produce *three* kinds of life (581c) depending on which part predominates: the philosopher's life, the life of honour and the life of gain. This fits very badly with the previous discussions of unjust souls and states (although the parts of the soul were clearly used there, in a way making this new introduction of them here very abrupt and odd). For in terms of what is said here, oligarch, democrat, and tyrant, all of whose lives are dominated by the lowest part of the soul, would be versions of the life devoted to profit! The passage does not harmonize with what has gone before; despite the talk of 'three proofs' Plato is actually starting again, ignoring the complications the city–soul parallels have introduced.

Secondly, although the proofs concern the just person (cf. 583b) it is the *philosopher* who throughout figures as the only candidate for being just, and the arguments hinge on this. Plato is carrying on from what the central books have established: to be truly just one must have knowledge, and this requires the kind of understanding that only comes with philosophical training. We shall also see that the shift between the practical and contemplative conceptions of the philosopher which was so noticeable in the central books recurs in these arguments.

Thirdly, the arguments try to prove what Socrates was never even asked to show, namely that the just person's life is more *pleasant* than the alternatives. Up till now we thought that he was going to show that it was happier, or more worth having. But these arguments are unambiguously about pleasure.

Almost universally, critics have complained that pleasure is irrelevant to the argument, and that anyway Plato is wrong about what pleasure is. These two criticisms are connected; for it is only if Plato is indeed wrong about what pleasure is that pleasure is irrelevant to the argument. In these arguments Plato is indeed not very careful about the nature of pleasure, and says some questionable things. But it is not so clear as many think that he makes a fundamental mistake about the nature of pleasure that totally vitiates the arguments; they are more defensible than is commonly allowed.

In the first argument (581c–583b) Socrates asks how, given that there are three kinds of life each with its own pleasures, we are to judge which is the most pleasant? Plato has tried to show us that by the objective standard of the Good the philosopher's life is *better* than that of the soldier or merchant, and he thinks that it is fairly obvious that it is more attractive and graceful (588a); but what if we ask *only* which life is the more pleasant (581e–582a)? All three kinds of men think that their own life is the most pleasant kind. How can we judge which is right? The appropriate way of judging is by 'experience, practical wisdom (*phronēsis*) and reason (*logos*)' (582a). The philosopher will have experienced all three types of pleasure, whereas the soldier and merchant lack the inclination and competence to enable them to taste the philosopher's pleasures. And wisdom and reason are the philosopher's special field of competence. So his judgement is the most authoritative, and since he prefers his own life, the life of seeking wisdom is the most pleasant.

Modern interpreters claim almost without exception that this argument does not get off the ground. They think this because they think that judgements about pleasure are subjective, whereas Plato is treating them as objective. A judgement is objective if its truth is settled by appeal to standards that are (in principle) public and agreed on between different people. If two people disagree on the truth of an objective judgement, then there is a real disagreement, which is (in principle) settled by reference to the public standards acknowledged. A judgement is subjective if its truth is settled by the claim an individual makes. If two people disagree about a subjective judgement, their disagreement is merely apparent; the truth of what each claims is settled by what he or she says, and there is nothing objective to disagree about. It is very commonly taken for granted that pleasure is subjective in this sense. That is, it is assumed that 'this is pleasant' is shown to be true when the person making the claim sincerely says that he or she enjoys what is claimed to be pleasant. No objective claim is being made that others could dispute. If this is right, then Plato's argument here is completely misguided. For the three kinds of person all sincerely prefer their own lives; so none of them can be wrong in thinking that their kind of life is the most pleasant life. In saying that his life is the most pleasant each is just claiming that he prefers it and enjoys it most; and he cannot be wrong about *that*. Even if we grant Plato that the philosopher has had experience of the other kinds of life and their pleasures, he cannot tell the others that their lives are less pleasant than they think. For there are no standards for the pleasantness of their lives other than what they think. The philosopher is, absurdly, telling them that they do not enjoy their lives as much as they think they do. But nobody else is in a position to tell them *that*; and when they claim that their lives are the most pleasant all that they are claiming is that they enjoy them most.

Perhaps, however, we are moving too quickly here. *We* find it obvious that 'my life is pleasant' cannot make any claim beyond 'I prefer my life'; so we take the argument to fail, because all the philosopher could be doing would be to tell the others that they do not really prefer their lives as strongly as they think. But it does not look as though Plato is making this assumption. He says nothing in the argument about people's claims about what they prefer. The criteria that are to be the relevant ones are 'experience, practical wisdom, and reason'. Plato clearly thinks that the pleasantness of a life is an objective matter; but he does *not* think that this commits him to denying any subjective claims about what people prefer. He is not denying that the soldier and merchant enjoy their lives as much as they think they do. He is, however, saying that this is not enough to show that their lives are as enjoyable and pleasant as the philosopher's. For a life to be properly called pleasant more is required than just that someone who has never thought very much about it, or experienced alternatives, should say (however sincerely) that he enjoys it. Lack of experience and thought disqualify a person from knowing what a particular kind of human life is like, what its possibilities are, what sources of pleasure it contains and what others are incompatible with it. People with experience and wisdom are taken to pronounce with authority that one life is really pleasanter than another, because they are in a position to weigh up rationally the advantages and capacities of each. Someone without experience and wisdom will be likely to pick their own life just because of unimaginative prejudice in favour of feelings they happen to have about their own life. (A simple example would be a person who has never travelled who refused to allow that any pleasure was added to a life by the possibility of travel.)

It is important that this is an argument about the pleasantness of a *life*; for what gives it its plausibility is the fact that the pleasantness of a whole life is not something that can obviously be authoritatively settled by anyone's say-so; here it is plausible that the person with wide sympathy and under-standing is at an advantage. People do, after all, go to older friends and careers counsellors to find out what to do with their lives. They are often ready to depend on the wisdom of others to find out what sort of life offers most chance of pleasure. None of this commits Plato to claims that *would* be absurd, such as that if I say that butter pecan ice cream is pleasant and you deny it, we should settle the objective truth of the matter by widening our understanding and experience to take in thirty-one other flavours. Particular tastes may very well be subjective. But judgements about the pleasantness of a life are not clearly subjective. Plato may not be right about all pleasures, but he is not obviously wrong about the pleasures that he is talking about. This argument is often compared with one of Mill's, in chapter 2 of *Utilitarianism*, where he claims that the judgement of the experienced can settle which are the 'higher' pleasures. That argument has some points of similarity with the present one, for Mill is prepared to let reason as well as experience settle the matter. But it is noteworthy that Mill is much less cautious than Plato here, for he makes the claim about a wide variety of 'higher pleasures', whereas the argument here implies only that in some cases, involving long-term assessment and complex activities over a person's whole life, it is not the case that everyone's opinion is equally worth having.

So the argument is not a totally misguided enterprise. There are difficulties, even so. Firstly, is Plato really entitled to claim that the philosopher has had experience of other kinds of life? I do not see that this is a very serious objection. Obviously he hasn't *lived* other kinds of life, and has never, for example, spent time buying and selling. But we need not be too literal-minded about 'experience'. Most of us would be prepared without hesitation to say that the life of a prostitute or a drug addict was not pleasant, undeterred by not having lived such a life first-hand. Of course we *might* be wrong; but to a great extent we are justified in relying on 'experience' in a broader sense: knowledge of the world that enables us to make imaginative projections about other kinds of life.

A more serious objection is Plato's unclarity as to how we should think of the philosopher. The way he and his aims are described, he sounds like the contemplator of eternal truths from the central books. (Cf. 581e, 582a–b.) If so, his judgement may well be a bit suspect, for why should he do justice to values that compared with his own are of no commensurable worth? How can a detached lover of learning do justice to the pleasures of gain? This is a familiar problem by now. However, the criteria for settling what was the pleasantest life included not just reason, but also experience and *practical* wisdom, and this is what we need: we want the philosopher here to be the ex-perienced and wise person who can make good practical choices and who therefore can be respected as a giver of advice about the pleasantness of lives. The tension in Plato's notion of the philosopher is nowhere more evident than in this argument. The philosopher is characterized as though he were con-templating eternal truths; but the argument, to get off the ground, requires him to be the practically wise just person. Aristotle, with his distinction between theoretical and practical reason, took up the latter aspect of the argument and developed it in his picture of the practically wise person as setting the norm for what is pleasant.

We find a similar tension in the 'third proof' (583b–588b); which falls into three parts.

Firstly Socrates claims (583b–585b) that the philosopher's pleasures are the only true, real ones. Activities that most people think are pleasant are not really so, only apparently, and owe the appearance to a contrast with pain. Smells are offered as an example of pure pleasures that do not require a preceding pain for them to be experienced as pleasant, and the pleasures of anticipation as an example of merely apparent pleasures (584b, c). Here we feel that a modest point is being questionably inflated. The acceptable point is that we do sometimes use the language of appearance and reality about pleasures when we are contrasting long and short term views of some pleasures and pains. When I say that a visit to the dentist's is not nearly as unpleasant as I think, I am contrasting a short-term view of its unpleasantness with a longer-term view which, more rationally, takes into account its importance in my life as a whole, and the pleasantness of spending long periods without worrying about toothache. But this is something that each person does for the pains and pleasures that he or she experiences. It is not clear that Plato is entitled to suppose that there is one single objective viewpoint, available to the philosopher, from which all pains and pleasures can be assessed as apparent or real. Judgements about the pleasantness of a whole life are one thing; judgements about an apparently unlimited range of experiences (from anticipations to smells) are quite another. Plato has an interesting idea here, but his claim is too hasty and unguarded to be accepted as it stands. How plausible it is to claim that a judgement about pleasantness is illusory depends on what the claim is being made about; Plato shows no awareness of that point here. The wise person is set up as a norm for every pleasure of every kind.

One thing is clear, though: this argument-section requires the practical conception of the philosopher. He is presented as being the person who makes a just estimate of pleasures because he can take the rational view of his life as a whole and the lives of others, and so makes no errors because of wrongly estimating the importance of any particular time or point of view. But the next section of the argument sees a dramatic shift to the contemplative view (585b–586c). Now we are told that there is a different way in which the philosopher's pleasures can be shown to be true. Hunger and thirst are kinds of bodily emptiness, and there is a corresponding emptiness of the soul, which is ignorance and foolishness. To be filled with knowledge and truth is to be more really and truly filled than to be filled with food and drink, since what fills the soul is more real and true than what fills the body. So the philosopher's pleasures are the most real, since they are pleasures taken in the most real kind of replenishment.

This bit of argument is, to say the least, controversial. Firstly, it jars with the previous stretch, for that distinguished real pleasures as those not depending on any relation to other things, a contrast cutting across the soul/body distinction and letting in smells as pure, real pleasures; whereas this argument consigns all pleasures arising from and depending on the body's workings to unreality. In this passage the philosopher's wisdom is wholly unworldly, and the pleasure the soul takes in learning is sharply cut off from the body. By the same token, bodily pleasures are spoken of as though the soul had no role in them and they were simply to be identified with the bodily replenishment (a point to which Aristotle objects at *Nicomachean Ethics* 1173b7–13). In a later dialogue, we can see Plato returning to the question, what role the soul and body play in any pleasure, and coming to more careful conclusions (*Philebus*, esp. 31b–55c).

But apart from the philosopher's abrupt jump from practical judgement to other-worldly contemplation, what is going on here with 'real' and 'true'? In the metaphysical arguments of the central books, *being*, it was claimed, was to be understood predicatively; something which is, is *F*, and something that unqualifiedly is, is unqualifiedly *F*. But here we are told that the soul and the soul's filling partake more of being than the body and the body's filling (585d); and this can hardly mean that knowledge is more truly knowledge, and the soul more truly the soul, than food is food or the body the body. In this argument *being* is actually introduced by the notions of changelessness and stability (585c). Something has true being if it is changeless and immortal, it is claimed, and is concerned with and comes about in what is changeless and immortal. We may wonder how what is changeless can *come about in* what is changeless, but the general point is clear: to be is to be stable and immortal, so that something that changes and perishes has less being than something that does not. That is why Plato moves (585d–e) from 'filled with what really is' to 'is really filled'; to be filled by what is stable is to be stably filled. This move makes no sense if what really is, is thought of as bearing its predicate unqualifiedly.

Two things are very odd about the way the objects of the philosopher's study are actually introduced by the notion of their being changeless, rather than by the arguments we have seen that relied on the notion of predicative being. Firstly, *being* is still treated in this argument as a matter of degree: some objects *are* more than others. But, while the previous arguments gave a sense to this, it is hard to see how being changeless could be a matter of degree. Secondly, it is not clear how this passage should be related to claims elsewhere about Forms. For the contrast drawn here is not one between Forms and other things, since it has as much application to soul and body as to other things (585d), and the soul is not a Form.

It is clear, anyway, that Plato is appealing to the contemplative conception of the philosopher, and the enormously greater value of the objects of his knowledge than that possessed by the objects of any other endeavours. And the familiar objections apply: why should grasp of the unchangeable make one a better judge between everyday matters of pleasure and pain?

At 586c we return to the superiority of the philosopher's practical reason. The familiar point that only reason cares for the whole soul is recast in terms of pleasure: when reason attains its proper pleasures, then all parts will be satisfied (586e) whereas dominance by the desires of another part upsets the whole ordering of the person's life, so that no part is properly satisfied or attains its own pleasures (587a). Abruptly returning to the tyrant, Socrates declares that the just person is 729 times more happy than the unjust tyrant (587b–588a), giving a numerological twist to the conclusion about the soul's three parts. Just people are the happiest because only in them does reason rule so as to produce the pleasure that each part of the soul seeks when it is performing its own appropriate role.

The arguments about pleasure are not the mistake they are often said to be. Plato is not making an obvious mistake when he claims that the pleasantness, as well as the goodness, of the just person's life is objectively superior, though philosophical training and insight may be needed to see this. If we disagree, it is up to us to argue, and not just assert, that pleasantness can *never* be an objective matter. The arguments go wrong rather in their lack of caution. Claims about pleasantness which have some plausibility when applied to a whole life are incautiously extended to all cases of pleasure. Further, the unresolved tension between the practical and contemplative conceptions of the philosopher makes his role in these arguments questionable. What should be a claim about the worth of good practical reasoning is often mixed up with a claim about the value of eternal objects of knowledge. Plato recognized later that these arguments were too hasty and that he had not considered the nature of pleasure carefully enough.

The rest of Book 9 rounds off the *Republic*'s main argument. At the beginning of Book 2, Socrates undertook to show that justice should be put in Glaucon's second class of goods, things desirable for themselves and for their consequences. By the end of Book 4 justice was shown to be worth having for itself, desirable as health is desirable, that is, whether or not it has any further good consequences. This was the conclusion of the discussion of the first four books, which moved from an act-centred theory of justice to an agent-centred one, and concluded that being a just person had a value not reducible to the value of good actions, and so was worth having for its own sake. After the 'digression' of the central books, which as we have seen introduced a major problem into the argument, Books 8 and 9 have taken up the second half of the challenge: to show that justice has good consequences. This has been done partly by displaying the disadvantages of the various ways of being unjust, and partly by the arguments that conclude that only the just person's pleasures are real. So justice has as its consequence a pleasant and happy life, and thus is desirable both for itself and for its consequences, and belongs rightfully in the second class of goods.

Plato's arguments about the consequences of justice are uneven in quality; they are bedevilled rather than helped by the analogy with the city, and they are unclear about pleasure. But one point comes out clearly. Happiness and pleasure result from the nature of justice itself, and could not result from the various kinds of injustice. Pleasure is different from what produces it, but there is no one thing, pleasure, that is produced indiscriminately by the activities of just and unjust, wise and money-grubbing. You experience a tyrant's unhappiness only by living a tyrant's life; we are told explicitly that all three parts of the soul have different pleasures because they aim at different objects. We are shown that the tyrant is unhappy by being shown what kind of life he leads; and we are shown how superior the philosopher's pleasures are by being shown how superior are the objects of his concern. Pleasure and happiness are intrinsic to the kind of activity and the kind of life that produce them. And so justice necessarily produces pleasure and happiness, because justice is the ordering of the soul that is brought about when all the parts of the person's soul are doing the appropriate things in the right conditions.

At this point we may well feel dissatisfied, and discover that by the end of Book 9 conviction has leaked away. For Plato is showing us that we will be made happy by having Platonic justice, that is, psychic harmony. And in the same way that that could not be equated simply with the common conception of justice, so the happiness it brings cannot be simply equated with the common conception of happiness or pleasure, as understood by all and sundry. For if justice is a state of one's soul, then the happiness that justice brings is the result of a state of one's soul; and this is not our ordinary notion of either happiness or pleasure, both of which we take to depend on a good deal more than the state of oneself. (We draw distinctions here between happiness and pleasure, which Plato does not draw, but I do not think that these affect the present issue.) The happiness which the tyrant can never have flows from a well-ordered soul; but Thrasymachus would not associate happiness with a well-ordered soul. He would think of it as being in a position to do what one likes and satisfy any desire one happens to have. If he is stubborn enough, he can say at the end of Book 9 that his claim was that the tyrant was happy in this common-or-garden sense, and that the results of psychic harmony are not relevant to that.

We should bear in mind, though, that this is not a separate problem with the arguments about pleasure; it is already implicit in Plato's shift to justice as an inner state, psychic harmony. Plato undertook to show that justice is desirable in itself and also for its consequences. He has shown that justice is essentially a matter of one's own inner state, not only the actions performed. But if justice has happiness as its consequence, and justice is psychic harmony, then happiness must be the result in a person of having psychic harmony. What else could it be, after all, once we have revised the notion of justice as Plato has done? He is bound to restructure our notion of happiness just as he did our notion of justice. It is not open to Plato at this point to treat happiness as something that everyone has already agreed on, and then show that justice leads to *that*. For he has already shown that justice is an inner state of the agent, and it is hard to see what grounds there could be for thinking that an inner state will lead to happiness as most people think of that. Happiness in most people's conception depends in large part on how the world happens to be, on one's surroundings being in a certain way favourable, and Plato cannot convincingly link *that* with psychic harmony. Rather, he wants to persuade us that happiness, like justice, is more in ourselves than we tend to think it is. He has been trying to show us that we do not depend on others, or circumstances, for our happiness; we can bring it about by the development of reason within us that makes us just. It is absolutely crucial that all the arguments about happiness and pleasure are cast in terms of the soul's parts and their ordering. Happiness, on this way of looking at things, does not lie in what others do to you. It lies in what you have already done to yourself. It remains for the more realistic Aristotle to insist that whatever one's inner state, and however satisfactory it is, there are *some* constraints on how the external world happens to be before one can be reasonably called happy. Plato does not face the question of whether one could be happy if one had psychic harmony but had to cope with external problems, like being terribly poor. This is no doubt because in the *Republic* he does not give extended consideration to the condition of a just person in an unideal society. He thinks of just people in the conditions that produce them, namely a just society; and of course *there* the just person will not be prevented by external factors from being happy.

Plato does not defend his redefinition of happiness even to the extent that he defends his redefinition of justice. He takes it as obvious that once one accepts that justice is really psychic harmony, then the happiness that results from it will likewise be seen to depend on the agent's state rather than the way the world happens to be. But, even if we accept that the happiness produced by a life is intrinsic to that life, and not obtainable by living any other kind of life, can happiness really be something depending entirely on the agent's inner condition? It is probably because we find this so implausible that we tend to be unconvinced by Books 8 and 9. Yet even though Plato produces no real argument, he at least raises a point of genuine difficulty, which modern ethical discussions tend to overlook. On the one hand, happiness surely cannot lie entirely in what the agent makes of his or her life; for this neglects the role of the environment, especially the social environment, and disasters and hostility do affect the agent's happiness. On the other hand, happiness surely must depend on what the agent does with his or her life; for to make it contingent on the favourableness of the environment seems to treat the agent merely as the product of the environment, and to leave out the fact that the agent *makes* his or her life, by the kind and quality of the choices that are made. How can my happiness, the result of my chosen way of life, be the outcome merely of luck? We have seen that Aristotle disagrees with Plato on this difficult issue, and the dispute continued in the Hellenistic schools of philosophy. How important are 'external' versus 'internal' goods? How far is my happiness dependent on what I do with my life, and how far is it contingent on luck and what others do? Modern moral philosophy does not take this to be a central question in the subject; but for an agent-centred theory of ethics it is one of the most important questions that there are.

Justice, then, produces happiness; but it is not a happiness that could be produced by anything other than being just; it is a consequence of justice that cannot be separated from justice and attained by being unjust instead. We do not tend to think of happiness this way; we tend to think of it as the utilitarians do, as something that can be attained in any number of ways regardless of their moral quality. The arguments of Books 8 and 9, then, would not convince anyone not already convinced by the arguments of Book 4. But this is not a fault in the argument, but a virtue. Right at the beginning we were told that justice was to be put into the second class: the argument was to show that it was desirable for itself and for its consequences. Now we see that there has been indeed a single argument to that conclusion. There have not been two logically distinct arguments, first to show that justice is desirable for itself, and then, separately, to show that it leads to happiness as independently conceived. Rather, Plato shows first that justice is psychic harmony, something that to a great extent changes our views on what is essential to justice; then he shows that, so conceived, it is the kind of thing that is bound to lead to a happiness which the unjust cannot have. It has the good consequences it has because it is the kind of thing it is. The two parts of the argument are distinct, but they do not fall apart into a deontological bit and then a consequentialist bit. There is a single argument which is neither, but is distinctive; the form of Plato's argument has remained just what he said it would be.

We find the first part of the argument more convincing than the second. The difference between act- and agent-centred theories of ethics is a deep one whose importance is recognized, even if we do not follow Plato in his priorities. But we are inclined to dismiss Books 8 and 9. There are good reasons for being dissatisfied with the arguments; they are hasty and casual about pleasure, and how it is related to happiness, and Plato is not nearly so concerned to show that his conclusions here do not outrage common sense as he is in the case of justice. But paradoxically, in spite of the weakness of the arguments, they are underestimated. They express a deep point which modern theories of ethics find hard to express: the point that the happiness and pleasure that can be got from a life of a certain moral type is in important ways intrinsic to that life. Utilitarians prefer to think of pleasure as something that can be got indifferently from any moral source, and so as something to be maximized and distributed to people, regardless of what they are like. Plato's ideas here about pleasure, though not particularly well put, are more profound than anything to be found in any utilitarian theory.

Book 9 ends with an image which sums up the argument and returns to the focus on the agent, and on justice as a state of the agent's soul, which has given the discussion its characteristic form. We are to imagine a person as being a man containing a little man, a lion and a huge multiform and unruly beast. These are the soul's parts, and the fact that reason is a little man within the big one repeats the point that reason's interests are those of the whole, that developing one's whole self with all its capacities is identifying with one's rational desires. To praise injustice, we are told, is to say that it is good to leave these parts in chaotic combat, with the man and lion outnumbered and overwhelmed. Praising justice is praising the orderly taming of the beast by the man with the lion's help.

The image is bizarre, and, like some other images of Plato's, has a visually incoherent, slightly nightmarish quality. But it serves to sum up very well many aspects of the main argument of the book – including some notable tensions. On the one hand, Plato makes clear, by means of the image, that justice is, contrary to what we might have thought, something internal to the agent: the things relevant to the agent's justice are all inside him. The agent produces justice in himself by identifying with the little man, the reason. The benefits to the agent of doing this are, we are told, obvious (589c–590a), so much so that it can only be ignorance that makes most people go wrong. This can all be fairly said to illustrate the revisionary aspect of Plato's account of justice. But he is also concerned, on the other hand, to show that he has not lost touch with what we recognize already as justice; for he stresses that many everyday condemnations are provoked by what we can now see to be lack of psychic harmony. He goes, in some detail, into the ways that different recognized faults spring from different kinds of dislocation in the psyche (590a–d).

The image brings out another tension too. For what makes the person just, and most fully human, is the identification with reason, which is portrayed as identifying with what is human-like inside you rather than what is bestial. For reason to rule is for the person's inner life to have the order and dignity which are characteristically human. But at 590c–d we are told that labourers, and those weak in reason, must have reason imposed on them to produce justice in them. Plato says in so many words here that even an imposition of reason amounting to one person's being another's slave does not prevent them from being 'friends'; what matters is that reason rule, and it should make no difference, be no cause for resentment, that is imposed by another rather than coming from within. The reason whose rule in the individual soul produces a truly human and dignified life is also the reason whose rule in Plato's state leads to people being treated in impersonal ways which precisely deny their dignity as humans. Plato brings these points out together, without reconciling them, in a single passage.

The final word, however, is that politics and the management of society on rational lines matter less than the individual and the personal struggle to be just. In spite of the prominence the city's justice has had, Plato ends by saying that it does not matter if the ideally just state is only a pattern 'laid up in heaven' (592b); what matters is its role in bringing about justice in the individual. We end where we began, with the question of why *I* should be just.

FURTHER READING

There is little on the parts of the soul in Books 8 and 9 compared with the discussion of Book 4. Most useful is Irwin, *Plato's Moral Theory*, ch. 7, sections 6–8, 15–19.

The arguments on pleasure are usually lambasted; for a typical write-off see Cross and Woozley, *Plato's Republic, a Philosophical Introduction*, ch. 11; for a somewhat more sympathetic though still negative view, Murphy, *The Interpretation of Plato's Republic*, ch. 5.

Plato's later dialogue *Philebus* is, though difficult and tortuous in parts, a useful supplement to the pleasure arguments here.

Chapter 13

Plato's Moral Theories

Book 9 forms the end of the *Republic*'s main argument, the attempt to answer Thrasymachus. There are many reasons for thinking that Book 10 is an appendage to a book whose main point has already been made. So it is appropriate to sum up Plato's argument at this point and consider certain outstanding questions about it.

Thrasymachus claimed that justice is 'another's good', a sacrifice of your own interests which benefits only the weak and stupid, and which would be rejected by the strong and intelligent. Socrates undertakes to show that justice itself, not its appearance, benefits the agent. In Books 2–4 and 8–9 he shows that justice is the only state in which all of a person's basic needs find harmonious fulfilment; unjust people are dominated by desires that cannot produce a truly unified person. This claim is backed by a theory of human nature and of the social conditions necessary for it to be properly developed. Justice, as thus presented, is worth having for itself, as the ordered state of health is preferable to the disordered state of disease. And it is also worth having for its consequences, because it brings happiness in a way not attainable through other kinds of life. This line of thought shows that justice is worth *my* while if I do not want to deny and frustrate the human nature that I cannot help but have.

In Books 5–7 Plato develops what is meant to be an extension of this line of thought, to take into account the implications of justice for our relations to others. But the line of thought developed turns out to be rather different. Now Plato claims that to be just one must be a philosopher – that the just person's knowledge requires philosophical understanding, and must be the product of a long training which begins with a recognition that some problems cannot be solved by unthinking reliance on experience, but must be worked through by pure thought. The just person comes to have insight into what is absolutely good and just, and will act in accordance with its impersonal requirements. But to achieve this understanding, and to conform oneself to its requirements, is to reject the idea that justice must be in my interests for it to be something that I have reason to have. Just people in a just state (the Guardians) will think and act in an absolutely impersonal way to achieve the common good, rationally conceived; and they will act to bring themselves and others as near as anything mortal can come to the state of the Form of Good. Although his account of knowledge, and the actual passages of argument that involve Forms, perfectly well allow Plato to develop a practical conception of the philosopher, he in fact opts for the contemplative picture, and stresses the ways in which devotion to this ideal will tear a person away from all normal concerns and interests.

I have stressed the way in which the absolute nature of justice's requirements in the central books undermines the kind of justification offered in the main argument. It will be clear by now to the reader that I take the developments of the central books actually to conflict with the course of the main argument. For if justice must be grasped as absolutely and unqualifiedly good, the requirements of justice will hold regardless of any personal points of view or interests; but Socrates undertook to show that justice was in the agent's interests, and Books 2–4 and 8–9 in fact try to show that it is something which is worth having *for the agent* both in itself and for its consequences. I have drawn the distinction here between the main moral argument and the development of the central books much more sharply than many would, and many would not agree that they are actually inconsistent. But the problems I have pointed out arise even for those who want to interpret Plato as holding a single coherent argument throughout Books 2–9.

It will also be clear to the reader by now that I think that the main argument, often summed up as the argument that 'justice pays', is a forceful moral argument, and that the central books' insistence on the impersonality of justice's requirements is a mistake. But is this not a paradoxical position? Surely the demand that justice be shown to be in my interests is a demand that I be given a non-moral reason for being just – or even an immoral one? For is it not giving me a self-interested, egoistic reason to be just? But self-interested reasons are the paradigm of reasons that are *opposed* to moral ones. Surely it is a requirement of morality that we take up an impersonal viewpoint such as is described in the central books? A very common way of characterizing moral reasons is that they are universalizable, and this is often understood to mean that they apply to all rational beings in an impersonal way. But if moral reasons are those that apply to all impersonally, then the demand for a moral reason to be just must be quite distinct from any demand that the agent be benefited by being just. If we look at the matter this way (which is quite common in moral philosophy) then it will be the main argument, that 'justice pays', which will be the mistake, and Plato will be offering a properly *moral* argument only in the central books. Since I have claimed that the opposite is nearer the truth, more needs to be said.

Firstly, we should be precise about the nature of the conflict between the main argument and the central books. It is not merely that Plato starts to defend the value of justice for everyone, and then ends up in the central books putting so many constraints on the knowledge required for justice that only a few can attain it. It is true that Plato's answer has élitist implications: only a few can be just, because only a few can have the knowledge that is required. But this is not peculiar to the central books; even if these did not exist it would still be clear that in the ideally just state only a few would be wise enough to be fully just. We do not need the further move, that the knowledge required is a philosopher's knowledge, to get us to that conclusion. And the present problem would arise even if Plato had thought that everyone could be wise, and so a Guardian. This would still leave him saying in the main argument that justice is in the agent's interests, and in the central books that justice does not offer the agent egoistic reasons favouring his or her own interest, or altruistic reasons favouring others' interests, but simply makes impersonal demands on all alike to do what is absolutely and objectively good.

I shall offer three reasons for thinking that Plato's main argument – justice benefits the agent – is a legitimate answer to a moral problem, and that, while not complete and satisfactory as it is, it can be taken seriously as a moral answer. I shall then try to indicate what is required to complete it, and how Plato goes wrong in the central books by offering not this, but the impersonality of the Good instead.

(1) Plato picks up, and treats as genuine, the demand that justice be shown to be in the agent's interests. This is necessary if he is not only to meet Thrasymachus' challenge but to deal with people like Polemarchus, who do the just thing but without any understanding of why they do it, and who are therefore vulnerable and intellectually insecure. Plato wants to show that justice benefits the agent, not only to show the moral sceptic that injustice is not really a good bet, but also to show the conventional that there are in fact good reasons for doing the kind of thing that they have been doing unreflectively. There are good reasons, because there are good reasons for being the kind of person who would do just actions, not merely because they are demanded, but with understanding. Even in the area of moral notions, which are greatly disputed, Plato's concern is not only to meet the sceptic, but to give the person with mere true belief some understanding of what it is that he or she has true beliefs about.

I can see no good reason for rejecting this demand as being irrelevant to morality. Many philosophers have a notion of 'morality' according to which morality excludes *any* appeal to self-interest; the two are thought of as mutually exclusive. But this is not a notion of morality that we all unproblematically share. We need to have good independent reasons for accepting it. Of course, most people find it intuitively true, and true on reflection, that morality excludes selfishness and making exceptions in one's own favour just because it suits one to do so. But self-interest need involve neither of these, and Plato's notion of it certainly does not. (We shall come back to this under (3).) But then it is not at all obvious why morality must exclude any reference to the agent's own needs and interests. The claim that it *must* do so, and that therefore the *Republic*'s main argument is not a *moral* one, is sheer dogmatism.

Further, a notion of morality that makes it illegitimate for the agent to demand that justice be shown to be something that he or she has reason to have, is in danger of making morality something that has no explicable connection with people's needs and natures, and this makes it appear blankly unintelligible why one should be moral at all. If I am assured that the moral thing to do is the course of action that has nothing to do with any of my interests, needs or projects, then it is a good question, why I should do the moral thing. This is not to require a selfish reason, merely a reason that shows why it is reasonable for me to act on moral requirements. After all, *I* am the one who *acts*. This is a platitude, but one that has important implications. If I am to perform an action, I must have a reason for doing it that is a reason for me, makes some appeal to desires that I have. If there is no reason for me to do the action, then it is not clear how I could ever be motivated to perform it. It is sometimes claimed that in morality this is not a problem: if a reason is a *moral* reason then I can and should be motivated to act in accordance with it even if I have no reason so to act and no appeal is made to any interests or desires that I have. A moral reason demands that something be done – and I am supposed to do it forthwith, regardless of my view on the matter.

Plato rejects this attitude to morality – and surely he is right to regard it as shallow and inadequate. If I am convinced that something is the moral thing to do, but see no reason for me to do it, then if I none the less act, my action has an unthinking quality; even if we waive the problem of how I am ever to be motivated to do the act, it can hardly be seen as a reasonable thing to do. If morality is seen as a set of external demands on the agent, then the person who responds to them with automatic respect is, in an important way, behaving irrationally, giving up on reason. Someone who respects moral rules but cannot answer the question, 'Why should I be just?' is someone who divorces morality from his or her deepest personal concerns. Plato thinks this is a scandal; it is because even conscientious followers of moral rules lack interest in and understanding of this question that they are powerless to avoid scepticism about the value of morality. In the *Republic* Plato has shown us how to avoid Thrasymachus' conclusions – but not by an ever more ponderous stress on the importance of morality, in a way that grants Thrasymachus' claim that morality thwarts the excellent development of human nature. Rather, he has sketched the kind of theory that grounds morality in fact and shows it to be a development and fulfilment of human nature. Plato sees the just person as someone who does just actions without conflict or strain: virtuous actions are a natural product of well-developed character. The shift from an act- to an agent-centred theory has rejected the idea that a person can be just if he or she acts simply because it is the moral thing to do, with a kind of chilly distance between the agent and the act required by rule.

We are bound to disagree strongly with many aspects of Plato's theory. But we should at least not confuse his demand for a reason for the agent to be just with a demand for a selfish or egoistic reason. That way of looking at things grants what Plato rejects, namely that a reason for me to be just must be a selfish reason, one opposed to morality. Rather, Plato is moving us towards a more profound way of looking at ethics. It is no longer enough blankly to respond to moral rules. It matters, and matters morally, what kind of person you are.

(2) But does Plato not recommend justice for the wrong reasons when he undertakes to show that justice will bring about happiness, and goes on to claim that the result will be a more *pleasant* life? Here we should remember exactly what it was that Socrates undertook to show. He said that he would show that justice itself, not its appearance, benefitted the agent. That is, the only consequences that would count as good consequences of being just were what were called there natural, as opposed to artificial consequences (pp. 66–7). They had to come from the nature of justice, not from a successful pretence of being just. At the time this seemed like a weakness in Socrates' argument, because the task seemed to be thereby made hopelessly difficult. But now we have seen the distinctive form of Plato's argument we can see that so far from being a weakness it is a strength. Plato has argued that justice is worth having both because it is in itself a worthwhile condition and because it makes the agent happy. But the happiness or pleasure brought by being just is not something that merely *happens* to be a consequence of justice, and could as well be sought some other way. It is a natural consequence of being just, something one can only get from actually being just and not any other way. Although the just person's pleasure is something over and above

the state of being just, still it is pleasure that can only come to the just, not to the unjust.

We have seen that Plato's arguments are not in fact very satisfactory, and that more attention needs to be paid to the nature of pleasure and happiness. None the less, it is clear that even in the *Republic* he avoids many problems that face modern philosophers who recommend justice (or anything else) because of the happiness or pleasure it produces. Many forms of utilitarianism, for example, give as our reason for being just the fact that this will maximize happiness. Now this appears to give the agent a reason for being just, since everyone has a reason to maximize happiness. But it is not a very reliable reason, since there are obviously many cases, which some Thrasymachus will always stress, where more happiness would be forthcoming if justice were not respected. (Of course utilitarians have various moves that they can make at this point.) The claim that someone seeking happiness has reason to be just is bound to be a fragile one – as long as happiness is thought of as something that can equally well be attained by just and unjust alike. Utilitarians have thought that it is obvious what happiness is, and that everyone wants it and is capable of it regardless of what kind of lives they lead to get it. If Plato had thought of happiness or pleasure this way, then he would have been recommending justice, most implausibly, as a good bet for anyone who wants to be happy. But we have seen that his argument is not of this form; happiness is something you get if you are just, but you only get it by really being just, and so the happiness which the just person gets has no appeal to someone who does not want to be just anyway. Happiness, therefore, does not figure in the argument in the way that it does for a consequentialist; after all, Socrates rejected the idea that justice belonged in the third class of goods, as being something worth putting up with for the sake of being happy. If that is how you think of happiness, and justice, then justice will indeed not be a good way of being happy; but Plato has been trying to persuade us to change the ways we think of justice, and of happiness, in significant respects. At the end of the argument, then, the appeal of justice is in no way egoistic. For to want justice merely as a means to one's own well-being is precisely not to see it as desirable in itself. But for Plato only the person who wants justice for itself is just, and therefore made happy by being just.

Once again it is important to stress the distinctive nature of Plato's claim, because his form of argument is not familiar to us from modern moral philosophy, and we are in constant danger of misinterpreting it. We tend to assimilate it to a deontological claim that justice is good, and worth having, whether it makes me happy or not; in which case the arguments of Books 8 and 9 become simply baffling. Or we assimilate it to a consequentialist claim that justice is good only to the extent that it produces happiness; in which case it is Plato's procedure in Book 4 that is going to leave us baffled. But both of these ways of looking at the *Republic*'s argument fail to do justice to the peculiar role of pleasure or happiness. Plato does not think of pleasure or happiness as utilitarians do, as being clear and definable independently of how it is attained, as being something equally well attainable by any kind of life, however noble or degraded. And because the just person's happiness can be got only by being just, with no short cuts, Plato has not, in appealing to happiness, made an appeal to egoism or selfishness. Happiness may be a prize for the just, but it is no incentive to someone who does not want to be just anyway. Plato has not given us an immoral or potentially immoral reason for being moral.

(3) However, Plato does think that justice makes for a satisfactory way of life that answers to one's desires and will (external disasters apart) make one happy. And is this not objectionable anyway? Why should justice have anything to do with my desires? Why should a life that satisfies rather than frustrates them be a *just* life?

But Plato is not arguing that a just life will take all existing desires into account. He is as aware as anyone that many existing desires are such that no life that fulfilled them could be just. But he does not (as many utilitarians are forced to) have to give moral weight to the satisfying of any and every desire. This is the point of his theory of human nature and the 'parts' of the human soul. What should be fulfilled is the unified and harmonious realization of a certain pattern of the sources of motivation that everyone has. No value is given to the fulfilment of particular desires unless as part of this pattern. Individuals and their actions are judged by their conformity to such a pattern of ideal functioning. By adopting such a theory Plato avoids having to give moral weight to every actual desire, whatever its object, while still founding his theory of justice on an empirical account of what people are like, and making actual human nature centrally relevant to his moral theory. So, again, there are no objectionably egoistic implications. Justice will provide a satisfying life for me – if I am functioning as a human being should.

It is all too obvious to us what is wrong in Plato's theory of human nature. For one thing, it is too monolithic. It imposes a single pattern on all people. One of its most signal failures is the way in which, although he in principle wants women to be genuinely equal with men, Plato thinks that the perfection of women's nature will simply lie in their being assimilated to the ideal of male nature. Further, not only is there one single pattern, that pattern has obvious deficiencies. We cannot wholeheartedly support Plato's intellectualism. He is mainly concerned with the havoc wrought by the passions and particular desires. We are bound to think of this as comparatively small-scale compared with the damage caused by too rational and intellectual an approach to human problems. Plato is too single-minded in his insistence that value is to be found in the renunciation of individual wants and their importance in favour of the overall, rationally integrated view of one's life. In the wake of utilitarianism and other theories that similarly insist on the desirability of rational 'life-plans' we are likely to be more concerned to reinstate the worth of particular attachments and commitments in the individual's moral life.

All the same, the defects in Plato's picture of human nature do not show that the whole approach, of founding morality on the desirability of realizing a particular pattern of desires, is quite misguided. It is often assumed that, if one rejects a monolithic pattern of 'human nature' such as the one Plato puts forward, one must therefore reject any attempt to ground the appeal of morality on human nature. But this does not follow at all. What is needed is rather a picture of human nature that is both more subtle than Plato's, and more pluralistic. We are hardly unfamiliar with the idea that the doing of particular

actions is judged according to the way it does or does not fit in
with a whole pattern of behaviour and motivation that the
agent accepts. People all the time judge what they do by
whether it would be 'bourgeois', 'feminine', 'uptight', and so
on. The fact that they do not judge their actions against one
single paradigm of human nature does not show that they do not
judge it against any paradigms. Plato is too hasty and too crude
in his view of what human nature is; but is not going in the
wrong direction entirely.

It might be objected that such an appeal to ideals, and
approved patterns of desire, does nothing to meet the point
that justice is supposed to have an appeal to *the agent*. Why
should I think that *I* have reason to be just, merely because
being just is required by some overall pattern of desires and
behaviour? The issues here are very complex, and I am not
under the illusion of having done more than raise them. But a
few points can be made. This objection does indeed seem hard
to answer if one is operating, as Plato is, with only a monolithic
notion of human nature. But this is precisely because it is too
crude and simple a notion. We do not feel impelled to be just
by the picture of Plato's just person (indeed, we find it repellent)
because we are not inclined to accept his theory of human
nature. But the same might not be true of a more realistic and
pluralistic theory. And even Plato's theory, for all its
inadequacies, has two points in its favour. For one thing, it does
appeal to facts about people the way they are. The argument,
that justice pays, relies on pointing out to people the fact that if
they are unjust they will suffer in recognizable human terms;
they will pay a price that they recognize both in self-esteem
and in relations with others. And this is much more appealing
than the claim that injustice should be avoided because of the
sanction of some externally conceived morality. Plato is at least
giving us the right *kind* of reason to have a grip on the agent. We
cannot help but be human, in our various ways; and reasons for
being just that appeal to this have a force that is entirely lacking
in appeals to sanctions that come from sources external to our
human nature. And secondly, the facts about us that Plato
appeals to, however crudely, are facts that hold of *everyone*; the
theory of the parts of the soul is meant to give us a picture of
human nature in general. So the argument that is to persuade

us to be just relies on facts that are equally true of everyone; and here we can see a plausible basis for what is needed, namely some move from the claim that justice benefits *me* to the claim that justice demands that I not act in ways that will prevent others being likewise benefited. For others are relevantly like me.

So to show that justice benefits the agent is not to reduce justice to egoism or selfishness. Rather, it produces a distinctively 'agent-centred' view, one both interesting and fruitful as a moral answer to the question 'Why should I be just?' Justice is to be shown as an intelligible demand on human nature, something in accordance with our potentialities for living creative and fulfilling lives rather than the lives that are likely to result if we spend them following an arbitrary set of external demands.

But the account of Books 2–4 and 8–9 is not yet a complete account of the grounds of justice. For there is a genuine problem, why justice should, as so conceived, make me respect the rights of others. Why should the best realization of my nature be constrained by the needs and interests of other people also trying to realize their own individual projects as best they can? We have seen that by the end of Book 4, when Plato has completed his account of justice as a harmony of the individual soul, he has also raised some doubts as to the extent to which this is really *justice*, which demands that the agent refrain from taking from others more than is his or her due. The main argument will not do as it stands. Plato does need to do something of the kind he attempts in the central books – to try to show what justice implies for the treatment of others.

Plato's answer here is that the demands of justice are recognized by a (fully trained) reason and that they apply impersonally to all, because justice is part of the bringing about of what is unqualifiedly and completely good, not good in a way relative to particular interests. In doing what justice requires people act, therefore, neither egoistically not altruistically, but impersonally, responding to an impersonal demand. Only the Guardians fully recognize what these requirements are, but both they and those that have less understanding of them must act in accordance with them, whether autonomously or under compulsion. Justice demands that one follow reason, and reason is universally present in human nature (though because it is very unequally distributed only some have enough reason to act on it without compulsion; others have to follow reason as it is imposed from without by others who have more).

Justice, then, requires that one adopt the impersonal viewpoint. But we have already seen at length that, in the central books, this turns out to have repellent and quite unacceptable results. How has Plato gone wrong? There is, I think, more than one way in which one can appeal to what is universally present in human nature in order to recommend a viewpoint that is 'impersonal', and it is here that Plato goes wrong.

One way of looking at the needs and interests of others is from a point of view which I shall call the 'impartial' viewpoint. (This is to contrast with the 'impersonal' viewpoint; I make no claim that this is how we usually use the words, but make the distinction only for the sake of clarity.) The impartial viewpoint is one from which one can see other people as agents with desires, interests, and attachments like one's own. Of course one has a special relation to one's own desires and commitments that cannot be transferred to others, but one can view others as having the same relation to their interests as one has to one's own. One regards the other person not just as a means to one's ends, or a nuisance to one's plans, or part of the scenery, but as a person like oneself. Accepting this viewpoint rules out certain attitudes and actions, like manipulating or exploiting them, for one knows that they will feel what one would feel oneself; one sees that there is no difference of kind, grounding a moral difference, between, say, his doing it to me and my doing it to him. (One may of course go ahead anyway, but one will not feel the same about it as one would in the case of an object lacking the same kind of feelings.)

The impartial viewpoint excludes selfishness – my giving myself and my own concerns a special place and treating others as means to what I do; it makes me regard myself as just one among others. But it is not impersonal in the sense of abstracting altogether from the personal viewpoint. I am an individual, with particular concerns and so are others: their concerns matter to them just as mine do to me. Regarding others impartially, I can still regard them as persons, with all the attitudes to their concerns that I have to mine.

But Plato's Guardians are led to take the literally impersonal viewpoint, one which demands that they abstract from any personal concern at all, for themselves or others. And those who are not Guardians are treated in accordance with that viewpoint, which they can only understand to the extent (perhaps very small) that they identify with their reason. Throughout the central books we have seen that people capable of knowledge have been encouraged to identify themselves with their reasoning part, and to reject as alien to them any concerns that involve the world of particular actions and people. It is no accident that Plato thinks that this will involve a communal way of life discouraging the development of deep commitments to particular people. The Guardians' final moral perspective is inhuman, because from it no real importance attaches to anything personal, either in their own case or in that of others.

The limitations of this view come out particularly clearly in Plato's political proposals. The individual weak in reason must be ruled absolutely by the person strong in it; the person strong in reason sees the need to give up personal fulfilment, and succeeds in accepting this without pain or resentment. No value is attached to *any* individual life apart from the fulfilment of a social role for the common good. Stress on the wholly impersonal viewpoint is responsible for much of what is inhuman about Plato's political proposals. People are seen from a perspective which avowedly ignores everything which makes for individual and personal commitment. When the Guardians advance to philosophical understanding, this is described as an advance from darkness into light; but the light bleaches out of the picture all the agent's concerns that made justice appealing, all the facts of human nature that the definition of justice as psychic harmony built on.

The impartial viewpoint, by contrast, has no such implications. It allows us to see people as individual sources of value, without measuring and judging this value on a single scale. The impartial viewpoint stresses what is common between people, the facts about human nature that make each person one among others, without losing awareness of the personal dimension: the fact that each person has a special viewpoint on his or her own life, one that cannot justifiably be ignored or replaced by a calculation of his or her contribution to some end or the extent to which he or she embodies rationality. We have seen that Plato has no real notion of rights, and this seems to be no accident. For theories of rights seem to rely on the impartial viewpoint rather than the impersonal one. They stress that each person has a unique and irreplaceable value (however hard this idea is to articulate). Rulers taking the impartial viewpoint would not be led to treat their subjects in ways that take into account as having value only their contributions to some social good.

These remarks are obviously crude and sketchy. I have tried to indicate only that the main moral argument, that justice pays, is a legitimate answer of a moral kind to a legitimate demand; that it needs to be supplemented by some consideration of others; and the best way to do this would be to recommend the adoption of a viewpoint that is impartial, and in accordance with one's theory of human nature. But Plato goes on to put forward the impersonal viewpoint. His doing so is unfortunate in two ways. It conflicts with the main argument, in ways I have tried to bring out. And it is objectionable in itself. We have to wait for the utilitarians before we find another moral theory that tells us that morality requires us to become so alienated from our own personal concerns as to regard them with indifference as means to the end of achieving some overall good.

Chapter 14

Book Ten

Book 9 ends the main argument of the *Republic*, and ends it on a rhetorical and apparently decisive note. We are surprised to find another book added on. And in Book 10 we find many disturbing differences from the rest of the *Republic*. We have already seen that it introduces somewhat dissimilar ideas from the central books on both knowledge and the Forms (pp. 191–4, 227–32). It also adds new and unexpected points about poetry and its role, the nature of the soul, and the kind of reward that the just person can expect. Several interpreters of the *Republic* have treated Book 10 as a 'coda' or 'appendix' and it certainly seems to have been composed at a different time (or perhaps a collection of different times) and added to a work essentially complete already. To make this judgement is to conclude that Plato failed as a literary artist, for we have no reason to think that the work we have is not the work as Plato finally intended it to stand. All the same, we are driven by the peculiarities of Book 10 to see it as an excrescence. Plato clearly wanted to add extra material on points that he felt had not been adequately or forcefully enough treated. And his solution of adding on Book 10 has the merit of collecting these matters at the end rather than spoiling the unity of the rest of the book by long digressions. But the result is that Book 10 itself appears gratuitous and clumsy, and it is full of oddities. We can see why Plato thought it relevant to the rest of the *Republic*; but the level of philosophical argument and literary skill is much below the rest of the book.

Book 10 falls into two parts: the banishment of poetry (595a–608c) and a ragbag section that renews the theme of the rewards of justice (608c–621d).

POETRY

Poetry has been discussed together with the other arts as part of education: nothing has prepared us for the statement that we are now to have a better justification, in terms of the soul's parts, for the banishment of all imitative poetry (595a). For at 396b–398b some, though restricted, imitation was left for the good person. In Books 2 and 3 poetry was just one of the arts, though the most important. Here Plato singles it out for attack in a way impossible to reconcile with Book 3.

In Book 3 only *some* poetry was imitative. Here *all* poetry is, but we soon see that something different is meant by 'imitation', for Plato's model of imitative art is now painting. Abruptly, we are given two arguments which claim that all that a painter does is to copy the way things appear, and then treat poetry as though this were what *it* did too. They are among the most famous, and outrageous, arguments in Plato.

The first argument claims to show that all artists lack knowledge (595a–602c). A craftsman copies a Form to produce a bed; the painter, more superficial, only copies the way the bed appears. We have already seen how odd the role of Forms here is (pp. 227–32). They are introduced here to emphasize the idea that the painter merely copies particular things, a fairly fatuous thing to do; he does not even achieve the level of the craftsman, who at least embodies general principles of function and design in his products.

Mimēsis or 'imitation' was introduced in Book 3 in the context of the performing arts, and was best thought of there as expressing or representing. But here it is introduced by what the painter does, and is rather the literal copying of one visual aspect of a particular thing (598a). It is explicitly said to be like holding a mirror up to reflect things (596d–e). Clearly no-one who does this requires knowledge or even true belief; mindless copying is possible if one lacks understanding of one's subject-matter and even if one has false beliefs about it. Plato is talking about *trompe-l'œil* painting (which actually takes more skill than he allows), not painting as he has talked about it before through the *Republic* (401a, 420c, 472d, 484c, 500–501). He could not be more insistent that imitation is an exact copying of the way things in the world look; it may take effort but it is not creative in any way, any more than mirroring the world is.

Plato now talks as though the same were true of poets like Homer (598d); he has already made the claim about the tragic poets (597e). They too are said to be mere imitators who produce something 'at three removes from real nature' requiring no comprehension of what is imitated.

But the claim just made about painting does not carry across to poetry, precisely because of the very narrow account given of what the painter's activity is. Poets do not do anything that can be compared to holding up a mirror to particular things, or capturing the perspective of the way a bed looks from one angle of vision. Plato just assumes that he can talk of poetry as being 'mere image', 'at third remove from real nature', and the like, without considering that these terms have only been given their sense within the metaphysical picture of Form, particular, and painting, and that this model does not fit poetry in any obvious way. In fact when Plato expands on the way in which the poet lacks knowledge, he does not use this picture at all, but a quite different one. Now (601c–602b) we are told that the person with knowledge and understanding is the *user*, the person with mere true belief but no understanding the *maker*; the imitator is the person with neither. So the poet as imitator is the person who neither makes nor uses what he is talking about; not the person who has no grasp of a Form. Forms, which are not objects of use, do not fit into the picture at all; the contrast is not between levels of reality, but between different ways of relating to things on a single level of reality, since one uses, makes or imitates the same kind of thing, like bridles or flutes. (Plato *could* have said that the poet only describes particular things, in contrast to the person with understanding who has turned away from the shadows on the wall towards the state of enlightenment that grasps only Forms; but he does not.) Plato's actual points against the poet's claims to knowledge are quite common-sensical (and similar to points he makes in other dialogues): the poet, he says, describes activities, like those of generals, about which he has absolutely no understanding, and therefore there is no reason for us to give his works the respectful attention which they get.

So the reasons for saying that the painter lacks knowledge do

not carry over to the poet. Plato has made a few points against
the poet's claim to have knowledge, but has done nothing to
show that he imitates in the way that a *trompe-l'œil* painter does,
or that his works are mere images and at third remove from real
nature. He has not established that the poet imitates in the
pejorative sense established for the painter. But this is the only
sense so far given to us in Book 10. We cannot appeal to Book 3
to fill out the sense in which the poet imitates. For in Book 3
imitation was not what the poet did, but what the person did
who recited or acted the poet's works; the distinction between
imitative and non-imitative was there drawn *within* poetry,
whereas in Book 10 *all* poetry is said to be imitative.

The second argument goes from 602c–605c. Scene-painting
relies on various kinds of optical illusion; flat surfaces can be
made to appear three-dimensional, just as straight sticks can
look bent in water, and concave surfaces appear convex. What
happens in cases like this is that part of the soul is taken in and
accepts the appearance at face value, but the reasoning part
does not; it relies instead on objective procedures for finding
out the true state of affairs, like measuring, counting, and
weighing. So we find two parts of the soul in conflict. The
reasoning part, relying on objective ways of finding out the
truth, is clearly the better part, so painting appeals to the
inferior part of the soul (whose worthlessness is dwelt on). Plato
now applies this point to poetry. Poetry appeals to and
strengthens the lower, desiring part of the soul, which is apt to
resist reason. It encourages us to give in to our immediate
feelings and emotions when reason would forbid their gratification because it is useless or harmful for the agent if he considers
his life as a whole and the true value of human attachments.

This distinction of reason and lower part of the soul, however,
appears to be a totally different one from the one appealed to in
the case of painting. How can the strength and importunate
nature of one's desires have anything to do with one's being
taken in by optical illusions? The lowest part of the soul to
which poetry appeals is one which itself gives scope for
imitation, since it is the tendency to be led by emotion which
provides most of tragedy's best plots. But this cannot be
identified with the part which passively and unreflectively
accepts appearances and is led to judge that a straight stick in

water is bent. It is absurd to suggest that this is a rich source of dramatic material! The argument from painting does not carry over to poetry because the parts of the soul distinguished are not the same in both cases; conclusions drawn from the conflict of reason and another part in the one case have no application to the other. Some try to escape this problem by claiming that Plato does not even think that the two contrasts drawn are the same; his language at 603a7 and 605a–b suggests that he may think of the part of the soul opposed to reason as being not a unity but a collection of bad tendencies. But this does not avoid the problem that *reason*'s role does not come out the same in the two cases. And anyway if the parts of the soul appealed to in the two cases are not the same, then Plato has no argument at all; he would have no semblance of justification for claiming that the worthlessness of painting proves anything about poetry.

These two arguments raise, incidentally, problems about how *either* of the divisions of the soul here fit with the divisions we have become used to throughout the book. None of the roles of reason and the lowest part of the soul have any perspicuous connection to their roles as seen so far in the theory of the soul's parts that Plato has used to establish conclusions about justice. Further, it is hard to see how the third part, spirit, is to fit in; its roles seem to be partitioned between the two factors distinguished here. The rational part in fighting grief and sorrow is said to obey *nomos*, 'law' or 'convention', in a way that makes it look like the kind of motivation developed in the Auxiliaries: the rational principle determines how it feels, but is seen as external to it. On the other hand, the emotions that have to be resisted, like grief, seem at least as conceptually complex as anger, the spirit's main emotion, and they are not very like desires for particular objects. Plato in fact is very vague here about the soul's lower part. It does not have its clear role of being a collection of particular desires whose reasoning capacity is limited to the attaining of particular satisfactions. It is treated as simply the trashy part, the part, whatever it is like, that opposes reason, the hero of the soul. Plato presumably fails to see that his argument will not work, that desire has nothing to do with optical illusions, because he thinks of the lower part of the soul as being *merely* the trashy and reason-resisting part. In this passage he always refers to it simply as the worthless part, keeping in the background the fact that to be consistent with its roles elsewhere it would have to be the *desiring* part.

In both these arguments we find Plato trying (unsuccessfully) to assimilate poetry to painting – and to a debased form of painting at that. This underlines the most striking and surprising feature of these two arguments. In Book 3 Plato was concerned to stress how *important* the role of the arts is, especially that of poetry. The poetry that surrounds people can decisively influence their beliefs, for better or worse. (Plato is mainly thinking of the effects on the developing minds of the young, but he is also concerned with people who have grown up; there is no relaxation of censorship for adults.) The arts, and particularly poetry, are important because the education Plato stresses is character education, not academic training. It is vital that the Guardians have not just the right beliefs but the right attitudes and motives, and so it is important that their characters be developed by exposure to the right kind of poetry and art. Existing poetry, like Homer, is attacked and severely censored because it is seen as dangerous. However, in these two arguments in Book 10 poetry has been presented as essentially *trivial*, as tacky as scene-painting, something that no serious person would bother wasting time over. Plato has gone from accepting that poetry is important and dangerous, to trying to prove that it is really trivial and marginal.

The forced and unconvincing assimilation to *trompe-l'œil* painting is vital for Plato's downgrading of poetry. Throughout this passage poetry is assailed in terms of contempt that have become famous. The poet, we are told, is despised because he devotes his life to making images instead of originals; he deals with images of virtue only; he and his works are at third remove from the truth; he lacks knowledge and even true belief because he deals only in images; he is an imitator and as such held in low regard; his imitation consorts with an inferior part of the soul, and he goes in for easy popularity because most people lack the discernment to see his products for what they are, mindless productions appealing to the mindless part of the soul. (Cf. 597e, 598e–599b, 599d–e, 600e–601b, 602b–c, 605a–c.) All these attempts to get us to see poetry as being trivial are given their sense by the assimilation to painting. We have seen that the way we were introduced to imitation in Book 3 did not suggest that imitation was trivial or contemptible; rather the reverse, in fact. We have seen that the assimilation Book 10 attempts does not work, and that Plato's real hits against poetry are not dependent on it; but it is the sole base for his denunciations of poetry as worthless and stupid.

Plato now adds a third argument against poetry; and to our surprise it reverts to the standpoint of Book 3, in complete contrast to the previous two arguments. The gravest charge against poetry, Socrates says, has yet to be brought (605c–608b). 'It is able to corrupt even good men, with very few exceptions, and . . . is a terribly dangerous thing.' (605c, Grube.) The arts, and especially poetry, encourage all our desires and make them hard to cope with in our own lives. The part of us that takes pleasure in watching actors lament is the part that longs to indulge our own griefs; taking pleasure in laughing at comedies tends to make us cynical and unserious in real life. The effect of poetry is to encourage the desires that ought to be suppressed in the virtuous life (606d). And Plato concludes, going beyond Book 3, that poetry is so dangerous, and so attractive, that it must be banished entirely from the ideally just state. He recognizes that this seems philistine, and perhaps absurd, but 'the struggle to be good or bad is important' (608b).

This argument is not merely a more rhetorical repetition of what was said in the second one. It may seem so, because it renews the point that poetry fosters the lower part of the soul against the rule of reason. But there are three important differences. Plato has reverted to the Book 3 attitude of recognizing the importance of poetry in people's lives (here he is thinking of the performances of tragedy and recitations of Homer). In the first Book 10 argument, Plato would have had us believe that poets are actually despised because they are not real moral teachers with knowledge (600c–e). Secondly, in this argument he has given up talking of poetry in visual terms derived from the forced assimilation to painting. He talks straightforwardly about what goes on in the theatre, and its effects on people. And thirdly, and most important, he has reverted to the idea that poetry is important and dangerous, not something contemptible and fatuous like mindless copying. Homer can make one stray from the right path, and that is why, although poetry has genuine pleasures, Homer is to be banished.

We thus get the odd spectacle of Plato arguing passionately for the banishment of poetry because of its danger to the moral life, on the basis of arguments that show (if they succeeded) that poetry is so trivial that it has no moral significance at all. This passage of Book 10 makes us aware of a serious problem. It is not just that it adds a discussion of poetry that changes the meaning and scope of 'imitation' and argues that all poetry should be banished, whereas Book 3 was more tolerant. The problem is deeper than that. Plato seems to hold two inconsistent views about poetry: that it is important and dangerous, and so should either be censored and tamed in the service of a truly moral life (Book 3) or expelled from the truly moral life altogether as being hopelessly untrustworthy (Book 10); and that it is a trivial and fatuous thing, too pathetic even to be immoral. It is the first of these views which Plato holds most consistently and which makes most sense of the development of the *Republic*. Plato is bound to be worried about the influence of poetry when he gives such weight to the education of people's desires and characters, and it is only realistic for him to bear in mind the important role of poetry in the popular education of his own day. (In a modern context he would be talking about other forms of popular culture; cf. p. 94.) By contrast, he has to try and *prove* that poetry is trivial. This he attempts in the first two arguments of Book 10; arguments that do not work, because they rely on a forced and unconvincing assimilation of poetry to a wholly distinct art form. (In any case they raise problems of consistency with what Plato says elsewhere about knowledge, Forms, and the parts of the soul.) It is therefore a mistake to take these two arguments as being the essence of Plato's 'theory of art', as is often done. In the course of trying to prove a conclusion, the triviality of poetry, which he elsewhere implicitly rejects, Plato puts forward a view of both poetry and painting which he endorses nowhere else. To find Plato's views on poetry, we would do better to look at Book 3, the third argument of Book 10, and other dialogues such as the *Ion* and the *Phaedrus*.

All the same, the arguments are there, and they are argued with such crude vigour that they have impressed many as defining Plato's view of poetry. Why does Plato argue in this way, revealing a deep split in the ways he thinks of poetry and introducing an unresolved tension into the *Republic*? He is deeply divided about poetry, and cares passionately about it in two quite inconsistent ways. On the one hand, he writes as the committed moral reformer, who is prepared to restructure society to get rid of nuclear families, and has no qualms about altering the content of poetry to achieve the truly just life. In this light poetry appears as a dangerous rival. It is attractive, and it imbues people with wrong beliefs and wrong ideals that are hard to get rid of. In Book 3 Plato tries to tame this rival and enlist the attractive force of poetry in the service of morality. Poetry that has a bad influence will be banned, but if it is not harmful it is retained, and the possibility is left open that there might be good poetry that makes a positive contribution to the education of good people. In Book 10 Plato is more pessimistic; all poetry is now seen as hopelessly corrupting; but it is still seen as a critical factor in how one lives one's life and acquires one's ideals and patterns of living. Its importance is still seen as lying in the moral influence it has. But on the other hand, Plato is not only a committed social reformer, he is himself a literary artist who knows from the inside what creative writing is, and according to one tradition was a poet himself before encountering Socrates. He sees that however important is the moral content and influence of poetry (and the other arts), still real poetry answers to its own standards, and cannot be composed to order in a way that will guarantee the acceptability of its content. In some dialogues (*Ion, Meno, Phaedrus*) he talks of the poet in a very Romantic vein as being a divinely inspired being. And though he is inclined to be sceptical about the poets' own attitude to their gifts, he takes poetry seriously in realizing that the good poet composes as the Muse or god tells him to compose. In a famous passage of the *Phaedrus* (245a) he stresses that skill alone will not make you a good poet; all the talent in the world pales into nothing beside the true poetry of inspired 'madness', the inspiration of the god. So Plato does realize that the poet is a true creator answering only to artistic standards. Hence the first two arguments of Book 10: to reduce the importance of the poet's claims, Plato denies him any real creativity. He compares

him to a person mirroring the world, and argues against his
pretensions in terms that reduce him to a mindless copier of
appearances. Such passionate, hopelessly bad arguments show
clearly that Plato was aware of the poet's creativity; for to show
that the poet is no real rival to the philosopher, he tries to show
that the poet has no creative gift at all. It is not possible to take
the first two arguments of Book 10 seriously as arguments about
the value of poetry, but they are extremely interesting for what
they show us about Plato. The extraordinary, hysterical
attempt to show that the poet is not really creative shows that
Plato was in fact aware of the nature of the poet's creativity,
and so, despite what some passages of Book 3 might suggest, he
is not to be numbered with people who think that art is valuable
only for its role in helping to produce some socially valuable
end. After having banished all poetry he allows into his ideal
city some civic verse, 'hymns to the gods and eulogies of good
men' (607a). Whether he is aware of it or not, there is no real
inconsistency here, for Plato is enough of a creative artist
himself to know that such productions are not real poetry.

THE ENDING OF THE REPUBLIC

The discussion of poetry has returned to the important struggle
to be good (608b) and Plato now takes up the theme of the
rewards of justice (608c). The rest of Book 10 deals with this in
three separate sections: (1) the proof of the soul's immortality
(608c–612a), (2) the just man's rewards in this life (612a–614a),
and (3) the rewards of justice in the afterlife (614a–621d), a
section commonly referred to as the Myth of Er. These sections
fit awkwardly together, and there are problems internal to each.
  (1) The proof of the soul's immortality (608c–612a) is
introduced in a very off-hand way, which might make one
wonder how seriously it was meant (608d) except that irony
seems pointless here. Nothing can be destroyed, claims Socrates,
except by its own natural peculiar evil – that is, whatever is bad
for the kind of thing it is (as rust is bad for metal and mildew is
bad for grain). But it is injustice that is the soul's natural evil,
and injustice does not destroy the soul; so the soul is
indestructible. So (611a) there always exists the same number
of immortal souls. There cannot come to be any less, or some
would not be immortal; or any more, since this could only

happen by some mortal items becoming immortal, with the result that everything would eventually become immortal, which is manifestly not the case.

This is one of the few really embarrassingly bad arguments in Plato, and though Glaucon is quickly satisfied with it, we have good reason not to be.

Firstly, the argument only works if each thing has *one* peculiar evil; otherwise we could not argue that if justice does not destroy the soul, nothing else will. Could not the soul have another natural peculiar evil besides injustice? We can see why Plato does not think of this possibility: he is thinking of the naturally best state for a soul as being one of unity, so that it is hard to see what could be characteristically bad for the soul other than the disruption characteristic of injustice. This is not made explicit, but it is in Plato's mind, because he will go on to face a problem this raises.

Secondly, even if we accept that a thing has only one naturally destructive evil, why should what destroys the soul be different from what destroys the body? When rust destroys metal, it destroys the saw or knife made out of the metal. What is to prevent the relation between body and soul being of this kind, destruction of the body carrying with it destruction of the soul? Plato insists vehemently that this is not so (610a–b), but only by assuming what is never argued for, that the soul is a different kind of thing from the body, and distinct from it in being unaffected by what happens to the body. But if one accepts *this*, one accepts already that the soul is indestructible, and the argument from peculiar evils is redundant. As in Book 1, we find a snappy little argument for a controversial con-conclusion depending on a question-begging premise which is never argued for.

Thirdly, even if the argument worked, why does it show not only that *the soul* is immortal but that there is a plurality of immortal souls? Plato makes the move without comment at 611a, not noticing that one might take the argument to show only the immortality of *soul* thought of as something present in different places but not divided into separate individual souls (as though 'soul' were a mass term). Both ways of looking at soul figure at length in Plato's works elsewhere, but they are very different conceptions.

And as a final grumble one can fault the way Plato at 611a supports the claim that immortal souls cannot increase in number. If they did, everything would become immortal in the end, a conclusion we are meant to reject as obviously false. But why should we? It is hardly a matter for common-sense experience what is and what is not immortal. Plato himself goes on to say that we don't perceive the true nature of the immortal soul. Perhaps we are similarly mistaken about the true nature of other apparently mortal things. Nothing in the argument rules that out.

Plato does not see, or is unmoved by, the question-begging nature of this argument. He goes on (611a–612a) to air a problem that this argument raises. The soul has throughout the *Republic* been treated as having parts, as being the area of psychological complexity and division. But the soul just proved immortal is *unitary*; this was implicit in treating the disruptive force of injustice as being the soul's *only* destructive evil, and apart from this Plato here betrays a tendency (cf. *Phaedo* 78b–c) to think of destruction as being a breaking-up and dissolution, so that anything indestructible must have no parts or internal complexity. However, if the soul has internal complexity, how can it be immortal? Plato's reply here is that the soul's true nature is immortal, and that our notion of it as being composite and liable to internal conflict is not a true view. What we see is like a beautiful sea-divinity rendered unrecognizable by damage and the growth of barnacles and rubbish (611c–612a). The striking image conceals a difficulty. Why should we think that immortal simplicity is the soul's true nature, rather than its perceived complexity? Fantastic as it seems, Plato is laying more weight on this ridiculous little argument than on the whole of the rest of the *Republic* with its use of the composite soul. No better grounds are offered for his doing so than his identifying the soul's apparent complexity with its association with the body. The true, immortal soul is identified with the love of wisdom that strives towards its like (611e). Anything else is consigned to the mucky accretion of the body.

Now this division of the pure love of wisdom from everything particular and perceptible was seen to be characteristic of the contemplative conception of the philosopher; once the love of wisdom is stressed, as it is in Sun, Line, and Cave, it is opposed to any individual concerns. But we have also seen that this conception introduces a severe conflict into the *Republic*'s main argument; for justice was to be a concern of *all* the soul's parts. This argument makes it starkly obvious that the contemplative conception identifies a person with his or her reason, not with the soul thought of as embodied in the whole person. Correspondingly, the practical conception requires that the person be thought of as having a complex soul, not an immortal, incomposite soul identified with the pure love of wisdom. Reason in its role as overseeing and unifying the interests of all the soul's parts – the basis of the account of justice as the virtue that unifies and harmonizes the soul – cannot be identified with something pure of the body. One important corollary of this is that this argument, and any conclusions drawn from it, are relevant only to the contemplative conception of the philosopher, not the practical one. But we have seen that the practical one is what is needed for the argument about the value of justice. Book 9 concluded the main argument with considerations about happiness and pleasure that involved all parts of the soul; the justice of the just person, shown to be worthwhile, was the justice that required practical wisdom, which judges about particular personal matters. So this argument, as a preliminary to an extra proof of the value of justice, is highly intrusive.

It does not even suit Plato's immediate purposes. For the whole point of arguing that the soul is immortal was to show that the prizes of virtue are great, because concerned with the whole of eternity (608c–d). Yet when Plato turns to the fate of immortal souls, in the Myth of Er, they are characterized by more than impersonal love of wisdom. The myth demands that between incarnations the soul retain enough characteristics of the person to be rewarded or punished for what the person did, in a way leading to change, and the soul chooses a new life on the basis of what happened in the last one, and its results. So these immortal souls are not simple instances of love of wisdom. They are in fact complex persons with conflicting motivations and a mixture of aims. Plato could of course respond that this is just a feature of the myth form: in fact, souls are simple, as he has argued, but in a narrative this fact cannot be properly represented. But if this is so, then the argument becomes irrelevant to the conclusion of the myth; yet that appeared to be the point of the argument as it was introduced at 608c. In fact an argument that removes from the true nature of the soul everything that gives sense to talking of its justice, as that was understood in Books 8 and 9, cannot fail to be irrelevant to the renewal of the question about the rewards of justice.

(2) Plato now turns abruptly to the rewards of the just man in this life (612a–614a). The connection with what has just preceded is obscure: if the body is so disgusting, and the true soul detached from it, then why show that justice brings rewards that can only concern it in its unfortunate and temporary connection with the body? After the intensity of the last argument, nothing could be more bathetic. It has occurred to more than one interpreter that this section was not originally meant to stand here, and the fact that Plato lets it do so is another indication of the generally lower level of artistic taste and skill in Book 10. We can discern a line of thought which Plato is pursuing: the soul's true nature is different from the way it appears in the person's lifetime (section 1); so the rewards of justice will apply not only in this life (section 2) but over eternity when souls are disembodied (section 3). But Plato does not take into account sufficiently the fact that section 1 is so negative about the body as to make section 2 of doubtful force, and so insistent on the soul's unity as to make problematic the interpretation of the myth in section 3.

This section also has internal problems. Socrates says that now that they have been shown that it pays to be just even if one has Gyges' ring (612b) it cannot be resented if the just man now has restored to him all the rewards that conventionally he does have. In fact, the just man is loved by the gods and *does* gain worldly rewards; and even if injustice has temporary success, the unjust man, like an overambitious runner, is shown up in the end for the loser that he is.

Verbally this passage recalls Glaucon's and Adeimantus's speeches in Book 2, where they demanded that Socrates show justice to be worth having for itself and for its consequences, excluding only *misthoi*, artificial consequences depending on fallible human institutions and capable of following the appearance of justice as much as the reality, and *doxai*, the opinions of others, which might be false. Now Books 2–9 of the

Republic have been a sustained defence of the thesis that justice is desirable in itself (being a harmonious state of the agent) and also such as to lead to the desirable consequence of being happy. Plato has done all he can to defend his views about the needs and interests of agents that make justice worth having in this way. Why does he now insist on adding the artificial consequences that everyone agreed were no guide to the truth? For he can hardly be claiming that the just man is always loved by the gods, and always wins out in the world as it is. In Book 6 we have seen at length quite how far from this is the state of the just man in any actual city. But if he is merely claiming that justice *usually* is a good bet, that the President Nixons of this world *usually* come to a bad end, then it is baffling why he should think the claim even relevant. It was agreed by everyone in Book 2 that it was of no interest that justice usually pays; *that* leaves it open that it might be seeming, not real, justice that is the real winner. In undertaking to show that it pays to be just even if you have Gyges' ring, Plato was rejecting the relevance of the 'realistic response' given here (pp. 69–70). What is said in this passage denies the very existence of the problem whose pressing reality led to the writing of Books 2–9.

(3) Plato now turns to show that the rewards of justice in this life are minor compared to those that await the soul after death. There follows the Myth of Er: a man allowed to see the underworld and return tells of what happens after death. Souls are rewarded in heaven or punished in the underworld for the person's deeds on earth; after an allotted time they are incarnated again and choose which life to lead. How they choose depends on what is available (there are only a limited number of lives to choose from) and also on how well they have learned the lessons of their previous incarnations and their results.

The Myth of Er is a painful shock; its vulgarity seems to pull us right down to the level of Cephalus, where you take justice seriously when you start thinking about hell-fire. It is not only that the childishness of the myth jars; if we take it seriously, it seems to offer us an entirely consequentialist reason for being just, thus undermining Plato's sustained effort to show that justice is worth having for the agent in a non-consequentialist way. Your present life determines how you fare after death, so it is unwise to be unjust, because short enjoyment on earth will be followed by tenfold torment in hell (615a–b). How can this be squared with the *Republic*'s sustained attempt to show us that justice is worth having for itself and for the rewards its nature brings about?

It is always hard to know what Plato intends to convey by using a myth. A common view is that he uses myth to express higher religious truths which are above the scope of arguments. Reason abdicates to the mystical vision. This view encourages us to read the myths on an aesthetic level, and, like Walter Pater, enjoy the description of coloured light rather than trying to extract a message. But the Myth of Er resists such treatment. It is a very cerebral myth, and its content is open to interpretation; we are told that it is important to believe its message, presupposing that we cannot miss what the message is (618b–d, 621b–d). In this it is very unlike the strange, indeed surreal, myths of the *Phaedrus* and *Statesman*, whose content and significance are hard to interpret. So we cannot avoid a rational consideration of the problem that overtly the myth has a different, and morally lower, view of why we should be just from the rest of the *Republic*.

Can the myth be defended? One common way of regarding it as an attempt to stress the *eternity* of the soul's existence (608c). So far we have only looked at the lives of individuals and their institutions. Even if justice *is* worthwhile, and the ideally just city *is* realizable, still this might be an accident of human nature. The myth puts the human race in a wider setting. Justice is guaranteed by the cosmic order; the universe is such that overall justice is rewarded and evil punished. The myth is not denying the importance of justice in an individual life, but it ignores this to stress that it is also part of the much grander workings of the entire cosmos.

This interpretation is very common; if correct, it aggravates the problem just mentioned, that the myth is a lapse from the level of the main argument. However, can it survive a reading of what is actually said in the Myth of Er? If justice is part of a cosmic pattern, it is not a very encouraging pattern. The soul's rewards and punishments do not provide an inspiring balance or outweighing of what happens on earth. Some of the afterlife punishments are salutary, and the souls end up sadder but wiser (619d), but (unusually for Plato) the stress is not on the useful improving power of punishment but on vindictive retribution; the very wicked are eternally tortured although they will never improve (615c–616b) and Plato's underworld is a sadistic hell, not a purgatory. More surprisingly, the myth is pessimistic about the heavenly rewards, which turn out to be two-edged; most of the souls who return from heaven to be incarnated make bad choices of life as a result of having got used to heavenly joys (619c–d). The Myth of Er shows us something that cannot be interpreted in terms of a Last Judgement at all. Its ideas come closer to a kind of fatalism: just and unjust are bound up together on the eternal wheel of reincarnation, and the rewards of justice even in other-worldly terms will only lead to a compensating increase in injustice as a result. The individual is likely to be depressed rather than inspired or frightened by such a vision. The best we can hope for in this life is to become philosophers; but this only ensures heavenly rewards for a time, and these will ultimately be compensated for by a lapse into injustice in a future life. The place of justice in such a vision of the universe is likely to make one give up rather than strive to become just. It may be retorted to this that we are supposed to forget our previous incarnations anyway (621a), so that there is no reason to be depressed by the fact that nothing any individual does makes any difference to the eternal cosmic pattern. But this is likely to increase, rather than decrease, our sense of the pointlessness of trying to be just in such a universe.

Perhaps we are taking the myth too literally, and should not tie Plato down to the most narrow way of taking what he says. At 618b Socrates breaks off his description of the souls' choice of life to address Glaucon directly, and urgently, stressing the need of wisdom to choose what leads to a just life, avoiding false values and making the most of what life provides. He is talking about the choices that *we* make. This suggests that the whole apparatus of reincarnation, heaven and hell, and so on, is not to be taken seriously as a story, but serves merely to dramatize what is at stake in one's choices *now*. Plato is not seriously suggesting that we have lived other lives and been through their consequences in heaven and hell, but only that our decisions, though they are bound to reflect the character we already have

(620a) reflect also our awareness of the kind of life we are choosing to live and its results. The myth is meant to jolt us out of the easy assumption that our day-to-day choices have no particular significance. On the contrary, the choices we make determine the kind of people we are, and the wise person will choose in knowledge of this. When we make decisions, more is at stake than we care to think, in the way of the effect on us and others, and the decisions are not to be accounted for as much as we like to think in terms of what has already happened to us. We are responsible for the people we are in making the choices we make, and the myth, with its apparatus of judgement-day eternally going on, makes us aware of the existential nature of decisions that make us the people we are. The myth does not show justice triumphing in the universe, because that would not be a realistic way of representing the background of our choices; and it does not represent the good person as escaping from the wheel of fate, because love of wisdom is not a guaranteed escape from the problems and tragedies of life.

If we take the myth this way, then Plato is saying that we punish or reward ourselves now in choosing bad or good lives. Our choices can to some extent be explained by our past lives, which were not entirely under our control (620a), and are limited by many factors, but in the end the decision is ours and we cannot blame anyone else (617e, 619b). And we have to live with the results. Justice is worth having because the just person will be the person with the insight into the results of various ways of living, and the balance and internal harmony, that enable him or her to make wise and balanced choices. Injustice is to be avoided because it will lead one to make ill-advised decisions that will leave one an ill-balanced and fragmented character. The unjust person lacks perspective and is blinded by passion into making choices that land him or her with a hateful life, with no inner sources of unity or harmony. The message of the myth, on this reading, is not basically different from that of the main argument: justice is worth having for the agent because it produces a life which is worth having for itself and for the consequences that come from its nature and not the opinions of others. Justice is worth living with; injustice is not.

It is hard to say whether it is legitimate to 'demythologize' the myth this way. (In the *Phaedrus* Plato shows himself dis-

inclined to demythologize traditional myths.) One is left with
the kind of residual doubt that attends similar demythologizing
of religious myths. If the myth is not threatening us with future
punishments in a terrifyingly impersonal universe, but bringing
home to us the importance of what we are doing to ourselves
now, why is it cast in the most misleading possible form from the
point of view of its message? Possibly Plato thought that, since
most of his contemporaries did not believe in reincarnation and
had a quite different picture of the afterlife, they would be
forced to look for a deeper interpretation. It is hard to tell about
this; cf. 498d. We simply cannot be sure about how Plato
expected us to interpret the myth.

Why did Plato not end the *Republic* with Book 9, instead of
tacking on this collection of further points, hanging together
rather awkwardly and most very problematic? We can only
make suggestions, and the most obvious is this. Plato always
wanted to show that justice was, Thrasymachus notwith-
standing, worth having both for itself and for its consequences.
There is more than one way that one might try to show this. The
bulk of the *Republic* is Plato's most successful attempt. But one
can also see the matter in terms of present success and ultimate
reward. And Plato is attracted to these views anyway, for what
appear to be personal reasons. Ideas that have powerful
expression in the main coherent body of the book are presented
at the end in a much cruder form, which Plato none the less
believes can add to our understanding. And so the *Republic*, a
powerful and otherwise impressively unified book, acquired
its lame and messy ending.

FURTHER READING

The account of Book 10 on poetry given here, an unorthodox
account, is defended at greater length in my 'Plato on the
Triviality of Literature' in *Plato on Beauty, Wisdom and the Arts*, ed.
J. Moravcsik and P. Temko (*APQ* monograph, 1982). Also in the
volume are Nehamas, 'Imitation in *Republic* X' and Urmson,
'Plato on Poetry'.

A 'unifying' view of the place of art in the *Republic* is defended
most influentially by J. Tate, '"Imitation" in Plato's *Republic*',
Classical Quarterly 1928 and 'Plato and Imitation', *Classical
Quarterly* 1932.

References to the vast secondary literature can be found in Nehamas (above). A stimulating if idiosyncratic introduction is given in Iris Murdoch, *The Fire and the Sun: Why Plato Banished the Artists*.

Select Bibliography

ADAM, J. The *Republic* of Plato, with critical notes, commentary and appendices. 2 vols. 2nd edition with introduction by D. A. Rees. Cambridge: Cambridge University Press, 1963.

ALLEN, R. E. (ed.) *Studies in Plato's Metaphysics.* London: Routledge and Kegan Paul, 1965.

—— 'The Argument from Opposites in *Republic* V' in J. P. Anton and G. L. Kustas (eds.), *Essays in Ancient Greek Philosophy*, State University of New York Press, Albany, 1972, pp. 165–75.

—— 'Participation and Predication in Plato's Middle Dialogues', in Allen (ed.), pp. 43–60 and in Vlastos (ed.), *Plato* I pp. 167–83.

ANNAS, J. 'Plato's *Republic* and Feminism', *Philosophy* 51 (1976), pp. 307–21.

—— 'Plato and Common Morality', *Classical Quarterly* 28 (1978), pp. 437–51.

BAMBROUGH, R. (ed.) *New Essays on Plato and Aristotle*, London: Routledge and Kegan Paul, 1965.

—— (ed.) *Plato, Popper and Politics.* Cambridge: Heffer, 1967.

BARROW, R. *Plato, Utilitarianism and Education.* London: Routledge and Kegan Paul, 1975.

—— *Plato and Education.* London: Routledge and Kegan Paul, 1976.

BRENTLINGER, J. 'Particulars in Plato's Middle Dialogues', *Archiv für Geschichte der Philosophie* 54 (1972), pp. 116–52.

BOLTON, R. 'Plato's Distinction between Being and Becoming', *Review of Metaphysics* XXIX (1975), pp. 66–95.

CALVERT, B. 'Plato and the Equality of Women', *Phoenix* XXIX (1975), pp. 231–43.

CHERNISS, H. 'The Philosophical Economy of the Theory of Ideas', in Allen (ed.), pp. 1–12, and Vlastos (ed.), *Plato* I, pp. 16–27.

COOPER, J. 'The Psychology of Justice in Plato', *American Journal of Philosophy* 14 (1977), pp. 151–8.

CORNFORD, F. M. 'Mathematics and Dialectic in *Republic* VI–VII', *Mind* XLI (1932), pp. 37–52 and 173–90, and in Allen (ed.), pp. 61–96.

CREED, J. L. 'Is it Wrong to call Plato a Utilitarian?', *Classical Quarterly* 28 (1978), pp. 349–65.

CROMBIE, I. M. *An Examination of Plato's Doctrines.* 2 vols. London: Routledge and Kegan Paul, 1962.

CROSS, R. C. and WOOZLEY, A. D. *Plato's Republic: A Philosophical Commentary*. London: Macmillan, 1964.

CROSSMAN, R. H. S. *Plato Today*. London: Allen and Unwin, 1963.

DAVIES, J. K. *Democracy and Classical Greece*. London: Fontana, 1978.

DEMOS, R. 'A Fallacy in Plato's *Republic?*' *Philosophical Review* LXXIII (1964), pp. 395–8, and in Vlastos (ed.), *Plato* II, pp. 52–6.

DENNETT, D. *Brainstorms*. Massachusetts: Bradford Books, 1978.

DOVER, K. J. *Greek Popular Morality in the Time of Plato and Aristotle*. Oxford: Blackwells, 1974.

FERGUSON, J. 'Sun, Line and Cave Again', *Classical Quarterly* 13 (1963), pp. 188–93.

FINE, G. 'Knowledge and Belief in *Republic* V', *Archiv für Geschichte der Philosophie* 60 (1978), pp. 121–39.

FORTENBAUGH, W. 'Plato: Temperament and Eugenic Policy', *Arethusa* 8 (1975), pp. 283–306.

GALLOP, D. 'Dreaming and Waking in Plato', in J. P. Anton and G. L. Kustas (eds.), *Essays in Ancient Greek Philosophy*. Albany: State University of New York Press, 1972, pp. 187–201.

GOSLING, J. *Plato*. London: Routledge and Kegan Paul, 1973.

—— 'Ta Polla Kala', *Phronesis* V (1960), pp. 116–28.

—— Comments on White, F. C., *Canadian Journal of Philosophy* VII (1977), pp. 307–314.

GREY, D. R. 'Art in the *Republic*', *Philosophy* XXVII (1952), pp. 291–310.

GUTHRIE, W. C. K. *A History of Greek Philosophy*. Cambridge: Cambridge University Press. Vol. 3, 1969; vol. 4, 1975.

HAMLYN, D. '*Eikasia* in Plato's *Republic*', *Philosophical Quarterly* 8 (1958), pp. 14–23.

HARE, R. M. 'Plato and the Mathematicians', in R. Bambrough (ed.), *New Essays on Plato and Aristotle*, pp. 21–38.

HENDERSON, T. Y. 'In Defense of Thrasymachus', *American Philosophical Quarterly* 7 (1970), pp. 218–228.

IRWIN, T. *Plato's Moral Theory*. Oxford: Clarendon Press, 1977.

—— 'Plato's Heracleiteanism', *Philosophical Quarterly* 27 (1977), pp. 1–13.

JOSEPH, H. W. B. *Essays in Ancient and Modern Philosophy*. Oxford: Clarendon Press, 1935. Ch. 1 is reprinted in A. Sesonske (ed.), *Plato's Republic: Interpretation and Criticisms*. California: Wadsworth, 1966, pp. 6–16.

KAHN, C. 'The Greek Verb "Be" and the Concept of Being', *Foundations of Language* 2 (1966), pp. 245–65.

—— 'The Meaning of "Justice" and the Theory of Forms', *Journal of Philosophy* 69 (1972), pp. 567–79.

KENNY, A. 'Mental Health in Plato's *Republic*' in Kenny, A., *The Anatomy of the Soul*, Oxford: Blackwell, 1973, pp. 1–27.

KIRWAN, C. 'Glaucon's Challenge', *Phronesis* X (1965), pp. 162–73.

—— 'Plato and Relativity', *Phronesis* XIX (1974), pp. 112–29.

KOSMAN, L. A. 'Platonic Love', in W. H. Werkmeister (ed.), *Facets of Plato's Philosophy*, *Phronesis* Supplement 2. Assen: Van Gorcum, 1976, pp. 53–69.

KRAUT, R. 'Reason and Justice in Plato's *Republic*' in E. N. Lee, A. P. D.

Select Bibliography 357

Mourelatos, R. M. Rorty (eds.), *Exegesis and Argument*, *Phronesis* Supplement 1. Assen: Van Gorcum, 1973, pp. 207–24.

LESSER, H. 'Plato's Feminism', *Philosophy* 54 (1979), pp. 113–17.

LEYS, W. 'Was Plato Non-Political?' in Vlastos (ed.) *Plato* II, pp. 166–73.

MABBOTT, J. D. 'Is Plato's *Republic* Utilitarian?', *Mind* XLVI (1937), pp. 468–74; rewritten for Vlastos (ed.), *Plato* II, pp. 57–65.

MACGUIRE, J. P. 'Thrasymachus . . . or Plato?', *Phronesis* XVI (1971), pp. 142–63.

MALCOLM, J. 'The Line and the Cave', *Phronesis* VII (1962), pp. 38–45.

MOLINE, J. 'Plato on the Complexity of the Psyche', *Archiv für Geschichte der Philosophie* 60 (1978), pp. 1–26.

MORAVCSIK, J. M. 'Recollecting the Theory of Forms' in W. H. Werkmeister (ed.), *Facets of Plato's Philosophy*, *Phronesis* Supplement 2. Assen: Van Gorcum, 1976, pp. 1–20.

—— 'Understanding and Knowledge in Plato's Philosophy', *Neue Hefte für Philosophie* 15–16 (1978), pp. 53–69.

MORRISON, J. 'Two Unresolved Difficulties in the Line and the Cave', *Phronesis* XXII (1977), pp. 212–31.

MULHERN, J. 'Population and Plato's *Republic*', *Arethusa* 8 (1975), pp. 265–82.

MURDOCH, I. *The Fire and the Sun: Why Plato Banished the Artists*. Oxford: Clarendon Press, 1977.

MURPHY, N. *The Interpretation of Plato's Republic*. Oxford: Clarendon Press, 1951.

NAKHNIKIAN, G. 'Love in Human Reason', *Midwest Studies in Philosophy*, vol. III. University of Minnesota, 1978, pp. 286–317.

NEHAMAS, A. 'Plato on the Imperfection of the Sensible World', *American Philosophical Quarterly* 12 (1975), pp. 105–17.

—— 'Self-Predication and Plato's Theory of Forms', *American Philosophical Quarterly* 16 (1979), pp. 93–103.

NEU, J. 'Plato's Analogy of State and Individual: The *Republic* and the Organic Theory of the State', *Philosophy* 46 (1971), pp. 238–54.

NICHOLSON, P. P. 'Unravelling Thrasymachus' arguments in the *Republic*', *Phronesis* XIX (1974), pp. 210–32.

OKIN, S. M. 'Philosopher Queens and Private Wives: Plato on Women and the Family', *Philosophy and Public Affairs* 6 (1976–7), pp. 345–69.

OWEN, G. E. L. 'A Proof in the *Peri Ideon*', *Journal of Hellenic Studies* LXXVII (1957, part 1), pp. 103–11, and in Allen (ed.), pp. 293–312.

PENNER, T. 'Thought and Desire in Plato', in Vlastos (ed.), *Plato* II, pp. 96–118.

POPPER, K. *The Open Society and its Enemies*, vol. 1. London: Routledge and Kegan Paul, 1945.

RAVEN, J. 'Sun, Divided Line and Cave', ch. 10 in *Plato's Thought in the Making*. Cambridge: Cambridge University Press, 1965.

ROBINSON, R. *Plato's Earlier Dialectic*, 2nd ed. Oxford: Clarendon Press, 1953.

—— 'Plato's Separation of Reason from Desire', *Phronesis* XVI (1971), pp. 38–48.

ROWE, C. *An Introduction to Greek Ethics*, London: Hutchinson, 1976.

RUSSELL, B. 'Philosophy and Politics', in R. Bambrough (ed.), *Plato, Popper and Politics*.

SACHS, D. 'A Fallacy in Plato's *Republic*', *Philosophical Review* LXXII (1963), pp. 141-58, and in Vlastos (ed.), *Plato* II, pp. 35-51.

SARTORIUS, R. 'Fallacy and Political Radicalism in Plato's *Republic*', *Canadian Journal of Philosophy* III (1974), pp. 349-63.

SCHILLER, J. 'Just Men and Just Acts in Plato's *Republic*', *Journal of the History of Philosophy* VI (1968), pp. 1-14.

SCOLNICOV, S. 'Three Aspects of Plato's Philosophy of Learning and Instruction', *Paideia* Special Plato Issue, 1976, pp. 50-62.

SPARSHOTT, F. E. 'Plato as Anti-Political Thinker', in Vlastos (ed.), *Plato* II pp. 174-83.

—— 'Socrates and Thrasymachus', *Monist* 50 (1966), 421-59.

STALLEY, R. F. 'Plato's Arguments for the Division of the Reasoning and Appetitive Elements within the Soul', *Phronesis* XX (1975), pp. 110-28.

STRANG, C. 'Plato and the Third Man', *Proceedings of the Aristotelian Society* Supplementary Volume 37 (1963), pp. 147-64, and in Vlastos (ed.), *Plato* I, pp. 184-200.

TATE, J. '"Imitation" in Plato's *Republic*', *Classical Quarterly* 22 (1928), pp. 16-23.

—— 'Plato and Imitation', *Classical Quarterly* 26 (1932), pp. 161-9.

TAYLOR, C. C. W. 'Plato and the Mathematicians: An Examination of Professor Hare's views', *Philosophical Quarterly* 17 (1967), pp. 193-203.

VERSENYI, L. 'Plato and his Liberal Opponents', *Philosophy* 46 (1971), pp. 222-37.

VLASTOS, G. *Platonic Studies*. Princeton: Princeton University Press, 1973.

—— (ed.), *Plato* I. New York: Doubleday, 1971.

—— (ed.), *Plato* II. New York: Doubleday, 1971.

—— 'Degrees of Reality in Plato', in R. Bambrough (ed.), *New Essays on Plato and Aristotle*, pp. 1-20, and in *Platonic Studies*, pp. 58-75.

—— 'A Metaphysical Paradox', *Platonic Studies*, pp. 43-57.

—— 'The Third Man Argument in the *Parmenides*', Allen (ed.), pp. 231-64.

—— 'Plato's Third Man Argument: Text and Logic', *Philosophical Quarterly* 19 (1969), pp. 289-301; revised for *Platonic Studies*, pp. 342-65.

—— 'Justice and Happiness in the *Republic*', in Vlastos (ed.), *Plato* II, pp. 66-95.

—— 'The Theory of Social Justice in the *Republic*', in H. North (ed.), *Interpretations of Plato*, Leiden: Brill, 1977, pp. 1-40.

—— 'The Individual as Object of Love in Plato', *Platonic Studies*, pp. 3-42.

WEDBERG, A. 'The Theory of Ideas', ch. 3 of *Plato's Philosophy of Mathematics*. Stockholm: Almqvist and Wiksell, 1955, and in Vlastos (ed.), *Plato* I, pp. 28-52.

WEINGARTNER, R. 'Vulgar Justice and Platonic Justice', *Philosophy and Phenomenological Research* 25 (1964-5), pp. 248-52.

WENDER, D. 'Plato: Misogynist, Paedophile and Feminist', *Arethusa* 6 (1973), pp. 75-90.

WHITE, F. C. 'J. Gosling on Ta Polla Kala', *Phronesis* XXIII (1978), pp. 127-32.

—— 'The "Many" in *Republic* 475e–480a', *Canadian Journal of Philosophy* VII (1977), pp. 291–306.

—— 'The *Phaedo* and *Republic* V on Essences', *Journal of Hellenic Studies* XCVIII (1978), pp. 142–56.

—— 'Plato's Middle Dialogues and the Independence of Particulars', *Philosophical Quarterly* 27 (1977), pp. 193–213.

WHITE, N. *Plato on Knowledge and Reality.* Indianapolis: Hackett, 1976.

—— *A Companion to Plato's Republic.* Oxford: Blackwell, 1979.

WILLIAMS, B. A. O. 'The Analogy of City and Soul in Plato's *Republic*', in E. N. Lee, A. P. D. Mourelatos, R. M. Rorty (eds.), *Exegesis and Argument*, *Phronesis* Supplement 1. Assen: Van Gorcum, 1973, pp. 196–206.

WILSON, J. R. S. 'The Contents of the Cave', *Canadian Journal of Philosophy* Supplement II, 1976 (*New Essays on Plato and the Pre-socratics*, ed. R. A. Shiner and J. King-Farlow), pp. 117–29.

—— 'The Argument of *Republic* IV', *Philosophical Quarterly* 26 (1976), pp. 111–24.

Index